AMERICAN EMPIRE
and the Politics of Meaning

AMERICAN EMPIRE
and the Politics of Meaning

Elite Political Cultures in THE PHILIPPINES *and* PUERTO RICO *during* U.S. Colonialism

Julian Go

DUKE UNIVERSITY PRESS

DURHAM AND LONDON

2008

© 2008 Duke University Press

All rights reserved

Printed in the United States of
America on acid-free paper ∞

Designed by Heather Hensley

Typeset in Monotype Janson by
Keystone Typesetting, Inc.

Library of Congress Cataloging-in-
Publication Data appear on the last
printed page of this book.

For Emily

CONTENTS

ACKNOWLEDGMENTS

This book aims to illuminate comparatively the cultural dimensions of American colonialism in Puerto Rico and the Philippines. One of its larger arguments, however, is that the task demands a careful reconsideration of what we mean by *culture* in the first place. This work can therefore be seen as bridging cultural sociology and comparative history. It is a work of comparative-historical sociology that pays close attention to power and meaning making. Fittingly, the origins of the book lie in the halls of the sociology department at the University of Chicago, where I was able to develop my interest in comparative-historical and cultural analysis under the guidance of George Steinmetz, Andrew Abbott, John Comaroff, and Martin Riesebrodt. I am grateful to them not only for nurturing my study of historical processes and culture, but also for encouraging me to pursue my interest in U.S. colonialism and empire when the study of such matters had been traditionally marginalized in sociology. Others at Chicago who provided indispensable support, by serving as either model thinkers, friendly critics, or attentive friends, include Kate Bjork, Neil Brenner, Robin Derby, Andreas Glaeser, and Moishe Postone. Marshall Sahlins, simply through his lectures at Chicago, taught me to think hard about culture and structure. Dipesh Chakrabarty taught me to think even harder about colonialism and how one might think about it in the first place.

Beyond Chicago, an array of area specialists and historians introduced me to Philippine and Puerto Rican historiography, guided me through its sticky terrain, and provided encouragement throughout various stages of the project: Patricio Abinales, Astrid Cubano-Iguina, Michael Cullinane, Rey Ileto, Martin Manalasan, Alfred W. McCoy, Resil Mojares, Vince Rafael, Michael Salman, Francisco Scarano, John Sidel, and Lanny Thompson. Monita Manalo taught me the nuances of Tagalog; David Rodriguez and Angel Quintero-Rivera at the University of Puerto Rico at Río Piedras graciously shared some of their research with me. Others who provided comments, guidance, and vital encouragement on certain ideas in this book include Julia Adams, Mabel Berezin, John C. Campbell, Michael Goldman, Neil Gross, Jason Kaufman, Michelle Lamont, Sally Merry, and Andrew Pickering. The comments of two anonymous reviewers at Duke University Press were indispensable, as was the editorial guidance of J. Reynolds Smith and Sharon Torian.

At the Harvard Academy of International and Area Studies, I was honored not only with the time and resources to push the project along but also by friendly commentary from John Coatsworth and Samuel Huntington. Other institutions who helped fund the research and writing of this book are the Social Science Research Council International Predissertation Fellowship Program (with funds from the Ford Foundation); the CASPIC-MacArthur Foundation at the University of Chicago; and the College of Liberal Arts and Sciences at the University of Illinois. The staff at all of the various libraries and archives I consulted were immensely generous. I would especially like to thank Magali Cintrón Butler (Centro de Investigaciones Históricas, UPR–Río Piedras); Marisa Ordonez (Lazaro Collection, UPR–Río Piedras); the staff at the University of the Philippines and the University of Chicago libraries; and Margaret C. Cook (Rare Books and Manuscripts, Swem Library, College of William and Mary).

My parents, Julian Jr. and Heide, have provided me with the background for my interest in U.S. colonialism in the Philippines (and, by extension, Puerto Rico). When I was a kid, my father used to jest now and again about the "colonial mentality" of the Filipino elite. At the time, I did not know what it all meant. But it would not be a stretch to say that his passing remarks eventually and subconsciously led me to this work. In any case, this book would not have been possible without their support, if not their subtle badgering ("you're *still* working on that book?"). Finally, I cannot extend enough heartfelt thanks to my partner, Emily Barman, who has lived with this work almost as long as I have. I do not know if this book has been more taxing on me or on her. If it has been more taxing on her, she has offered no evidence of it. Even as she was enmeshed in her own scholarly labors, she was interminably patient with my ceaseless need for assurance. My best friend and most insightful critic — this book is dedicated to her.

COLONIALISM AND CULTURE IN THE AMERICAN EMPIRE

At the end of the nineteenth century, the United States embarked upon a new stage in its career. By seizing the Philippines and Puerto Rico in the wake of the Spanish-American War, it became an overseas colonial empire not unlike England, France, or Spain. But America's new colonialists nonetheless fashioned their project as distinct. They declared that, rather than only governing Puerto Rico and the Philippines, they would also transform them. They would give their colonial subjects lessons in self-government and teach them the ways of American-style democracy. Supposedly, neither Puerto Ricans nor Filipinos were yet fit for democratic self-government. "While they deal in high sounding phrases concerning liberty and free government," asserted William Howard Taft, the first governor of the Philippines, about the Filipinos, "they have very little conception of what that means."[1] Tutelary colonialism would fill the gap. It would enable Puerto Ricans and Filipinos to "assimilate American ideas and American institutions" and learn "our best American thought and methods of administration."[2]

Keeping with the rhetoric, American officials built extensive public school systems. They also set up American-styled elections and governmental forms modeled after territories at home. They retained ultimate control for themselves but let Puerto Ricans and Filipinos vote, hold local office, and formulate legislation in national assemblies. In this way, colonial occupation would itself serve as a "school of politics," and the colonized would receive a "practical political education" in self-government. American rulers would offer a "course of tuition . . . under a strong and guiding hand," while Puerto Ricans and Filipinos would internalize the lesson and be transformed into "truly American types."[3] As Elihu Root, one of the main architects of the project, explained: "[We are] trying to train the people . . . in the first lessons of ordered liberty and teach them how to govern themselves."[4]

This period of tutelary colonialism marked a formative moment for the countries involved. Puerto Rico and the Philippines had been previously subjected to centuries of Spanish rule, but they now faced a new imperial master. On the other side, the United States embarked upon a presumably exceptional project of "exporting democracy" that would resurface in subsequent years in various countries — most recently in Iraq.[5] Still, we know comparably little about this portentous exercise in tutelary colonialism and its effects upon local political cultures. What exactly were the modes and mechanisms of tutelary colonialism? Did tutelage induce the kind of change its proponents projected, erasing the Puerto Ricans' and Filipinos' prior political culture and replacing it with the meanings and models of the American authorities' idealized vision of liberal democracy? Or was tutelary rhetoric only rhetoric, unfulfilled on the ground, or perhaps a mask for other imperial interests? What exactly were the effects of tutelary occupation upon local political cultures, whatever tutelage's supposed intentions?

To address these questions, this book focuses upon and compares the first decade of U.S. rule in Puerto Rico and the Philippines. It examines the operations of the tutelage project, both in its theory and in its practice, while tracking how one group in each colony — the Puerto Rican and Filipino elite — received, engaged, or otherwise negotiated it. The overarching approach is comparison. This book traces tutelary occupation and its cultural effects while looking for points of similarity and difference, convergence or divergence between the two colonies. At the same time, it aims to *explain* whatever similarities or differences we find.

Such a comparison has yet to be offered in existing studies of U.S. colonialism. While existing scholarship offers invaluable insights on U.S. colonialism in one or another place, it has not typically undertaken the task of comparing across places and spaces. Perhaps this is not surprising. Any attempt to compare the complexities of tutelary rule and its political-cultural impact in two different colonies faces seemingly insurmountable obstacles. Colonialism everywhere was a messy and multilayered process. It reshaped colonizer and colonized alike, affecting diverse groups in different ways on various registers, and its effects are not always easy to discern. A comparison of U.S. rule in Puerto Rico and the Philippines would be further complicated by the fact that we are dealing with three diverse countries having their own distinct histories—even if their histories were eventually conjoined under the rubric of empire. Is comparison therefore viable at all?

This book does not and cannot purport to account for everything about U.S. colonialism in Puerto Rico and the Philippines. Nor does it aim to trace all of colonialism's multilayered effects for all periods. The focus is comparably narrower, yet precisely motivated. Foremost, rather than speaking of tutelage's impact upon all colonized groups, this book restricts its attention to the Puerto Rican and Filipino "political elite"; that is, the wealthiest, most educated, and most politically powerful of local society. The structure of the tutelary colonialism itself warrants this focus. American officials first targeted the elite for "political education." The elite then took up new offices and participated in the new elections, enlisting as tutelage's primary "students" and collaborators at once. Examining the elites' activities through the first decade of occupation (ca. 1898–1912) thereby enables a sustained examination of tutelage's impact upon a single generation. We can more clearly trace the experiences of this cohort and how—if at all—the Americans' proffered political ideas and forms were woven into the fabrics of local meaning systems and political practices.

This focus upon the elite and political tutelage during the first decade of rule also approximates a controlled comparison that enables explanation. As we will see throughout this book, American colonial authorities in Puerto Rico and the Philippines enacted the same tutelary project. In both countries they incorporated the local elite into the colonial state, subjected them to political education, and endeavored to impose the same set of political ideas, concepts, and institutional forms. This similarity thereby offers opportunity to compare trajectories and cultural effects while isolating the factors that shaped them. With a sustained comparative focus, we can better illuminate what made certain processes and outcomes possible, others less likely.

While the focus of this book is relatively narrow, its comparative-historical analysis might nonetheless illuminate issues of broader concern. By examining America's first attempt to occupy and reconstruct foreign societies, we might obtain some larger insights on the multifaceted character of American power extended abroad, the different ways in which subject peoples have dealt with it, and the potentially diverse trajectories and fates of local cultures subjected to empire's projects of power. Furthermore, examining tutelage's cultural impact in the two colonies might yield a fresh understanding of culture and its relation to imperial power. To be sure, one of this book's many conceits is that its comparative examination offers opportunity to rethink what we mean by *culture* in the first place. Traditional discussions have treated culture as deep and durable subjective values, beliefs, and norms. Pat descriptors like "Hispanic culture" or "Filipino culture" follow from this notional concept. Other discussions of culture treat it as something people use instrumentally to realize their goals, or a malleable formation that powerful institutions readily shape and reshape. The present study conjures a different approach altogether. Summoning a range of innovations in culture theory across the social sciences, it will consider culture as a *semiotic system-in-practice*, a matter of signs, cultural schemas, and meaning making. This book's overarching claim is that such an approach to culture can alert us to dimensions of American empire otherwise overlooked while also helping us best explain tutelage's impact in Puerto Rico and the Philippines.

First, however, some ground needs to be cleared. As will be elaborated upon later, to talk about culture is to talk about meaning. But when talking about colonialism, why talk about culture at all?

CULTURE AND COLONIALISM

Cultural Power

To some readers, it might sound odd to speak of "culture" and "colonialism" in the same breath. Traditional scholarship has examined colonialism for everything *but* culture, focusing upon, for example, the modes and means of economic production during colonialism rather than the production of meaning.[6] Other traditional studies have treated colonialism as primarily a matter of violence. Colonial regimes attained "dominance without hegemony," sustaining themselves only by the sword.[7] "All empires," noted Edmund Burke long ago, "have been cemented in blood."[8] But different strands of scholarship have looked beyond these logics of capital and coercion. Together, this work reveals that what social scientists cover under the category "culture" was an important part of colonialism, too. The work of Bernard Cohn (1996) and Edward Said (1979) is perhaps most seminal. Both disclosed the categories by which dominant groups defined subordinate peoples, places, and spaces. Both also showed that these categories were more than justifications for intervention but rather enabled colonizers to name and identify what it was they were penetrating in the first place. "Colonial discourse" was not just talk.

Other works, however, reveal that culture was important in other ways besides its articulation as colonial discourse. Some have shown, for instance, that culture was often a *tool of rule* on the ground. While colonial regimes surely resorted to brute force, they did not always have the resources to do so, nor did they always prefer to. Working on the cheap and on the spot, rulers typically sought collaboration from local elites.[9] They aimed for legitimacy, or at least consent and compliance, and to meet the task they engaged in a panoply of symbolic practices. They devoted crucial resources to ceremonies and state rituals—punctuating the rhythm of rule with the articulation of symbols—while pronouncing promises of civilizational development and benevolence.[10] Related scholarship has shown that culture was an important dimension of colonialism in yet another way. Culture was typically a terrain or *target* of colonial rule. Colonial regimes aimed to control, manage, and sometimes transform local meaning systems; as colonial rulers sought compliance and legitimacy, they also strove to colonize the consciousness and cultural practices of subordinate groups. Nearly everywhere, in fact, colonial regimes engaged in a range of transformative projects targeting local cultural systems.[11] As studies inspired by Foucault's concepts of discipline and governmentality have shown, policies regarding sanitation and the health of the population, schooling, urban planning, and economic modernization—all of these were aimed at reorganizing local ways of life, restructuring habits and values, and imposing new classificatory schemes. As Timothy Mitchell thereby concludes, "colonizing" refers "not simply to the establishing of a European presence" but also to "the spread of a political order that inscribes in the social world a new conception of space, new forms of personhood, and a new means of manufacturing the real."[12]

The point in highlighting these cultural dimensions of colonialism is not to deny colonialism's violence or to downplay its economic features. Even Fanon, who had witnessed the naked brutality of French colonialism in Algeria firsthand, recognized the transformative projects of colonial regimes and their cultural character.[13] The point rather is to call attention to dimensions of colonialism that would otherwise go overlooked. It is to underscore that colonial power operated at multiple registers, in diffuse and subtle ways. It is to suggest that colonialism involved what we might call *cultural power* — exercises by colonial rulers to marginalize, manipulate, or control meanings while also imposing preferred cultural forms and practices.[14]

How do these matters of culture matter for U.S. tutelage in Puerto Rico and the Philippines? Few would dispute that the imperatives of capital accumulation partly shaped the dynamics of U.S. empire in the late nineteenth century or that colonial rule facilitated economic exploitation. Nor would they dispute the fact that American rule involved brute violence.[15] After all, America's occupation of the Philippines began with a war of conquest that cost at least 400,000 Filipino lives. Still, a number of important studies have deepened our understanding of U.S. colonialism at the turn of the twentieth century by unpacking the ways in which matters of meaning also mattered for U.S. colonialism. Work inspired by Said's analysis of colonial discourse, for example, has disclosed the cultural constructions of colonial subjects and the racialized knowledge that guided American occupation.[16] Related studies by Reynaldo Ileto, Warwick Anderson, and Vicente Rafael have disclosed that seemingly neutral state technologies (such as the colonial census) and ostensibly benign projects like sanitation and colonial medicine were important cultural dimensions of American colonial power in the Philippines.[17] All such technologies and projects served as ways for reshaping local practices and marginalizing local narratives and meaning systems that challenged American authority. Local cultural systems were not just derided as markers of backwardness, they were likewise targets of new technologies of power.

The chapters to come are informed by this novel work, but they also elaborate upon it. As we will see, while American officials entered the colonial scene with certain classificatory schemes that guided their policies and practices (not least racial schemes), they also used culture as a tool for rule. American authorities in both Puerto Rico and the Philippines sought to cultivate compliance and consent through a myriad of signifying practices, using signs and symbols so as to win hearts and minds. If empire was cemented in blood — as Burke had it — we will see that American officials also tried to cement it with signs. We will further see the ways in which the tutelage project was itself a matter of cultural power.[18] We should not let terms like *tutelage* or *political education* occlude the fact that American colonialism targeted Puerto Rico and the Philippines for cultural transformation according to the colonizers' own terms. As one official put it, tutelary colonialism was to "serve as an instrument of instruction constantly at work training the habits, methods of thought and ideals of the people."[19] American authorities sought to impose their own political conceptions and invented traditions. All the while, local practices, forms of authority, and meaning structures — derided by American officials as retrograde, backward, and uncivilized — were to be uprooted. In this sense, democratic tutelage marked not an absence of power but a subtle form of power altogether — a cultural power that worked alongside the coercive power of the sword. Culture thus mattered for U.S. colonialism in the sense that U.S. colonialists made it a matter of direct concern.

Colonialism's Cultural Impact

Elucidating these otherwise elusive cultural dimensions of tutelary colonialism, however, is only the first step in our story. The larger goal is to address the critical questions raised by the reckoning. Given that colonial rulers tried to manipulate signs and symbols, what resonance did their efforts have among receiving populations? And if occupying regimes aimed to colonize local culture and induce cultural change, to what extent were they successful? More precisely: how exactly did the targets of tutelage in Puerto Rico and the Philippines receive the Americans' symbolic exercises, and did tutelage have the kind of cultural impact its proponents projected? A more complete understanding of colonialism and culture would have to confront these questions. Otherwise we are left to assume that legitimacy was as simple as raising a flag; that effecting change was as easy as constructing schools, giving speeches, and handing out ballots; that, in short, cultural power never faced limits or tensions.

This question of colonialism's cultural impact is indeed critical. Recent debates on American influence and power in the world, animated by America's occupation of Iraq since 2003, raise it with urgency. Can the United

States expect to effectively implant its preferred ideas and institutions on foreign terrain? Can a new political culture be imposed from above, replacing preexisting local practices and cultural forms? Can American empire do effective work? Debates over these issues implicitly or explicitly raise the question of colonialism's impact, but the answers subsequently offered run into a questionable dichotomy. On the one end, some insist that yes, foreign political cultures can indeed be transformed by the work of imperial hands. It only takes the proper will and commitment. The implication is that the United States should never hesitate to carry out a liberal imperialism. As long as Americans have the proper will, the United States should export ballot boxes along with Coca-Cola.[20] Skeptics run to the other end of the pole. They point to the power of local cultures to resist foreign rule. In this view, attempts to transform local societies are hopeless. Rather than successful transformation, colonialism leads to an inevitable culture clash — if not a "clash of civilizations." In short, in these current debates, empire either brings assimilation or invokes diametric resistance. It heralds either an easy cultural accommodation or an irreconcilable culture clash.

But are the effects and correlates of foreign occupation reducible to these terms? A different scholarship on colonial encounters around the world offers a more nuanced view. This scholarship, probing a variety of colonial settings, reveals processes that are more fluid than current terms of debate on American empire's success or failure imply. Rather than simple success or failure, this work speaks of complex processes of exchange: "transculturation," "hybridization," "appropriation," and "localization." Nonetheless, taken as a whole, this scholarship's findings also tend to run between two opposed poles; it is just that the end points are different. On the one hand, some studies complicate views of colonial power by showing its multidimensional character — how it works on the micro level rather than being a simple outcome of rulers' motivations from the top down. Through a range of "disciplinary" institutions, power permeates local spaces and works through colonial subjects in ways that no single imperial ruler controls. But these studies nonetheless suggest that colonialism everywhere induced significant cultural transformations. Studies of European colonialism in Asia and Africa inspired by Foucault, for instance, imply that through the magic of colonial discipline, local spaces and subjects were colonized through and through. Disciplinary power, when exported abroad, worked exactly as it worked in Europe, turning colonized peoples into "isolated, disciplined, receptive, and industrious political subject[s]" bestowed with the very same classificatory schemes and ethos as their imperial masters.[21] Supposedly, even anticolonial resistance attests to the success rather than the failure of colonialism's cultural power. Presumably, so complete was the erasure of preexisting forms that anticolonial resistance could be expressed only through the terms and idioms imposed by colonial masters.

A different line of scholarship points in another direction altogether. Rather than demonstrating effective impact and the inevitability of cultural transformation, this scholarship illuminates how colonized groups tame the otherwise disruptive force of foreign intrusion while nonetheless accepting some of its terms. Studies of first contact and religious conversion in the early imperial period are indicative. Rafael (1993b) shows that during early stages of Spanish missionary activity in the Philippines, Tagalogs scrambled the missionaries' messages—a process Rafael refers to as "localization."[22] Studies on modern colonial periods reveal similar processes. Eileen Findlay shows that American officials in Puerto Rico at first enacted marriage and divorce laws as part of their "civilizing" efforts, but Puerto Rican women—guided by "their own [prior] definitions of marriage and its responsibilities"—appropriated the laws for their own purposes.[23] Similarly, Ileto and Rafael show resistance on the part of nonelite groups in the Philippines that did not follow from the categories imposed by American rulers.[24] As opposed to Foucauldian studies of resistance, these works show that peasants and urban workers articulated their own categories unscathed by the disciplinary power of the American state. This alternative scholarship on colonialism's impact therefore shows that the signs and tools of cultural power indeed permeated local societies; it is just that they were domesticated, appropriated, or indigenized in ways that tamed their otherwise powerful impact. "While subjugated peoples cannot control what emanates from the dominant culture," stresses Mary Louise Pratt, "they do determine to varying extents what they absorb into their own, and what they use it for."[25] By the same token, these studies hint that cultural reproduction rather than transformation was the norm. As colonized peoples appropriate, localize, or indigenize the artifacts and signs of colonial power "in terms of local meanings and practices"—as Sally Merry puts it—those local meanings and practices are perpetuated rather than erased.[26] At most, local cultures articulate with imposed meanings and models, creating novel "hybrid" forms that ultimately unsettle the binary of colonizer versus colonized, which colonialism induces in the first place.[27] In short, mainstream scholarship presumes cultural transformation and successful cultural power portray local cultural systems as "soft" or easily penetrated, manipulated, and malleable, but these alternative studies imply that targeted cultures are "hard" — much more resistant to alteration or manipulation, and more difficult to deteriorate or destruct. *then about did any change?* *what can in Aou the sp small pot?*

A LOOK AHEAD

The story told in this book is partially guided by this fruitful work on cultural impact. Rather than looking for unqualified success or diametric cultural resistance, forthcoming chapters uncover processes in-between. But our story nonetheless digs deeper while also looking beyond. For the most part, existing studies on colonialism's cultural impact are case-specific. They focus upon one or another colony and one or another outcome. The focus provides rich insight into processes unfolding in particular contexts, but it has nonetheless impeded a more precise differentiation between processes or cultural outcomes that might be disclosed by investigating multiple sites. Countless concepts are proffered, but they are not often put into comparative light that might in turn offer conceptual refinement and empirical specification. The cultural historian Peter Burke therefore stands puzzled at the variety and elusiveness of the terms invoked in existing studies: "Cultural borrowing, appropriation, exchange, reception, transfer, negotiation, resistance, syncretism, acculturation, enculturation, inculturation, interculturation, transculturation, hybridization (*mestizaje*), creolization."[28] In contrast, the comparative examination in this book might help to better specify differences between the processes to which these oblique terms refer. First, by looking at different colonial contexts and how groups therein dealt with colonial intrusion, we might be able to clarify different forms of negotiation and interaction. In turn, the sustained comparative focus of this book facilitates a critical-realist analysis that might *explain* the differences.[29]

Stresses the importance of comparative 2-approach

Such a comparative analysis would be vital for building upon existing scholarship on colonial encounters and local reception. Without explanations rooted in comparative analysis, we are left in a pickle. If, as some scholarship suggests, colonized peoples are so easily seduced by imposed signs — and if local cultural systems are so easily transformed — what about the processes of localization or appropriation revealed in studies of first contact? If colonizing forms or signs are thereby localized or appropriated, and if local systems are thereby reproduced (as other studies suggest), how might colonized peoples ever adopt new cultural schemes and cast off their prior ones? If local cultures are "hard," how do they change during colonialism if at all? The comparative examination of the elites' reception to American tutelage offers one way to reconsider — and propose answers to — these pressing questions.

To be sure, throughout this book we will find some processes similar to those already detected in the foregoing scholarship on cultural impact. The first part of the book addresses how the elite received tutelage during the early years of occupation (ca. 1898–1903). As we will see, during these years the elite in both colonies *domesticated* tutelage. They received American occupation and everything it imposed, but they did so in terms of preexisting local meanings. The American authorities tried to impose their own concepts, models, and associated modes of conduct regarding democracy, liberty, self-government, and elections, but the elite made sense of and engaged it all in accordance with their own local schemes. In this way, the elite inadvertently thwarted the impact of the Americans' preferred methods, modes, and meanings while reproducing their own preexisting ones.

This stage of the story thereby discloses processes similar to "localization," "indigenization," or "appropriation" discussed in studies of first contact. Yet we will also see that domestication in Puerto Rico and the Philippines was somewhat distinct. Existing scholarship reveals how such things as Bibles or European commodities were localized or indigenized by subaltern populations. By contrast, in Puerto Rico and the Philippines, political offices, ballots and ballot boxes, and political concepts fashioned by American rulers as distinctly "American" were domesticated as well. Furthermore, while much existing scholarship analyzes indigenization by supposedly supine natives untouched by foreign influences, neither the Puerto Rican nor the Filipino elite had been more strongly exposed to global circulations of ideas before U.S. arrival. In fact, they had already espoused modern discourses of democracy and self-government. We will see, then, that domestication occurred in part because of these preexisting influences rather than in spite of them. We will also see that this domestication was not a matter of motivated resistance. In fact, the elite did not always know that they were domesticating at all — and neither did the American officials.

The analysis will not end with this examination of domestication. The second part of this book shows that, after the first few years of occupation, there was a significant *divergence* in the elites' cultural trajectories. On the one hand, the Puerto Rican elite stopped domesticating tutelage and instead expanded their cultural repertoire. They learned and used the cultural meanings that tutelage imposed while marginalizing their own preexisting ones. Thus, the initial domestication and reproduction gave way to a *structural transformation*. On the other hand, the Filipino elite followed a very different path. Rather than adopting the Americans' meanings as tutelage proceeded, the elite continued to domesticate them just as before. The only difference is that this continued domestication was concomitant with a *revaluation* of the elites' preexisting political culture. As the elite continually domesticated tutelage in accordance with their prior cultural system, they complexified that system at the same time. This form of change is significantly different from structural transformation in Puerto Rico. While the Puerto Rican elite abjured their prior political meanings and adopted new ones, the Filipino elite continually employed their own while elaborating upon them.

Tracking these processes will thereby serve to show that domestication can give way to change, and that change can take different forms. They will also reveal some of the different ways colonized peoples can negotiate the imposition of new things and the different cultural outcomes of colonial occupation. Furthermore, and most critically, they raise the question of *why* they occurred. Why did the elite in both colonies domesticate tutelage and reproduce their prior political culture, even though they later affected different forms of change? What accounts for the elites' initially similar and later divergent cultural trajectories? Addressing this issue is the final task of the book. In these late chapters, theories of culture come into play. This is where we need to be careful about what we mean by *culture* in the first place.

THE TASK OF EXPLANATION: THINKING CULTURE

Culture theory across the social sciences merits attention because it would readily offer various different hypotheses for meeting our task of explanation. Furthermore, and perhaps most importantly, existing scholarship on U.S. colonialism often deploys these very same theories of culture, however implicitly at times. Consider traditional studies of U.S. colonialism in the Philippines. These studies made two claims. They first argued that American officials brought with them a distinct set of "American values" that conflicted with "Filipino values." American officials brought distinctly liberal-democratic beliefs, but, supposedly, the Filipino elite had been socialized into patron-client "norms" and "orientations" rooted in "Malay" traditions and their Spanish past. Second, these studies suggested that as the Filipinos' patron-client values and orientations were ostensibly incommensurable with the values the Americans tried to impose, tutelage was bound to fail. Rather than effective transformation under America's guiding hand, tutelage inevitably led to a dysfunctional culture clash.[30] Note that these claims are not simply a matter of historical record. They are a matter of interpreting the record through an implicit theoretical lens; in this case, structural functionalism and its approach to culture. Structural functionalism treated "political culture" as subjective "orientations," beliefs, norms, and "values" that give meaning to political action and political systems.[31] It was tied to modernization theories that claimed that some values were more congenial to and functional for democracy than others.[32] To speak of "culture clash" between American values and Filipino values is to silently if not loudly summon this way of thinking about culture. It is to treat meaning as a matter of subjective beliefs and values; action as a matter of cultural norms and orientations.

Can this approach help us meet our task of explanation? We will see that the patron-clientelism pinpointed in traditional studies is indeed evident in the Filipino elites' discourse and conduct during American rule. But we will also see that the approach is deficient as an explanatory framework. Treating patron-clientelism in terms of subjective values and norms, for example, elides the ways patron-clientelism can take on different forms and meanings and manifest as very different kinds of practices. Nor can the approach account for the elites' initially similar and later divergent cultural trajectories during tutelary rule. According to the theory, values are instilled through socialization; they are engrained, deep, and therefore durable. If cultural change occurs at all, it occurs only after a new round of socialization, hence with a new generation. Yet, as we will see, structural transformation in Puerto Rico occurred within the *same* generation. These shortcomings relate to structural functionalism's larger problems as culture theory. By conceiving of culture as cohesive values, orientations, and beliefs, the structural-functionalist approach treated culture as "totalizing, coherent, and normative" while overlooking relations of power.[33] It also carried a questionable conception of the relationship between meaning and action by portraying social actors as overdetermined by culture. Supposedly, culture is a unilateral force upon action — values shape orientations and norms that in turn determine conduct — and cannot be cast off or reconfigured dialectically by agents. Finally, the approach ran the risk of psychological subjectivism that in turn raises problems of validity. It theorized meaning as something deep in people's hearts, which makes culture difficult to analyze. Values are not directly observable; hence cultural analysis is not falsifiable.

Of course structural-functionalism's approach to culture as values has not been the only option for cultural analysis. Since the 1980s, social scientists critical of structural functionalism but nonetheless interested in retaining a focus upon meaning turned to Clifford Geertz for new hope. Geertz approached culture as "public vehicles of meaning"; social scientists then adopted this insight to suggest that culture is observable rather than hidden, and cultural analysis could provide "thick descriptions" without digging for deep values.[34] Fittingly, Geertz's innovation helped to spawn a host of new cultural studies across diverse fields.[35] But Geertz's approach carried problems, too. One criticism is that Geertz's approach does not fully cast off the structural-functionalist legacy. His was not a rejection of the values concept of culture but rather a new way to measure it. Values and beliefs remained the source of meaning; symbols simply encode or reflect them.[36] A related criticism was Geertz's assumption of cultural cohesion and the associated occlusion of agency, history, and process. In order to analyze symbols, Geertz had to presume that their meaning was shared by all. Culture involved *shared* meaning systems. In turn, meaning is not forged by social actors but always already there. It was as if everyone in Balinese society shared the meaning of the cockfight, but no one in particular created it. Thus, in *Negara* (1980), Geertz analyzed political symbolism to argue that "power served pomp, not pomp power," but he nonetheless overlooked the possibility that those subjected to pomp's power might have challenged it or that target populations might have created alternative meanings that might have exploded the otherwise seamless web of meaning. Power may serve pomp, but Geertz occluded the possibility for pomp to be appropriated in resistant ways.[37]

The problems with Geertz's approach are palpable when considering our task. While it offers methodological insights on how to wrestle culture from the depth of people's hearts, it offers less guidance for thinking about how local populations receive or negotiate foreign intrusion.[38] To assume "shared meaning systems" obliges us to presume that colonizer and colonized alike shared the same meaning of the same symbols. Nor did Geertz offer a theory of cultural transformation and its different forms. To "thickly describe" cultural systems demands analytically freezing culture in time, not tracking meanings in motion.[39] For understanding the impact of America's tutelary regimes and cultural transformation on the ground, Geertz's approach provides a promising beginning, but not an end.

Because of the problems with structural functionalism and a general unease with Geertz's interpretative approach, scholarship in the social sciences has offered up other approaches. These approaches follow from the criticisms they register. Rather than locating meaning in subjective values or in thick descriptions, these alternatives downplay matters of meaning and locate its dynamics in external logics; better, then, to understand those externalities rather than worrying about culture's internal logics. One such alternative has been to treat culture as an instrument: an "irresistible strategic resource" that utility maximizers use depending on their preferences and incentive structures.[40] In this view, political elites manipulate culture as a tool, employing symbols to cultivate constituencies and power; they then shift the meanings they use according to which meanings provide added utility for realizing their goals. This approach urges us to shift our lens from values in people's hearts to the calculations in their minds. It also makes attempts to explain cultural change where previous approaches did not. Cultural change follows not from generational change but from shifts in interests or incentives.[41] A second alternative approach comes from political scientists who specify the role that states play in shaping cultural outcomes — a focus upon supply rather than demand. Studies of colonialism in Africa, for example, have explained cultural identities by reference to colonial state policies or strategies of rule. Strategies such as "indirect rule" solidified certain norms and cultural meanings rather than others.[42] As David Laitin summarizes this top-down, state-centered approach: "states have enormous power to restructure culture."[43]

These approaches have been primarily developed in political science, but both also implicitly underlie some existing case-specific studies of U.S. colonialism that have eschewed the analysis of culture as deep values and beliefs. Some studies on Puerto Rico, for example, treat the elite as colonial *compradors* whose actions can be explained by reference to the elites' politico-economic interests.[44] Parallel work on the Philippines similarly conceives of the Filipino elite as "oligarchs" and "caciques" who cynically manipulate symbols to better realize their political-economic goals.[45] Both sets of studies thereby insinuate the instrumentalist approach to culture. Alternatively, a different set of studies implicitly summon the state-centered, top-down approach to culture. These studies shift the focus away from the elites' interests to the actions of American colonial rulers. In these studies, if there was anything problematic or incomplete about tutelage's cultural impact, it was due to the shortcomings of the Americans' policies, the weaknesses of their ruling strategies, and the contradictions embedded in the tutelage project from the outset. In this view, the outcome of cultural impact depends on the action of colonial rulers; local cultural outcomes are determined from the top down.[46]

Because these approaches to culture have often been employed to analyze U.S. colonialism, they will merit closer attention as we proceed. But ultimately, the analysis will reveal the need for a different approach to culture altogether. Rather than treating culture as values, strategic instruments or utility, or as a thing shaped from the top down, we will see the value of treating culture as a *semiotic system-in-practice*. This approach has been induced from the empirical analysis in this book, but some of its main contours have also been broached in diverse sectors of scholarship — from the "new cultural sociology" to Bourdieu's theorization of structure and practice; from historians' work on colonial discourse and cultural meanings in the Philippines to anthropologists' attempts to theorize culture and temporality.[47] How does this approach to culture differ from extant theories? The basic elements are worth elucidating.

First, a system-in-practice approach locates meaning not in values and beliefs or in people's heads and hearts, but rather in patterns of opposition and contrast between signs. These patterns form an internal logic; they are relatively autonomous from the world and thereby enable people to make meaning of it. As "the world" — that is, the events, happenings, things, and other people to which cultural users refer — is infinitely complex, signifying patterns allow people to give it palpable form. Second, the semiotic or cultural "system" in this view does not necessarily adduce to a coherent uniform "culture." It rather consists of multiple, layered, and diverse cultural structures; that is, classificatory schemes, cognitive lenses, narratives, scripts or "key scenarios."[48] These cultural structures or schemas can thereby serve to produce different meanings of the same thing. Culture in this sense is a repertoire of possibly incoherent meanings and models, even though culture remains a system in the end,[49] for we cannot mistake lack of coherence for lack of system. To say that models or meanings are "incoherent" is to say that they are different: they are incoherent in the sense that they contrast with each other. But this is merely to say that they obtain their specific meaning in relation to the other, such that, taken together, the different incoherent models form a pattern of contrasts or opposition — that is, an overarching system of differences. Culture, then, is more precisely a *systematic* repertoire.[50]

A system-in-practice approach also highlights meaning making where other approaches do not. Culture enables meanings to be made, but it does not make meaning itself, nor does meaning flow directly from engrained values and beliefs. Instead, *people* make meaning. Meaning has to be created by social actors through their concrete, social, communicative acts.[51] Through "semiotic practices" — discourse, speech, and signifying gestures — social actors use available signifying patterns to classify the world, to define and narrate it. They draw upon cultural structures to render the world palpable, making meanings that in turn guide (but do not fully determine) their conduct.[52] In this sense, culture is indeed a "tool." But unlike an instrumentalist approach, a system-in-practice approach insists that culture is enabling *and* constraining. Culture enables meaning making because it provides the cultural structures by which people order the otherwise orderless world. But in order to use a schema, category, or narrative, cultural users must already have them in their repertoire. The schemas they use and hence the meanings they make must be familiar, available, and retrievable. Cultural systems thereby delimit the possibilities of instrumental usage. People do things with signs, but not under conditions of their own choosing.[53] Furthermore, this constraint is not about essentialism or determinism. It is not a matter of people blindly following the "norms" or "values" that society imposes upon them. Constraint instead emerges from the history preceding concrete semiotic practices.[54] Over time, some cultural schemas, codes, or narratives become routinized and thereby interdependent with the world they refer. They become institutionalized, fixed in practice. This institutionalization thereby delimits the width of the systematic repertoire upon which people draw. Because certain cultural structures have been previously institutionalized, cultural users will draw first upon those cultural structures rather than others when making meaning.[55] They do not do so because culture tells them to; they do so because those cultural structures — by virtue of their institutionalization — are the most available, retrievable, and familiar.[56]

There is a final added element to a systems-in-practice approach that is worth highlighting; that is, it incorporates an examination of power. Since the world is not transparent itself, and since culture provides the basis for making meaning of it, how people define and manage power relations in the first place depends on the meanings they make. Culture itself becomes a ground of struggle. And because people *make* meaning rather than being fully determined by it, people can challenge, invert, or subvert codes. They can formulate alternative or oppositional meanings within the overarching cultural order — even as powerful institutions and actors endeavor to marginalize alternative meanings or suppress them altogether. Thus, culture is not a sideshow to the analysis of power but "central to questions of power and its effects."[57]

All of this remains abstract, of course. It will take the rest of this book to show how a semiotic systems-in-practice approach fares best for understanding tutelage's cultural power and the uneven impact it had upon elite political culture in Puerto Rico and the Philippines. The task will also involve further theoretical refinement as we proceed, for in order to employ the foregoing approach to culture to account for the elites' initially similar cultural trajectories and the different forms of change that followed, we will have to inductively elaborate upon the basic points outlined above and push them further.

Before turning to the concrete details, however, it is necessary to set up the story by introducing the main actors and the contours of our comparison.

TUTELAGE AND THE POLITICAL ELITE

As Jean and John Comaroff (1991; 1997) have pointed out, colonialism was much more than a story of a monolithic "colonizer" facing an equally monolithic "colonized." On both sides of the divide, there were internal divisions and complexities. Similarly, the actors in our story are not "Americans" and "Puerto Ricans" or "Filipinos" broadly, but two subgroups more specifically: American colonial officials and associates on the one hand, and the Filipino and Puerto Rican "political elite" on the other. As noted, this focus is warranted because we are primarily interested in the political-cultural dimensions of tutelary rule and its efforts in "political education." It is likewise warranted by the structure of tutelary rule itself.

On the American side, tutelary rule was administered by a tight imperial hierarchy that concentrated power in the hands of a comparably small group. In Washington, responsibility for the colonies was initially put into the hands of the Department of War. To head the Department of War, President McKinley appointed Elihu Root, a lawyer from New York. Root's Department of War thereby became the de facto colonial office. Administration and power were likewise concentrated on colonial ground. Both Puerto Rico and the Philippines were initially run by the military, and military governors had full charge. When the military governments were replaced by civilian administrations, the Department of War remained the home office and the new civil administrations centered around a comparably small group of officials. These officials included the colonial governor and the members of the executive bodies in charge of all legislation (the Philippine Commission and the Executive Council in Puerto Rico), handpicked by Root and the president. There were typically about eight members of each of these executive bodies. All of them except one were members of the Republican Party (which held the presidential office until 1912).[58] In addition, these officials in both colonies came from comparably similar backgrounds. Together, their prior occupations clustered around three interrelated professions: work in elected political office, law (e.g., judges), or academia (e.g., scholars or heads of bureaucracies).[59] Furthermore, the officials in Puerto Rico were similar to the officials in the Philippines. Officials with legal and academic backgrounds formed the majority (appendix, table 10). Finally, the officials shared certain ideological orientations. Most had been educated at elite universities or had taught at them; most were from northern and northeastern urban centers and, as said, were members of the Republican Party. Nearly all had been part and parcel of the growing Progressive reform movement at home. They might have had their distinct opinions and views, but they nonetheless shared a Progressive-era repertoire.

As we will see, the shared background of the officials proved important for the formulation, contours, and content of tutelary rule. It also contributed to the fact that the officials in Puerto Rico and the Philippines embarked upon the same tutelage project involving the same economic, education, and infrastructure policies. In fact, officials constructed very similar colonial states in the two colonies. In both, they set up local governments and a national legislative assembly to be staffed by Puerto Ricans and Filipinos while monopolizing ultimate authority for themselves. They likewise initiated a program of "practical political education" in both colonies. This was aimed at the more privileged, educated, and wealthier segments of the population, whom American authorities classified as in need of "as much education in practical civil liberty as their more ignorant fellow-countrymen in reading, writing, and arithmetic."[60] Accordingly, while the American officials allowed Puerto Ricans and Filipinos to vote and hold offices, they initially put restrictions on both. Voters and officeholders had to meet certain requirements (e.g., prior office holding during Spanish rule, literacy, [male] property holding), and those who qualified became "the eligible class," ready to "receive instruction in the principles and methods of government . . . in the practical school of experience."[61] They were the voters, party leaders, legislators, and officials in the tutelary regime and were the key players in colonial politics through the first decade of rule. In short, they constituted the political elite.[62]

Relative to their respective societies, the political elite in each colony formed a small group. In the first municipal elections of the Philippines during U.S. rule, only 2.44 percent of the Filipino population could vote, and only some 5 percent of Puerto Ricans could participate in their first election under U.S. rule.[63] In the Philippines, the proportion of native political officials to the total population was 1:801. For Puerto Rico, it was 1:709. The political elite were also organizationally cohesive. In Puerto Rico, most political officials were from the same political party. The dominant political party for the first years of rule was known as the Federal Party. In 1903, the party changed its name to the Union Party, but it was a change in name only: leaders and members, with a few exceptions, were continuous with the previous party. In the Philippines, party politics was more complicated — as we will see — but organizational cohesion emerged nonetheless. On the one hand, the diversity of the archipelago meant that the political elite came from different provinces, often with distinct languages and cultures. On the other hand, U.S. rule helped to further consolidate them all as a political class with various connections and organizational ties.[64] At the onset of rule, a party known as the Federalistas (not to be confused with the Federals in Puerto Rico) dominated. Their power lasted only a few years, and later, a party called the Nationalist Party was formed (the Nacionalistas). Many Federalistas joined, previous parties slowly dissipated in importance, and the Nationalist Party took up most of the posts in the local regime.[65]

The political elite in each colony were also a continuous group from the end of Spanish rule to the end of 1912. They formed a cohort.[66] Most of the key political leaders during U.S. rule had been political leaders during late Spanish rule. The leaders of the dominant party in Puerto Rico had led the dominant party during the Spanish period, and key political figures in the Philippines had been politically active at the tail end of Spanish rule.[67] A look at the elites' demographics further discloses the continuity. Less than 10 percent of native officials in each colony were under twenty years old when the Americans first arrived. The majority were born in the 1860s and 1870s. This means that the elite who first came of political age during late Spanish rule also dominated office during American rule (appendix, table 11). The elites' previous office-holding experience shows the same thing. In Puerto Rico, 60 percent of the officials during U.S. rule had also held office during Spanish rule. In the Philippines, 52 percent had held office during Spanish rule (appendix, table 12).[68] This continuity therefore offers a unique opportunity to analyze elite meaning-making activities. We can trace elite political culture from the end of Spanish rule through the beginnings of American rule, thereby examining and comparing the effects of tutelage upon the same cohort.

Beyond the foregoing, other factors further facilitate the comparison. Both Puerto Rico and the Philippines had been previously subjected to centuries of Spanish rule before American acquisition. Spanish rule had its own particular inflections in each of its colonies, as we will see; but generally speaking, both colonies were governed according to the same basic principles and political forms. Both colonies also saw similar economic and political reforms during the late nineteenth century. The Spanish Empire was weakening at the time, and the liberal Spanish party took the seat of power in Madrid in the 1890s. Consequently, the local elite in both colonies were allowed to hold office in the colonial state and were granted increasing local power by Madrid. In turn, the elite became politically vocal and active. In both colonies, they led political movements demanding reforms from Madrid. In the process, they each formed new political and social identities while articulating new ideologies of self-determination and democracy.[69]

Both colonies also had relatively similar socioeconomic features. Both were largely agrarian, as were most countries at the time, but they had also been incorporated into the world market during Spanish rule. This shaped the social structure of the two colonies in similar ways. In Puerto Rico, the mass of the population were peasants or tenants, connected to a relatively small class of export-oriented landlords (about 7 percent of the population); a group of merchants who mediated between landlords and the global market, and a smaller burgeoning professional class. Doctors, lawyers, and teachers — typically from prominent landed families — constituted about 1 percent of the population engaged in gainful occupation.[70] A similar social structure is found in the Philippines. This too was a world of peasants and export-oriented landowners, with a small class of merchants and professionals (as in Puerto Rico, less than 1 percent of people engaged in gainful occupation were professionals). Literacy rates in the two colonies were also similar. In both, the percentage of the population that could read and write was 20 percent. In the United States at the time, the percentage was close to 90 percent.[71] Finally, both colonies had seen a remarkable growth of export production before U.S. occupation. This further served to concentrate wealth and power in both colonies, and it gave the local elite a significant base of socioeconomic resources. Hacienda-style production and a high concentration of land was typical.[72] Appropriately, the political elite in both colonies were most often tied to landed wealth. Close to 50 percent of officeholders in Puerto Rico during U.S. rule and close to 60 percent in the Philippines were landowners (appendix, table 13).[73] Even the officials who were primarily nonlandholders — doctors, journalists, lawyers, or merchants — were tied to the landed class. Many had been brought up on estates and stood to inherit land from their parents; others married into wealthy families or served as clients of wealthy landowners.[74] In both colonies, the political elite was truly a class based in land.

This is not to suggest that the two colonies were exactly the same. There were important differences. While a small portion of the elite in both colonies had been educated abroad (typically in Europe), the proportion of Puerto Rican political officials educated abroad was higher, and a small handful had been educated in the U.S. (appendix, table 14). While both the Puerto Rican and Filipino elite in the nineteenth century had come into political consciousness to lead reform movements, only in the Philippines had those movements resulted in revolution. In Puerto Rico, the elites' movement was aimed at full incorporation into the Spanish system. Finally, internal linguistic and ethnic differences were more marked in the Philippines than in Puerto Rico. This was related to the diversity of Philippine geography. The Philippines consisted of thousands of islands, while Puerto Rico consisted of one major island and a small group of outlying islands. It was also related to the influx of Chinese immigrants to the Philippine archipelago during previous centuries. The influx meant that a large portion of the elite in the Philippines were Chinese mestizo, alongside Spanish mestizos and provincial natives of various ethnicities, while the elite in Puerto Rico were largely Spanish mestizo or criollo.

These and other differences will be considered throughout this book. But what is remarkable is that the elites' cultural trajectories during the early years of U.S. rule were the same. As chapters 2 and 3 will show, the elite in both colonies initially domesticated tutelage despite the various differences just noted. We begin, however, by more closely scrutinizing the cultural dimensions of American rule and the operations of tutelage's cultural power.

Chapter 1

TUTELARY COLONIALISM AND CULTURAL POWER

The [American] Ideal is this you see, that every people in the world should
have self-government and equal rights. This means, when reduced from
windy oratory to common-sense, that they consider these Malay half-breeds
to be capable . . . of understanding the motives, and profiting by the institutions which it has taken the highest white races two or three thousand years
to evolve. . . . When I come to think of it, America with this funny little
possession of hers is like a mother with her first child, who . . . tries to bring it
up on some fad of her own because it is so much more precious and more
wonderful than any other child any one else ever had.

MRS. CAMPBELL DAUNCEY, *AN ENGLISHWOMAN IN THE PHILIPPINES*

Mrs. Campbell Dauncey, British citizen and diplomat's wife in the
Philippines, came to her incredulity of American colonialism
after witnessing it firsthand. She had watched as U.S. officials set up
local elections and let Filipinos hold political office, part of their
larger effort to teach Filipinos the ways of American-styled democracy. But Dauncey was not alone in her critical skepticism. In Puerto
Rico, where U.S. occupation also took a tutelary form, American
settlers were just as critical. "There are plenty of native men who can
make fine speeches on the subject of liberty and free government,"
they complained upon hearing that the Puerto Ricans were allowed
to hold office, "but precious few know anything about the intricate

science of administering the same. It is like putting a big business, that requires old heads and experience, in the hands of apprentice boys."[1]

If tutelary colonialism had its skeptics, proponents on the ground were unmoved. Policy planners and officials were determined to follow through and transform Puerto Ricans and Filipinos. "It seems to me obvious," wrote Governor Luke Wright in the Philippines, in response to criticisms that the Filipinos had been given too much political control over local affairs, "that in purely local matters at least we must give the people of the various municipalities a reasonable hand in directing their own affairs and endeavor, by precept, example and constant watchfulness, to develop them along American lines. This I appreciate is a work of time and labor. I must think, however, that it is worth our best efforts."[2] How could this be? What was behind the officials' determination to teach the colonized the "art and science of self-government" and turn them, as they themselves insisted, into "truly American types"?[3] And what exactly was involved in this seemingly contradictory attempt to transform subject peoples into liberal democratic subjects?

Traditional scholarship offers contrasting views on this issue. According to one view, tutelage was a ruse masking deeper imperial interests. American colonialism was fundamentally about capital and coercion; the officials' tutelage discourse was but ornamental rhetoric — perhaps aimed at appeasing anti-imperialists at home. A different view takes the tutelage discourse more seriously and adopts a culturalist perspective. The attempt to democratize the colonies was not a ruse but a reflection of America's political traditions, democratic values, and anticolonial beliefs. It was a valiant and exceptional project, reflecting America's own exceptional political culture.[4] The examination of tutelary colonialism in this chapter offers a different approach altogether. On the one hand, tutelage was not simply a ruse. It was a concerted and determined policy, guided by certain cultural logics and aims. On the other hand, these cultural dimensions of tutelage do not boil down to the formula offered in existing culturalist scholarship. Rather than subjective beliefs or values, the cultural dimensions of tutelage were about signifying structures and meaning-making practices. Colonial authorities — when making sense of colonized populations, and defining issues, problems, and solutions — drew from particular cultural schemas rendered salient to them by their specific background and experiences. These schemas then served to enable the tutelage project while also shaping its contours and content (not least its definition of what constituted "democracy" in the first place). Furthermore, American officials did not transpose a "culture" or set of "American values," they *used* culture as a tool and target. Culture was something that they sought to manipulate and manage, control and transform on the ground.

In short, by explicating these processes and practices, the goal of this chapter is not to treat the cultural dimensions of tutelage as ornamental rhetoric that masked presumably deeper interests. But neither is the goal to treat tutelary colonialism as a reflection of America's ostensibly exceptional cultural values to thereby portray American officials as heroic figures. The goal instead is to highlight cultural aspects of American rule typically occluded in existing studies. Tutelage, rather than a sideshow to coercion and capital, and rather than an expression of America's exceptional culture, constituted a cultural project in its own right. It was a matter of *cultural power*.

THE BASES OF TUTELAGE

"There are two classes [of residents] here," wrote Cameron Forbes, a member of the Philippine Commission and would-be colonial governor, "those that believe in the effort to educate and help the Filipinos. . . . and those who say the Filipinos are hopeless and that we'd best exploit the Islands for our own benefit. I am glad to say none of the Commission feel that way and none of the higher officers of the government feel that way."[5] Forbes's statement, etched in his personal diary, echoes a larger point: in public forums as well as in internal memos and private correspondences, the new American colonialists insisted that tutelage should be the rule of colonial rule. But how should we understand this? How could the American officials have insisted upon teaching the colonized the ways of democracy through the undemocratic means of colonial rule? Part of the answer can be founded by examining the specific cultural schemas that underwrote the tutelage project. The other part of the answer lies beyond the American officials' cultural schemas and in processes on colonial ground. Specifically, it lies in a principle of colonial state-building everywhere: the drive for legitimacy. To better understand the Americans' presumably exceptional project in tutelary colonialism, both of these issues merit close attention.

Schemas for Rule

The officials who formulated and carried out tutelage came from particular social backgrounds, operated in a larger domestic and global milieu, and worked from particular classificatory schemes and narratives befitting their social position and experiences. These cultural structures rendered tutelage possible, practical, and palpable. They also gave tutelage its specific contours and content. The first set of schemas had to with *racial difference*. Drawing upon already existing racial classifications at home — which had become all the more potent by the late nineteenth century — policy makers, the press, and the public typically claimed that the Puerto Ricans and Filipinos were unfit for self-government due to their racial makeup. "Savage blood, Oriental blood, Malay blood," argued Senator Albert Beveridge about the Filipinos, "are these the elements of self-government?"[6] As many studies have shown, these racialized claims were unsurprisingly common.[7] Still, the authors and proponents of tutelage deployed a more specific set of racial schemas that demand analysis, for even within the overarching discourses of race at home there circulated distinct meanings.

On the one hand, some thinkers in the new sciences of race had emphasized the strictly biological side of racial inferiority. A proto-eugenicist conception, the accent here was upon genes, blood, and stock. Senator Beveridge's appeal to "savage blood" and "Malay blood" exemplifies this conception. On the other hand, different thinkers had offered another view, focusing upon the environmental production of racial inferiority. For example, in Lamarck's theory of the inheritance of acquired characteristics, an organism's traits developed in response to the environment, and these traits were then passed down to inheritors. The emphasis was less on nature than on nurture, more on history and environment than on genes or stock.[8] These understandings of racial difference in turn carried respectively different practical implications. As the strictly biological view rooted inferiority in blood or biology, it classified lesser races as incorrigibly lesser. Inferiority was interminable. By contrast, the Lamarckian scheme did not classify the so-called lesser races as so incorrigible. As the issue depended upon history and environment, differences in behavior (however indexed phenotypically) could be reduced, given the proper external stimuli and surrounding conditions.

Those deemed lesser could be uplifted. Critics thereby labeled this view the "equality fallacy," which "belittles race differences and has a robust faith in the power of intercourse and school instruction to lift up a backward folk to the level of the best."[9]

The architects of tutelary colonialism clearly espoused the so-called equality fallacy. Elihu Root claimed that Puerto Ricans and Filipinos were "still in political childhood" and were therefore unfit for self-government, but he added that this unfitness was due to their "rudimentary stage of political development" rather than biology.[10] Apparently, centuries of Spanish colonialism had served to develop Puerto Ricans and Filipinos beyond "savagery," but it had not completed the job. Officials in Puerto Rico claimed that Spanish rule had not offered mass education, leaving the majority of the population "ignorant, credulous, and child-like." They also claimed that while Spanish rule had allowed privileged groups to receive higher education, it had not given them proper political experience. The "highly centralized" form of Spanish rule in Puerto Rico meant that "the development of a distinctive local civic life" had been "discouraged and even violently repressed"; the people had been "deprived of the invigorating and elevating influence of direct participation in local affairs."[11] Supposedly, Spanish officials had been corrupt and self-aggrandizing, which meant that Puerto Ricans "have not been trained in a good government school."[12] "The people of this island," claimed the early officials, "have been long and thoroughly taught an unfortunate object lesson. They have seen the island governed and exploited by a class in the interest and for the benefit of a few. The Spanish governing element has disappeared, but their example remains. There is no lack of natives of learning and ability ready to take the place of their former masters, step into their vacant shoes, and take up the government laid down. And, having power, would they not use it as their predecessors did? So long have the people been accustomed to this kind of control and absolute subordination that the most of them would accept it as a matter of course."[13] Root condensed the view:

> The most important fact to be considered is that the people have not yet been educated in the art of self-government, or any really honest government. In all their experience and in all their traditions, law and freedom have been ideas which were not associated with each other, but opposed to

each other; and it is impossible that a people with this history — only 10 per cent of whom can read or write — should have ever acquired any real understanding of the way to conduct a popular government. I do not doubt their capacity to govern themselves; but they have not yet learned.[14]

Views on the Filipinos' inferiority were the same. The first investigative commissions pointed out that Spanish rule had failed to offer mass education while also failing "to accomplish even the primary ends of good government — the maintenance of peace and order and the even administration of justice." It had been "an engine of oppression and exploitation of the Filipinos."[15] Thus, even privileged and educated Filipinos had acquired "tyrannical" traits. "The politicians here are, with a few exceptions," wrote Governor Taft to his friend at home, "venal and corrupt to the last degree and as tricky and uncertain as were the statesmen in the days of George the first and Queen Anne."[16] While the elite spoke a modern democratic language, they did not yet fully comprehend the meanings of what they said. "Round phrases, including 'liberty,' 'independence,' 'the development of the Philippines,' come with ease to their lips," Taft opined, "[but] the only example of government which they have had is the Spanish."[17]

The idea of developing, democratizing, and transforming Puerto Rico and the Philippines followed from these neo-Lamarckian conceptions. If nature did not explain inferiority, then nurture could lift the colonized out of it. Capacities could be built upon, "development" could be hastened, and Puerto Ricans and Filipinos could become self-governing subjects. "Unlike the sparsely settled regions of New Mexico and Arizona . . . ," claimed officials, "Porto Rico [sic] has many alert, intelligent people, who, though bowed down by centuries of oppression, still retain the spirit and capacity for higher and better conditions. This capacity and these conditions can be developed only under a system which will wisely control, guide, and support them until they attain sufficient vigor to support and control themselves."[18] Taft explained to Congress, when recommending tutelary government in the Philippines: "While there is to-day a palpable unfitness for self-government, there is in them a capacity for future development, for future preparation for self-government."[19] So confident was Taft in the "capacities" of colonial peoples that he claimed that the Philippines might one day become a state in the union: "It is the duty of the United States to establish . . . a government suited to the present possibilities of the people, which shall gradually change, conferring more and more right upon the people to govern themselves, thus educating them in self-government, until their knowledge of government, their knowledge of individual liberty shall be such that further action may be taken by giving them statehood or . . . if they desire it, by independence."[20] In this sense, Mrs. Campbell Dauncey was not entirely incorrect in her criticism of American empire. Proponents of tutelage indeed acted like "a mother with her first child." The only difference is that tutelage's proponents, by transposing neo-Lamarckian racial schemes to the colonies, took this to mean that the child could be nurtured into adulthood.

While neo-Lamarckian meanings fed the tutelage idea, however, there was nothing inherent to neo-Lamarckian logic that called for tutelary colonialism. So-called lesser peoples might be uplifted, but this did not mean that such uplift was practically feasible or desirable. Hence the other factor shaping tutelary colonialism: a certain *style of government*, an ethos of reformism and transformism, that had circulated both globally and domestically. Indeed, the global context of imperialism had already been undergoing significant modification by the time the United States acquired its colonies. European powers advanced new models for colonial governance, racial uplift, and so-called civilizing missions. European writers like Rudyard Kipling thereby urged Americans to join in the new efforts and take up the "White Man's Burden." American policy makers, proimperial scholars, and officials were clearly attuned to this global discourse. They read up on European colonial experiences and affirmed the idea of racial uplift.[21] Some affirmed it on the basis of a cross-Atlantic racial rapprochement. Influential thinkers like Franklin Giddings argued that Britain and America together would lead the world as an Anglo-Saxon empire, fending off the Chinese and the Slavs. His fellow scholar John Burgess asserted: "The teutonic races are instructed with the mission of conducting the political civilization of the modern world."[22] Others who affirmed the new ethos asserted that imperialism was inescapable, so the only question was how to best use it for the purposes of civilizing. Bernard Moses, who served in the Philippines, and Woodrow Wilson, whom colonial officials often cited, together argued that the domination of all "less developed races" by the "higher races" was inevitable due to the forces of modern globalization. Any notion that lesser races could develop autonomously was simply "utopian." "The East," wrote Wilson, "is to be opened and transformed, whether we will it or no; the standards of the West are to be imposed upon it."[23] The only hitch to them was that the United States, by its special history and exceptionally democratic character, was particularly well suited for the task. Wilson argued that while imperialism by the powerful white nations was inevitable, the United States also had the "peculiar duty to moderate the process [of imperialism] in the interests of liberty; to impart to the peoples thus driven out upon the road of change . . . our principles of self-help; teach them order and self-control; impart to them . . . the drill and habit of law and obedience which we long ago got out of the strenuous processes of English history."[24]

Models of uplift, however, were not only drawn from the global field. They were also drawn from schemes of reform and transformation circulating among particular social groups in the United States. Historians have already intimated connections between the Americans' discourse of Native Americans, African Americans, and colonized populations overseas. This discourse, however, was largely restricted to American military officials, soldiers, or statesmen at home (who viewed affairs only from afar). By contrast, civilian officials responsible for devising an administration explicitly disavowed such connections. They instead found inspiration in the discourse of reform movements at home that were aimed at multiple groups and society as a whole.[25] The most important was the Progressive reform movement. The movement was internally differentiated, but what it shared was a particular style or approach to the world. Specifically, it sought to alter the government to change society, and as such it carried an inflated sense of empowerment and efficacy. It classified the otherwise overwhelming forces of the world as objects to be tamed, managed, remolded, and transformed; the problems attendant with capitalism, urbanization, industrialization, and immigration could be easily solved through proper intervention and engineering.[26] No surprise that progressivism was concomitant with the emerging social sciences, especially the new science of government. This new science proposed that "good government" could solve all ills. Administration could be separated from the turmoil and seemingly crude realm of city politics; it could change the polity and hence society as a whole. Administration could "clear the moral atmosphere of official life," claimed Woodrow Wilson.[27] It could help to reduce the power of corrupt politicians and courts, and to uproot petty political feuds and partisan games — all of which seemed to contribute to society's problems. Social scientists thus allied with progressive activists and pinned unswerving hope on impartial expertise, objective analysis of government, and nonpartisanship.[28]

One of the main social targets of the progressive reformers included immigrants and the urban political machines and bosses that the immigrants' putative ignorance supposedly fostered. Both posed a putative threat to American democracy.[29] But with America's rising imperialism, the progressivists' approach was also extended to targets abroad. Progressive reformers like Wilson claimed that reform at home went hand in hand with the colonial civilizing mission.[30] Proimperialists added likewise that the key to America's colonial success was "administration," suggesting that such administration "is nature's method for the spread of civilization."[31] James Hyslop, in fact, contended that administration in the colonies for the purposes of transformation would be easier than administration and transformation at home. The kind of "efficient and successful government" most needed in America's municipal governments could be swiftly produced overseas, because in the colonies power was concentrated in the hands of a few American officials, while at home power was divided among different groups. If progressive reformers categorized the world as an object to be transformed, and if colonialists categorized the colonies as objects to be transformed as well, for Hyslop the only difference was that transformation in the latter would be quicker and more efficient.[32]

On colonial ground, too, the progressive style was clearly at play. When considering what kind of policies and governmental forms should be implemented in the colonies, the McKinley administration relied upon expert commissions, thus rendering a parallel with the progressivists' ideal of commission-based city government. In fact, most of the commissioners had been taken from universities.[33] Furthermore, to formulate and administer colonial policy, McKinley appointed personnel with strong progressivist credentials. Many of the colonial officials were academic experts or had served in the progressive movement. Root was appointed secretary of war in charge of all colonial administration, and his reformist credentials had been already displayed.[34] Taft was appointed first civil governor of the Philippines, and he too had taken on the role of progressive reformer in Cincinnati.[35] Taft's fellow Yalies fittingly bragged that Taft was the perfect progressive reformer for the imperial job, chanting:

> When Dewey's guns gave Uncle Sam the Filipino's lands,
> We found we had a grouchy proposition on our hands;
> A governor was needed there; the job as not a graft,
> So a Yale man was selected and his name is Bill Taft.[36]

Officials also cited key writers of the new government of science when discussing how to solve problems of colonial government and drew inspiration for their programs from policies proposed by progressives at home, such as civil service and the Australian ballot system.[37] In these ways, the progressivists' style and its attendant schemas of control and engineering significantly fed the tutelage scheme. It made the idea of transforming foreign lands not only seem possible but also palpably promising and practical.

THE DRIVE FOR LEGITIMACY

A final factor helped to spawn and sustain tutelary colonialism. When the Americans contemplated what their colonialism should look like, they aimed to organize colonialism according to perceived local demands and interests. This was not because American authorities were especially liberal or benign, it was only because organizing colonialism to partially fit with perceived local demands would ensure an efficient occupation. The *drive for legitimacy* thus converged the American officials' particular schemas to finish the contours and content of occupation on the ground.[38]

The drive to legitimate rule is seen most clearly in the Philippines, where resistance to American sovereignty from armed revolutionaries had been strong. Indeed, the first commissioners insisted that American rule, rather than relying upon coercion alone, would fare better to demonstrate benevolence. They reckoned that not all Filipinos wanted to overthrow American sovereignty and thus asserted that, to best win the war, the regime had "to create a situation where those in favor of peace can safely say so, and can argue with their brethren in the field not only that our intentions are good but, by pointing to accomplished facts, show the advantage of accepting our authority."[39] Jacob Schurman thus suggested that replacing the existing military

drive for legitimacy entail the winning of hearts and minds.

government with civil government "would do more than any other single occurrence to reconcile the Filipinos to American sovereignty."[40] But winning hearts and minds would not only help to establish American rule, it would also help to sustain it in the long run. When Schurman cabled his views on long-term occupation to Washington, he asserted that it could not rely on coercion: "Americans and Filipinos will have to trust each other . . . while the Filipino stops at nothing nor thinks of death when influenced by hatred resentment or revenge, he is much moved by sympathy and generosity of powerful superiors, whose power he has felt. Believe magnanimity our safest, cheapest, and best policy with Filipinos."[41] He and his fellow commissioners then concluded that such "trust" and "magnanimity" could be best established by taking into account the Filipinos' own needs and interests and coordinating them with colonial policy. "To secure the confidence and affection of the Filipinos it is necessary not only to study their interests, but to consult their wishes, to sympathize with their ideals and prejudices even."[42]

Accordingly, as the commissioners pondered what kind of colonial government should be established, much of their initial activity was devoted to gathering information from inhabitants. While the war raged in the countryside, they held hearings and conducted interviews in Manila with "eminent Filipinos." They also collected information from their commanders in the field and dug into "articles, constitutions, proclamations, and other documents emanating from the insurgent Tagalogs and from pacific organizations of other Filipinos."[43] Such data collection was difficult and time consuming, but according to the commissioners it was "of the most vital significance":

> The United States can succeed in governing the Philippines only by understanding the character and circumstances of the people and realizing sympathetically their aspirations and ideals. A government to stand must be firmly rooted in the needs, interests, judgment and devotion of the people, and this support is secured by the adaptation of government to the character and possibilities of the governed — what they are, what they have it in them to become, what they want, and, not least, what they think they are entitled to have and enjoy.[44]

Statecraft in Puerto Rico followed the same logic. Even though war with the people had been averted from the outset, the first rulers strove for legitimacy. They were first instructed by Washington "tactful and conciliatory" when dealing with the people, and military commanders on the ground responded affirmatively.[45] They warned against arbitrarily arresting individuals, for example, because they worried that such arrests would threaten the image of American occupation. "The command that you will exercise [over municipal districts]," they told field agents, "is one that requires for successful administration the utmost tact, firmness, activity and sound judgement on the part of yourself and your officers and men."[46]

Legitimacy was also the goal of civilian rulers. Leo Rowe, head of the Puerto Rican code commission, claimed that legitimacy was definitive of civil rule. "Civil authority is unable to command the same obedience, or to exercise the same highly organized supervision which characterizes military rule." Civil rule "involves the co-operation of the native element, not only when in harmony with the executive but as a permanent, obligatory feature of the system." It must "use persuasion where the army may use command."[47] Accordingly, the first investigative commissions in Puerto Rico devoted much time to ascertaining local interests, just like their counterparts in the Philippines. The Carroll commission toured the island and held hearings, and their subsequent report to Washington, laying out their recommendations for policy, contained a section titled "What Porto Rico Expects from the United States."[48]

The result of this drive for legitimacy in both Puerto Rico and the Philippines was no minor matter. The forms of colonial government the commissioners recommended (and eventually instituted) partially incorporated the "interests" and "wants" of the colonized. Consider the recommendations for Puerto Rico. From its investigations, the Carroll commission found that the Puerto Ricans had been highly critical of Spanish rule. Apparently, the Puerto Ricans complained that Spanish rule had been too centralized, preventing Puerto Ricans from holding high positions; that it had not provided public education; and that Spanish economic policies had served only the interests of Spanish bureaucrats and residents. According to Carroll, then, what the Puerto Ricans wanted was not so much full independence as a more liberal form of colonial government—one that would give Puerto Ricans direct participation in the colonial state and modernize the island's economic and governmental system. More specifically, they wanted American control leading to statehood in the American union.[49]

Carroll's recommendation for colonial government followed. Carroll suggested that colonial policies should be devoted to building public schools, infrastructure, and helping agricultural industries. He further contended that the colonial government should give the Puerto Rican elite political participation and offer the opportunity for eventual statehood. His idea was to model the colonial government after the territorial governments that had already been established at home; that is, the territorial governments of Louisiana, New Mexico, and so on. This kind of government would serve a dual purpose. For one, it would establish legitimacy: "We do not need to promise statehood to them, [but] we certainly ought not to forbid them to aspire to statehood. It is an honorable aspiration and would put them on their best behavior." For another, it would help to educate the Puerto Ricans in self-government and thus realize local demands:

> They will learn the art of governing the only possible way — by having its responsibilities laid upon them. . . . The father who wishes his son to learn to swim does not row him all day upon the lake, but puts him into the water and the child's fear of drowning will stimulate those exercises which lead to the art of swimming. Let Porto Rico have local self-government after the pattern of our Territories and she will gain by her blunders, just as cities and States in our own glorious Republic are constantly learning.[50]

The plan finalized by Root reflected the recommendations. Directly modeled after territorial governments at home, however with colonial modifications, a tutelary government with the potential for eventual statehood would realize "the interests of the people" and "afford them an opportunity both to acquire and to demonstrate capacity for the conduct of government."[51]

The recommendations of the Philippine commissioners were similar. From their investigations, the commissioners concluded that the Filipinos who had not rebelled wanted "the tutelage and protection of the United States" rather than independence. They wanted a more liberal form of colonial government than Spain had provided, one that would (a) "respect the rights" of Filipinos, (b) give them an active part in the colonial state, and (c) attend to education, infrastructural development, and economic accumulation. The commissioners then asserted that the Filipinos who had rebelled against American sovereignty wanted the same thing. The commissioners studied the documents of the Philippine revolution and concluded that the revolutionaries despised Spanish rule for its disregard of the Filipinos' rights and the tyranny of Spanish friars. "What the people want above every other thing, is a guarantee of those fundamental human rights which Americans hold to be the natural and inalienable birthright of the individual but which under Spanish domination in the Philippines were shamefully invaded and ruthlessly trampled upon." The only hitch, according to the commissioners, was that the revolutionaries were too "self-seeking" and uneducated to be able to fully realize these rights under an independent government. A tutelary government was thus necessary. This would win over the revolutionaries and realize their interests in spite of themselves.[52]

> If these abuses [from Spanish rule] are remedied, if a capable and honest government is instituted, if the Filipinos are permitted to the full extent of their ability to participate in it . . . if church is separated from state, if public revenues are used solely to defray the legitimate expense of government. . . . if, in a word, government is administered in the Philippines in the spirit in which it is administered in the United States, the people of that archipelago will, as already a few of them foresee, enjoy more benefits than they dreamed of when they took up arms against the corrupt and oppressive domination of Spain.[53]

The commissioners ultimately recommended a colonial government modeled after territorial governments at home. Here the model was drawn not from treatment of Native Americans but from governmental forms that applied to fledgling states and their populations as a whole. The commissioners quoted Jefferson's statement in 1803 that the inhabitants of Louisiana were "as yet incapable of self-government as children," and stated that the Filipinos should be given political participation in local offices and a national assembly in the same tutelary fashion that was applied to Louisiana. This kind of government would serve the Filipinos' interests and, hence, the Americans' own interests in establishing a liberal form of colonial government. "It has been a leading motive with the commission in devising a form of government for the Philippines to frame one which, to the utmost extent possible, shall satisfy the views and aspirations of the educated Filipinos." It would also give the Filipinos an education in how to properly govern themselves. By following "Jefferson's lead" and "adapting it to the condition of the natives," the Filipinos would be set upon "a course of development under American training [and] eventually reach the goal of complete local self-government." They would then have "contentment, prosperity, education, and political enlightenment."[54]

In part, then, tutelage was motivated by the need to accommodate perceived local demands and thereby meet the requisite of legitimacy. This is not to say that the drive for legitimacy itself determined tutelary policy. American officials may have wanted to realize legitimacy and thus partially concede to local interests, but if they had not classified the colonized as eventually capable of learning self-government (i.e., if they articulated a racial view rooted in biology, blood, and stock), their concessions might not have affected policy. If they had not brought with them a reformist and transformist ethos, the idea of tutelage might have seemed impossible. Tutelage was born from a happy coincidence, a contingent convergence between the perceived demands of the colonized on the one hand, and the Americans' racial and reformist self-classifications on the other.

DISCIPLINE AND DEMOCRATIZE

While the American officials' particular cultural repertoire provided the elements that made tutelary colonialism possible, palpable, and practical, it also delimited what tutelary colonialism was to impose and create. Tutelage was supposed to teach "liberty," "democracy," and the "art of self-government," but the meanings of such signifiers were guided by authorities' own particular cultural structures — the preexisting set of parallels and oppositions familiar to them.

One of these oppositions was straightforward enough: democracy or self-government on the one hand, and monarchical or hereditary rule on the other.[55] Still, authorities also worked from a more specific set of schemas within the overarching opposition. These schemas put a distinct set of valences upon what would otherwise be presumed as essential or coherent "American" democratic values. After all, as historians of the Progressive era have noted, the meaning of democracy itself had been in contention in the United States at the time. America's political culture was neither singular nor uniform.[56] Thus, American officials did not make meaning by transposing a "traditional" or essential notion of democratic self-government; rather, they worked from their own particular schemes shaped by their specific experiences and institutional backgrounds.

For starters, democratic self-government in the American officials' conception did not mean only the absence of monarchy or hereditary rule. It denoted more precisely what Taft often called "popular" self-government — that is, government by the people, rather than by a handful of self-interested and unrestrained elites. The "self" in self-government had to be a collective self, and the collective self had to be a popular collectivity. This is why the Americans claimed that the Malolos government of the temporary Philippine Republic (constructed by the revolutionaries) was not actually a democracy. It had instituted some "ceremonies" of democracy — such as elections and a constitution — but it was incomplete. Putatively, political offices in the Malolos government had been monopolized by the most privileged and educated Tagalogs (sometimes known as *ilustrados*). These elites then vulgarized power for their own ends in disregard for the rights and opinions of the mass of the population.[57] "There wasn't a clause in the whole thing," complained Cameron Forbes about the Malolos constitution, "giving poor people representation or rights." For Forbes, this proved that the Filipinos "do not understand the American idea of government." Their idea of independence was the "freedom of a few to oppress the many," and so the Philippine Republic was actually an "oligarchy" (or, at best, a "Malay despotism" and "tyranny").[58] Officials used the same schema when discussing Puerto Rico. Root asserted that while there were a few "public spirited and patriotic" Puerto Ricans, there were "not enough of them to make a working government which would be anything but an oligarchy." The elite, like their Spanish rulers, were far too self-aggrandizing and corrupt.[59] If anything, they were like the caciques of Latin American republics — a wealthy, greedy, and aristocratic class of officeholders who vulgarized government for their own ends.[60]

Authorities also added another opposition to the series. Democratic self-government did not only mean government by a collective self, it also meant that the collective self, or the "people," had to be "enlightened." This was the other reason colonial authorities saw oligarchic and despotic tendencies in the two countries: most of the population was "ignorant, credulous, and childlike," as Taft described them. The "masses" were easily dominated and exploited by the elite, which in turn constituted tyranny. Necessary for proper self-government, then, was an informed and "rational" citizenry — a people that would be able to "know their civil rights and maintain them against a more powerful class," and thereby resist the "absolute control . . . frequently exercised over him by the local cacique."[61] Without this resistance to absolute control, Orville Platt wrote, "there may be a republic in name, but in fact it will only be a dictatorship."[62]

"Reason" and enlightenment was also something that political leaders and government officials had to have. This did not only mean that leaders and government officials had to have formal education. Officials repeatedly claimed that while the Puerto Rican and Filipino political elite were educated, they were not fit for self-government because they did not base their actions on the decisions of the majority or on considerations of the public good. As oligarchs and tyrants, the elite instead pursued only "selfish ends" and based their actions upon personal, familial, or narrowly partisan considerations. "The present incapacity of the people of Porto Rico for the enjoyment of complete self-government," asserted William Willoughby, "is due to this failure rather than to the lack of education on the part of the majority of the population":

> The more highly educated classes of the population show little if any desire to subordinate selfish ends to public considerations. After centuries of effort to create such a public opinion [even at home], success has only been partially achieved. It is not remarkable, therefore, that when we turn to a country such as Puerto Rico, inhabited by persons having none of the traditions of self-government behind them, with temperaments more excitable, with the custom of valuing immediate rather than ultimate results, and with the characteristic firmly ingrained in them of emphasizing personal, family and other considerations at the expense of public interests, to find that these fundamental bases of real democratic self-government should be largely lacking.[63]

Here the colonialists' specific Progressive-era schemes, rather than a coherent American political culture or essential set of traditional values, are most clearly disclosed. Not only did the officials classify the elite as oligarchs and caciques, they also equated with the bosses of political machines at home.

As intimated earlier, the Progressive reform movement took these bosses as one of their many targets. In so doing, it tried to elevate a specific culture of democracy—a liberal democracy based upon sovereign individuals—over and against political machines. The American officials were part and parcel of the Progressive movement, so they operated from the same spirit and schema. In their view, the problem with bosses at home was the same problem with the Puerto Rican and Filipino elite. Both attained power by the "ignorance" of the people (e.g., immigrant voters at home and "child-like" masses in the colonies), and both conducted government through patronage and parties, personal passions and interests, and organic ties of family, ethnicity, and clan. Both, in other words, posed an affront to liberal democracy; that is, a polity wherein people were freed from organic loyalties and could act as "rational" sovereign individuals.[64] Thus, just as Boston reformer Robert Woods complained that "ward politics" was "built up out of racial, religious, industrial affiliations; out of blood kinship; out of childhood associations, youthful camaraderie, [and] general neighborhood sociability," so too did Willoughby in Puerto Rico assert that "real democratic self-government" demands considerations of "public interests" rather than "personal, family and other considerations." Just as reformers decried the political corruption in ethnic wards, so, too, did the Americans in the colonies decry the corruption of the Puerto Rican and Filipino elite. The key "defect" of native officials during Spanish rule had been their "lack of any sense of responsibility . . . to the public at large" and their use of office "as a source of private profit and as a means of gratifying private desires."[65]

Critical for proper self-government in the colonial authorities' view was "rational politics"—a politics based upon informed ideas, issues of public good, and criteria of efficiency, not personalism, patronage, and partisan passions. "In time," wrote governor William Hunt, laying out his vision of proper self-government in Puerto Rico, "the overwhelming importance attached to everything political and the phenomenon of purely personal politics . . . will be superseded by rational politics based upon principles of administration and honest differences in opinion on important questions rather than on the personal difference of the various leaders."[66]

This emphasis upon liberal democracy and rational politics was concomitant with the final aspect of the officials' meaning structure. If self-government meant collective self-rule, which was realized when the collectivity consisted of sovereign and rational individuals, those individuals in turn had to exercise self-restraint. They had to suppress their passions and "selfish ends" and submit to higher considerations — political principles, for example, or the "public good." Thus, collective self-government was also parallel with *individual* self-government: the government of the individual self by the self. Power was not to be exerted from above or outside — by a king, tyrant, cacique, or boss — but rather from within. Power had to circulate in and through sovereign individuals, rather than being imposed upon them.[67] Foucault detects this kind of *self*-government, this "self-subjection" and "self-discipline," as critical for modern liberalism.[68] But long before Foucault American progressives and their imperial counterparts conceived of it. Root articulated it during his lectures on citizenship at Yale. In modern democracies, he claimed, government no longer works through a "superior authority claimed by divine right, selected by inheritance [or] supported by a small governing class." This "repressive and directive" power, claimed Root, has been replaced by new "modern systems of popular government" in which repression functions as "self-repression." For Root, popular self-government connoted "organized self-control."[69]

Root and the other American colonialists transposed this classification of self-government overseas. They equated the absence of self-discipline, the lack of self-restraint and self-control, with the Puerto Rican and Filipinos' corruption, partisan and personalized politics; and they equated the presence of self-discipline with "rational politics." "What is necessary for self-government," asserted Willoughby in regards to Puerto Rico, "is not only mass education but also public opinion and self-restraint."

> No system of self-government upon a democratic basis can be other than a pretence [*sic*] or mere form unless there exists in the community, not only an effective public opinion demanding that those in public office shall exercise their powers for the welfare of the community as a whole rather than for the attainment of selfish and party ends, but the people themselves must possess those qualities of self-restraint, tolerance, obedience to law and constituted authorities, and acquiescence in the decision of majorities which are the absolute prerequisites of the successful operation of popular government.[70]

Officials in the Philippines similarly claimed that what the Filipino elite lacked, and what they needed for proper self-government, was self-discipline. Theodore Roosevelt wrote, "The educated people themselves, though full of phrases concerning liberty, have but a faint conception of what real civil liberty is and the mutual self-restraint which is involved in its maintenance."[71]

Given this emphasis upon self-discipline, it is not surprising that the American colonialists put heavy emphasis on legal-rational action and formal procedure. Political thinkers have long equated the rule of law and liberal democracy, but for the American colonialists, the rule of law was especially critical. It was an index as well as the guarantor of individual self-discipline. According to William Willoughby, the Puerto Rican elites' disregard of the public interest and their pursuit of personal and party interests was due to the fact that, during Spanish rule, law had been administered "in an arbitrary and illegal manner."[72] John Taylor claimed that the despotic character of the Malolos government lay in the fact that the ilustrados exercised a political control over the people that was "absolute, and . . . outside the law." Evidently, what the elite needed was to internalize the force of law, thereby exercising self-discipline.[73] Wilson summarized the scheme in a passage oft-quoted by colonial officials: "Self-government is not a mere form of institution, to be had when desired, if only proper pains be taken. It is a form of character. It follows upon the long discipline which gives a people self-possession, self-mastery, the habit of order and peace and common counsel, and a reverence for law which will not fail when they themselves become the makers of law; the steadiness and self-control of political maturity. And these things cannot be had without long discipline."[74]

In short, the meaning of democratic self-government articulated by tutelage proponents was particular indeed. Differing from other meanings both abroad *and* at home, it referred to collective and individual self-government and entailed a particular set of cultural models and schemas of conduct. It followed that as the American officials made meanings by reference to this cultural structure, conjoined with their racial schemes, they concluded that the Puerto Ricans and Filipinos were not yet fit for self-government. The elite may have wanted democracy, but the American officials classified them as lacking it. It also followed that while tutelage was supposed to realize local political interests, it was only to realize them as the American officials defined them. Tutelary colonialism meant the imposition of the officials' own distinct conception of self-government at the expense of all others.

CULTURE AS TERRAIN: THE PRACTICES OF RULE

In later chapters we will see that there were alternatives to these particular conceptions of democratic self-government. But for now we might wonder. What exactly was involved in carrying out tutelary colonialism? How was tutelage to do its work and realize stated goals? An analysis of the regimes' practices shows that while culture provided the schemas by which tutelary policy was conceived and then adopted, it was also a critical dimension of enacting and fulfilling it on the ground. More than a systematic repertoire enabling and guiding rule, it was also the very terrain upon which colonialism was to do its work.

Signify and Subject

As noted already, American officials and policy makers were intent upon establishing and sustaining the legitimacy of their rule. Their idea to institute liberal colonial governments and facilitate native participation was in part motivated by this concern. But the attempt to win hearts and minds extended far beyond the construction of liberal states. It was a sustained effort, permeating the rulers' actions and involving various other practices. When, for instance, General Miles first arrived to Guanica on the southern shore of Puerto Rico, he immediately issued a proclamation. The proclamation asserted that the American military had come to the island "in defense of Liberty, Justice, and Humanity," bearing "the banner of freedom" and bringing "the fostering arm of a free people": "The chief object of the American military forces will be to overthrow the armed authority of Spain and to give to the people of this beautiful Island the greatest degree of liberty consistent with this military occupation. We have not come to bring war against a people which has been oppressed for centuries but . . . to bring protection . . . to promote your prosperity and bestow upon you the guarantees and blessings of the liberal institutions of our Government."[75]

The proclamation was precisely motivated. Miles had previously received reports that there was "considerable disaffection among the people in the southern part of the island [with Spanish rule]" and that the Puerto Ricans had been asking Madrid for political reforms and more participation in government. Miles recorded that, in light of this information, "I deemed it advisable, if possible, to encourage this feeling, and also to impress the people of the island with the good intentions of the American forces."[76] But the point is not that the proclamation was purely cynical. Colonial authorities were indeed planning to transpose certain elements of "the liberal institutions" of the United States to the island.[77] The point instead is twofold. First, American rulers wanted to win minds by portraying American occupation as something that fit local concerns and demands. Thus, Miles's proclamation was aimed at appealing to the Puerto Ricans' own "sentiment," as he perceived it. Second, this tactic of representing American occupation as fitting into local interests necessarily involved signifying activity. Rendering U.S. rule legitimate to local populations necessitated communicating that colonial occupation would be appropriate and beneficial.

Authorities in the Philippines relied upon the very same signifying means. True, with the war raging in the provinces, the task was all the more urgent. But in fact, even before the outbreak of Filipino resistance, imperial agents had proclaimed America's ostensibly benign intentions. Soon after the Treaty of Paris, President McKinley issued his "benevolent assimilation" proclamation (December 21, 1898). The proclamation announced that "the earnest wish and paramount aim of the military administration to win the confidence, respect, and affection of the inhabitants of the Philippines by assuring them in every possible way that full measure of individual rights and liberties which is the heritage of free peoples, and by proving to them that the mission of the United States is one of benevolent assimilation, substituting the mild sway of justice and right for arbitrary rule."[78] After the first shots of the Philippine-American War were fired, the Philippine Commission proceeded to use words as weapons. The commissioners concluded that the goals of the rebellion were not unlike America's own colonial goals, and that the rebellion was due to the "ambitions of a few and the misunderstanding of the many." Thus, "to clear away such misunderstanding," they issued yet another proclamation, on April 4, 1899. The proclamation, "prepared with great care and after [a] diligent study [of the] situation," asserted that the United States would install "an enlightened system of government"; "spread peace and happiness among the Philippine people . . . guarantee them a rightful freedom, protect them in their just privileges and immunities, accustom them to free self-government in an ever-increasing measure; and to encourage them in those democratic aspirations, sentiments, and ideals."[79] To first insinuate colonial power, rulers relied upon the power of signification.

To be sure, the regimes devoted much effort and material resources to signifying activity. They issued countless proclamations and made many speeches. The Philippine Commission translated their proclamations into Spanish, Tagalog, and other local dialects (there were 25,000 copies of their first proclamation), and they exerted precious time to propagating the tutelary mission. "Much of the time of the Commission during the last few days," noted Moses in his diary, "has been taken up in explaining to conspicuous Filipinos the purposes of the Commission, and in giving them some idea of the kind of government that will be established here after the return of peace."[80] But the colonial rulers did not only use words, they also engaged in acts and gestures self-consciously symbolic. Military officers in Puerto Rico made it a point to employ local labor and rent oxcarts and oxen from local farmers. As one officer explained, the goal was to show that "we stood for order, good behavior, and a peaceful resumption of business."[81] They also reappointed Puerto Ricans to the lower-level municipal posts that they had held during Spanish rule. Guy Henry explained to President McKinley: "If I had pursued any other course, putting Americans in position or forcing the military upon them, a very strong feeling against the Government would have been aroused."[82]

Authorities in the Philippines did the same thing. An amnesty proclamation decreed that as long as insurgents surrendered and took an oath of allegiance to the United States, they could participate in the new tutelary order. This was an effort to win hearts and minds in order to win the war, but even after the war the American officials remained intent upon portraying their benevolence. Governor Taft repeatedly insisted that Filipinos rather than Americans should be appointed to bureaucratic posts as much as possible. "We are very anxious," he wrote to one department head, "to have the Filipino understand that we are not here for the purpose either of spoils or place."[83]

Govern and Transform: The Mechanisms of Tutelage

Written and spoken words; benevolent acts and deeds — together they constituted a continuum of signifying practices deemed necessary for establishing a colonial rule. But as noted already, American officials also had more ambitious goals. Puerto Ricans and Filipinos were supposed to submit to tutelary colonialism, and signifying activity was supposed to aid the process, but the colonized were also to be changed and transformed in the process. By what magic was this to occur?

Part of the answer comes from Theodore Roosevelt. "Only the exceptional people," he said, "have ever succeeded in the experiment of self-government because its needs, its interest, and its successful working imply the existence within the heart of the average citizen of certain very high qualities. There must be control. There must be mastery, somewhere, and if there is no self-control and self-mastery, the control and the master will ultimately be imposed from without."[84] In other words, to become fit for self-government, colonial peoples had to first submit to an external authority. Like students to a schoolteacher or a child to a parent, they had to be subjected to what Root called a "course of tuition under a strong and guiding hand." Then, by this course of tuition, the students would internalize the external authority, adopting the meanings and schemas imposed. "Under the wholesome and salutary influences of just laws and a sympathetic administration," claimed Woodrow Wilson, "they will after a while understand and master themselves." Vicente Rafael (1993a) and Michael Salman (1995) have therefore suggested that the discipline of schooling was the metaphor and model of tutelage in the Philippines.[85] But to this it must be added that was also a matter of "governance." The distinction is important. While discipline works directly upon individual bodies, governance works from afar and above, coordinating spaces and structures rather than bodies so as to lay down the conditions for presumed laws and regularities to work on their own accord.[86] Governance is thus akin to the progressive reformers' conception of "administration." In regards to tutelage, it meant creating the conditions necessary for the linear process of development and improvement — the process of building upon the capacities of colonial peoples — to best unfold.

For instance, officials in both colonies placed emphasis upon economic and infrastructural development. Taft suggested that the influx of "Yankee capital" to the Philippines would bring "Yankee ingenuity, Yankee enterprise, and Yankee freedom." In regards to Puerto Rico, officials claimed that "with the development of commerce comes an influx of democratic ideas."[87] Economic development would thus change the conditions on which the colonized lived, thereby facilitating Americanization. Officials similarly put emphasis on public schooling. As Taft put it, the goal was to teach the so-called ignorant and credulous masses "how to exercise their rights against a more powerful class," and while each individual school employed disciplinary measures, colonial rulers did not themselves act as disciplinarians. They instead oversaw the process from afar, providing funds and directing the school system so as to help create an enlightened citizenry on a mass scale.

A final and related governmental program was "political education" — the focus of the present study. This was targeted at the Puerto Rican and Filipino elite, who were to get their own kind of education.[88] It involved a two-tiered process: (a) the transmission of political meanings through the imposition of yet more signs, and (b) giving the elite direct experience in political affairs so that they could learn hands-on. Both of these involved changing the conditions under which the elite lived. The first involved making the authorities' ideologies available and recognizable. The second involved turning the colonial state into a "school of politics" so as to transmit and institutionalize the authorities' schemas and meanings in local practice.

American authorities exerted much energy trying to transmit American political principles and ideas through preaching and pedagogy. This was considered crucial. Putatively, while the Puerto Rican and Filipino elite "deal in high sounding phrases concerning liberty and self-government," they did not *really* know what those things meant. "In public speech," wrote one observer of Puerto Rican politicians, "the [political] orator is usually verbose . . . enabled to pronounce a great many words in an address without the necessity of furnishing many ideas."[89] Thus, American officials tried to teach beloved political concepts through the written and spoken word. They sought to make their political meanings available and desirable. Hence, at inauguration ceremonies, officials gave speeches that tried to convey not only a sense of colonial authority and benevolence, but also how to practice office in a democratic government. Governor Allen in Puerto Rico used his inauguration speech to stress that elected officials had to be "men of high sense of honor who will not seek to advance their own fortunes at your expense and who will not allow others do so; men who will see that justice and straightforward honesty will be meted out to all, and who will have a sole regard for the welfare of Porto Rico and the honor of the American Government in its relations to it."[90] Governor Hunt added in his inauguration speech: "This is not a personal government, but a government by law."[91] American authorities in the Philippines gave similar speeches at public meetings with the local elite. When Taft and his fellow commissioners first established local governments, they traveled through the islands as part of their educating efforts. They gathered the local elite together, read aloud the new provincial and municipal laws, and then preached the Progressive-era gospel. "You must have in mind the public weal," Taft told them, "you must . . . serve only the public good and not personal gain. If each officer administers his office so as to benefit the general public and not his individual interest there would be no difficulty in maintaining law and order and giving to the people contentment and prosperity, but if any official shall regard his office solely as a means of gratifying either his personal desire for revenge or to benefit particular friends, then the government would be a failure."[92] The colonial states in both countries also sponsored occasional conventions of local officials — another prime opportunity to preach. "Always make good use of your votes," urged Governor Hunt at one such convention, "for you are responsible, in casting them, for the good or bad government of the country, for the quality of the government which you have chosen."[93]

Besides the spoken word, colonial authorities relied upon the circulation of written texts. Both regimes inaugurated the *Official Gazette*, translated into Spanish (and in the Philippines into local dialects, too). The journal was transmitted to all local officials. It contained the laws and codes of the land and reproduced the speeches of officials, thereby making the American officials' verbal lessons further available.[94] The regimes also distributed memos and circulars. "In order to permit American customs and policy to take root in this island," said one, "it is desirable to set aside personal politics."[95] Tutelary states thus became signifying machines. In 1902 alone, the executive office in the Philippines distributed more than 200,000 copies of laws, orders, and speeches. The number increased to 663,927 in 1904. The same year the Bureau of Printing used up 7,201 reams of paper. In 1913, the number of reams increased to 14,203.[96] These levels of symbolic production made the availability of American meanings comparable between the two colonies. In Puerto Rico, for example, there were 1.3 copies of texts produced by the bureau for every one literate adult male; in the Philippines, there were 1.2 copies.[97]

While American officials inundated the colonized with signs, they also claimed that hands-on experience was the best educating method. The "art of self-government," Root asserted, "does not come to men by nature, it has to be learned; facility in it has to be acquired by practice."[98] Hence the other part of political education: "practical political education."[99] As officials noted, this idea derived from Tocqueville. Taken to the colonies, it meant granting the elite political and governmental participation so that they could get the political experience and practice they putatively needed. "Instruction in the principles and methods of government can be imparted," claimed Willoughby, "in the practical school of experience."[100] Accordingly, authorities let the elite hold municipal offices and gave them some autonomy. "The towns are to be let alone and free to administer their own affairs," General Davis wrote to Root. "I fear they will not at first do this well, but they will learn, and while experience may prove to be dear schoolmaster, they will ultimately learn the lesson."[101] American authorities did not hesitate to clarify the purpose to their students. During the commission's trip through the municipalities, governor Taft quoted Tocqueville to stress that, in town governments, "civil liberty and a free government [find their] formulation." The town government is where "the seeds of popular government might be sown."[102] Authorities also instituted legislative assemblies staffed by elected natives and modeled after the House of Representatives at home. Puerto Ricans and Filipinos were supposed to learn the principle of the separation of powers and how to formulate legislation along American lines.[103] Colonial officials further let Puerto Ricans and Filipinos vote for their own assemblies through regular elections.[104] The foremost goal was to produce "rational" and sovereign voters and, accordingly, the Americans in both colonies instituted the Australian ballot system. This was the system already used by progressive reformers at home to protect "the sanctity of the ballot" and prevent corruption by tyrannical bosses.[105]

On the other hand, these efforts in granting autonomy went only so far. American officials instituted a number of mechanisms for maintaining ultimate control in the belief that such control was necessary for the elite to learn their lessons properly. For instance, authorities kept the highest posts of government for themselves. Following the territorial model at home, they occupied the Philippine Commission and the Executive Council for Puerto Rico, choosing a few select natives to act as advisers. These bodies served as the executive branch and upper legislative house at once, and American appointees of the president thus had ultimate veto power over all legislation. They further constructed a system of surveillance to ensure that native officials would receive their lessons properly. In Puerto Rico, American authorities retained the power to remove officials at will and intervene into municipal affairs as needed. In the Philippines, the governmental hierarchy was more complicated, for there was an intermediate level of provincial governments between the central government and the municipalities below, but authorities nonetheless took concerted steps to ensure control and compensate for the problem of geographic distribution. The Philippine Commission, for example, appointed Americans to provincial posts. These Americans served as local field agents, performing certain administrative functions and directly supervising Filipino officials.[106] Finally, authorities in both colonies instituted an American-controlled bureau of civil service agents that would check into the financial affairs of local governments. This would serve to give the native officials "a political education which will show them the possibility of the honest administration of government."[107]

All the while, American authorities fashioned themselves mentors and models offering "object lessons" in good government. This idea of "object lessons" drew from theories of learning and development articulated by G. Stanley Hall. Hall, known as the founder of American psychology, had argued that both children and the "lesser races" learn through example. American colonial officials likewise believed that their presence and governmental activities would serve the educating process. Colonial governments were to be "administered in such a way as to constitute a valuable means of educating and instructing the local officials in the art of government and administration, by pointing out errors [and] encouraging higher ideals." The people would then "outgrow the remembrance and practices of the past and look upon such efficient, disinterested, and impartial administration of affairs as the normal one to be expected and insisted upon in the same way as they formerly looked upon the old regime, where personal motives and interest had full sway, as the natural and unavoidable one."[108]

Finally, there was a larger system of incentive and reward. At one register, there were incentives and rewards for individuals. In both colonies, American authorities promulgated strict provisions against local political corruption — bribery, graft, and so on — and officials found guilty were to be removed from office. This was akin to disciplinary power: individuals, when deviating from the system, were to be punished. The other register, however, operated a higher level of abstraction and was the key to the operations of tutelage. Tutelage itself was to be a kind of reward system for the elite and the society as a whole. The idea was that as the people slowly learned their lessons in the art of American-styled self-government, American control and supervision would be decreased over time, leading ultimately to complete self-government. As Taft put it, "practical political education" meant "the extension, step by step, of political control to an eligible class."[109] Root summarized: "A form of government should be provided which will assure the kind of administration to which we are accustomed, with just as much participation on the part of Porto Ricans [*sic*] as is possible without enabling their inexperience to make it ineffective, and with opportunity for them to demonstrate their increasing capacity to govern themselves with less and less assistance."[110]

In short, while tutelage sometimes employed discipline, and while it sought to install it as the premise for self-government, it typically relied upon manipulating spaces, structures, and conditions so as to allow the invisible hand of development to do its work. The colonized were to be subjected to new ideological conditions, as colonial officials inundated them with new political ideas and concepts. They were subjected to new political structures — as American authorities fashioned their colonial states as "instruments of instruction." The ultimate goal was transformation. Tutelage in the Philippines, claimed Forbes, would serve to "uproot or modify all impediments to democratic institutions." "Hispano-Malayan" forms of authority would be replaced with so-called American forms.[111] In this sense, culture was much more than a sideshow to colonial power; nor was it merely a manifestation or reflection of America's presumably exceptional values and traditions. Culture was colonial power's very target and terrain, an object that colonialism was to manage, work upon, and recreate.

But then we might wonder. If such exercises in cultural power were a critical part of occupation, did they always, if ever, do their projected work? Or do we assume that colonialism was constituted by the colonizers' utterances and projections alone?

Chapter 2

DOMESTICATING TUTELAGE IN PUERTO RICO

"They call themselves 'Porto Rican, American,'" General Guy Henry happily reported to President McKinley not long after first arriving at Puerto Rico.[1] He was not exaggerating. Nearly all sectors of Puerto Rican society warmly welcomed the American forces. When General Nelson Miles's ship first landed on the southern coast in June 1898, crowds amassed on the shore and cheered loudly. As the troops proceeded inward, townspeople showered them with cigars, fruit, and flowers, hollering "Viva los Americanos!" "The natives," recorded one soldier, "seemed to have gone mad for joy."[2] Even the more privileged among the population gave a warm reception. Municipal officials, comparably wealthy and educated, greeted the troops with extended hands. They swiftly submitted to the new authority and offered their services.[3]

The people were eager to see Spanish rule end. But they were also eager to see American occupation begin. While locals referred to themselves as "Porto Rican, American," municipal officials renamed streets after prominent American statesmen — Washington, Lincoln, and even General Nelson Miles. They renamed streets after the day when the troops first arrived to their town and issued proclamations declaring that the Americans' arrival marked "a new era of progress and liberty for the country."[4] The elite even accepted the idea of tutelary rule and its transformative designs. One political leader urged his peers to participate in the tutelary regime in order to regenerate local life: "Puerto Rico, which by good fortune has been emancipated from the odious domination of Spanish, and which today, by even more fortune, forms part of the U.S. of North America . . . needs the assistance of worthy men to help in the great labor of political and administrative regeneration."[5] The elite also called for full incorporation into the American union. They acknowledged that a period of tutelage was to come first but hoped that it would eventually lead to self-government in the form of statehood.[6] "I accept with all my heart annexation to the U.S. of America," they told American authorities.[7] General Henry concluded, "They want to be Americans in every way."[8]

The Puerto Ricans' reception to American occupation and tutelage had critical consequences. Popular images in the U.S. portrayed the Puerto Rican people as desperate for external authority. When American statesmen justified colonial rule, they employed these same images, using them as proof that U.S. rule would serve the Puerto Ricans' own interests. Furthermore, the Puerto Ricans' warm reception made for a swift transition to American sovereignty. In the absence of resistance to American occupation, the United States was able to oust Spanish rule and establish a new colonial government on foreign terrain, almost overnight.

Why did the Puerto Rican elite so swiftly and warmly accept the tutelage project? Part of the answer lies in the Americans' symbolic efforts and exercises in cultural power. As we saw in chapter 1, American authorities from the very beginning used signs and symbols to establish the legitimacy of occupation. Scattered reports suggest the efforts were successful. Journalists reported that one of the reasons why the Americans "landed in triumph" was because of General Miles's proclamation offering "the guarantees and blessings of the liberal institutions of our Government." The Puerto Ricans continued to accept U.S. occupation because the military commanders "played the conquerors with tact, with power, and like gentlemen. They recognized the rights of others and they forced others to recognize their rights."[9] Members of the Puerto Rican elite themselves acknowledged the success of signs. According to Jose de Diego, he and his peers had initially wanted to resist the Americans when the Spanish-American War broke out and had asked the Spanish governor for arms. But they "dropped the idea" when they read Miles's proclamation and heard his "magnificent speech."[10]

But if the elite had been seduced by signs, what exactly did they see in them that made them submit to occupation and its tutelary designs? The answer cannot be assumed. Nor can it be read off the symbolic practices of rulers or a few scattered reports. We would fare better to closely investigate the meanings the elite made. By doing so, this chapter will show that when the Puerto Rican elite received the Americans' messages and symbolic exercises, they first drew upon their preexisting cultural structures. Before American rule, the elite had already formulated a distinct set of schemas on what democratic self-government meant, and narratives for how to conduct it. When the elite classified tutelage, its signs, the American officials, and the Americans' actions, they did so by first drawing upon these previously institutionalized schemas and narratives. They *domesticated* imposed signs and forms. The correlate of this domestication was twofold. On the one hand, the Americans' attempt to win hearts and minds by manipulating signs was effective. As the American officials proclaimed that tutelage would bring democracy and self-government, and as the Puerto Rican elite received the Americans' discourse and actions in accordance with their prior concepts of the same, the tutelage project resonated among the elite and the elite thereby affirmed it. On the other hand, while the Americans' signs resonated, they resonated in a particular way. The elite made meanings of American occupation in terms of their prior cultural schemas, but the particularity of those schemas — conditioned by their prior history of formation — meant that the elite produced distinct meanings that escaped the ones assumed and authorized by the American rulers. Cultural power worked on one level, but only because it failed on another. Rather than initiating cultural transformation, tutelage confronted cultural reproduction.

THE PUZZLE OF RECEPTION

Existing studies present two arguments for why the elite warmly accepted American rule. One argument connects with structural-functional studies of culture. Some, for example, have suggested a congruence between the elites' subjective beliefs and the tutelage project. The claim is that, prior to American rule, the Puerto Rican elite had already come to value democratic institutions. During the last decade of Spanish rule, they had adopted democratic ideals and had demanded self-government from Spain. They had also come to believe that democracy needed to be further developed with the help of an outside civilization. The Puerto Rican masses were ignorant, the island was backward, and so the island's political system needed external civilizing influences. The elites' preexisting beliefs and values thus had an affinity with those of the new American rulers, which helps explain why they accepted American occupation.[11]

Another argument suggests that the elite accepted tutelage because of their economic goals. The elites' export economy had long depended upon Spanish capital and markets, but facing the end of Spanish rule, the elite lost those privileges. The solution was for the elite to subject themselves to tutelage and become incorporated into the United States. Incorporating as a state in the union would increase the flow of goods and capital between the island and the mainland: the United States would provide markets and capital, just as Spain had offered before. In this argument, accepting tutelage was a means to regain lost economic privileges.[12]

Both of these arguments help identify important dimensions of the elites' acceptance of American rule. First, the elite had indeed proclaimed democratic ideals before American occupation. During late Spanish rule, they had repeatedly demanded democracy from Spain. They had also insisted that, due to the character of the ignorant masses, democracy could only be realized with the help of Spain's external hand. The elite had not demanded independence from Spain but had instead requested self-government within the Spanish federal system. In their view, democracy as self-government was perfectly compatible with Spanish rule — the latter could accommodate the former by making Puerto Rico an equal province in the Spanish system. Furthermore, when American occupation began, the Puerto Rican elite praised the potentially civilizing influence of American occupation on the same grounds. They praised American democracy as an exemplar of civilization and insisted that they should be a part of it.[13] The elite insisted that American rule would help regenerate the island.

It is also true that the elite faced serious economic problems that could be solved with the help of the United States. In 1896, the price structure of the international coffee market collapsed; prices for Puerto Rican coffee dropped by 50 percent.[14] The elites' main source of income was thereby halted.[15] Furthermore, when news of the Spanish-American War broke out in 1898, Spanish financiers packed their bags and transferred their capital back to

Spain.[16] This was disastrous because the elite had been dependent upon outside capital. Finally, the elite faced a loss of future markets. Their coffee had long circulated within the protectionist umbrella of the Spanish Empire, but if Spain was ousted from the island, so too would the elites' protected markets.[17] For the elite, therefore, accepting American rule was the only solution. Accordingly, alongside the elites' affirmation of American occupation were repeated requests for economic help. They begged American authorities to set up agricultural banks supplied with American capital, thereby filling the void left behind by the Spanish.[18] They also requested free trade between the United States and Puerto Rico, which would open up America's doors to Puerto Rican exports. Free trade, claimed political leaders, was the "only possible solution," the "only remedy for our ills."[19] In fact, the elite made it clear that accepting tutelage was essential for realizing their economic goals. For example, they proclaimed their desire for the American military regime to end sooner rather than later and for it to be replaced by a more stable government. This was because, in their view, only with a stable government would American capital come to the island. As long as military rule continued, they felt that "little money will come to Puerto Rico for investment."[20] They also hoped that military occupation would lead to what they called "territorial government"—a status that Louisiana and other territories had had before obtaining full statehood in the American union. They wanted this status because territorial government would imply free trade between the United States and Puerto Rico.[21]

In short, existing studies that focus upon subjective values and political-economic incentives offer some insight into why the elite accepted tutelage. But a closer look reveals that they are also incomplete. They cannot account for the entirety of the elites' reception. Note that if the elite accepted U.S. rule due to their values or economic interests, we would be obliged to predict the following: not only would the elite have accepted American rule, they would have also learned and adopted the lessons of political education. If the elites' values were amenable to the Americans' project of development—congruent with tutelage's transformative designs and content—the elite would have had little hesitation in learning and adopting the Americans' political meanings and models. If the elite had a political-economic interest in eventual statehood, they would have had further interest in learning about tutelage's "lessons" and putting them to use. The Americans' meanings and models would have been an irresistible strategic resource, adopting them a key strategy for realizing their primary goals. To be sure, by learning and adopting the Americans' political models, the elite could demonstrate that they were capable of incorporation. Military rule would end, territorial government would begin, and statehood would follow — the elite would realize their political demands and achieve their economic goals at once. This was the very idea of tutelage in the first place, and the American authorities made it clear and public. In countless speeches and proclamations since the very beginning, American officials told the islanders that the peoples' conduct would be closely scrutinized and that the elite had to demonstrate their political fitness. Only if they proved their fitness would military rule end and statehood follow.[22] "You may never know," stated the first governor, "the anxiety with which your experiment is being watched. . . . Every step will be criticized."[23] Not only did the elite have an interest in learning about tutelage's lessons and putting them to use, they also had clear incentives to do so.

Yet the elite did not do this. To the contrary, during the first years of occupation — when all awaited Congressional legislation that would officially declare the island's future political status — the elite acted in every way contrary to their own stated goals and against their presumed values. They welcomed tutelage but remained impervious to its so-called lessons. First, as we will see in greater detail below, the elites' discourse during this period did not incorporate the Americans' signifying patterns. In none of their party platforms, public speeches, newspaper editorials, or even private correspondences did the elite reiterate the Americans' meanings on what democratic self-government involved. Second, the elite did not conduct tutelary office or elections according to the models of political conduct American authorities offered. Instead, during the first years of occupation, local officials conducted all kinds of political corruption. American authorities noted that they were "abusing" their power, using offices and police forces as "political tools," cultivating patronage and favoring their "friends and enemies." And during the first series of elections, they used money and sometimes coercion to win votes.[24]

If the Puerto Rican elite wanted territorial government and then statehood so as to remedy their economic ills, this was hardly the way to do it. In the face of the corruption, American journalists sent home the message that the

Puerto Ricans' conduct proved they were ignorant of the "true meaning of equality and liberty" and were like the bosses of "ward politics" at home.[25] Further, American officials in private correspondence told Washington that the corruption further attested to the Puerto Ricans' unfitness for statehood. Commander Davis noted the corruption and then concluded that "these people have no true conception of the use to be made of political rights" and that, therefore, military occupation should continue "for some time to come."[26] The elite, rather than demonstrating fitness as they claimed they should and would, wound up demonstrating incapacity.

The elites' failure to act in accordance with their presumed values and proclaimed goals cannot be explained by reference to the availability of the Americans' meanings and models, as if tutelage's requirements were not retrievable. Tutelage was like a panopticon, and the elite surely felt its presence. To be sure, the elite were not uninformed about what was to be expected of them. In speeches, proclamations, memos, and other public pronouncements, American authorities laid out the new municipal codes and regulations, all of which forbade the abuses and illegalities discovered. They also told the local officials what they should do to prove their fitness. They stressed that local officials had to follow the "American methods that have resulted in the success of the American nation" by being "honest," showing "zeal and attention to duty," and using political office "for the public good."[27] Furthermore, authorities made the tutelage narrative clear in their proclamations and speeches, and the elite took it to heart. Articles in the elites' own press organs referred directly to these speeches and proclamations. They urged their readership (consisting of, among others, local political officials across the island) not to "give the idea to the American metropolis that the military government should be prolonged for years and years. We need now, more than ever, to give proof of our capabilities." Editorials in the elites' papers also stated that if local municipal officials did not show their fitness for self-government, they would send a negative message to Congress. By failing to show fitness, their conduct would "harm future legislation for the country."[28] Many editorials even added that, in order to obtain statehood sooner rather than later, all local officials should "imitate" American ways of governance: "Never is the road most great than when the example of the greatest is imitated. And the people of the U.S. are giving us great teachings."[29]

It follows that a focus upon values, goals, or incentives — or even a focus upon culture from the top down — cannot account for the elites' curious conduct. The elite had a self-expressed interest in and incentive for learning the Americans' models, and the colonial regime made their models available. An approach that examines culture as a semiotic system-in-practice might fare better. Rather than locating meaning in subjective values or reducing it to calculations of utility, this approach would consider how users *make* meaning by employing available cultural structures. It would propose that when cultural users make meaning, they are constrained to first employ the cultural structures with which they are most familiar — that is, the cultural schemas and narratives previously institutionalized and hence interdependent with their fields of reference. This approach would also suggest that such semiotic practices in turn serve to shape political conduct. As people relate to others around them, as they conduct themselves in the world, they are guided by the meanings they make. Below we will find that this approach fares best for understanding the elites' reception to tutelage. We can better see why the elite accepted tutelage *and* why they nonetheless appeared impervious to its lessons.

ELITE POLITICAL CULTURE PRIOR TO U.S. RULE

We must begin by considering the elites' particular meanings on democracy and self-government before American occupation. Tutelage sought to implant certain ideas and practices of governance, but during the last decade of Spanish rule, the Puerto Rican elite had already discussed politics, formed political parties, participated in colonial elections, and held offices in the Spanish colonial state. Through this experience, the elite had constructed a systematic repertoire of political meanings, models, and methods regarding *democracía* ("democracy") and *gobierno propio* ("self-government" or "self-rule"). These meanings would be elusive to us if we were to reduce them to a set of subjective "values" or "orientation." But the elites' meanings were not of this sort. They were first made possible by elemental interrelations: patterns of opposition and contrast constituting various cultural schemas. Nor were these meanings static or untouched by outside influences. To the contrary, the external influences were multiple, and they obtained salience not because they marked an essential "Puerto Rican culture" but because of the particular context of Spanish rule and local social relations that had helped to fix them in practice, thereby institutionalizing them. A look at those local contexts and the cultural schemas that embedded them thereby merits attention.[30]

Cultural Structures in Practice

One key context in which the elites' political meanings were first forged lies in the world of agricultural production. The Puerto Rican political elite were not only a group of politicians. They were part of the socioeconomic elite, intimately tied to the island's expanding export economy. Most of them had been tied to coffee production, which rose to dominance during the late nineteenth century. Coffee has served as the material and symbolic base of elite power. The world of agricultural production was the world with which the elite were most familiar. In turn, this world of agricultural production was structured by particular social relations and attendant schemas of conduct. While the island had been articulated with the world capitalist system, it had not been fully subsumed by free wage labor. Surplus instead accrued through a series of personalized exchanges between landowner and tenant, and merchant-financier and landowner. Production was based upon patron-clientelism and concomitant codes of obligation, debt, and honor; signs of mutual dependence and paternalistic affection.[31] Most laborers in the island, for instance, were tenants bound to the land and the landlord. Tenants gave the landlord portions of their crop and offered personal loyalty, and in turn landlords let the workers and their family live on the land. These exchanges were highly unequal, for tenants were infinitely indebted to the landlord.[32] But paternalistic displays sustained the relationship. Landlords provided plots of land, clothing, and food; they served as ritual coparents of the tenants' children; sponsored weddings and funerals; and provided workers with a fiesta at the end of the harvest season. They acted as true patriarchs, each serving "as father, counselor, physician, and judge of his people," the very "personification of authority" to the laborers.[33] Novels thus portrayed hacendados treating their laborers "with the pure affection of a father."[34]

Such schemas of personalized dependence and exchange also guided relations within the wealthy class. Intra-elite relations often took the form of familial patron-clientelism: landed families intermarried, and siblings, sons, or cousins served the patriarch as overseers, doctors, or lawyers.[35] When relations between merchants and landlords were not familial, they were familiar nonetheless. Merchants continually extended credit for production, and landlords were continually indebted. It was "an economy of trust," a series of transactions "implying an element of confidence" that contributed to and sustained the expansion of agricultural production in the period.[36]

These patron-client schemas in the social field were transposed onto, and became reciprocal with, governmental conduct. At the municipal level, officials cultivated their domains like hacendados did. Municipal mayors controlled and dictated nearly all municipal affairs and fashioned themselves as the grand patrons of their localities. They sponsored town fiestas and religious celebrations of the town saint; they founded local charitable organizations, elite social clubs, and funded schoolhouses. To further ritualize their paternalistic benevolence, they sometimes renounced their salaries in grandiose public declarations.[37] They also cultivated personal followings by filling petty offices with families and friends and used the local police force as extensions of their personal power.[38] Municipal officials also extended patronage outward, building upon familial and economic networks to capture higher state resources and even control the local courts. The result was a series of exchanges among the political elite later derided by American observers: "Personal favor was bestowed for money. It appeared in the form of payment for privileges, the sharing of salaries, participation in profits, downright bribes, gratifications, and every sort of tribute that Power could exact."[39] This governmental conduct was facilitated rather than hampered by legal restriction. The municipal law in the 1890s granted municipal officials with a wide range of powers, and the laws were so complex, layered, and internally contradictory that, in practice, the law was whatever the official declared it to be. It was easily manipulated or ignored altogether.[40] In such a context, schemas of patronage and personalized authority were fostered and normalized as common and accepted ways for conducting government. The guiding schemas are even discernible in explicit discourse. A short pamphlet in 1898, written for popular instruction, proclaimed to lay out the "rights and duties of the citizen." But in so doing it referred to and thus personified political officials as "Authority." It then defined Authority as "the law in action and the law in practice."[41]

Municipal mayors (alcaldes) thus acted like hacendados; townspeople were classified akin to tenants; and political officials related to each other as did wealthy families. Such homologies between the social and governmental field were also mutually reciprocal. Officeholders were drawn from the economic elite, such that governmental and social relations were intertwined.[42] Accordingly, when the Spanish authorities opened up elections to fill local posts, electoral conduct was guided by the cultural models made available by social and governmental conduct. Votes were exchanged for favors and cash, and patron-client exchanges followed from the lines of agricultural production and circulation. Political leaders held their meetings in the commercial warehouses of the larger towns, and from there the networks expanded outward to the rural areas to form rural political machines.[43]

By the 1890s, all of these patron-client practices were further institutionalized to the benefit of the local elite. Coffee production accelerated, sugar production (the peninsular Spaniards' longstanding base) declined. This meant an expansion of the Puerto Rican elites' social power.[44] It also fed aspirations. The elite began demanding more economic and political control. But there were fetters. First, the Puerto Rican elite did not control finance capital. Peninsular Spaniards, many intra-imperial itinerants, owned the largest merchant houses of the island.[45] Second, Spanish financiers and other Spanish residents had long allied with the colonial state to form a conservative regime. With Spanish governor-generals appointed by Madrid, they constructed a network of patronage to their own favor. For instance, when elections for the provincial deputation had opened up in the 1870s, resident Spaniards formed their own political party, the Incondicionales. That party became the government party. The governor doled out bureaucratic offices to Incondicionales and appointed them to mayoral positions, thus impinging upon the Puerto Rican elites' municipal power.[46] Patronage from the top down posed an obstacle to the Puerto Rican networks from the bottom up.

It was in this context that the Puerto Ricans began to mobilize for the first time. Beginning in the 1880s, the elite reached out to other groups in the island and formed their own political party. Their movement was known as a movement for *autonomía* (autonomy), or full incorporation into the Spanish system. It called for Puerto Rico to be on equal par with Spanish regions in the metropole. In the process, the elite forged a new political discourse.

The signifiers that went into the elites' political movement were drawn from discourses circulating in the global context. They included terms like *autonomía*, *sociedad*, *patria*, and, later, *democracia*. But the elite constructed specific meanings of these terms. When using the signifiers, they articulated them with the cultural structures most familiar and available; that is, the classificatory schemes of patron-clientelism fixed in social and governmental practice.

Consider elite discourses of society and community. As the autonomists mobilized and tried to pose a cohesive front before the Spanish colonial state, they formulated a singular identity — the collective entity that would receive autonomy, the "self" that would govern itself. They scripted this entity as a hierarchically ordered, developing organism whose elements were bound together through mutual obligations. For instance, Salvador Brau, a widely influential leader, suggested that the main elements in Puerto Rico's society were corporatist — landlords, laborers, and merchants. He then suggested that landlords, or "the superior classes," as he called them, were obliged to treat their laborers with paternalistic affection. As laborers provided labor and loyalty, landlords were obliged to give "moral education," "protection," and "the farsighted and intelligent direction which only you [the landlord] can give them." In Brau's view, landlords and laborers "form two entities who complete each other, who are mutually dependent, one unable to dispense with the other." Brau extended the schema to classify the community as a whole. All social elements, he wrote, "love each other, support each other, live as one, work harmoniously like organs of a single body."[47]

This conception of the community as a hierarchically ordered entity of obligations was typically signified through recurrent familial keywords. Brau scripted Puerto Rico *sociedad* as the *gran familia puertorriqueña* — the great or large Puerto Rican family — and it was this term that the autonomist movement repeatedly employed.[48] Furthermore, when autonomist leaders spoke of the *familia*, they equated the love for it with love for the patria, that is, love for Spain. "To love the patria it is necessary first to love one's family," said Matienzo Cintrón.[49] Movement members additionally referred to each as *hermanos* and "sons of the patria" and the patria as the "mother country." In turn, the autonomists hitched particular meanings of political authority to this classification of the community. They claimed that "governing and governed are all members of the same family" — but, of course, families need heads.[50] Authority was essential, and submission to it meant not a denial of one's rights or freedom but their realization. Francisco Cepeda asked in his *Catechismo Autonomista*: "What is necessary to be a free man? To be honorable, true, and deferential; to obey and respect your fathers, to work and pay your debts, to fulfill your obligations and personal duties."[51]

In accordance with this schema, autonomist leaders divided the Puerto Rican "familia" into two categories: the "masses" (or "directed" classes, i.e., laborers) and the "directing classes." Putatively, the masses were inarticulate and unable to represent themselves. According to Luis Muñoz Rivera, one of the foremost autonomist leaders, the masses were the "productive crowd," a "passive multitude" — the "unconscious masses."[52] On the other hand, landowners, professionals, and merchants constituted the "directing classes." Just as Brau had suggested that hacendados should give "farsighted and intelligent direction" to their workers, so too did Muñoz suggest that the directing classes were the ones who could best articulate and realize the family's desires and interests, where the "unconscious masses" could not. Finally, Muñoz suggested more specifically that political leaders should necessarily come from this larger directing class. "There are, among the directing classes, thousands of individuals who are inhibited from action . . . [they] should one day form the head of the army." This political elite would then be "the directorate" holding "executive power within the collectivity." Wielding their "virility," they were endowed with the power to "order and command" the gran familia.[53]

The autonomist leaders classified themselves and their landed allies as having this privileged ability. Muñoz Rivera recollected his entry into politics as follows: "One afternoon, people followed me to my house and made me speak; I addressed them from the balcony, without having prepared my thoughts; and the fact is, they flowed with ease and I was able to say what I wished."[54] The leading elite newspaper, *La Democracia*, reported on a mass celebration of the Autonomist Party in the town of Mayaguez as follows:

> All Mayaguezian society, without distinction nor color, have rendered gallant tribute to the merits of [Luis] Muñoz [Rivera] and to the high aspirations of his politics [through] popular bands, triumphant arches, banners, applause, acclamations, flowers, speeches. . . . In such instances eloquence

spurts forth, and all are stirred and moved by its mysterious power. In Mayaguez the popular masses vibrated upon hearing the ostentatious word of our orators. . . . Never has Muñoz felt more energetic, nor Matienzo (Cintrón) more profound, nor Guzman more exquisitely correct, nor Casanova more reflexive. Yesterday [at the celebration], we . . . saw a clear demonstration of the ties that unite the [party] cause with the cause of the people; because the people were people in their true state . . . raising a pedestal to our men, a monument to our Ideal, a column of triumph to our regional culture.[55]

Spanish satirists were thus quick to deride the gendered and hierarchical self-image: "They [Muñoz Rivera and other 'directors'] let the people call them wisemen, while the negritas rock them in the hammocks."[56]

But if the political community was a gran familia, and if it was a matter of mutual exchanges and obligations injected with natural hierarchy, what could democracy and self-government mean?

The Emergence of "Democracy"

Neither the creole intellectuals nor their lesser peers in the autonomist movement wrote long treatises on the meaning of democracy. But they did make references to it. The earliest references employed very basic oppositions, particularly the opposition between some form of representation on the one hand, and no representation on the other. Salvador Brau in the 1880s, for example, claimed that whenever the Spanish Crown had taken the wishes and interests of the Puerto Rican people into account when it made policy, the Crown manifested a "democratic spirit."[57] But later, other autonomist leaders elaborated upon this opposition while retaining the underlying sense. Muñoz Rivera built upon it when articulating the only explicit definition of democracy in the 1890s. The definition came in the form of an editorial, "The Democratic Doctrine," published in 1893 in the autonomist's party organ, *La Democracia*. Unlike the time when Brau was writing (the 1880s), this was a time when the Autonomist Party had been expanding its ranks and had begun to participate in local elections. It was also when references to the "gran familia" and talk of "unconscious masses" proliferated. Unlike Brau, therefore, Muñoz defined democracy in accordance with these categories.

Muñoz began by noting the need for communities to have leaders. "A collectivity of any kind — nation, party, guild — meets, mediates, deliberates. It needs a man who is elected by all, who channels the thoughts of all, who carries the word of all. [The collectivity] looks around, studies the majestic personalities who stand out by talent, by perseverance, by energy, by *civismo*. And after this preliminary . . . analysis, the collectivity that wants to give to their acts the greatest number, votes. It then has a jefe."[58] Muñoz then suggested that the election of this jefe itself constitutes democracy:

> And what is a jefe? An inviolable figure, sacred, almost divine, similar to a God . . . not able to be mistaken or deceive us? No: he is an entity in which is condensed and synthesized the opinion of his *compañeros*, his compatriots, his *correligionarios*. In their name does he move, speak, write, make pacts and governs. But he should follow, always and always, the inspirations of the majority, which is the supreme power. In the old organisms . . . the jefe — a monarch, proconsul, pontifice — exercised illegitimate power. . . . In modern organisms the jefe . . . interprets the general sentiment and obeys it. Today, power is recognized because of its constancy, talent, energy, civicism that is asked to be demonstrated every moment in representing the masses. . . .
>
> In democratic societies it is not permissible that the jefe constrains the impulses of those who, with their vote, elevate him to the summit. There he will remain as long as he is responsive to his great debts [*deberes*], as long as he is deserving of universal confidence. From there he will step down when decadence is discovered in his conduct, when his character weakens, when his history is blemished, or his rectitude is perverted, or his will declines; when for whatever reason he is not the most faithful guardian of the ideals, interests, and honor of his brothers [*hermanos*].[59]

Here Muñoz worked from the basic opposition that Brau had used; that is, between some kind of representation on the one hand and, on the other, no representation at all. The jefe represented the "thoughts of all," thereby making for a democracy. Through the jefe, representation of the collectivity was assured, and as long as the jefe sustained that representative character, democracy persisted. Still, Muñoz elaborated Brau's opposition in several respects. First, unlike Brau, Muñoz suggested that voting was necessary for democracy. The jefe had to be chosen. Second, Muñoz drew upon schemas of hierarchy and authority. Indeed, Muñoz's claim that collectivities need a leader who "channels the thoughts of all" relied upon the classification of society as hierarchically ordered unity. The jefe was someone with a privileged ability that the unconscious masses lacked. At most, the collectivity could vote for the privileged person, choosing among their "brothers" who would be the head of the family. But even then, the jefe, once chosen, was the one who did the important work of representation and condensation. He was the one who "spoke for all."

Finally, Muñoz drew upon existing schemas of personalized authority and law. Note that Muñoz said little about what the jefe was to do in office, as if elected political leaders, like municipal officials, had little restraint. As long as the jefe condensed and interpreted the will of the majority and thus enjoyed "universal confidence," the jefe could legitimately stay in power. This approach to democracy thus approximates what Guillermo O'Donnell (1994: 59–60) calls "delegative democracy." In this model, according to O'Donnell, a political leader is "entitled to govern as he or she sees fit" without formal constraints of law, and serves as a "paternal figure . . . taken to be the embodiment of the nation and the main custodian and definer of its interests."

To be sure, when Muñoz's fellow autonomists made references to how political leaders should act in office, they employed schemas of patronage and paternalism rather than legal rationality. It was not only that directors like the jefe had to interpret the will of the masses of the collectivity, they were also supposed to paternalistically care for them and attend to their needs, just as a good patron — a good hacendado and father — should. Jose de Diego, for example, contended that the primary task of political officials, as patrons, was to ensure the aggrandizement of agricultural wealth, thereby serving as the "sweet hope of agriculture." Holding state power, they would enact policies and programs that would help landlords expand production, decrease the circulation time of commodities to market (by providing modern infrastructure), and thus, by implication, continue to exert their social power over tenants and other clients.[60] In this view, then, state leaders would serve as the apex of a large patron-client pyramid constituting the collectivity. State leaders would be the heads of the gran familia. Fittingly, when Diego discussed what the autonomous government should look like, he suggested that the state should have an executive power (i.e., a governor or jefe) aided by a

"Ministry" or "Council." This latter body was to be a kind of informal legislature. While Diego likely modeled it after parliamentary systems, he referred to the council more precisely as the "Council of the Family." The councillors would serve as "masters of the great home," with the jefe at the top. According to Diego, together the jefe and the "masters of the home" would "facilitate, fulfill and realize the desires of the gran familia."[61]

The concept of paternal care, embodied in a benevolent authority figure, was articulated by other autonomist leaders as well.[62] Transposing schemas of practice from the municipal level to the insular level, they suggested that the rulers should dole out patronage directly to clients by giving them employment in bureaucratic offices. Patron clientelism was the way in which political leaders were to "condense" the will of the family and fulfill their obligations to it. Jose de Dominguez, for instance, argued that in an ideal autonomic state, Puerto Ricans should be appointed to the colonial bureaucracy. They would thereby replace the members of the Spanish government party who monopolized the posts.[63] It followed that political leaders who did not faithfully realize the will of the gran familia in this way were unworthy of office. Indeed, Puerto Rican autonomist leaders classified the Incondicionales who monopolized offices as exactly such unworthy figures. Muñoz Rivera lamented the fact that the Incondicionales dominated the mayoral positions of the municipalities by referring to them as illegitimate family members: "The [Spanish] alcaldes. I have here a large subject. They are so many! And so pernicious! They administer so poorly! What family are they! What progeny!"[64]

Parties, Elections, and Democracy as Autonomía

By the late 1890s, as the autonomists pursued their political demands, these meanings took on further accents within the context of colonial politics, parties, and elections. In this context, the Puerto Rican elite eventually constructed a meaning of democratic government as more than a matter of jefes and "directors" commanding the gran familia. They classified it as a matter of single-party rule and, more specifically, the rule of the Puerto Rican elites' own party, the Autonomists (or "Liberal Autonomists").

Consider, first, electoral conduct and the organization of the existing political parties in the island. The political field in Puerto Rico was essentially divided between two major parties: the Incondicionales or Spanish party, on the one hand, and, on the other, the Puerto Ricans' party, the Autonomists, headed by Luis Muñoz Rivera and his colleagues. This had two implications. One was that elections—when conjoined with the government party's monopoly over the state—became highly charged affairs marked by intense partisan competition, party violence, and manipulations of the electoral machinery. Since the Spanish authorities controlled state power, they had initiated it. During the first decades of elections, the Spanish colonial government employed devious methods to secure victory for their preferred party. They manipulated registration lists, intimated the rival party using the state's armed forces, or stuffed ballot boxes.[65] To counter such activities, the Autonomist Party had to mobilize its forces and respond in kind. One way the party responded was to try to expand the suffrage. The greater the number of laborers who could vote, the more votes the Puerto Rican elite could control, for those laborers were the tenants of the hacendados in the party.[66] Accordingly, the autonomists consistently demanded that Madrid loosen restrictions on the suffrage. In addition, the Autonomists instituted strict party discipline. In the face of the electoral violence, loyalty to party was critical and even took on a religious tone. Fellow party members referred to each other as "correligionarios" who had a "duty [*derecho*]" to each other and an "obligation" or "debt" to the party committees.[67] The party also organized itself into a quasi-military organization, with party leaders as military commanders. The autonomists consistently referred to elections as "battles," not just "contests," while party circulars proclaimed that "political parties can acquire its force only through . . . strict discipline and the proper and necessary obedience to the authority and direction which they voluntarily impose upon themselves." Other party documents insisted: "We need cohesion, unity, and discipline." Party members had to "obey the commands of the jefe" and the other "directors of the collectivity."[68] Muñoz even evoked Louis XIV by uttering, "El partido soy yo"—"I am the party."[69]

The other implication of the structure of the political field was that the Puerto Rican elite classified their party as the only legitimate expression of the will of the familia puertorriqueña. Because the political field had been so long divided between the Incondicionales and the Puerto Rican Autonomists, they classified their party as the only true representative of the family. "If our men govern," uttered Muñoz, "it is clear that the Puerto Rican people govern."[70] This had two correlates. The first was a particular classification of elections. In local conception, elections were not the mechanism for adding up the choices of sovereign individuals to ascertain the peoples' choice, for the people's choice was predetermined, known from the outset. The "choice" was the Autonomist Party. About this there was no question. The only question was whether or not the elite would be able to publicly confirm this predetermined status through an electoral victory and consequently take hold of the government. Fittingly, when leaders like Cepeda at all defined the meaning of "election," they called it the "electoral battle," which involves "the *representation* of a collectivity through the suffrage."[71] This meaning did not treat elections as a formal procedure used to adduce the choices made by sovereign individuals. Election was about "representing" a collectivity, a moment for displaying the people's already assumed choice, for *re*-presenting it or presenting again. An election was a ritual of confirmation and confidence.[72]

The second correlate was that democratic self-government meant the victory of the elites' party and thus the institution of the privileged directors and jefe who would attend to the needs of the gran familia. Self-government meant that the Autonomists, as the people's true representatives, would become the new government party. They would oust the Incondicionales from the seats of state and institute their own extensive patron-client pyramid over the island. An American observer later derided this approach to government: "The general government itself was regarded as simply a place to which the more favored following of the party in the power should be assigned with a view of reaping a rich harvest and gathering quick and profitable returns."[73] But autonomists suggested that such patronage was perfectly logical and a necessary dimension of self-rule. Cepeda explicitly declared that the Incondicionales, monopolizing bureaucratic jobs, should be replaced by the Puerto Ricans:

Who are the enemies of Puerto Rico?
The Incondicionales.
What party is that?
It is not a party, it is a group of impudents . . . who prosper by taking all of the jobs.
Who should occupy the public offices?
The insulars [e.g., native-born Puerto Ricans].[74]

The demand for autonomy itself condensed this meaning of self-government. On its face, the demand for autonomy was a demand to make Puerto Rico equal with regions or provinces in Spain; that is, to fully incorporate Puerto Rico into Spain by making it an equal province. Puerto Rico would have "identity" with existing Spanish provinces and would no longer be an inferior colony. But this also meant that, with autonomy, the Puerto Rican people would govern themselves. Autonomy meant that "the country [will be] administered with the consent of its inhabitants."[75] As Cepeda put it: "What is colonial Autonomy? The government of the pais by the pais, under the sovereignty of the [Spanish] Nation."[76] Fittingly, party members wrote to each other saying that if their party ever took power and if autonomía was granted by Spain, it would be a recognition of "our aptitudes and right to rule ourselves."[77]

Political Validation and Final Institutionalization

Recognition finally arrived at the end of the 1890s. The cultural structures delimiting the meanings of democracy, self-government, and autonomía were validated in practice, hence further institutionalized. First, throughout the 1890s, the Autonomist Party led by Muñoz Rivera had been able to slowly accumulate political power in the island. This was effected in part through a tactic they employed known as *retraimiento* ("retirement" or "abstention"). The tactic was widely known and had a typical sequence. The protesters demanded something from the ruler — calling for "justice" and the recognition of Puerto Rican *dignidad* — and if the ruler did not concede, the protestors abstained from elections or resigned from office. This carried the threat of revolt, and so a concession by the ruler was necessary. Concession would restore political equilibrium. The Autonomists used this tactic consistently in the 1890s and, due to the weakened Spanish Empire (always threatened by revolt in Cuba and the Philippines), it had always worked.[78] For instance, the autonomists used it to demand an expanded electoral suffrage and thereby secure their rural base, and the Spanish rulers conceded.

Second, the Autonomists' slow accumulation of power reached an apex by 1898. Previously, conflicts in the metropole between the conservative Crown party and the Liberal Party, headed by Mateo Sagasta, had held out hope for fundamental change. Muñoz's autonomists saw the opportunity and aligned with Sagasta's Liberal Party, changing their name to the Liberal Autonomists. The idea was that if Sagasta emerged victorious and took power in Madrid, he would replace the rule of the Incondicionales with the rule of the Autonomists. "Incorporation [with Sagasta's party in Madrid]," proclaimed Muñoz, "is effective, fair, and logical so that a party of the [Spanish] nation can be able to lift [our party] to the spheres of government and official influence."[79] As it turned out, Sagasta did emerge victorious, and under his reign Puerto Rico was given the Autonomic Charter. The Autonomic Charter called for elections with an even more expanded electorate than the conservative regime had previously granted. It also called for the victorious party to take up the reigns of the newly organized colonial state.

A brief discussion of the elections under the Autonomic Charter is informative, for the elections condense all of the categories and schemas already outlined. Note first that the expansion of the suffrage immediately brought about a split in the Puerto Rican family. Jose Barbosa, an urban professional competing with Muñoz Rivera (who represented the landed interests), broke with the latter's Liberal-Autonomist Party to form a new party, the Reformists-Orthodoxos. Barbosa hoped to mobilize other middle-class professionals, along with urban workers and clerks. His party was small. But the problem was that, after the split, both Barbosa's new party and Muñoz's Autonomist Party claimed to be the true representations of the gran familia. Both believed that they were the people's choice.[80] Hence, during the election, neither party paid heed to formal electoral procedures and corruption proceeded on an expanded scale.

The Liberal Autonomists dominated, however. They controlled the rural areas and had the support of Sagasta. One of Barbosa's followers thus complained that the masses in the countryside "believe that there is a God, called Sagasta, whose prophet is Muñoz."[81] Indeed, nearly all of the so-called masses voted for the Liberal Autonomists, not least because many were their tenants.[82] Furthermore, the island's new governor, appointed by Sagasta, used the state's powers to help the Liberal Autonomists. Officials tampered with registration lists and used various other methods, sometimes violent. The Liberal Autonomists won the elections by an overwhelming number.[83]

With the preordained victory of the Liberal Autonomists and Sagasta in Madrid, Muñoz Rivera and other party leaders were installed as the new "masters of the great home" under the Autonomic Charter. They took up seats in the Autonomic Council, the very kind of body that Diego had called for and referred to as the "Council of the Family." They then proceeded to consolidate a new network of patronage, replacing the Incondicionales in local office with their own and excluding Barbosa's Orthodox-Reformist party. In local terms, neither of these parties truly represented the familia, and both could be legitimately marginalized from the spheres of government.[84] "Muñoz has been given all he wished," complained a Barbosa follower, which is also to say that Muñoz was installed as the jefe of the gran familia.[85]

By the Autonomic government, then, the "democratic doctrine" was finally instituted. "The enthusiasm that reigned that day in all of the Island cannot be adequately described with my humble pen," wrote one Autonomist when the charter was inaugurated. Spain had "recognized in the Puerto Rican people the political maturity to govern itself by itself."[86] In other words, the Puerto Rican elite achieved self-government, and their models became further interdependent with the fields they referred. Yet, just months after the Autonomic Charter had been granted, the Spanish-American War broke out. Thereafter came the American military—vanguard forces of a rising colonial empire from the North.

MEANING MAKING DURING U.S. RULE

We have already seen in chapter 1 what the American officials did when they first arrived. After learning that the Puerto Ricans had demanded self-government from Spain, American authorities tried to incorporate those demands and interests into their legitimating speeches, proclamations, and their overarching colonial project.[87] We have also seen that the Americans worked from their own particular cultural conceptions and racial schemes—the schemas with which they were most familiar given their institutional background. They heard the elite use terms like *self-government*, and they heard them register demands for it, but they assumed that there was only one kind of self-government and that theirs was it. They saw in the elites' discourse incomplete and imperfect concepts, not different ones. In this sense, the Americans' symbolic efforts were predicated upon a kind of misunderstanding.

Given the foregoing analysis of the elites' institutionalized political culture, we might therefore wonder: was the Puerto Ricans' warm reception to

American occupation predicated upon a similar misunderstanding, just from the other way around? Were not the elite also constrained to make meaning according to their previously institutionalized culture?

Accepting Tutelage

Consider first the elites' reception to the Americans' initial proclamations. As noted, when the Puerto Rican elite first heard General Miles's proclamation, they disavowed notions of resisting American occupation and instead cooperated with the regime. They responded affirmatively to the military authorities, who in turn reinstalled them into municipal office. This was a happy coincidence for the military rulers, who were intent upon ensuring a smooth transition to American rule. But a closer look at the elites' discourse shows more precisely what the elite saw in Miles's proclamation. Note, for example, the discourse of the reappointed Puerto Rican officials. After the American district commanders appointed them to office, and after the officials took their oath of loyalty to the regime, these officials gave their own speeches and proclamations, which reiterated the discourse of the Spanish regime. At the inauguration ceremony in Yauco, Francisco Mejía Rodríguez, the newly appointed municipal mayor, lowered the Spanish flag at the district commander's behest and then announced from the balcony of the Alcaldía: "Puerto Ricans! We, by the intervention of God, now enter the bosom of Mother America. . . . Sons of America: General Miles has been sent to us in her name, and to her we should send in turn our salutations and loving affection. Long live the Government of the United States of America! Long Live American Puerto Rico!"[88]

Mejía used preexisting categories to classify the United States and the island's relationship to it. Just as Mejía and others among the elite had referred to Spain as their "mother patria," so too did he then refer to the United States "Mother America." And as the elite had referred to Puerto Ricans as the "sons of Spain," so too did Mejía refer to Puerto Ricans as "Sons of America." Mejía thereby constructed a series of parallels between Spanish rule and U.S. rule — as if the United States was like Spain previously; as if it might grant the island autonomía as Spain had. When making meaning of tutelary occupation and its initial proclamations, Mejía drew upon previously institutionalized schemas.

To be sure, immediately after Meija's speech, the councillors took the stand and explicitly equated U.S. occupation with a movement toward autonomía. They proclaimed that they would work "within" autonomy—that is, they would work under an Autonomic Regime, not "autonomously" (as in freedom of action): "Major D. E. Clarke of the Sixth Regiment of the Infantry of the United States of America [has reappointed] the honorable proprietor D. Francisco Mejía Rodríguez for the government and administration of the interests in the jurisdiction of this district. [Mejía] is authorized to nominate the necessary employees for a good administrative regime in all of its manifestations, promoting and doing everything possible within *autonomía* for the betterment of the entire jurisdiction."[89]

The discourse of other municipal officials is profoundly similar. Across the island, councils issued proclamations that referred to the United States as "our Mother Patria" and then classified U.S. occupation as a movement toward autonomía:

> The [American] invasion had been effected and we are subjected to the decisions of the American government, and since its representative here offers us the opportunity to continue at our posts, we should accept the suggestion. By so doing, we fulfill an ineluctable duty to the Puerto Rican people. . . . We shall continue in our posts as long as our mission is to heed and obey the just dispositions of the American nation, which is not the conqueror or our nation *but the protector of our autonomic rights*, rights which, in the future, we wish to see expanded to obtain the most absolute independent and *autonomic regime*.[90]

But if the elite classified American occupation as a movement toward their preexisting ideal of autonomy, it would have followed that they also classified the American rulers as akin to the Spanish rulers during the autonomic regime. They would have then expected the American authorities to do what the Spanish authorities under Sagasta had done; that is, favor the dominant party that truly represented the familia. In fact, this was the very view that Muñoz Rivera and his copartisans in the Liberal-Autonomist Party articulated when they, as the Autonomic Council, were inaugurated as advisers to General Brooke. They saw their appointment as a sign of their party's privileged place. "The Secretaries of the Autonomic Council," wrote Councilor Juan Hernandez, "were received by the commander-in-chief [General Brooke] with favored attention and distinction. To me it seemed that the American military commander saw in us the official and genuine representation of the people of the Puerto Rico."[91] The Liberal Autonomists were the true representatives of the people, and the Americans, like Sagasta, ostensibly knew it. *La Democracia* thus added: "General Brooke . . . knowing that the Liberal [Autonomist] Party was valued by and represented the island, put government in the hands of the Liberals."[92]

The Liberal-Autonomist's islandwide assembly, the party's first public assembly during American occupation, even more clearly discloses the association they made between autonomía and tutelage. At the assembly, the party changed its name from the Liberal-Autonomist Party to the Federal Party and issued a new platform. The platform narrated the present as a reproduction of the past, equating the Autonomists' Spanish-rule aims with their present goals. As the narrative moved forward in time, it shifted from the Spanish signifier for "self-government" (*gobierno propio*) to the English signifier, thus uprooting the latter from the Americans' discourse and tying to local signifieds:

> We come, as an organized political force, from the assembly of Ponce of 1887 [the founding meeting of the Liberal-Autonomist Party]. There the Puerto Rican patriots affirmed our energetic aspiration for gobierno propio. From that instant the Autonomist Party fought, with more perseverance than with fortune, for the triumph of its ideas. It was a fruitless labor: the European Spaniards, aided by their fellow countrymen in Madrid, dominated in all situations. . . . But the road remained: that of seeking efficacious alliances [with Sagasta's party] in the old metropolis in order to attain the goal of our principles, in order that *self government* would be established [original in English], in order that the sons of Puerto Rico administer Puerto Rico for themselves. . . . Our ideal has never changed. Being liberals, we are subsequently autonomists, because we were and still are in the habit of hating that tyranny which consists in imposing upon weak peoples an authority that does not have its origin in the consent of the citizenry.

The platform then narrated the arrival of the Americans as the beginnings of autonomía and further equated autonomía with "democracy":

Upon arriving to our shores the invading army [of the United States] . . . was received as a liberating army. The American flag floated in the masts of its boats and in the lines of its battalions, symbolizing the greatest and most perfect democracy [*democracía*] in the world, and we . . . caught a glimpse of the certainty of a sincere *autonomía*, a guaranteed right, an overflowing prosperity in the bosom of a new nation. In such manner, without any resistance, to the contrary with the uproarious delight that the solemn majesty of the historical moment was not repressed, the people received, between its applauses and its palms, not their conquerors, but their saviors.[93]

The Puerto Rican elite had indeed received the Americans' discourse, and they thereby accepted tutelary rule. But they also saw in both their own political meanings. As Juan Nieves declared in his popular pamphlet, issued soon after the Americans had arrived: "The Puerto Rican people turned their backs on their former mother *patria* because they expected to be constituted as a State, free within the American Union, and enjoy *autonomía*."[94]

Narrating Autonomía

But how could the Liberal Autonomists (the Federals) legitimately claim that the U.S. rule would grant the kind of autonomy that Sagasta's regime had granted previously, especially if they believed they would be incorporated into a full-fledged state in the union? Was not American rule novel, having a certain "majesty" (as the platform above put it) and marking a "new era" (as municipal councils put it)? Would not American occupation bring with it an entirely different political system, and would not that system mean something else than a directing class, patronage, or single-party rule?

The answer lies in another set of preexisting cultural structures, this time having to do with Spanish federalism. During Spanish rule, federalism had referred to the system by which the regions of Spain enjoyed relative independence from the Crown. Each region or territorial unit ruled itself under the wider umbrella pitched in Madrid. Local rulers in the distinct units were clients of the Crown, and local populations were subjects of both. Thus, each of the units in the system had an identity with other units, in the sense that they were all treated equally by the Crown, but each also had its own "regional identity" akin to an individual nation. This had been the concept underlying the Liberal Autonomists' demands for autonomy in the 1890s. It had also been manifest in the Autonomic Charter. Puerto Rico was set to receive autonomía within Spanish federalism, akin to other Spanish regions.[95]

The federal system in the United States was not entirely distinct from this, because it too consisted of different states with equal standing. But the Puerto Ricans classified the two systems as identical. Note, for example, that besides calling the United States their "Mother Patria," they also called it the "State of states." "The United States is not a nation, even though it calls itself a nation: it is called the United States! Thus the people . . . do not say: *Oh Lord Bless our Nation*, but they say: *Oh Lord Bless these United States*. The America of the North is a state of States, a Republic of Republics . . . the great Federation of America."[96] Note, too, that when the Federals stated in their platform that U.S. rule would give them autonomía, they used the very same idioms of regionalism and identity that they had previously used in their demands for autonomy during Spanish rule:

[We] do not need to change [the previous Autonomist Party] platform. From that we proclaim the principle of identity. In identity our patriotism is incarnated, which is not the sentiment of the nation . . . but the intense and profound sentiment of the region; a region built and organized with wise independence in the form of a federal state, with self-government, combined and united within a wonderful variety of other regions . . . by the action of a superior, strong, and powerful organism [the United States].[97]

In local conception, American and Spanish federalism were the same. The United States was a large collection of fully autonomous states, just like the Spanish Empire.[98] As the Federals' newspaper announced: "There, in the [American] metropolis we see the absolute independence of powers, and the strict protection of autonomía in the life of the regions."[99]

In what sense, then, did American tutelage mark a "new era" in the Puerto Ricans' view? For the Puerto Rican elite, the difference between U.S. federalism and Spanish federalism was that the former was a more generous and perfected token of the latter type. It had taken three hundred years of colonial rule before Spain had finally granted autonomy to Puerto Rico, but in the elites' view, the history of U.S. expansion on the continent meant that the "Republic of Republics" was more willing to grant autonomy to its own territories.[100] Thus, the real novelty was not that U.S. tutelage would bring completely new political concepts and methods, it was that the U.S. would be a more generous Mother Patria than Spain had been, granting Puerto Rico autonomy sooner rather than later. In fact, this is why the Liberal Autonomists changed their name. No longer the Liberal-Autonomist Party that had aligned with Sagasta's Liberal party in Madrid, they changed the name to the Federal Party, ready for incorporation into the American federal system: "Upon meeting today, the old liberals [autonomists] conform their hopes and look for a name that corresponds to the methods and traditions of the federation [of the United States]. . . . And they want to be called the FEDERAL PARTY, because they continue believing in their autonomist ideal, and because there does not exist on the planet an autonomy so ample and so indestructible as that created when the patriarchs of the America of the North wrote their laws for its states and territories."[101]

Not surprisingly, when party leaders gave suggestions to authorities on what kind of governmental forms should follow military occupation, they employed models of the Autonomic regime. In fact, when Muñoz Rivera wrote to Elihu Root in 1899 and suggested a transitional government toward statehood, he used the Autonomic regime exactly. The transitional government, in Muñoz's view, should have municipal councils elected by the people and a governor appointed by the president aided by a "Government Council." The council, then, was to be like the Crown-appointed council of administration (or Autonomic Cabinet) during Sagasta's regime.[102] Similarly, when Federal Party organs discussed municipal governments, they agreed that the municipalities should be similar to the kind of state governments established in the United States, but they then equated those governments with the municipal governments in Puerto Rico during the Autonomic Regime: "The *autonomía* of the municipalities is the federation of the country, just as the *autonomía* of the States is the federation of the [American] Metropolis."[103]

Even when the elite tried to convince American authorities that they were capable of territorial government and eventual statehood, hence of self-government, they employed their preexisting categories on autonomía. For instance, when Congress was legislating civil government for the island, party member Lucas Amadeo suggested to a Congressional committee that military rule should be replaced by a "territorial government." This was a common suggestion among the elite, and Amadeo explicitly equated territorial government with self-government. Territorial government, he said, would allow Puerto Rico "to take the manage of its own internal affairs in its own hands." But to justify why Puerto Rico was fit for such self-government, Amadeo did not employ the Americans' categories. He did not refer to "impartial politics," legal-rational action in office, or "self-discipline" and "self-control." He did not try to convince the American committee by appealing to the committee's own terms. Instead he asserted:

> The first argument which I have . . . is, referring to the history of my country, summed up in two words, a state of constant peace and continual labor. . . . Besides which, on becoming acquainted with the better class of Puerto Ricans — the educated class — one becomes convinced that the island has men of sufficient capacity to guide or take the reins of government in their hands. When a country . . . has a directing class of men of acknowledged capabilities, it is easy for the directing class to carry the masses along with them in the right way, more especially if this mass has been trained to be docile and follow the example given.

Later in his testimony, Amadeo gave a more specific example of what he meant by this idea of a directing class "carrying" the masses. He said that the masses "follow the counsels of the people who are immediately above them. For instance, peons — farm hands on estates — will be governed more or less by the owners of those farms." To Amadeo, this was a perfectly acceptable situation because the farm owners "have the good of the country at heart."[104] For Amadeo, all that was needed to convince the Americans of the Puerto Ricans' capacity for self-government was to appeal to loyalty and deference.

Muñoz himself constructed the same signifying parallels. In an interview with an American journalist in October 1898, just months after the Americans had first arrived, Muñoz offered his opinions on the island's condition and its future. The journalist first asked if Spanish rule had "retarded the progress of country." Muñoz responded in the affirmative, agreeing that progress had been "retarded." But he then added that "justice" had been realized when Spain finally implemented the Autonomic regime: "Finally, the sons of the colony rose to power. . . . Under that autonomy the development of the country began to be initiated." The journalist then asked a more pointed question. "At what point do you think that the Puerto Rican people will be capable of self government such as the kind enjoyed by the States in the American union?" Muñoz replied: "I think that my country is already able to govern and administer itself, and that is the aspiration of all of the creoles [in Puerto Rico]. *There are the most competent directing elements and an obedient and sensible people who back them up.*" For Muñoz, all that was needed for self-government was a class of competent "directors." Then, after asserting that Puerto Rico was "already able to govern itself," Muñoz concluded by referring again to autonomía: "The general desire can therefore be condensed into this formula: a very brief military occupation, lasting while the parliament meets in Washington; during military occupation the laws which reign and the organisms that function today should be respected: afterward, the declaration of a territory, with the associated legislation; but never less *autonomic* and free than what we possess; much later . . . the declaration of statehood."[105]

Conduct Reconsidered

The preceding discussion reveals that the Puerto Rican elite made meaning of tutelage in accordance with their own preexisting schemas and narratives on autonomía. But the elites' meaning-making activities were not only about words. They also had implications for the elites' strategies and conduct. "Symbolic forms," notes Johnson (1997: 8), "operate indicatively to focus the attention of actors, directing it toward a certain range of alternatives and away from others."[106] Thus, by narrating tutelage through the symbolic form of autonomía, the elites' attention was likewise guided by it. Understanding this sheds clearer insights into the elites' so-called corruption, where theories of culture as values or strategic resources cannot.

As noted, American authorities, after setting up the first municipal governments, discovered that the Puerto Rican officials were engaging in all kinds of corruption. They found, for example, many instances of blatant financial mismanagement and abuse. Local officials were using public monies to enhance their own salaries or simply dipping into public funds for themselves. This meant a neglect of basic duties like infrastructural care. By making "extravagant expenditures for their salaries," the municipal officials were "failing to make any adequate provision for the carrying-on of [public] works."[107] Authorities also found repeated abuses of power. Local officials were collecting "illegal or unauthorized taxes" while failing to collect legally sanctioned ones and imposing fines or collecting taxes arbitrarily. Furthermore, municipal mayors concentrated executive, judicial, and legislative functions into their own hands—controlling the local courts, using municipal police forces for their own special needs, and failing to "impartially" administer the law. In some towns they arbitrarily removed municipal councillors from their seats.[108] The "abuse of power," reported one American agent, was "universal."[109]

All of this is surprising considering the elites' goals of demonstrating fitness. It is also surprising if we treat the elite as having values predisposed to American democracy. It is not surprising, however, when we look more closely at what was going on in relation to what happened during Spanish rule. Indeed, it is as if the elite, by their so-called corruption, were conducting tutelage just as they had conducted politics before, when Mateo Sagasta had granted autonomía and elevated Muñoz's party to the status of the new majority party. In fact, the officials conducting the corruption were of Muñoz's Liberal-Autonomist Party precisely. American military commanders had initially appointed the incumbents they first found back to local office, which served to reinstate the Liberal Autonomists. At the central level, too, the American authorities perpetuated the Liberal Autonomists' previously privileged place. After Spain had formally surrendered, and General Brooke had been inaugurated the first military governor of the island, Brooke decided to employ key Puerto Rican elites as advisers. He reckoned that Muñoz Rivera and the other members of the Autonomic Council were the most appropriate.[110] Yet these members of the cabinet were the very "directors" of the Liberal-Autonomist Party. As we have seen, Muñoz and his colleagues took it as a sign that they were members of the "privileged" party. That is, the appointments publicly projected a continuity between the Autonomic past and the American present. They signaled that the new American rulers, like the Spaniards of the Sagasta regime before, were favoring the majority party.

It followed that the majority party had every right to proceed as it had before—consolidate its grip over the gran familia, marginalize the unrepresentative "minority" party (Barbosa's Orthodoxo-Republicans), and fulfill their self-fashioned role as the "directors" through patronage—all of which would realize the "democratic doctrine" under the jefe just as during the

Autonomic Regime. To be sure, a closer look at the corruption shows that it was guided by the very patronage and partisan codes that the elite had associated with autonomía. For example, the Americans found that while municipal officials indeed legislated "extravagant salaries," they also found that the officials then used the funds to create "an unnecessarily large number of employees" and "petty offices" for their friends and partisans.[111] This was the logic of party patronage with which the elite were already familiar, and which had been followed under the Autonomic Charter. In addition, while officials collected illegal taxes, they only collected them from the members of their own party while leaving their own followers untaxed. Thus, as before, tax collection was used to favor friends and punish enemies.[112] Furthermore, municipal mayors used the police force not simply as personal henchmen but as political tools, organizing them "on a strictly partisan basis" and "as a weapon to favor the political party to which [the mayor] belonged, and to oppose those of the opposite political faith."[113] Even the so-called arbitrary removals of lower-level officials by municipal powers were not arbitrary: mayors removed municipal councillors who were of the opposed political party.[114]

Also suggestive is the fact that the elite did not conduct the corruption behind each other's backs, relegating their conduct to hidden spaces. The corruption was not a matter of free-riders, each individual official pilfering power and funds for himself while hoping that others would realize the group's larger goals. The corruption, noted observers, was "open and notorious." In fact, the local officials even conducted the corruption in the presence of American field agents, acting as if it was perfectly acceptable to all.[115] The "especially discouraging feature" of the corruption, concluded Willoughby, is that "it seemed to the Porto Ricans [*sic*] quite the natural and proper thing."[116] Was not tutelage a movement toward autonomía? And did not autonomía mean single-party rule and patronage?

At the same time, Muñoz Rivera was active in playing the self-conceived role of jefe, just as he had done under the Autonomic Regime. General Brooke, after inaugurating Muñoz Rivera and leading members of the Liberal-Autonomist Party as an advisory council, discovered that Muñoz was using his high position in ways that were "antithetical to American politics," as Brooke put it. When Brooke authorized central funds to be loaned to municipal governments so that they could build infrastructure, he discovered that Muñoz ordered that only members of his party should be employed. In return, local branches of the party wrote letters of praise and adhesion to Muñoz, referring to him as their "beloved jefe."[117] Furthermore, Muñoz tried to exercise "absolute control" over the government and, according to many observers, even "over the Military Governor [General Brooke] himself."[118] In turn, everyone else saw Muñoz as Muñoz portrayed himself. Despite proclamations announcing the military governor to be the executive authority, municipal officials acted as though Muñoz was the only authority, and thus they followed only his directions. General Henry complained: "There seems to be feeling in the island that at present they [the Puerto Rican people] are ruled by one man in power, which is a relic of Spanish system."[119] Rumors also circulated in local papers stating that, once Puerto Rico was granted a civil government, President McKinley would appoint Muñoz as the first civil governor. Ostensibly, Muñoz and the president were "in the box" together, as if President McKinley was Mateo Sagasta reincarnate.[120]

In short, the elite in office were indeed trying to demonstrate their fitness for self-government so as to obtain eventual statehood and thereby realize their economic goals, but they were constrained to demonstrate their fitness as they conceived it; that is, in terms of their prior cultural understandings of what self-government meant. Coll Cuchi, a colleague of Muñoz, later recognized this constraint in his memoirs. Muñoz and the other elite, he noted, "neither comprehended nor could comprehend American methods of government."[121] Not surprisingly, the corruption persisted even after the initial appointments, and as the elite continued to narrate tutelage as a movement toward self-government/autonomía. For example, the Liberal Autonomists, now renamed the Federal Party, emerged victorious in the first elections held in 1899, and this served to further confirm their self-conception as the true representatives of the gran familia. Indeed, after the elections, they proceeded as if it was all a reenactment of the Autonomic Charter. Muñoz's partisans on the local level dismissed the members of the minority party — the Republicans (formerly Barbosa's Orthodoxos) — from municipal offices and put in their own.[122] American agents reported that Federal Party members were filled with the expectation that they, and they alone, would be given bureaucratic positions in the local governments. "They have grown to feel that they have an inherent right to office," complained one agent.[123] Furthermore, and accordingly, the few Republicans who were not thrown off municipal councils swiftly resigned. They recognized "the futility of all their efforts against such overwhelming odds."[124] Evidently, the Republicans knew what everyone else around them assumed: that American occupation was a reenactment of the Sagasta regime, and to the victor goes the spoils.

The elite even conducted elections in accordance with their institutionalized meanings. The American officials had hoped that elections during military occupation would serve as "an education, a sort of kindergarten," giving the people an "object lesson in civil government under a Republic."[125] To meet the goal, the regime issued "cards of advice and explanations, registration blanks, and numberless circulars of information" to the people.[126] These laid out strict rules and warned against "fraudulent activity."[127] But the Puerto Ricans had already seen electoral regulations before, during Spanish rule, and at that time no one had paid them any mind. After all, elections were not a matter of formal procedures to adduce the choices of sovereign individuals, but of *re*-presenting the party's power. The electoral conduct of the past was reproduced in the tutelary present. American authorities were appalled, for example, to find blatant bribery. Proprietors paid taxes of "poor people" for their vote, and local officials extended all sorts of favors to put voters under their "obligation." As before, these lines of exchange followed the lines of agricultural production and commerce.[128] The Americans were further appalled to find that there were always "several attempts at fraud on the part of officials and individuals."[129] People "not qualified to vote" were sent to the polls, and in one town, even a donkey and a cat were registered to vote.[130]

Accompanying these "subtle arts of the politician," as the Americans referred to them, was party-based competition of the illicit sort.[131] Initially, the military rulers tried to subdue party-based bias through the use of election supervisors who represented the two major parties (following electoral codes laid down by Progressive reformers at home). But the plan did not bear fruit. Some supervisors simply prevented members of the rival party from registering to vote. Others rearranged the voting lines such that members of the opposite party could not vote in time for the count.[132]

Electoral campaigns also remained intense party-based affairs, just as they had been during late Spanish rule. In the campaign for the elections of 1899, the Federal Party held a meeting to demonstrate its "power [*fuerza*]" and "enthusiasm." Conceiving themselves as the sole representatives of the gran familia, the Federals proclaimed that "our adversaries [i.e., the Republicans] . . . make war upon us by all means; persecute us with concerted hate. [We must always] be disposed to the fight."[133] "Great excitement attended these elections," reported one American official, "party lines were drawn strictly. The bitterness was extreme."[134] Partisan abuses of state power were common as well. Mayors did what they had done during elections under the Autonomic Regime: they used the police to threaten and intimidate electors of the opposite party.[135] Violence between the parties thus marked some elections. In the town of Ciales, Republican campaigners were "attacked by a mob of men [from the Federal Party] armed with clubs. Conversely, in Fajardo, Federal Party members were attacked with "fire arms, machetes, and sticks," a skirmish that resulted in one dead and six wounded.[136] There were countless other incidents from across the island, amounting to what American authorities perceived as a "general condition of lawlessness."[137] The excess of meaning left behind the Americans' discourse yielded an excessive amount of electoral violence.

In short, as the elite made meaning of tutelage in terms of their preexisting schemas, they engaged the tutelage situation accordingly. As they narrated tutelage in terms of autonomía, jefes, directing classes and unconscious masses, and as they classified themselves as the true majority party and the American officials as their patrons, these meanings guided their conduct in office and elections. This had serious consequences. Not only was the political machinery disrupted by the elites' party politics and corrupt activities, so too were the American officials struck with fear by the elites' electoral practices. "The intensity of party feeling," wrote administrator Rowe, "soon became a menace to peace and good order."[138] So concerned were the authorities that they had to pass a law expressly prohibiting provocative language during elections. "Down with — [the opposite party]" and "Death to — [the rival party's leader]" became banned utterances.[139] Still, the threat of disturbance persisted, and it clouded the Americans' initial complacency. Governor Allen wrote to Washington after one set of elections: "There was a great deal of political excitement throughout the island, and the American members of the administration were naturally very much concerned that public order should be maintained. Party feeling among the people was very pronounced; there were, on the part of the executive, many anxious days and wakeful nights."[140]

MEANING MAKING AND THE
TROUBLES OF TUTELAGE

Admittedly, in the end, the elites' meaning-making activities ultimately served the Americans' own purpose. By classifying American rule as a movement toward autonomía, the Puerto Rican elite supported occupation. Does this suggest that the American rulers were astute semioticians, aware of the elites' preexisting meanings and deliberately playing upon them? It cannot be doubted that American rulers tried to manipulate meaning. Consider some shifts in the Americans' discourse. Miles's first proclamation, for example, had used the term *self-government* rather than *autonomy*. But then his successors slowly came to recognize that the Puerto Ricans tended to equate the former with the latter. Accordingly, they began to incorporate the term into their own speeches and proclamations.[141] In one of many proclamations, for example, they publicly announced that if the municipal governments proved "their capacity and ability to govern themselves," military rule "will lead directly to self-government and full *autonomy*."[142] The trouble, however, was that while the American officials tried to manipulate signs, they did not fully comprehend the polyvalence of the signs they uttered. To the contrary, they too made meanings in accordance with the constraints of their prior schemas, and so when they discussed "autonomy" they referred to the relative independence of town governments from central interference.[143] They did not recognize that, in local conception, the term *autonomy* was associated with the autonomía of the entire island. Furthermore, when some American officials later reckoned that the elite indeed used *autonomy* to apply to the entire island, they classified it as American "territorial autonomy" — the relative freedom from the federal government that territories on the continent were given in preparation for full statehood.[144] They still did not acknowledge that autonomía in the elites' conception referred to single-party rule. Only later, after a decade of occupation, did American authorities have a sense that their use of "autonomy" had a different resonance than they had earlier assumed. When Governor George Colton left office in 1911, he wrote a memo advising his superiors in Washington that, during the first years of occupation, "the term 'autonomy' was understood differently here from in the United States." Colton did not explicate the different meanings, but he warned his successors to be careful of the term.[145]

By the time of Colton's reckoning, though, it had been too late. During the first years of rule, both the Americans and the elite recognized certain signs (*self-government*, *autonomy*, etc.), but by their respectively different cultural repertoires and the constraints they posed, the two sides made of those signs different meanings. This was important not only because it marked domestication on the part of the elite, but also because it posed serious troubles for the tutelary project at the same time. Even though the differential interpretation contributed to the legitimacy of occupation, it also thwarted tutelary aims. It even served to disrupt the otherwise smoothly operating machinery of colonial state. Tutelary elections were supposed to be a "sort of kindergarten"; the rulers' parental authority was to be assured, their mentorship, teachings, and discipline well received. But as the Puerto Rican elite made their own meanings of the Americans' signs, gestures, and structures, such wishful thinking remained wishful at best. Intense party loyalty and its subsequent violence, intimidation of voters, fraud and corruption — all of these practices of the past persisted into the early years of American rule. The forms of America's beloved electoral democracy were thereby domesticated, subsumed by local schemas.

At the same time, nearly everything else about tutelage was domesticated too. According to tutelary planners, the colonial state was to serve as a school of politics. Muñoz and his colleagues were to be willing collaborators, the Puerto Rican elite eager students, and the American authorities were paternalistic mentors. All of this was to have facilitated a "steady assimilation" of the "best American thought and methods of administration." But the elites' meaning-making activities served to subvert tutelary power, taming its effects by the power of local culture. Tutelage, rather than producing cultural change, wound up as cultural reproduction. The cultural schemas of autonomía and gobierno propio, of "directing classes," "unconscious masses" and single-party rule, were not uprooted but perpetuated. Colonialism's cultural power was thus stopped short in its tracks. It served to win hearts and minds, but only because the local elite made of its discourse and gestures their own preexisting meanings while reproducing those meanings in the process.

Why did this domestication and hence local reproduction occur? By reducing the elites' meanings to deep subjective values, utility maximization and incentive structures, we would not be able to provide a sufficient answer. The elites' values may have already been amenable to tutelage's lessons, and learning them would have provided added utility for realizing their goals, but the elite nonetheless remained impervious to the meanings the American authorities tried to impose.[146] We have induced a better answer. Domestication was not due the elites' cultural values, incentives and interests, or even the actions of the American officials alone; it was rather due to the constraints posed by the elites' preexisting institutionalized cultural system. The elite had already had a particular set of schemas and narratives on democratic self-government before American arrival. These were not dictated by deep values or beliefs, they were about signifying patterns fixed in practice. Thus, when the elite first made meaning of tutelage and everything it offered (including the American officials themselves), they were constrained to employ these particular cultural structures. They employed the schemas and narratives which were most familiar, available, and retrievable — specifically, the cultural structures on democracy and self-government that had been previously created and then institutionalized by their social and political practice during Spanish rule. This is why the Puerto Rican elite accepted tutelary rule while remaining impervious to its imposed models, messages, and meanings. As they classified tutelage in terms of directing classes, jefes, single-party rule autonomía, they paid selective attention to what tutelage offered. They did not seek out the Americans' meanings — although those meanings would have provided added utility — because they presumed they already knew them. In short, understanding the elites' reception to tutelage demands an analysis of their meaning-making activities, hence the signifying patterns they employed and produced. Understanding those meaning-making activities in turn demands recognizing the constraints posed by culture's prior history of institutionalization.

But there is another way to explore this idea. We could compare the Puerto Rican elites' meaning-making activities with another case where the receiving elite had different values, interests, and incentives. Fortunately, we have such a case in the Philippines.

Chapter 3

WINNING HEARTS AND MINDS IN THE PHILIPPINES

When the American military defeated the Spanish navy at Manila Bay in May 1898, some among the Filipinos were hesitant. Having led a revolution against Spain, they were pleased to see the Spanish navy defeated, but they were also unsure of America's intentions. They knew little of the Americans' designs or the United States at all. The situation was tense. American forces occupied Manila, while Filipino regiments watched cautiously from the outskirts. Then, on February 4, 1899, a few Filipino soldiers unwittingly crossed American lines. American patrols shouted out warnings, but they went unheeded. Shots were exchanged. The Philippine-American War had begun.[1]

Not all of the local population participated in the war. Some had accepted American rule from the beginning. Nonetheless, the initiation of the war led to an influx of American military power. From 1899 to 1902, the United States shipped about 70,000 servicemen to the archipelago.[2] Guns and bullets thus preceded ballots and ballot boxes — an irony not lost on anti-imperialists at home. "It appears gentlemen," quipped Williams Jennings Bryan as news of the war reached the States, "that our destiny is not as manifest as it was a few weeks ago."[3]

Historians have fruitfully analyzed various aspects of the war.[4] This chapter probes the lesser examined circulation and reception of signs during the war and in its aftermath. As seen in chapter 1, the

American authorities aimed to win hearts and minds, employing signs and symbols rather than only swords. They issued proclamations, gave speeches, and set up elections and local governments in an effort to signal tutelary benevolence. While the war was a matter of brutal coercion and conquest, it also entailed the use of words, symbols, and communicative acts. And as the war waned, authorities began a concerted effort to instill the Filipinos "with the American spirit," give them a chance to "demonstrate a fitness for self-administration," and provide an "education" in the ways of American-styled democratic government.[5] So what did the Filipino elite make of these efforts?

This chapter focuses upon the Philippines, but it is guided by comparison. In both Puerto Rico and the Philippines, American agents tried to solidify their power through the power of signs. In both, the Americans proclaimed tutelary colonialism and targeted the elite. But there were key differences. The Americans' efforts in Puerto Rico unfolded amid peace; in the Philippines they unfolded amid war. The Puerto Rican elite sought eventual statehood, while many among the Filipino elite sought independence. The Puerto Rican elite were cosmopolitan, many having been educated abroad; the Filipino elite, with a handful of exceptions, were comparably provincial. And Puerto Rico was geographically close to the United States while the Philippines was far away. Existing theoretical approaches to culture would seize upon these differences. They would point to them as marking different cultural values, goals, or incentives between the elite. These approaches would then predict differences in outcome. If the elites' subjective values and associated orientations, beliefs, or norms were different, or if their interests and incentives were different, their reception to tutelage would also be different.

In this chapter, however, we will see that there was not such a difference in outcome. Just like their Puerto Rican counterparts, the Filipino elite received tutelage by domesticating it, classifying its signs, actions, and attendant forms in accordance with their preexisting cultural order. As in Puerto Rico, the Filipino elite eventually accepted tutelage, but only as they saw in it their own preexisting meanings. The result was that their preexisting cultural order was reproduced rather than transformed.

ELITE POLITICAL CULTURE, 1880s–1890s

When American agents first arrived in Luzon in the late 1890s, they found that Filipino leaders were already versed in Western political discourse, discussing concepts like "independence," "rights," "liberty," and "self-government." American observers nonetheless took the elites' utterances as empty rhetoric. "I am afraid," wrote Brigadier-General Frederick Funston, "[that] the word 'independent,' which these people roll over their tongues so glibly, is to them a word and not much more."[6] Ostensibly, the elite uttered signifiers without concepts, words without substance; they were poor mimics of Western political modernity. But if American colonialists did not see meaning in the Filipinos' discourse, the Filipino elite surely did. The elite had constructed their own political culture before American rule, which is also to say that the signifiers they uttered, rather than meaningless, took on particular meanings from an overarching system of oppositions and contrasts that went unrecognized by American authorities and soldiers.[7] It is worth considering this systematic repertoire in some detail.

Of course, the elites' political culture had diverse influences, both local and global, and drew from various streams (including Spanish Catholicism and French political thought). Our goal here is not to track all of these diverse influences, nor is it to posit a static cultural system untouched by outside influences. Rather, we do what any analysis of meaning systems must do: take a snapshot of the elites' semiotic system, attending to its complexity and its patterns while also highlighting the social, political, and economic contexts in which it was forged and through which it was institutionalized. The approach is sufficient to its object. As we will see, the elites' political culture had an internal structure of its own, even as it was first constituted in specific fields and enjoyed an interdependence with them.[8] An examination of the schemas evident in those fields is a good place to begin.

Schemas of Practice: Idealized Reciprocity

The elites' political meanings had a structure of their own, but they were first forged in relation to schemas of patron-client practice in the social field. These schemas have already been discussed in existing scholarship; they turned upon debt and idealized reciprocity. Landlord-tenant relations are paradigmatic (and, after all, the Filipino political elite were part and parcel of the landed elite). In these relationships, landlords let tenants use their land for cultivation, and in return tenants gave the landlord *buwis*, a portion of their crop signifying tribute. The exchange was unequal, but sustaining the relationship was a continual extension of material and affective surplus on the part of landlords and public loyalty and deference on the part of tenants.[9] Tenants referred to their landlord as their "benefactor" and "protector"; and to refer to the debt that they owed to their landlord, Tagalog tenants used the phrase *utang na loób* — a "debt of gratitude" or "debt of the soul [*loób*]" that could never be fully repaid.[10] This was the same term that children used to refer to the debt they owed to their parents for the gift of life.[11]

Evident in these social relations, then, is an idealized reciprocity. It was idealized in the sense that landlord-tenant relations ultimately benefited the landlords' material position, and landlords could always resort to coercion if necessary. But coercion was not the first resort nor was it in the patrons' best interest. When landlords did not sufficiently provide for their tenants, or when they employed excessive force to maintain subservience, they ran serious risks. They were deemed *walang hiya* ("without shame"), a charge which then justified disobedience and, on a large scale, peasant rebellion.[12] In this schema, coercion marked not the absence of idealized reciprocity but its logical opposite. Recourse to coercion followed from the logic of patron-clientelism while reinforcing its meaning.

Schemas of debt and reciprocity were also transposed to governance, as the landed class and its allies had monopolized local political posts under the aegis of Spanish rule. Filipinos staffed the municipal positions of *gobernadorcillo* ("little governor"), *cabeza de barangay* ("barrio headman"), and other petty offices. The officials wielded special honorifics and symbolic capital — the title *Don*, tasseled gold-headed canes, and preferential seating at religious and governmental ceremonies — which were not taken away after they left their posts.[13] Existing and former officeholders together were known as the *principalía*, and they kept many of their privileges (such as the right to vote) long after they left office. This implied that political power was as much about the person as the office and, indeed, with relative autonomy from the central colonial state, local officials exercised their posts in a highly personalized manner. They cultivated a network of friends and followers and a retinue of official deputies ("pompously termed a 'ministry'") that included the local police force. All of these followers were more or less personal servants–cum-clients who owed their loyalty to the official, and officials then used these personal relations to sustain and aggrandize their power. They captured the local state apparatus, manipulated or otherwise ignored legal restrictions, and thereby accumulated more land and wealth. These practices were open and common; even Spanish provincial governors and Manila bureaucrats engaged in them. The "thousand bribes and illegal exactions," noted one foreign observer, were typically sanctioned as "custom."[14] They were also guided by patron-client codes. The gobernadorcillos' followers, for instance, lent him their personal services, but the gobernadorcillo had to provide them with protection and material resources in turn. Even the police, for example, were not paid by official salary. The gobernadorcillo gave them daily rations of food along with token "piddling sums," or exempted them and other followers from taxes or labor services demanded by Spanish bureaucrats.[15]

Homologously, local officials treated the townspeople and the town as a whole also as a base of clients. On the one hand, they collected money as taxes but pocketed them (a portion of the taxes was allotted to them as their salary, but they often took more than their allotted share). They also imposed fees and fines as they wished, or called upon townspeople to perform whatever labor services they chose, whether to repair roads or buildings, or even build their houses and cultivate some crops.[16] On the other hand, to receive such deference, loyalty, and labor in the first place, the official had to consistently display their paternalistic power. If they wanted labor to be performed, they held a barangay feast and a fiesta before announcing which projects were to be done, just as landlords sponsored feasts, fiestas, or weddings for their tenants. From their own personal pockets, officials also financed schools, town celebrations of the patron saint, donated lands to the local church or sponsored the rebuilding of the public market. They also doled out small loans or offered legal aid to distressed workers and peasants.[17] In this sense, the so-called taxes that the official collected from the townspeople were not actually taxes. In Tagalog, the only signifier that approximated "tax" was *buwis* (in Spanish, *tributo*), yet *buwis* was the word used to refer to the portion of crop given to a landlord by a tenant in exchange for letting them use the land. It signified tribute. Not surprisingly, in lieu of money for buwis, officials were known to collect hens, eggs, and portions of the rice crop.[18]

Patron-client schemas also guided electoral conduct during Spanish rule. The highest positions of the Spanish colonial state (the governor-general and the provincial governors) were appointive positions, but Filipinos had been allowed to elect their own gobernadorcillos. The electorate was restricted to the principalía, and the electoral procedure consisted of a series of ritualized steps ostensibly reinforcing the symbolic power of the Spanish Crown.[19] But the local elite fashioned elections in particular ways. During electoral campaigns, candidates held social functions and banquets where they wined and dined the potential electors, thereby displaying their generosity. Candidates also distributed money, offering small advances to be expanded later if the candidate emerged victorious; or they paid the delinquent taxes of potential voters. Candidates thereby cultivated personal clients, and when a candidate won, it was a confirmation that they were the better patron, the privileged one who had been better able to initiate and follow up on ostensibly reciprocal exchanges.[20] Fittingly, immediately after the election, the official spent for lavish feasts and celebrations for the entire town, thereby cementing relations of dependence between the new patron and his subjects.[21]

Yet there was a darker side to elections. Campaigning sometimes involved bribery, intimation, and coercion. Incumbent gobernadorcillos seeking to return to office threatened to imprison or dispossess those who refused to vote for them, or they simply cheated.[22] Yet this dark side was still the dark side of *patron-client* schemas, rather than other ones. Coercion and intimidation constituted the excess of patron-clientelism in practice for, in practice, communities were typically divided into competing patron-client networks or clans. If a member of one faction tried to initiate an exchange with a member of an opposed faction to bring him in, and if the latter refused, they classified the latter as deserving of derision, unequal treatment, and perhaps vengeance.[23] In this sense, the cheating and coercion of elections were not deviations from the system of patron-clientelism, they followed from it.[24]

PATRON-CLIENTELISM IN DISCOURSE:
RECIPROCITY AND RAZÓN

Schemas of debt and personalized reciprocity served as implicit guides of conduct, but they also surfaced in elite discourse, beginning in the 1880s when some of the more educated elites (known as *ilustrados*) initiated new reform movements and registered criticisms of Spanish rule. This decade saw a discursive explosion and, by the mid-1890s, a revolutionary movement had emerged alongside the reformist one. In the process, Filipino elites produced new ideas on their society, their nation, and their future.

The discourse was multivocal. Reformists and revolutionaries did not share the same meanings. But they did share an overarching structure of parallels and oppositions that delimited the meanings in the first place — a *structure* of meaning that was interdependent and hence homologous with schemas embedded in lived relations. The discourse of Apolinario Mabini is exemplary.[25] Mabini's scheme first turned upon a classification of society as an organic entity of reciprocating elements. As opposed to Anglo-Saxon liberal philosophies that individuated society into self-enclosed actors, Mabini classified society as consisting of individuals relating together through personalized mutual help and mutual exchange:

> Society is an association of men who are together for mutual help, so that each could enjoy the highest possible well-being [*bienestar*]; a situation that can never be arrived at by the sole efforts of individuals without the aid of others. . . . A man cannot live alone; alone, he cannot build a house, knit his clothes and produce foodstuffs and other things of necessity; he has to join with others . . . so that through exchange . . . various needs can be fulfilled.[26]

Just as exchanges between patrons and clients constituted the community, so too did they constitute society in Mabini's view. In fact, for Mabini, such personalized exchange was a given fact of life, both a social law and God's law of nature. He reasoned that men cannot exist in isolation from one another; to survive, they necessarily have to engage in "mutual help" and exchange.[27] Mabini clarified using a body metaphor. "Society is nothing more than a large individual," for like the separate "members of the body," social elements, by their mutual help and exchange, move in "simultaneous and uniform movement."[28] Without such mutuality, "the harmony that exists among different members of the human body" would be destroyed and the social body would "fall prey to disease and death."[29] By the same token, Mabini also claimed that adherence to mutual help and exchange was as much a moral necessity as a natural necessity. Mutual exchange was a moral act, while nonreciprocity, or the failure to pay one's debts to another, was immoral.[30]

Attendant with this model of social relations were other key terms: specifically *razón*, or "reason," and its parallel, *inteligencia*, "intelligence." These terms were appropriated from the Spanish enlightenment, but they took on particular inflections. Mabini, for example, defined reason as a kind of faculty, a power that allowed one to know God's natural laws. By the same token, he saw it as a regulative power that allowed for man's self-preservation. But for Mabini, self-preservation demanded reciprocal exchange, thus adherence to God's natural law. *Razón* and its parallel term, *inteligencia*, then, referred more specifically to the faculty that facilitates and sustains reciprocity. As the earthly manifestation of God's natural law, reason and intelligence signified mutual help and mutual exchange.[31] Contrasting categories followed, and further effected a homology with patron-clientelism in lived relations. Mabini suggested that while razón was the faculty that facilitated and sustained the law of mutual exchange, the law was not always fulfilled. Sometimes people employed coercion, appropriating "by force or by deception the means of living of their partners."[32] This, then, was a violation of the law of mutual exchange, a transgression of reciprocity and hence razón. Coercion manifested a skewed or inoperative razón, a kind of irrationality.

Such was the cultural structure that reformers articulated in their criticisms of Spanish rule. As is well known, the foremost targets in this discourse were Spanish bureaucrats and especially Spanish friars (who had been proliferating across the island, impinged upon municipal affairs, and at times seized land). The discourse claimed that these actors disobeyed central state authorities, impeded the dissemination of the Spanish language to the populace, and were draining the country of its wealth. They were corrupt, "looking only after their own interests at the expense of communal good and of the Patria."[33] But most notable about the discourse is that it was replete with charges of "ingratitude." The friars were "ingrates, harmful to the country and to the Government"; they tried to "inculcate the sentiment of gratitude from the country and the government to them" while "they are the ones who should be giving thanks to the Government and to the country."[34] Similarly, the bureaucrats were "venomous serpents who corrupt with poison the whole archipelago! They consume but do not produce!"[35] The critical problem registered in this discourse, then, was that Spanish friars and bureaucrats were taking but not giving. As ingrates, they were failing to pay a debt, erring on their side of what was supposed to be a mutual exchange. In other words, the true abuse, the real corruption, was their transgression of mutual help and reciprocity dictated by razón.

To be sure, new invented histories of Spanish colonization produced by ilustrados had scripted past relations between Spain and the Philippines as a matter of mutual exchange. According to the story, when the Spanish explorer Miguel Lopez de Legaspi had first come to the Philippines, he had initiated a series of exchanges with the natives. Specifically, Legaspi had made an agreement with the local Filipino chief, Sikatuna, to establish the first Spanish settlement in the archipelago; Spanish rule was thus predicated upon a "blood compact" of "mutual obligation" between the Spaniards and Filipinos.[36] The "promise between Legazpi and Sikatuna" in particular was that Spain would bring "civilization" to the Philippines (in the form of education, wealth, and national development) and the Filipinos would lend their loyalty and gratitude in return for this "civilizing procedure" (as one ilustrado put it).[37] This, then, was much like the gratitude one owed to one's parents or landlords, and, not surprisingly, reformers still referred to Spain as their "loving mother." But the problem in the reformers' view was that Spain had been faltering on its obligations and failing to pay its debts: "What happens [today] between Spain and the Philippines is precisely everything that creates obstacles to Spanish-Filipino exchange. . . . [Spain] has established insurmountable barriers for exchange. What exchange . . . could there be between Spain and the Philippines with this regime of mutual alienation?"[38] Spain was violating razón, showing a lack or reason and imperfect intelligence.

The leading ilustrado reformer, Marcelo del Pilar, articulated this very idea when criticizing the Spanish policy of deporting Filipino dissidents from the archipelago. Pilar wrote that "deporting residents without prior notice constitutes an outright act of arbitrariness and the law that supports it does not prevent it from being a violation of natural law [*derecho natural*]." Here, Pilar claimed that the Spanish were violating natural law, that is, the law of mutual exchange dictated by reason. Pilar then added that General Blanco, one of the high Spanish rulers, had stopped the deportations, thereby offering a "respite from this arbitrariness" and making Blanco worthy of praise. But General Blanco was to soon be replaced, hence the problem:

> General Blanco, however, cannot stay much longer in the Philippines. The expiry of his term of office approaches with fatal velocity. . . . It is possible that General Blanco's successor may have the same qualities of prudence, rectitude, and point of honor. However, it is also possible for him not to

have these qualities, whether from true cowardice, which springs from *obtuse intelligence* [*hija de obtusa inteligencia*]; [or] whether from cowardice brought about by those who abandon all feelings of rectitude [*rectitud*] and sensitivity [*delicadeza*]. . . . Would the Filipinos resign themselves once again to a life of anxiety, intranquillity, and mistrust of their own honor? Would they resign themselves once more to having the frailocracy wield in their hands, and at their whims, the means of destroying the joy of families?[39]

The fear expressed was that General Blanco's successor would reenact the policy of deportation and therefore violate "natural law." Blanco's successor would then repeat the violations of razón, showing that he had an "obtuse intelligence" or a skewed razón. Conversely, on the other side of the cultural opposition, a good ruler should have proper intelligence. This ruler would properly access and enforce the "natural law" of reason. Hence Pilar's use of the term *rectitud* to refer to a good ruler. *Rectitud* translated into English as "rectitude," but it also carried the meaning of "uprightness" or "straightness," as in a nonobtuse or "straight" intelligence. One had rectitude when one had proper reason; that is, when one fulfilled their debts and obligations. The translation of *rectitude* into Tagalog shows the same meaning. *Rectitude* translated into Tagalog as *katwiran*, a word that meant "reason" as well as "right; justice; loyalty; lawfulness; uprightness; exactitude; straightness; moderation."[40]

If ilustrado reformers initiated this cultural schema, however, even revolutionaries later shared it. The difference is that the revolutionaries claimed that the Spaniards' failure to uphold their side of the exchange justified revolution. After all, to the revolutionaries, the Spaniards were erring not only on the terms of reciprocity, they were employing reciprocity's opposite, coercion: "Although the compact made by the Spanish leader, Miguel López de Legaspi, with Sikatuna, king of part of the Philippines, was one of friendship and for the purpose of Christianising the Filipinos — to which in times past the Spaniards as a Christian nation devoted themselves — yet when they had established themselves in the Philippines, *they changed the government founded upon this compact to one of armed force.*"[41] The cultural structure of razón and reciprocity was not at stake in the divide between reformers and revolutionaries. At stake was whether the Spaniards' violation of razón justified revolution.

Neither reformers nor revolutionaries restricted their discourse to criticisms of Spanish rule. At the same time, they formulated concepts of rights and liberty, articulating them with the overarching cultural structure of razón. Consider Pilar's complaints about the states' repeated deportations of dissidents:

> Deporting residents without prior notice and without granting the deportee a hearing of any kind constitutes an outright act of arbitrariness and the law that supports it does not prevent it from being a violation of natural law. No human power on earth has the legal permission to trample this right, and no honorable conscience may condone a similar system. The tyranny and the despotism this represents is a constant threat to peace in a home and incapacitates the exercise of one's right to a domestic life and the happiness of a family.[42]

Admittedly, deportation without "a hearing of any kind" was probably classified in many societies at the time as a violation of rights. But Pilar more specifically equated "right" with the right to "peace in a home" and "domestic life." He did not complain about violations to the right of private property, for instance, and instead claimed that the primary "right" violated by deportation is the right to "a domestic life." Pilar added in another article:

> We reiterate once more to the governing class that the aggressive system of that regime threatens the peace of Filipino residents as well as the colonial future of Spain in the Far East. To govern means to procure the well-being of those governed. It means guaranteeing the free liberty of their rights, to assure the peace of the home and the families. If, instead of all this, the government becomes a simple institution of domination, symbolizing the eternal violation of individual rights, what unity, what loyalty can be expected from those governed in favor of the governors? Is it possible to sustain a colonial government for a long time when it runs counter to the well-being and peace of the towns?[43]

Deportation violated rights, but only because it "incapacitates" one from "exercising one's right" to a happy domestic life. Deportation was not a violation in itself, it was a violation because it cut one off from the circuits of mutual help and exchange constituting the "happiness of the family" (viz., from the utang na loób, or the debt of the soul, that children owed to parents in exchange for the gift of life). Hence, according to Pilar, government should guarantee "the free liberty of their rights, *to assure the peace of the home and the families.*" Furthermore, Pilar suggested that when one is denied a happy domestic life, when one is cut off from the natural circuits of mutual exchange in familial life, one is denied their rights. Separation from the "happiness of a family" becomes a matter of "tyranny" and "despotism."

Rights and razón were intertwined. Mabini classified the violation of right with violations of razón and its dictates of reciprocity. More precisely, he classified the use of coercion, the opposite of reciprocal exchange, as a "mocking of the rights that all have been given by nature."[44] But Mabini took the parallels and oppositions further still. He equated the violation of rights with a violation of freedom and liberty, which is also to say that, for Mabini, freedom and liberty meant that everyone adhered to the law of mutual help and exchange laid down by razón:

> Many believe that liberty is to act without full restraint, for good or for evil. True liberty is only for what is good and never for what is evil; it is always in consonance with Reason [*Razón*] and the upright and honest conscience of the individual. The thief is not free when he steals for he allows himself to be led by evil and becomes a slave to his passions; when he is punished, it is precisely because he did not use true liberty.[45]

When one is using "true liberty," one is acting "in consonance with Reason." That is, freedom and liberty referred to a situation when everyone adheres to razón: everyone engages in reciprocal exchange, and everyone keeps up with their debts and obligations. Exchange is mutual, neither forced nor coerced.

A similar meaning is seen in a "Catechism" printed in *El Heraldo de la Revolución*, a Spanish-Tagalog paper of the revolutionary government. It is worth including both the given Spanish and Tagalog translations of the keywords: "What is liberty [*libertad/kalayaan*]? It is the faculty to work in accordance with the dictate of reason [*razón/katwiran*]. Can this liberty be employed for evil? No, because if it will be employed for evil, it will be against reason [*razón/katwiran*], which says that evil cannot be the end of our acts."[46] As in Mabini's scheme, liberty is the realization of razón and reciprocity, a condition of perfect mutual exchange. It could not be used for "evil," which, by definition, would be "against reason." Note, too, that "liberty" is translated into Tagalog as *kalayaan*. This also made an equation between liberty and a condition of perfect reciprocity. As Reynaldo Ileto shows, the term *kalayaan* comes from the root *layaw*, which means "satisfaction of one's needs" by a patron or "pampering treatment by parents" of a child.[47] Liberty was the ideal state of perfect reciprocity.

Government and the "Directors" of Society

The final element in this cultural structure had to do with authority and governance. Given the fact that razón could be transgressed, and therefore that rights and liberty could be impinged upon, the social body needed a head or authority that would ensure the proper operations of razón. Mabini wrote that there was:

> [The] necessity of having a person who, by superior razón, will prevent individuals from usurping the rights of others. . . . Who will be that power that will direct the rest and to whom obedience is necessary? . . . God does not come down to earth to meddle in the affairs of men. Who, then, should this person be? There is no other alternative but that of the members of society electing something amongst themselves someone whom they consider most suitable to command and direct [*dirigir*] the others and administer justice as God's Representative on Earth.[48]

Governmental authority, or a "director," as Mabini put it, would not only adhere to reciprocal exchange on their own, they would also ensure that people do not use coercion and thereby usurp the rights of the others. By their "superior razón," a superior intelligence or ability that gave them special access to God's natural law, they would "command and direct" society, ensuring that reciprocity was realized on earth. The elite thereby inserted hierarchy into the ideal state of reciprocal exchange. The revolutionary thinker Emilio Jacinto said, "In every community and society there is need of a head, of one who has power over the rest for direction and good example, and for the maintenance of unity among members and associates, and who will guide them to the desired goal. . . . This head is called government."[49] Mabini added that without this authority, the social body would become a corpse. There would be no one to "apportion specific work," and individuals "would not know what the other is doing." Without "directors" with privileged access to razón, "nothing will be accomplished."[50]

Yet the "directors" did not stand above the mutual exchanges in society, they occupied privileged nodal points in them. The government and the people, the directors and directed, were all bound by reciprocal obligations and duties. The people would choose their ruler, lend their loyalty to the ruler, and then subject themselves to the rulers' benevolent direction and dictates. In return, rulers would perform their tasks and paternalistically care for those who had chosen them. "A superior is a superior," said Emilio Aquinaldo, president of the Philippine Republic, "only so far as he promotes the welfare of his subordinates."[51] Jacinto added that this benevolence would result in the "love and esteem" of followers, such as the kind a proper patron deserved. This meant that the director had to adhere strictly to the rule of razón rather than use force:

> The power of those who govern depends upon the love and esteem of the governed, and these obtained by a just and prudent conduct [on the part of authority]. Those who believe that they can maintain their power by means of force and the gun make a great mistake. . . . He who governs owes duties to the people, namely to work for its prosperity and execute its will. . . . The happiness of all is the only duty of the ruler. . . . The welfare of the people, and nothing else, is the real reason and object, the alpha and omega, the beginning and the end, of all the duties of those who govern."[52]

It followed that a subject's adherence to such a benevolent government — that is, a government staffed by the "directors" of razón — would not mark an absence of liberty. It would secure it. "Liberty," claimed Mabini, "does not mean that we shall obey nobody, for it specifically demands of us that we should submit our conduct to the government of razón and the restraints of justice. Liberty does not provide that we should obey everyone, but it demands that we should always obey the power which we have elected and recognized as the most capable of directing us. In such a situation, one is only obeying Reason [Razón]."[53]

Local officials had sometimes scripted themselves as having privileged access to razón, therefore portraying themselves as benevolent rulers. In one postelection speech, a gobernadorcillo declared:

God, Maker of all things, created animals and rational human beings; animals are perfect in all except in reason [*razón*], which was given to man in order that he may know God, respect his elders in authority and government, teach his children to do no harm to others, give to each one what properly belongs to him, and share with the poor what he has. All these sacred principles vanished, however, since the time man sinned against God. For that reason, tribes elected Kings; since it is impossible to find Kings in all communities, He created judges to represent the latter. And so, today, you have me.[54]

Ilustrado reformers had also taken up the self-classification. They often praised each other for carrying the virtues that good rulers needed. One ilustrado praised Pilar for having a "powerful intelligence . . . assisted by reason [*razón*] that was brought to him," such that he "never refused to defend the unfortunate."[55] But as the revolution erupted in the late 1890s, these self-classifications proliferated and guided revolutionary discourse. In the discourse, Spanish rulers had too long erred on their debt, they had too long employed coercion rather than reciprocity, and they therefore had to be replaced by a new authority that would reinstate the proper operations of razón, hence reciprocity, rights and liberty. "A revolution," said Mabini, "is the violent means utilised by the people . . . to destroy a duly constituted government, substituting it for another that is more consonant with Reason [*Razón*] and Justice."[56] Aquinaldo, in his message to the people on June 23, 1898, exclaimed similarly: "taking reason as the only standard for their acts . . . the nation calls on all Filipinos . . . to solidly unite, with the object of forming a noble association."[57] Revolutionary elites then categorized themselves as best fit for the task. By their superior reason and intelligence, they would be the new directors-cum-patrons of the nation. The wife of the revolutionary Andres Bonifacio claimed that Bonifacio's choice to revolt "was motivated not by treachery, but by his adherence to what was *rational* [or, in Tagalog, *ng katwiran*]. The Revolution, representing reason, was ranged against forces representing avarice."[58]

The structure and practice of the revolutionary government at Malolos manifested and institutionalized the schema. On the one hand, the executive power resided in the president, in this case Emilio Aguinaldo.[59] On the other hand, the power of the executive was circumscribed by a national legislature.

The members of legislature included the most educated and wealthy land-owners, and the legislature was declared paramount. The reason for this was not simply because the Filipinos appropriated parliamentary forms of government. It had to with their classification of the legislature as the "brain" of the body, representing in turn the "brains of the nation." Mabini clarified: "Society should have a soul: authority. This authority needs an intellect [*razón*] to guide and direct it: the legislative power. It also needs a will that is active and will make it work: the executive. It needs a conscience that judges and punishes what is bad: the judicial power."[60]

Mabini privileged the legislature because the legislature was the embodiment of razón. "The power to legislate," he stressed, "is the highest manifestation of authority, just as the intellect is the noblest faculty of the soul." The executive and judiciary had to be subordinated to it in the same manner that both the will and conscience are subordinate to the intellect." Because the legislature embodied razón, it was the branch that accessed and regulated the mutual exchanges in society. It was to guide the other branches in "order and harmony" such that "the greatness of society and the well-being of its members" could be furthered. As the "brains of the nation," the legislature was the "nerve center" for the circuits of exchanges throughout the social body.[61] One assemblyman, Felipe Calderon, thus referred to the legislature as the "oligarchy of intelligence" representing "the most intelligent elements of the nation."[62]

Local governments also codified the schema. In a sense, local officials were the representatives of razón for their own little districts.[63] The establishment of local governments began with a town fiesta, akin to the fiestas when an official was inaugurated during Spanish rule to cement relations of dependence.[64] The position of the officials was honored and represented through elaborate symbology. Municipal officials carried a staff with black tassels; provincial officials carried a staff "with a handle of gold and tassels of silver." The upper part of the handle was engraved with "a sun and three stars"—the sun, like the sun of the government's flag, representing the light of razón.[65] The Malolos government inserted the privileged bearers of razón at the top of state, and lesser bearers at the local level. Razón was to be realized, as were rights and liberty in association. Some among the leaders thus claimed that the Malolos government represented "self-government."[66]

The only hitch is that the Malolos government was short-lived. As a result of the Americans' war of conquest, it was dismantled by force. But is this to say that the elites' cultural structures were dismantled by American occupation as well?

AMERICAN RULE AND RECEPTION TO TUTELAGE

The Work of Cultural Power

Fighting began in February 1899, as the first shots fired in Manila echoed in other parts of the islands. But as revolutionaries resisted American sovereignty, American authorities likewise endeavored to win them over with words and deeds. In April 1899, for example, the Schurman Commission issued its famous proclamation on behalf of President McKinley. The proclamation declared that the revolution was based upon a "misunderstanding" and that the United States would bring "a rightful freedom" to the people, "protect them in their just privileges and immunities . . . accustom them to free self-government in an ever-increasing measure; and encourage them in those democratic aspirations, sentiments, and ideals which are the promise and potency of a fruitful national development."[67] American authorities also set up local governments in the "pacified" areas, supposedly symbolizing benign intent. Governor Taft also encouraged the formation of a new Filipino political party that would stand for peace. The party, known as the Federalistas, was headed in Manila by some of the more cosmopolitan elites who had accepted U.S. sovereignty, and with whom the American officials had cultivated close ties. Taft ended up appointing leading members of the Federalistas to high positions in the government, in part to demonstrate that Filipino rebels would be rewarded if they surrendered and came out for peace.

The authorities' words and deeds did not fall upon deaf ears. The Schurman commission's proclamation "attracted large attention" throughout the Islands. Evidently, the people in Manila "gathered about the posters [of the proclamation] in groups," while copies of the proclamation "passed from hand to hand among the natives" and reached into the interior.[68] In fact, the proclamation convinced the revolutionary government to call for a temporary armistice and send emissaries to learn more about it. Thereafter came a series of meetings between the emissaries and the American commissioners. At the meetings, the commissioners went over the proclamation with the emissaries "word for word" and handed them a draft of their plan for civil government.

They discussed the draft "article by article, and explained any points [that the emissaries] did not understand." "This made our position with them very strong," recorded commissioner Worcester.[69] To be sure, dissension subsequently surfaced at Malolos. One faction, upon hearing the emissaries' report of the meeting with the commission, opted to drop their arms. They swiftly headed for Manila and conceded to American sovereignty.[70]

Even many of the revolutionaries who did not immediately surrender did so soon enough. The reasons for their surrender are complex. They include the elites' economic interests and the fear of America's brutal force. But many surrendering elites colored their public explanations with references to the Americans' proffered signs.[71] At a meeting held in Manila, defectors from Malolos gave speeches that called upon Filipinos "to work for peace." They stated that "McKinley announced that the Americans came to these Islands not to enslave but to liberate the people" and urged, "Let there be no more lack of confidence in the promises and statements of intentions on the part of the United States."[72] Others claimed that they surrendered out of the belief that U.S. occupation would bring "a just, liberal and democratic government under the sovereignty of the United States of America."[73] The testimony of Felipe Buencamino is suggestive. He was captured by the Americans in November 1899 but refused to take the oath of allegiance—until, that is, he was "converted" upon reading a copy of the U.S. Constitution. He related the following story during an interview with the commissioners:

[While a prisoner] I got hold of an American almanac in which was the Constitution of the United States, and with the aid of a soldier who was on guard, and who had a slight knowledge of Spanish, I was able to understand it and to make a translation. Having seen and read those grand principles which it contained, and which were in accordance with their rights and desires, I changed my mode of thinking and abandoned the *insurrecto* cause. . . . Therefore my conversion was principally due to having studied the American constitution. . . . it was one of the noblest documents ever written by a man; . . . I had never seen in any laws or constitutions of European powers sentiments so noble as those expressed in that. In none of those documents had I ever seen the expression "rights of liberty." These were details which had convinced me that they [his fellow insurgents] should surrender themselves to the Americans.[74]

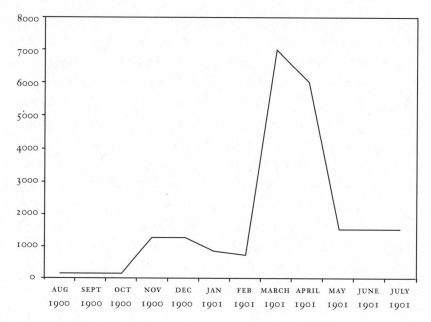

FIGURE 1 Number of surrenders, August 1900 to July 1901
SOURCE: Gates 1973: 229.
Relevant dates:
November 6, 1900: News reaches Philippines that McKinley has defeated the anti-imperialist William J. Bryan in presidential election
February 6–12, 1901: Passage of Municipal and Provincial Government Acts
February 12 to mid-March 1901: American officials tour pacified provinces to help popularize local government acts
March 29, 1901: General Emilio Aguinaldo captured by U.S. forces

The new local governments were also received positively. Many commanders surrendered only to then join the Federal Party and occupy seats in the new governments.[75] Consider Manuel Quezon's conversation with one such commander, Ricardo Paras. "It was his sincere opinion," Quezon reported about Paras, "that the only way of promoting freedom as well as the welfare of the Filipino people was by cooperating with the American Government . . . He pointed out to me that the founders of the Federal party . . . were already taking part in the highest council of the civil government, and that the steps taken so far by the United States all confirmed the policy enunciated by President McKinley that America had come to the Philippines not to subjugate but to train the Filipino people in the art of self-government so that in due time they might become a self-governing nation."[76]

The observations made by T. H. Pardo de Tavera, the leader of the Federal party, are also indicative of a positive reception of the Americans' word. Tavera reported that as the revolutionaries heard the Americans' proclamations and witnessed the new "state of affairs," "there was spread throughout the country, if not an absolute confidence in, at least a more favorable idea of, the Americans." Tavera added that the trips taken by Taft and the commission across the countryside to inaugurate local governments were of particular importance. The trips helped to "diffuse among the Filipinos . . . sentiments of confidence."[77] A look at available data offers some corroboration (see figure 1). The highest number of surrenders occurred between February and early March 1901. This was before General Aguinaldo was captured, but immediately after Taft had passed the local government acts and traveled across the country to set them up.[78]

In short, the revolutionaries, along with other Filipinos, indeed saw something in the Americans' signs and deeds. But what exactly did they see?

The Americans as Legaspi

Something of an answer can be glimpsed in a fiesta in Manila. Organized by Pedro Paterno, a former member of the Malolos government, the purpose of the fiesta was to celebrate the amnesty proclamation and promote peace. On the morning of the fiesta, commission secretary Daniel Williams passed by the fiesta site and noticed that arches had been constructed for the affair. "Upon two or three of the arches, the pictures of [Emilio] Aguinaldo [president of the Philippine Republic] and McKinley were placed side by side [and] bore inscriptions signifying 'Independence under an American Protectorate.' "[79] The American officials later discovered that such calls for "independence under an American protectorate" had been proliferating widely among the Filipino elite. Filipinos in the countryside had been giving speeches advocating it, sometimes equating it with another term, *autonomy*.[80]

The calls for independence under a protectorate irritated and angered the Americans. In the Americans' view, it was inciting enough to hold up a picture of President McKinley alongside a picture of Emilio Aguinaldo (leader of the revolution). It was still more inciting to call for independence, whether under an American protectorate or not, because guerrilla warfare persisted in the provinces. When not irritated, the Americans were bemused. They took the calls for independence under a protectorate as yet another sign of the elites' political ignorance. Taft found it funny that advocates "united the expressions, 'Independence under a protectorate.'" How could there be independence and protectorate status? Would not independence mean the full absence of American interference? Taft concluded that the Filipinos used the term "'independence' in an oratorical way without having thought out what the giving of it involves."[81]

Yet the American officials' condescension simply reflects their own narrow lenses. The Filipino elite indeed had an understanding of what independence meant; the Americans just did not know it. As intimated already, before U.S. rule Filipino elites had equated independence with terms like *liberty* and, in Tagalog, *kalayaan*. Together, these terms referred to a state wherein the laws of razón were in perfect operation, a state wherein reciprocity was realized between social elements and between rulers and ruled. Independence therefore connoted a condition that could have been realized even during Spanish rule, if the Spanish rulers had upheld their obligations dictated by razón. When speaking of protectorate status under U.S. rule, the elite conjured the same concept. Independence could be realized even under the rubric of American control, as long as there was reciprocal exchange between ruler and ruled. American rule would then be what Spanish rule should have been but was not: a realization of razón.

Was this the classification underlying the elites' requests for independence under an American protectorate? We should not make hasty assumptions.[82] Indeed, when some Filipino elites clarified to the Americans what they meant by the arrangement, they presented independence under a protectorate as a simple and practical matter, not a grand issue of razón. Some Filipinos suggested that it meant that the Filipinos would control internal affairs and the Americans would protect them internationally — for example, in cases of aggression by another country. Major-General E. S. Otis said that he spoke to a former revolutionary and "all [the revolutionary] said was this: They wanted the protection of the United States, and they wanted to control the internal affairs of the island, and they would turn over to us the custom-houses in payment for the protection which we would give them on the outside."[83] While this would be an exchange between Americans and Filipinos, then, it would not necessarily mean the kind of mutual exchange associated with razón or kalayaan. It would simply mean payment for protection (which is how the Americans saw it).[84]

On the other hand, even if the elite had meant only payment for protection, this is suggestive in itself. By turning over the customs collections to the Americans to pay for protection, the Filipinos would be offering a kind of tribute, such as the kind tenants gave landlords, or the kind Filipinos had given to the Spanish crown. The United States would then be a patron akin to Spain, only better. It would offer protection, upholding its debts, and in return the Filipinos would give loyalty. Independence under a protectorate would realize mutual exchange and mutual dependence.

Other discourse of the elite suggests that they indeed classified U.S. rule in these terms. While not all of them called for independence under an American protectorate, they all scripted U.S. rule as a matter of reciprocal exchange and debt. After General Mariano Trias surrendered, for example, he penned the following public explanation: "If the country is to advance with firm steps to the height of happiness and prosperity it needs nothing less than assistance; and for this purpose, there is nothing better than [the assistance of] the United States, which, I am convinced, has no other aim than to unite its forces with ours for the intellectual and commercial progress of the Filipino people."[85] Trias's claim that the United States would contribute to the "progress of the Filipino people" reproduced preexisting narratives about the reciprocal exchanges between Spain and the Philippines. It classified American rule as doing what ilustrados in the 1890s had believed all good governments should do, and what Spain should have done: initiate the progress of the archipelago, bring it prosperity, and ensure the happiness and bienestar of the people. When *El Renacimiento*, a leading ilustrado newspaper in Manila, learned that Governor Taft was asking the U.S. Congress for funds to carry out developmental programs (the kind of programs the elite had been clamoring for during Spanish rule), it insinuated that Taft was indeed attending to the bienestar of the people, as good rulers should: "From the Filipinos has come the idea of asking the Civil Commission for approval of a law to set up an agricultural bank. . . . These recommendations have been benevolently received by Governor Taft, who, always attentive to the general bienestar of the people, has already announced that three million pesos voted by Congress will be given."[86]

When Taft and the commissioners traveled across the towns to inaugurate the local governments, they received similar praise from recently appointed Filipino officials. The new officials claimed that the United States was meeting its patronage obligations by granting local control to the Filipinos. A mayor in Pangasinan proclaimed:

> Like the light of dawn which announces to the living world a day of heaven's own clear and serene blue, the Honorable Civil Commission, representing American sovereignty, has come to Pangasinan to inaugurate civil provincial government, the precursor of a thousand blessings and of a happy future for its inhabitants. And as this signifies much to me, I confess, gentlemen, that I cannot find words to express my gratification and satisfaction, especially when it is taken into consideration that this province is one of the first to which is offered the enjoyment of the benefits arising from the provincial civil law enacted by eminent men of wide experience whose only desire is the progress and happiness of this country. . . . Then let us this day engrave upon our hearts that in the future we will prove ourselves worthy of the favor done us by the Commission. . . . Long live America! Long live the Honorable Commission! Long live the representatives of the Federal Party. Long live the military commander of this district! Long live President McKinley! Long live the Governor General of these Islands![87]

An official in another town gave a speech in which he directly associated tutelage as a more perfected form of Spanish rule. He first criticized Spanish rule and asserted that the "new government" under Americans is "modeled on the principles of Rizal [the ilustrado hero of the 1890s]." He then proclaimed:

> We now have a civil government, the workings of which must satisfy the aspirations of a people desirous of their liberty and individual rights, which we blindly thought to secure through the use of arms, without bearing in mind that the occasion which brought their [the U.S.] flag to these islands favored our very ideals. . . . We can now entertain the confidence that the promises of America are no longer promises, but tangible deeds, evidencing the good intentions, which in an evil hour we doubted. . . . With respect to this province, so soon as the rainbow of peace appeared above its

horizon the honorable Civil Commission assured this condition of things by immediately creating a civil, paternal government, which will satisfy the desires of all, and whose platform is none other than that the government is for the people and not the people for the government, as was wisely said by one of the members of the honorable commission at the meeting. . . . May the people of the United States be our protectors forever![88]

The Filipino elite also associated tutelary rule with the realization of rights and liberty, classifying them in terms of preexisting cultural structures. Consider the discourse of Felipe Buencamino (who had read the U.S. Constitution as a prisoner and had been attracted to its discourse of "rights of liberty"). When Buencamino was asked in an interrogation what he meant by "liberty," he responded by using a familiar definition. According to the clerk at the interrogation, "Buencamino replied that . . . the definition of liberty was 'life, honor, family, home and property.'"[89] This was the definition of liberty that had been laid out by Pilar in the 1890s: liberty meant the right "to a domestic life and the happiness of a family." Apparently, Buencamino had seen in the U.S. Constitution Filipino concepts. Fittingly, Buencamino later wrote a letter to Taft stating that the Filipinos "believe that the American Government will be a true protector of the rights and liberties of the Philippine people."[90] He also gave public speeches claiming: "The Filipino people hungered and thirsted for justice when they rose against Spain. They also thirsted for liberty before all things. Today, the government of the United States is giving the Filipino people both these benefits."[91]

But if the Americans were indeed the new patronage rulers, would this not mean that the Filipinos had obligations in return? Indeed, the local officials referred to "the great American nation" as their new "mother" in whom the Filipinos "confide."[92] They also approached American officials and told them they owed "a debt of gratitude" — an *utang na loób* that tenants owed landlords and children owed parents.[93] The Filipino officials also had special praise for Governor Taft, head of the Philippine Commission and hence the personification of American patronage. After one local official was inaugurated by Taft, he declared in his inauguration speech: "My sense of gratitude to a great and just government, that has made this occasion possible, is represented here in the person . . . of a just man [Taft], who brings to us justice to all."[94] Federal Party leader Cayetano Arellano gave similar speeches, praising the Americans for the "seventy good laws" passed by the Philippine Commission and urging his listeners to fulfill their side of the exchange:

> Did you not demand acts, deeds [from the Americans]? You have them now, America gives you a foundation upon which to erect your greatness. The best guarantee for the future of the Filipino people, is the brilliant mode of procedure of the Commission, which in a short time has given us seventy-five new laws conceived and based upon a highly democratic spirit. In the face of this evidence are we not going to respond? Since the Commission has responded with patent and beneficial acts, ought we not answer it? Have you no obligations?

When Arellano gave this speech in Bulacan, a member of the audience replied in the affirmative: "Bulacan will reply with deeds. . . . We would do this as evidence of good faith and of our desire to return something for what has been done for us."[95]

True, these meaning-making activities served only to realize imperial interests. By scripting the Americans as patrons, and by classifying tutelage as the realization of their preexisting ideals, the elite offered public loyalty and gratitude. The effect was palpable to Taft. Upon returning from this trip across the towns, he wrote home: "It is not too much to say that we have received ovations in our trips to the provinces to organize provincial governments. . . . The effect of it is wonderful."[96] Still, tutelary colonialism was not only a matter of relations between Americans and Filipinos. It was also about the organization and conduct of government, and how the Filipinos would relate to each other. What meanings did the elite make of this dimension of tutelary rule?

A Government of, by, and for Razón

A series of public hearings held in 1899 in Manila are informative. In their proclamation of April 1899, the American commissioners had invited witnesses and "prominent persons" to give them information and present local opinions on American occupation. The hearings were slated to meet the task.[97] One of the common themes that emerged from the witnesses is seen in an exchange between the commissioners and Enrique Lopez, a Manila physician. Lopez, like his peers, suggested that U.S. rule should provide an autonomous government under an American protectorate, and the commissioners asked Lopez to "state briefly the scheme of government" he had in mind. Lopez responded:

> Answer [Lopez]: The American commission undoubtedly has the greatest desire to give proper liberties to the people, and I wish to present my plan to you. . . . The plan is to have five governors, under the sovereignty of America. The governor-general should be an American, and the sovereignty undoubtedly should be in the United States, without speaking of the Army or Navy, or anything else.
> Question [Commission]: The political sovereignty?
> Answer [Lopez]: The Political sovereignty and the immediate government of the islands should be a government of the country itself.
> Question [Commission]: In what way?
> Answer [Lopez]: My plan is to have five ministers. A minister of the treasury, of internal affairs — five different ministers of the general government, and they are to be Filipinos partly, Filipinos according to the greatest amplitude of the autonomy.
> Question [Commission]: How would you have the governor-general appointed?
> Answer [Lopez]: An American, from the United States, by the United States government.
> Question [Commission]: How would you have the five chiefs appointed?
> Answer [Lopez]: My private opinion is that for the first time the five ministers should be appointed by this commission.[98]

On the one hand, Lopez's scheme of government acknowledged American sovereignty. He said that the governor-general should be an American, and that "undoubtedly sovereignty should be in the United States." Lopez thus deferred to American control. Moreover, his scheme of having five different ministers along with a governor-general was not unlike the commission's own plan of having a governor-general and a consulting body (e.g., the Philippine Commission). Lopez's scheme therefore accords with the Americans' tutelary design. Indeed, Lopez left open the possibility for tutelary rule to eventually impose American methods. Even if he had scripted the United States and the Philippines as locked in mutual exchanges dictated by razón, this relationship could just as well facilitate the Americans' tutelary goals. The Filipinos would give their gratitude and loyalty to the Americans, and the Americans would in turn teach them new methods and schemes of governance.

Nonetheless, as the exchange between Lopez and the commissioners proceeded, and as Lopez began to elaborate what the tutelary government should look like, his scheme clearly diverged from the Americans' scheme. Lopez stated that the five ministers should at first be appointed; then, after this first appointment, they should be elected:

> Question: And after the first time, how would you have them [the ministers] appointed?
> Answer: Afterwards, the five ministers should be elected by the people — the intelligent people, people capable of casting an intelligent vote.[99]

Surely there is nothing noteworthy about Lopez's use of the word *intelligent* to describe qualifications for the suffrage. The American administrators also believed that any election under tutelary rule should at first have a restricted suffrage, and they planned to restrict it to those who could read and write or who had a certain amount of education (and paid a certain amount of taxes). This implied that the Americans also wanted to restrict the suffrage to those who were "intelligent." But Lopez, unlike the American authorities, put a particular accent on the signifier. The Americans' view of intelligent and/or educated Filipinos was mostly negative, and at best ambivalent. The "educated mestizos," said Governor Taft, "have acquired a good deal of superficial knowledge of the general principles of free government . . . [and] are generally lacking in moral character."[100] To American officials, *intelligence* signified a lack but also the capacity to make up for it. It referred to a quality that rendered someone a good receptor of political education: "There is no doubt that the exercise of political power is the best possible political education and ought to be granted whenever the pupil has enough intelligence to perceive his own interest even in a rude practical way."[101] In contrast, consider what Lopez said. After proposing that the electorate should be restricted to the intelligent, the commissioners probed further:

> Question [Americans]: What qualification would you have for voting?
> Answer [Lopez]: People in a good station in life, well-known people, people who have property. I do not mean the peons or lower classes.

Question: How much property ought they have to entitle them to vote?

Answer: I would not place a limit in actual dollars, *but decent people.*

Question: Can't you name a figure that would be a basis for voting, $100, $1,000, or $500?

Answer: A person that has property, any property bringing in an income, or any diploma of a profession, or license to practice a profession.

Question: If we said all the men who own $500 worth of property should vote how many of them would vote here in Manila?

Answer: My idea was to have 50 men choose the ministers, 50 men to represent the people.[102]

Lopez placed value on "intelligent people" without qualification. He equated them with "decent people," not with immoral and ignorant oppressors, as the Americans did. This is why Lopez was unconcerned with the particular details regarding property or income to narrowly specify the boundaries for the electorate ("Can't you name a figure . . . $100, $1,000, or $500?"). For Lopez, intelligence was a self-evident category of goodness, a value-in-itself. It meant "decent people" who could then "represent the people."

It is informative that Lopez valued "intelligence" in this way. As we have seen, intelligence had obtained a peculiar meaning for the educated elite before American rule. It had been the ilustrados' crucial criterion for proper political authority, the privileged ability to access and ensure the natural law of razón. Lopez, by stressing intelligence as the criterion for the election of ministers, persisted in this schema. As the "oligarchy of intelligence" in the Malolos government was to represent the people, so too did Lopez hope that the "intelligent" and "decent people" during American tutelage would do the same. Accordingly, when Lopez further elaborated his scheme to the commissioners, he clarified that "intelligent" electors should choose five ministers, and the five ministers in turn make laws for the archipelago and control the towns across the province, just as the legislature during Malolos did. As Lopez clarified this, the Americans became skeptical, and the initial convergence between Lopez's scheme and American design diverged:

Question: Is it your scheme that these 50 men should make laws for all the islands; if not, for what island?

Answer: No, sir; the 50 are only to elect the 5 ministers. They are to appoint the ministers.

Question: But these 5 ministers are to conduct the affairs of all the islands, are they?

Answer: Yes, sir; acting as a central government in Manila. The minister of *Gobernación* to appoint local presidents in the different towns and provinces and to collect the taxes and tributes and turn them in to the central government in Manila.

Question: You don't give the Philippine people much voice in their own affairs?

Answer: I have noticed that the lower classes, the poor, in the Philippine Islands will obey the orders of any government as long as it is a government; that *they will follow whatever they are told to follow by authority.*

Question: You would not give the Philippine people more representation?

Answer: I will draw up a detailed plan of the government I propose in regard to provinces and all details there, and will take great pleasure in presenting it to you.[103]

The Malolos government had had a similar structure, and it followed that Lopez did not see his proposed scheme — with power centralized in the hands of the "intelligent" element — as a violation of the liberties promised by American rule. He did not hesitate to say that the mass of Filipinos "follow whatever they are told to follow by authority." The American members of the commission found this offensive; hence their query: "You would not give the Philippine people more representation?" But for Lopez the plan was guided by local meanings of *razón* and *libertad*. As ilustrados had said in the 1890s, to follow the orders of the constituted authority was perfectly acceptable, as long as the constituted authority had intelligence and thereby embodied razón. Following authority would be a state of "liberty" precisely.

Lopez was not alone in accenting intelligence by inserting the signifier into preexisting cultural patterns. When asked about governmental or social questions, nearly all of the interviewed ilustrados at these hearings uttered the term without being prompted to by the Americans. They used it as the basic organizing category for classifying political questions and even for measuring political capacity. Asked if the provinces were "capable of governing themselves," one ilustrado replied: "To a certain extent, yes. In certain provinces, as, for example, Pampanga, the people are sufficiently enlightened to govern themselves in a certain manner." Asked if there were "capable men sufficiently qualified to be sent as representatives to a general parliament . . . in all the islands," he replied: "I do not know all the provinces, but I think it very profitable that in each of them there would be found one or two men of sufficient enlightenment."[104] Governor Taft recorded later that some elites had approached him and told him that the Filipinos were capable of self-government because "a count of the educated people in the islands showed that they were twice as numerous as the offices to be filled in the central, provincial, and municipal governments, and they, therefore, afforded two shifts to fill them, so that when one set became unsatisfactory, the other might take its place."[105] Even those elites who did not think that all Filipinos were ready for full participation in the government used "intelligence" as the yardstick. The Filipino people were not ready to govern themselves because "the enlightened classes are [only] in the proportion of 1 to 10,000"; and many towns did not have enough municipal officials "with sufficient intelligence" to be self-governing.[106]

Evidently, the elite received the signs and structures of cultural power, but only in accordance with local signifying patterns. American rule was about intelligence, a regime of razón, guiding relations between Americans and Filipinos and also among the latter. But in this semiotic context, what possible impact could "practical political education" and disciplining for democratization have?

"A School of Politics"

As we have already seen, the American authorities had initially set up local governments as part of their effort to win hearts and minds. But thereafter, they were also hoping that the local governments would serve as "a school of politics for the education of the people."[107] As Taft explained: "We have thought by establishing a form of municipal government practically autonomous, with a limited electorate, and by subjecting its operations to the scrutiny and criticism of a provincial government in which the controlling element is American, we could gradually teach them the method of carrying on government according to American ideas."[108] Accordingly, during the commissioners' trip across the islands to set up the new local governments, they had gathered the new officials in each town together, gave them speeches highlighting the Progressive-era qualities officials had to acquire, and read the new laws and codes delimiting the officials' duties. Edith Moses, wife of commissioner Bernard Moses, had accompanied the commission on some of these trips and found the discourse boringly routinized. She recorded in her journal: "The public session in Capiz began as usual with the reading of the Provincial law, which I am sure I can repeat now from memory."[109]

But the new "schools of politics" soon enough ran into some trouble. After the first year of operation, the commissioners discovered that municipal officials had been engaging in all kinds of corruption. They learned that the officials had been pocketing funds for themselves in direct violation of the new municipal code, thereby showing "a disposition . . . to vote all of the available funds for the payment of their own salaries and [to] leave nothing for the improvement or repair of roads, the construction of buildings, or the payment of school-teachers, and this although the law . . . by mandatory provision, have set aside certain definite shares of the public funds for such purposes."[110] Such conduct was common. Putatively, local officials across the towns had been deploying the office for their own "private profit," "private desires," and "personal aggrandizement."[111] To make matters worse, local officials had been abusing their authority, collecting "illegal taxes" and "voluntary contributions" from their subjects. These were collected such that "the people seem to think the local presidentes have the power of kings or despots."[112] Taft complained: "The presidente fails to observe the limitations upon his power, and the people are too submissive to press them."[113]

We have seen a similar outbreak of corruption in Puerto Rico. But we have also seen that it was not so much an outbreak of something new as it was an extension of prior cultural schemas. The same goes for the Filipinos' so-called corruption. Consider a disparity in the Americans' own reports. The Americans complained that local officials were filling their own pockets with public funds and collecting illegal taxes, but they also found that the same officials were using the "voluntary contributions" to secure "money, material, and labor" for public works.[114] Forbes learned, for instance, that the mayor of the town of Jaro (whose treasury was empty) had "macademized the public roads, put in permanent concrete culverts over all the waterways and at street crossings. . . . [and] obtained money enough to build a new school, and a market partly of concrete."[115] Municipal mayors throughout the islands also constructed public schools, using funds from their own personal pockets.[116]

While local officials pocketed money for their own "private profit," therefore, they also put some of that money back into their districts. The only hitch is that they did this against the dictates of the municipal code and instead personalized the process. It is as if the "illegal taxes" they collected were a kind of tribute or buwis, just as in the days of old. To be sure, locals continued to refer to taxes as buwis, and one investigation found that their collection had the appearance of legitimacy to the people: "The custom of collecting so-called 'voluntary contributions' for public and semi-public purposes exists in many municipalities of the islands. . . . In towns where it is desired to raise money by voluntary contributions, it not infrequently happens that each person is assessed a certain amount, and told that such sum is his share of the contribution which must be paid. [These people] are thus led to look upon all contributions as taxes."[117]

Moreover, the Americans found that local officials did more than build infrastructure from their own pockets. Evidently, they also gave out political appointments to friends and provided legal service to commoners.[118] As in the Spanish days, therefore, the Filipino officials used their privileged positions to initiate a series of personalized exchanges with people in their locality, cultivating a following as bearers of razón were expected to do. Not surprisingly, the Americans found that the local officials did not pay their municipal police forces with salaries. As in the past, local officials ran the municipal police as their own personal servants and henchmen, providing payment in forms that eluded the Americans' category "salary." Moses recorded in his diary:

> In Manila, as well as in the provinces, the native policeman is little more than the servant of somebody above him. In the provinces the native police run at the order of the Presidente without regard to the nature of the business which he demands of them. They are, consequently, little more than personal servants of the Presidente. This was illustrated on our trip [across the towns]. At Baong we were entertained in the tribunal by the Presidente and the police acted as servants, running here and there for fodder for the horses, for food for our company, and served us at table.[119]

No doubt such practices served the officials' own interests. But an appeal to naked interests alone cannot explain the remarkable fact that local officials acted as if their conduct was not in the least bit transgressive. Forbes investigated conditions in one province and then recorded: "The police were nothing but the servants of the officials and the natives did everything they asked and never expected pay. It was very difficult to make the Filipinos understand that this is not right."[120] He continued: "One of the principal difficulties with which the Governor [of the Philippines] finds himself confronted is keeping the native officials from oppressing those under them. They seem filled with the belief that this is the purpose for which they were elected or appointed."[121] The officials even acted as though their conduct was expected of them. Daniel Williams reported a discussion between a *presidente* (mayor) and the commissioners, in which the presidente had suggested that the municipal board members in his town should receive a higher salary. Williams stood amazed because the presidente had made this suggestion "based on the theory that they [the municipal officials] would be so beset by churchmen and landowners generally that they should have big pay."[122] Evidently, the presidente expected to use office to pay off friends and followers and believed that the Americans in turn expected him to do so.

Nor is it the case that the Filipinos' corruption was an unconscious habit. In fact, in explicit discourse, the officials classified themselves and their office in terms of prior categories. Something of this is seen in an incident that occurred when the commissioners were first drawing up the municipal code. Pedro Paterno (who had organized the amnesty fiesta for protectorate status) had caught wind of the commissioners' meetings and then paid them a visit to offer his own suggestion. His suggestion was that the American regime should bestow "decorations and orders of nobility" to the municipal officials.[123] The American commissioners found the suggestion ridiculous. They hoped to permit the Filipinos to hold office so that the officials could learn the ways of democracy, not aristocracy. But for Paterno, the suggestion must have been perfectly acceptable — otherwise he would not have registered it. After all, Filipino officials during Spanish rule had always received such honorifics, and the revolutionary Malolos government had bestowed similar honorifics and decorations upon its officials. Hence Paterno, in demanding honorifics and decorations from the Americans, demanded the same sort of recognition that local officials had always received. To him, Filipino officials under tutelary rule were to be the privileged bearers of razón.

A report to the American officials from Aguedo Agbayani, the provincial governor of Ilocos Norte, reveals a similar classification. The report came soon after the establishment of the first provincial governments, and in it, Agbayani claimed that "intelligence" should be the measure of worth for the municipal governments below him. He added that they should not employ coercion, that is, reciprocity's opposite: "The establishment of the provincial government in Ilocos Norte. . . . and the entry upon office of the provincial officials . . . have caused a feeling of general satisfaction among the inhabitants. The municipal governments must be composed of competent and intelligent men, worthy of the honor which is done them, and capable of performing the duties of their office, as the most powerful element for obtaining the prosperity and the happiness of the pueblos is now *intelligence and not force.*"[124]

Not long after Agbayani's report was made, an editorial in the newspaper *El Renacimiento* took such ideas further. The editorial is notable because it was among the first editorials about the new provincial governments. The editorial commented more specifically on the appointment of the first Filipino provincial treasurer in Negro Occidental:

> This [the appointment of the Filipino treasurer], then, opens up the period of testing the moral aptitude and diligence of the Filipinos in the discharge of that eminent official post, the first step taken to appraise the moral virtues and qualities of intelligence. . . . Upon the conduct of that first Filipino treasurer will depend the judgement that is formulated about the moral and intellectual coefficient of our race. The trial and observation begins. It all comes down to avoiding disappointment; disappointment to the government and disappointment to the *pais.*[125]

In this sense, the Filipino elite surely classified tutelage as the Americans did: as a trial of the Filipinos' political capacity for self-government. But to the elite, the trial was whether or not local officials truly had "qualities of intelligence" and a "moral and intellectual coefficient." Tutelage was a test of the Filipinos' razón.

Given these meanings, it is not surprising that the elites' electoral conduct, just like their conduct in office, reproduced the schemas and practices of the past. American residents scripted the electoral judges, ballots, and ballot boxes attendant with the new electoral system as "symbols of progress and modernity," but the Filipino elite engaged the new system by all the old rules.[126] Consider what William Freer witnessed. Discussing a campaign in the town of Mirasol, where Freer had been residing as a public school teacher, Freer recorded:

> During his campaign for reelection, any voter might go to Capitán Domingo [the incumbent candidate] and be sure of an attentive ear to his complaint; if he was in personal trouble or financial straits, no one was so willing to help him. Near the close of campaign, the Capitán always gave a *baile* [dance] and supper on a magnificent scale to the leading people of the town; during the last fortnight, he had frequent suppers at his home for the electors of less prominence.[127]

Freer observed the very same kinds of campaign activities that had been carried out during Spanish rule. In fact, Freer not only found that Capitán Domingo had held a "supper on a magnificent scale" but also that he had distributed favors, gifts, and money to voters. And evidently Domingo was not alone. Freer claimed that the "rival candidates adopted the same custom, and the voters . . . were invited to a round of feasting."[128] American authorities found that the same activities were being carried out across the archipelago, even though they were prohibited by law. "It is difficult," complained one official, "to make the candidates understand that ancient methods may not be resorted to in order to control the votes of electors, and equally difficult to make the electors understand that such control and direction is not perfectly reasonable and in accordance with law."[129]

Countless cases of so-called bribery surfaced as well. An American reporter living in Pampanga found that votes were being bought "at 12 pesos each." He also learned that candidates were paying the delinquent taxes of many people in the town so that they could qualify to vote. To his surprise, he learned too that the Filipinos were "[talking] of such things as mere matters of business, many of them having no idea that bribery is a crime."[130] Furthermore, authorities found that the Filipinos were blatantly cheating during the elections. In one town, "there were more ballots in the box than there were electors qualified to vote."[131] These "bold frauds" emerged quite often, compelling an American reporter to equate Filipinos with corruption at home:

"The average Filipino is no novice at political-wire pulling; he is just about as crafty in the art of politics as is the average American ward heeler and other political bosses. . . . I shall not be surprised if I hear in the future that some Tomás or other, lately emigrated from the Philippines, has captured the votes of the largest ward in New York City over the head of some redoubtable Patrick."[132]

It is also suggestive that there were no major political parties for the municipal elections. The Federal Party had many members, but it mainly operated in the capital. For municipal elections, the Federalistas were absent, as were other political parties. But this is not surprising. As was the case during Spanish rule, candidates did not run on political platforms of a party, they were representatives of the different factions of the town. An American in the town of Basco, for example, noted that "there were no political parties, only the partisans of rival cattle dealers."[133] Elections were competitions between different patron-client networks, battling on "personal" issues, making "personal enemies of the other," and creating "political feuds." "There are always two strong factions in the towns," complained the executive secretary, "which produce much friction at election times."[134] From this followed interfactional intimidation and threats, unsettling what was supposed to be a matter of formal procedures for adducing individual preferences. In one town, the incumbent mayor and candidate attacked those who refused to vote for him. In other towns, voters were forcibly prohibited from voting, and all such tactics were repeated throughout the archipelago. Rumors proliferated in one district that whomever was elected mayor would be assassinated by the followers of the losing candidate. Apparently, the townspeople did not see this as a transgression of the normal state of affairs, nor even as a transgression of electoral practice in the U.S. They told one American reporter that they believed President McKinley himself had been "assassinated by one of the rival party."[135]

This corruption and factional fighting proved immensely taxing to the regime. Due to repeated electoral irregularities, authorities had to order that elections be held over and over. In some towns, they had to be held six times. Complained the executive secretary, all of this "only causes strife and annoyance and interferes with business."[136] Indeed, the Americans recorded instances of electoral corruption in "about one-half of the municipalities" for the 1904 elections.[137] "As matters stand," summarized the executive secretary, "it is simple truth to say that in many instances there is disclosed lack of respect for and obedience to the ascertainment of the popular will, and that improper and dangerous influences and methods are exerted which tend to make elections far from satisfactory, and in some cases a farce."[138] Yet the "farce" was only a farce in his terms. Seen in light of the Filipino elites' meaning-making activities, it marks the reproduction of prior cultural structures.

THE EARLY ENCOUNTER EXPLAINED

We can now approach a better understanding of the incipient stages of America's tutelary empire. American officials tried to win hearts and minds. They also sought to implant their own preferred meanings and models of governance. But the former attempt was successful only because the latter failed. The elite in both colonies accepted American occupation, but they did so as they domesticated it. They classified American rule, its agents, and everything it offered according to familiar types and tales, thereby accepting tutelage while remaining impervious to its imposed meanings. Note that this domestication was not about a clash of values. It was rather about differences in interpretation and meaning making. Note, too, that domestication occurred in *both* colonies, despite differences between them. Domestication happened in both despite the fact that the elite had different backgrounds and presumably different cultural values; it happened despite the fact that tutelage began amid peace in one colony and war in another; it happened despite the fact that elite in the two colonies proclaimed different goals of statehood or independence and therefore faced different incentive structures.

Why, then, did domestication occur in both colonies? To explain the similarity, we must locate something the two colonies shared. By probing the elites' meaning-making activities and signifying patterns, we have found it: the elite in both colonies already had a previously institutionalized set of schemas on democracy and self-government before American rule. Thus, as the elite in both colonies made meaning of tutelage, they were constrained to first employ their previously institutionalized schemas. As those schemas had been routinized and fixed in practice, they were the most retrievable, available, and familiar, so the elite employed them to first classify and narrate the tutelage situation. This constraint thereby determined domestication. Despite the elites' respective interests or incentives, and regardless of other differences between the two colonies, domestication occurred due to the elites' previously institutionalized schemas and the constraints thereby posed upon meaning-making practices.

But then we wonder: if the elite in both colonies initially domesticated tutelage due to the constraints of their institutionalized meaning systems, were the constraints ever lifted?

Chapter 4

BEYOND CULTURAL REPRODUCTION

Since the outset of occupation, the American officials made new meanings, models, and modes of democratic self-government available. Through their speeches, proclamations, memos, and publications they offered tutelary texts that articulated their own Progressive-era ideas on democratic self-government and how it should be conducted. Tutelary rule thereby opened up the possibility that the Puerto Rican and Filipino elite would learn new signifying patterns and effect a transformation in their local political culture. But as we have seen, the elite in neither colony realized this possibility. Due to the constraints of their previously institutionalized cultural system, they first approached the new texts as familiar rather than foreign. They domesticated tutelage and thereby reproduced their preexisting cultural schemas.

Studies have revealed similar processes in other colonial contexts, showing that colonized peoples often responded to colonialism by "localizing" or "indigenizing" it—receiving its signs, artifacts, and the event of intrusion itself in terms of their preexisting cultural categories. Such processes of "reverse appropriation" (as Steve Stern calls them) are important to note, for they reveal the limits of colonialism's cultural power.[1] Still, the question arises: How might these processes lead to cultural transformation? Are colonized peoples forever condemned to employ their preexisting cultural categories to make meaning? Might they not learn and deploy new ones, thereby expanding their cultural repertoire? As critics have pointed out, without addressing these questions our analyses would fall into the trap of "culturology." We would be left to assume that colonized peoples are cultural dopes, forever condemned mechanically to employ their inherited meaning structures.[2]

These questions are also important in light of what happened in Puerto Rico and the Philippines as tutelary rule proceeded beyond its first years. As the next chapters will show, while domestication in the U.S. empire indeed happened, it did not proceed interminably or evenly. On the one hand, the Puerto Rican elite eventually stopped domesticating tutelage and instead opened themselves up to it. They paid attention to the American authorities' messages in a way they had not previously done, seeking out and learning the signifying patterns which tutelary rule had long been introducing to them. The Puerto Rican elite thereby expanded their cultural repertoire; the constraints of their inherited culture were lifted. Conversely, the Filipino elite continued in their domestication as tutelage proceeded. American officials continued to offer novel meanings, and the Filipino elite continued to receive them in terms they already knew.

This divergence in the elites' cultural paths had a critical impact on the American officials' perceptions. Initially, American authorities had suggested that the Puerto Ricans might not be ready for statehood or citizenship for decades to come. But as the Puerto Rican elite ceased domestication, some in American circles of authority proposed that the elite would be ready for statehood sooner rather than later.[3] The divergence is further significant because it eventually led to two different forms of change. On the one hand, as the Puerto Rican elite paid attention to the Americans' discourse in a way they had not before and expanded their repertoire, they also put the new lessons learned to use, marginalizing their prior schemas in the process. They thereby effected a *structural transformation*. On the other hand, as the Filipino elite continually drew upon their preexisting schemas to make meaning of tutelage, they reproduced their prior political culture while changing it in a very different way. Rather than abjuring their prior schemas for new ones, they modified them so as to *revalue* their preexisting system. What began as reproduction in both colonies ultimately gave way to two different forms of change.

We will see these different forms of change in subsequent chapters. This chapter begins the explanation for them. What accounts for the fact that the elites' initially similar cultural paths diverged? How and why did domestication in Puerto Rico and the Philippines give way to two different forms of change?

THE DILEMMA OF CULTURAL CHANGE

It is worth clarifying the task of explanation. The goal is not simply to explain why the elites' cultural paths diverged; it is, more precisely, why they diverged from the same starting point of domestication. This means that we must pinpoint *emergent differences* between the two cases. Without pinpointing *differences* between the two cases, we cannot explain why structural transformation happened in Puerto Rico while revaluation happened in the Philippines. Yet, without finding an *emergent* difference, we cannot explain why the initial domestication in either case ended up as change. In short, we must locate a turning point that can help us better explain why the elites' paths diverged from the same footing.

It follows that intuitive references to persistent differences between the two cases do not suffice for an explanation. Intuitively, for instance, we might conclude that the Puerto Rican elite later adopted the Americans' meanings while the Filipino elite did not because Puerto Rico elite were already more open to them. The Puerto Rican elite was geographically closer to the United States and sought eventual statehood in the Union. But this explanation cannot account for why the Puerto Rican elite at first received tutelage just as the Filipino elite had — that is, by domesticating it. It cannot explain why the Puerto Rican elite opened themselves up to tutelage's lessons only *later*, as U.S. rule proceeded, while their Filipino counterparts remained along the path of domestication. Something happened differently in the two colonies over time so as to push the elites' cultural paths in different directions. We need a proper explanation of what it was.

Another intuitive explanation would point to differences in elite constitution. On one level, the Puerto Rican and Filipino political elite were similar to each other. They constituted the wealthier and more educated in each colony; they occupied tutelary posts and led political parties; and they had backgrounds and connections in land and merchant capital. Still, there were vast differences between the elites on other counts. On the one hand, the Puerto Rican elite were more organizationally cohesive. One party with roots in the Spanish period, the Federal Party, remained dominant and persisted through American rule (first as the Federal Party; later as the Union Party). On the other hand, in the Philippines, party organizations had not developed before American rule; and during the first years of American occupation various political parties dotted the landscape. Relatedly, the Filipino elite were more culturally and linguistically disparate than the Puerto Rican elite: they came from different regions and provinces, each having their distinct languages and local cultures, while the Puerto Rican elite shared Spanish. Taken together, these differences might account for differences in cultural outcomes. Given the weaker organizational and linguistic connections among the political elite in the Philippines, it might have been more difficult for new foreign concepts to transfer to and disseminate among the Filipino elite as a whole.

These differences, however, are not enough to account for the elites' divergent cultural trajectories. First, while the provincial elites in the Philippines spoke regional languages, they also had Spanish as their lingua franca and American texts were disseminated in Spanish as well as in local languages.[4] The Filipino elite also communicated with each other through archipelago-wide newspapers and journals, which proliferated in the colony as U.S. rule proceeded. These factors would have enabled inter-elite communication and the transmission of American concepts and ideas in a manner not unlike in Puerto Rico. To be sure, as we will see in subsequent chapters, disparate elites across the archipelago typically responded to the same American speeches and events in Manila, thereby showing that the Americans' discourse was more available and retrievable than geographical and linguistic differences would imply. Second, while inter-elite party organization in the Philippines was initially weaker than in Puerto Rico, the Filipino elite did in fact develop overarching organizational ties as tutelage proceeded. The Federalistas first incorporated various elites from across the provinces. Later, the Nacionalista Party emerged to replace the Federalists and it did the same, taking in defectors from the Federalistas and other parties to serve as an overarching umbrella for most of the political elite. Finally, the Filipino elite from across the provinces mingled and communicated with each other at various meetings and events in the capital, such as the provincial governors' assembly in 1905.

The establishment of the Philippine Assembly in 1907 was but a culmination of a larger process of elite formation.[5] Therefore, as tutelage proceeded, elite cohesion in the Philippines more closely approximated elite cohesion in Puerto Rico. If anything, we would expect a *convergence* in cultural trajectories between the two colonies rather a divergence. Yet this convergence did not happen. Instead, the elites' cultural trajectories diverged.

Beyond intuition lie some theoretical hypotheses. Do existing approaches to culture fare better for meeting the task of explanation? The structural-functionalist approach, which theorizes culture as subjective values, beliefs, and orientations, is clearly insufficient. This approach explains change by a shift in generations. For cultural change to occur, newly socialized people must replace the prior generation. Yet, structural transformation in Puerto Rico occurred within the *same* generation; and the structural-functionalist approach offers no way of explaining this intragenerational change.[6] Other theories would pinpoint different factors. An instrumentalist or strategic-uses approach would suggest that the elites' preferences dictated the meanings they made. To account for the divergence in the elites' cultural paths, this approach would predict shifts in the elites' interests or incentives.[7] Alternatively, state-centered approaches to culture argue that cultural outcomes follow from state policies or structures. Existing studies of colonial politics in the Philippines insinuate this theory by arguing that the Filipino elite never "learned" the Americans' lessons because of what the Americans did. To maintain colonial control, American authorities constructed patronage relationships with the elite and a particular political party (the Federalistas). This strategy then belied the American authorities' educating rhetoric. Presumably, it served to teach the elite that politics was little else than a matter of playing patronage games.[8] To explain the different cultural outcomes in Puerto Rico and the Philippines, therefore, this approach would look for differences between the Americans' tutelage policies or collaborative patterns between the two colonies.

These potential explanations do not suffice either. First, we will see that the elites' interests did not shift over time. From the beginning, the Puerto Rican elite wanted statehood while the Filipino elite wanted eventual independence, and throughout the period of divergence they remained true to these goals. Nor did incentive structures differ over time or between the cases as tutelage proceeded. In fact, in both cases the elite faced powerful incentives for adopting the Americans' meanings. Finally, we will see that the Americans' collaborative patterns and ruling strategies did not differ. American officials in both colonies enacted the same tutelage policies, programs, and collaborative patterns on the ground. When their ruling strategies shifted over time, they shifted in similar directions. It follows that this similarity cannot account for the elites' divergent paths.[9]

The inability of existing case studies and theoretical approaches to predict the elites' divergent cultural paths invokes the need for an alternative approach. The approach should be able to guide us toward a specification of emergent differences between the cases, thereby orienting us to a better explanation of the elites' divergent cultural paths. Might we find such guidance in the semiotic systems-in-practice approach to culture? In the first half of this book, I have shown that a semiotic systems approach can help us understand the elites' initially *similar* paths. In this half, I show that an elaboration of the approach can also help us understand why the elites' initially similar cultural paths diverged.

SEMIOTIC SYSTEMS AND CULTURE'S PREDICTIONS

At first glance, an approach that conceives of culture as a semiotic system-in-practice would appear ill equipped to explain the different forms of change in the elites' political culture. The idea of system or cultural structure emphasizes constraint and reproduction rather than transformation. "The more emphasis upon system," notes Peter Burke, "the more difficult it is to explain change."[10] The problem is palpable when considering the story told in previous chapters. If the elite were constrained to first make meaning in accordance with their preexisting institutionalized cultural structures, all novel events would get subsumed by those meanings, and the elites' cultural order would be continually reproduced rather than transformed. Still, the approach does offer a better beginning than others. The key lies not in disavowing the notion of system and constraint but in better understanding it. Specifically, we must consider the "predictions" registered by meaning making and whether or not those predictions are validated in practice.

To understand this, return first to the constraining character of culture. Culture is constraining because it is limited. Over time, some cultural schemas get institutionalized rather than others, and cultural users are first constrained to employ those particular schemas. This is what accounts for the initial domestication in the two colonies. But a closer examination of this very same phenomenon of constraint also compels us to recognize that while culture constrains users to make particular meanings of the world rather than others, it likewise constrains them to make particular claims *about* it at the same time. To use a cultural schema is to make meaning by classifying, categorizing, or narrating the world (that is, the things, people, people's interactions, and events and happenings to which cultural users refer).[11] Therefore, making meaning serves to reduce the world's unfamiliar complexity into familiar types and stories, "imparting a view of how the world actually is and how it operates — the sorts of entities it contains [and] how those entities can be expected to behave."[12] In other words, meaning making serves to make tacit claims about how the world operates, how events will unfold, and how people will act. It servers to register *predictions* of the world.

Narrative schemas are the clearest example of this. Narratives have beginnings, middles, and ends, so using an already familiar narrative to render a situation meaningful carries the implicit expectation that the situation will unfold according to the story.[13] Other kinds of schemas like codes or classificatory schemes are similarly predictive. To classify a thing, a person, a set of social relations, or an event is to insert them into an already existing type. Such typification therefore carries the implicit expectation that the objects referred to (including happenings or people) will fit into that type.[14] Every act of meaning making is therefore also an implicit prediction. Roger Keesing's notion of culture as a "theory" condenses the point: "Culture is not all of what an individual knows and thinks and feels about his world. It is his *theory* of what his fellows know, believe, and mean, his theory of the code being followed, the game being played."[15] More precisely, meaning as theories predicts that the referential fields encompassed will respond as they had before — that is, when the schemas and the world had been interdependent and when those schemas had been institutionalized.

The hitch is that theories do not always prove true. Herein lies the second point. While uses of culture serve to register predictions of the world, the world might fail to conform to them. This follows from the premises of the approach to culture already outlined. As cultural schemas are relatively autonomous from the world, so too is the world relatively autonomous from culture. Referential fields (i.e., the events, people, and things referred to by signifying patterns) move according to their own logics and dynamics, regardless of the schemas that any single semiotic community might extend onto them to render them meaningful. People classified by schemas operate according to their distinct concerns and interests; contingent events sometimes erupt in expected ways. The world, therefore, is under no obligation to prove culture's predictions true. There is no guarantee that events will unfold according to the narrative or that people referred will act according to the type. Simply put, the world might be *recalcitrant* to the meanings people make. Cultural users employ familiar schemas, but the field, by failing to conform to predictions, resists the meaning altogether. The implicit theory registered by meaning making is invalidated in practice.

Recognizing this possibility for recalcitrance offers added value for meeting our task of explanation in several respects. First, it allows us to imagine different paths of meaning making that begin from the same point. The starting point is that cultural users make meaning in accordance with previously institutionalized schemas. But different paths can then be opened up from this same point, depending on the invalidation or validation of culture's predictions. One path, for instance, is that cultural users make meaning in accordance with previously institutionalized schemas, and the people, things, and happenings referred to affirm the meanings made. People act according to predicted types; events unfold as narratives had forecasted. In this case, cultural schemas are validated and the predictions registered by semiotic practices are proven true. Yet, as noted already, a different path is also possible. That is, cultural users make meaning in accordance with previously institutionalized schemas, and the world repeatedly invalidates the meanings made from all sides at once. Rather than proving culture's predictions true, the things referred to (or the world) proves recalcitrant.

Second, recognizing recalcitrance as a possibility enables us to conceive of further variations on the same theme. One variation is *convergent recalcitrance*. A cultural schema typically refers to and makes predictions of a number of things, people, relationships, or events at the very same time. A patronage schema refers to patrons and clients, but it might refer to patronage relations in the social field (e.g., between landlords and tenants) and in the political field at the same time (e.g., government officials and their friends). Only some of these referents might pose recalcitrance, while others might still conform. Convergent recalcitrance, however, would mean that *all* referents meaningfully encompassed pose recalcitrance. Social actors extend their preexisting categories or models onto the changed situation, but those categories or models face recalcitrance from the world on *all* sides and sites. Nothing about the world bends as predicted.[16] Another variation is *recurrent recalcitrance*. Existing studies of cognition suggest that even in novel situations, social actors are likely to first employ their already familiar cognitive structures. Despite the emergence of new events, people will render them meaningful by employing what they already know.[17] This research therefore affirms the premise of cultural constraint already affirmed in previous chapters. It suggests that the constraints of culture remain even during novel events or unexpected situations. We can therefore pose an additional scenario: even when first faced with recalcitrance, cultural users would still employ previously institutionalized cultural materials to make meaning. Yet recalcitrance might occur *repeatedly*. Given the fact that the world is never reducible to the classifications any single group applies to it, it is possible for recalcitrance to happen over and over again. People make meaning of the world according to their prior schemas, and the world does not oblige; in response, they further extend or employ their prior schemas (thereby registering further predictions about the world), but still the world does not oblige. In this case, recalcitrance is recurrent. The world fails to validate predictions over and over again.

Recognizing recalcitrance and its variations also offers added value because it allows us to hypothesize emergent differences between cases at hand regardless of the factors pinpointed in other theoretical approaches. Recalcitrance could happen in one case but not the other regardless of the actors' interests or incentives, or regardless of whether interests and incentives change over time. The issue would be not a change in incentives but whether or not meanings face recalcitrance. Similarly, recalcitrance could happen in one case but not the other, even if state policies or ruling strategies are similar across cases. The difference here would be not ruling strategies or policies but the type of cultural schemas at stake. After all, recalcitrance is a conjuncture — a *relationship* obtained between particular cultural schemas and specific events. In order for a strategy, policy, or course of action taken by rulers to prove recalcitrant to a cultural schema, *it must be recalcitrant to that schema precisely*. A different schema applied to the same event might not face recalcitrance at all, because the different schema would have registered different predictions of the event. Therefore, there can be recalcitrance in one case and not in another, even if policies or ruling strategies are the same between them. The difference instead would lie in the particular predictions registered, hence differences between cultural schemas.

This approach thereby builds upon the lessons learned from previous chapters while also opening up the possibility for divergence. Social actors are constrained to employ their prior cultural structures as they initially generate meaning — resulting in reproduction and domestication — but from this same point different paths can follow, depending on whether or not the predictions registered by those cultural structures are validated. Therefore, the first question for our analysis is simple enough: were the elites' schemas validated or invalidated as tutelage proceeded? The rest of this chapter offers an answer.

THE MAKING OF DIVERGENCE

By domesticating tutelage, the Puerto Rican and Filipino political elite also made predictions of it. They registered implicit or explicit claims about how tutelage would unfold, what the American officials would do, and how people around them would behave. Due to the specific cultural schemas at stake, the elite in each colony made predictions about two fields of referents at once. One field was political, having to do with the tutelage project and its overseers. By domestication, the elite in both colonies classified American occupation as a token of the Spanish type: American occupation would be better than Spanish rule, because it would bring what Spanish rule had not — democratic self-government. The elite also classified American rulers as better patrons than Spanish rulers. The Puerto Rican elite classified the American rulers as akin to Mateo Sagasta, who had helped their party realize autonomía; the Filipino elite classified Taft as the patron to whom they owed a debt of gratitude (the patron who would realize the promises that the Spanish had broken). These classifications therefore carried the expectation that tutelage would move toward self-government as the elite conceived it, and that American rulers would act as the patrons the elite classified them to be. In the Philippines, Taft and other American officials would ensure the bienestar of the people by securing outside resources and distributing them to the elite as "directors" of society, while also giving the directors autonomy to carry out their self-fashioned roles. In Puerto Rico, President McKinley and officials on the ground would prop up the Federal Party, give them autonomy and privileges, and cultivate single-party rule. In so doing, they would realize autonomía, and tutelage would lead toward statehood.

The other field was social and economic. By domestication, the elites' categories did not only posit things about tutelage and self-government, they also referred to social relations. Who is to be governed? The "unconscious masses." With whom do patrons exchange, and over whom do they thereby rule? Clients, or "the directed classes." The elites' categories thereby assumed certain social relations and material resources. Patrons are patrons only in relation to clients, and clients are obtained only by providing them with resources. The implicit prediction here was that social relations and the resources endowing them would persist as they had during late Spanish rule, when the elites' patron-client schemas of governance had been institutionalized in the first place. The related prediction was that the so-called directed classes would act as they should. As long as the elite provided them with resources, the "unconscious masses" would remain subservient clients who — as one Puerto Rican landowner and official had put it — "follow the counsels of the people who are immediately above them."[18]

The elite thereby registered predictions of two referential fields at once. But there was no guarantee that those predictions would prove true — their cultural schemas were put at risk. The elites' schemas predicted things about their clients in the social field, and therefore presupposed that the resources needed to maintain patron-client relationships would persist, but the resources that had previously propped patron-client relations in both colonies had been dependent upon the expanding export economy and the character of agricultural production. There was no guarantee that these conditions would continue as U.S. rule proceeded. Similarly, while the elite classified the Americans as a familiar type, the American officials had their own distinct backgrounds, designs, and goals, not to mention their own particular schemas on what proper self-government entailed. As they continued in their "political education" efforts, therefore, there was nothing to guarantee that tutelage would unfold as the elites' narratives predicted.

The risks to the elites' meaning-making activities were high. But as we will now see, the risks were realized only in Puerto Rico. The Puerto Rican elites' schemas faced resistance from both referential fields at once, and recalcitrance happened over and over again. The cultural structures by which the elite domesticated tutelage therefore faced *convergent and recurrent recalcitrance*. As for the Filipino elite, we will later see that their schemas met a fundamentally different fate.

DISJUNCTION IN PUERTO RICO

Recalcitrance in the Social Field

By domesticating tutelage, the Puerto Rican elite classified themselves to be the patrons, or "fathers," of the gran familia. They likewise categorized their party, the Federal Party, as the organizational channel for patronage practice. This classification therefore involved two interrelated predictions. First, the members of the familia would continue to be dutiful clients, giving their loyalty and labor. Second, party leaders would have the resources to act as proper patrons, thereby securing the loyalty and labor of their clients. Given the elites' history, these implicit predictions were warranted. During Spanish rule, the elites' resources had been abundant. Due to the continually expanding coffee economy, the elite had easy access to surplus, so they had been able to cultivate and maintain a large patron-client network. But during the first years of American rule, these happy conditions were threatened. Export production, upon which the elite had long relied, faced unprecedented troubles.

We have already seen that the elite faced economic problems during the transition from Spanish to American rule: the elites' productive base in coffee had been threatened by falling prices and the loss of Spanish markets. In part, this was why the elite accepted American rule and hoped for a territorial government leading to statehood. But an unexpected event worsened things further. In August 1899, a hurricane named San Ciriaco swept through the island. It was the worst natural catastrophe the island had ever seen, causing 2,500 deaths and infrastructural damage estimated at $20 million. "There only remains of this Antillean isle," wrote local newspapers in the hurricane's wake, "heaps of rubble spread everywhere . . . tears, death, and misfortune."[19] The hurricane deepened the elites' economic problems. It hit the coffee regions especially hard, causing short-term and long-term damage. Conjoined with the lack of capital and markets, it caused a further deterioration in coffee production. In 1896, the total amount of coffee exported from the island had been 579,613 quintals. For the years 1898 to 1900 together, it was only 640,730. Landowners lamented: "Our plantation is mostly ruined. We have a plantation only in name."[20]

The crisis had a devastating economic impact, but it also had an important social impact. *Jornaleros*, the small mobile labor force that had emerged in the late 1890s, were suddenly left without work, and they did not even have small plots of land for subsistence production.[21] Destitute, they roamed the countryside in dire need. Many flooded the urban centers, and the elite in San Juan and Ponce began complaining about the sudden emergence of "vagabonds" and "paupers."[22] Tenants suffered as well. Unlike the jornaleros, tenants had relied upon subsistence crops, but the hurricane made subsistence production difficult.[23] Ninety-six landowners in the municipalities of Mayaguez, Las Marias, and Maricao reported that, due to the crisis, the "the poor classes" who had once been dependent "on the work given by the agriculturist" were "reduced to the utmost misery."[24] To worsen matters, landlords could not extend basic provisions and resources to them as they had done in the past, for they were lacking resources themselves. Justo A. Mendez Martinez, an official and landowner in Lares, complained that he was unable to provide food for his tenants, adding: "A few years ago we were in a better position owing to the high prices of coffee but to-day we are utterly helpless."[25]

At first, the elite dealt with the crisis by drawing upon their preexisting patron-client schemas, mustering their meager resources to use as patronage. A landowner and official in Utuado gave one of his last remaining cows to one hundred tenants who had asked him for help, while municipal councils organized relief committees to gather and then redistribute food.[26] The Federal Party leadership mobilized similarly. They requested loans from the military authorities and hired destitute tenants to work on state-funded infrastructural projects.[27] They also secured a program from American officials that offered 10 centavos a day to the unemployed in order to help them meet subsistence needs. They further secured some resources from a planters' relief program inaugurated by the military government.[28] These were logical responses to the crisis, but they involved the continued use of preexisting schemas of patronage and party. After receiving funds for the public works programs, Muñoz Rivera told municipal officials not to hire members of the Republican

Party. Both political parties tried to manipulate the planter relief program in order to secure relief for their partisans only.[29] All the while, municipal officials not only made demands for loans, monies, and patronage, they acted as if it was all part of their due. "The alcaldes," complained American authorities, "are dissatisfied unless some money is coming to pay peons and other bills."[30] Even as the elite faced crisis, they dealt with it in accordance with their prior cultural structures, a process part and parcel of continued domestication.

The temporary relief measures, however, were only temporary. As the military government was financially strapped, funds for the local officials to enact patronage and public works projects were not enough.[31] The elites' ability to use state resources to replace their own private resources diminished significantly. The *San Juan News* reported:

> For generations the people have been accustomed to look to the alcaldes [mayors] and the municipal authorities to relieve their reasonable wants and to redress their grievances. . . . Unfortunately, at the present time the municipalities of the island have not got in their power to assist the people. Local treasurers are empty. Worse than that, the majority of the municipalities are involved in debt. . . . The fact remains that no expenditures for local improvements can be made, no scheme for the immediate relief of the people can be carried out owing to the scarcity of funds. . . . Deterioration must result if some means of relieving the situation is not found. It is unnecessary to cite instances. In almost any district of the island there are towns where municipal improvements have been commenced but uncompleted . . . because there is no money. If these works could only be undertaken, a number of people would find employment.[32]

The socioeconomic crisis was palpable. The alcalde of Utuado woke up at four in the morning to find "between six and seven hundred persons" outside his home asking for work on public works projects which he could not provide.[33] Local officials' networks of friends and followers could not be sustained either. Municipal mayors had typically constructed petty offices as patronage but, with the crisis, mayors no longer had sufficient funds to maintain their patronage posts.[34] To worsen matters, the elites' personal economic resources continued to deteriorate. Indebted to merchants, they had no more income; and future prospects remained bleak. *La Gleba*, a novel written in 1912, posthumously captured the situation in the character of Don Feliciano:

"When he had his coffee hacienda and could distribute money among his friends. . . . Don Feliciano was a great figure, with a social reputation that was unmatched. . . . After, he was not left with any more respect and consideration than his old friends, [he was] ruined."

If the situation remained dire for the elite, it likewise remained dire for the elites' clients. As the crisis proceeded, more and more tenants became destitute, and their ranks added to the growth of the unemployed in the cities.[35] The situation was unprecedented. General Davis reported to Washington: "[The] condition here is now much worse than it ever was under Spain, [and] is apparent to all."[36] *La Democracia* added:

> Begging has always existed in Puerto Rico, but never in the form it exists today; there had been a number reduced to the state of vagabonds, and others disabled, but a relatively small number; there had been poor workers in the farms, but at least they did not need charity. When the Americans came, they found a poor people, but not a starving people. For centuries a bad and ignorant government reigned this colony, but the colony never was the victim of misery. It's been more than a year since the American flag has floated in Puerto Rico, and during that period of time the decay has come slowly, but without receding a single iota. The prolonged agony of the people can be seen in all respects. Was this what we had hoped for?[37]

The overarching impact of the crisis was twofold. First, the circulations of exchange that had constituted and structured the gran familia puertorriqueña were short-circuited. The world that had benefited the elite, and by which the elite had forged their schemas in the first place, began to fall apart. For instance, American officials had first decried the "class distinctions" and "clear division" in the island between the elite and the laboring poor. But due to the crisis, the Puerto Rican elite complained that such distinctions had become blurred: "The disaster that has immersed all citizens in the most terrible misery without distinction between classes nor hierarchy is well known; it is clear that since the landowner lacks the most elementary things to maintain his family, the . . . working classes are in an even sadder situation. The harvests destroyed, urban and rural property lost, planters and merchants lacking credit; what outlook awaits us? What future, so full of difficulties can be sketched? What can be done before such a depressing picture?"[38]

Second, and relatedly, the elite began to lose their preexisting legitimacy among the gran familia. No patronage, no power. The earliest signs of this had come immediately after the hurricane. The hurricane had been completely out of the elites' control, but local populations nonetheless blamed the directing class for it. In the city of Ponce, a large crowd of "several hundred indigent natives" gathered in the plaza of Ponce to demand the removal of the alcalde. He should have known about the hurricane, they clamored, and he should be doing more to help them.[39] Similar demands for resignation were made in other cities, striking the elite with unprecedented fear.[40] "Owing to the ruinous state of agriculture," complained one landowner, "the working classes are in a state of deprivation, with no hope and no means of subsistence, and the day will come when they will declare themselves in open revolt."[41]

This talk of "open revolt" was a portent. Some violence had already erupted during the Spanish-American War. Roving bands had attacked the signs and structures of Spanish authority. But as the economic crisis spread, many acts of violence aimed at the local elite surfaced. Landowners, many of them also local officials, received anonymous threats to their lives. Haciendas were robbed; plantations pillaged and in some cases burned; rumors of large-scale peasant plots circulated.[42] The nature of the incidents attests to the larger disruption of preexisting patron-client relationships. When plantations or the homes of landowners were pillaged, the culprits soiled their faces with coal to conceal their identities, thus receiving the designation *tiznados* (literally, "the soiled ones"). These attempts to conceal identities suggest that the assailants were former tenants of the hacendado.[43] Indeed, as officials complained, the bandits typically proved to be "farm laborers who hold a grudge against their former employers."[44] "Almost every case of burning of a plantation," reported authorities, "is traced to the hired men on the plantation."[45]

Outbreaks of disorder were not confined to rural areas. The cities, filled with destitute workers from the countryside, also saw disturbances. Town plazas, traditionally the free space of leisure and sociability for privileged families, were plagued by protests, harassers, and robberies.[46] They also became the site for political protests. During one such protest, a band of so-called "immoralists" paraded through the streets, chasing a man dressed up as a crazy woman. The cries from this group were clear: "Down with the tyrants" and "Death to the '*loca*' [crazy woman]." *Loca* here referred to Muñoz Rivera, and the carnivalesque critique was potent.[47] The jefe of the gran familia, supposedly the one who could best articulate the family's will, was emasculated and rendered insane. In fact, this was not the only incident against Muñoz. Previously, the printing office of Muñoz's newspaper had been torched by "a mob of fifty or sixty men" who first "pulled down the doors . . . penetrated into the building and destroyed the press." Around the same time, shots were fired at Muñoz's urban residence in San Juan.[48]

The number of these incidents cannot be tracked over time with precision, but American reports claimed in 1899 "disorders and outrages were of a nightly occurrence."[49] The larger point, at any rate, is that the directors of the gran familia felt an unprecedented and frightful sense of threat. To be sure, party leaders wrote countless editorials and tracts complaining about the violence and disorder. One was aptly titled "La Anarquía en Puerto Rico" ("Anarchy in Puerto Rico").[50] Another told the story of a once prominent hacendado forced to flee the island because of the "corrupted and disgraceful [Puerto Rican] collectivity."[51] Newspaper editorials complained about the urban protestors, calling them "false democrats" who mistake "liberty for licentiousness" and who "insult the familia puertorriqueña and mock the Federal [Party] jefes."[52] The elite also complained that the social disorder and violence was unprecedented; the "state of terror" was "entirely new to Puerto Rico."[53] *La Democracia* exclaimed: "Since the invasion not only have we lost all that we had in civil and political order, but to the surface have come crimes and passions that we have never [previously] witnessed, in which we could not believe a people as moderate (well-mannered) as this would be wrapped up."[54] The elite had classified their tenants as docile and willing members of the gran familia who obediently followed the directing class, but the unconscious masses now showed signs of an agency over which the elite could no longer claim control.

The elite did not sit passively in the face of the disorder. Some tried to control it by continuing in their claims to be the paternalistic figures of the familia. One mayor issued the following proclamation: "All riot manifestations should be stopped forever, as it only carries with it intranquillity to our homes, division to the society in which we live and loss of confidence on the part of the government. . . . I appeal to the regard of the people, to their sincere and spontaneous affection, to cease all collective acts of protests against determined individuals. . . . I order it."[55] These proclamations tried to evoke a familial sense of "affection" to quell disorder and, in the end, conjure coercive power ("I order it"). But they went unheeded. Local officials continued to complain about social disorder, and they even pleaded to the American authorities for police protection.[56] "City officials lack moral power to conduct the affairs properly," cabled one mayor to the governors' office. "[We] request that Insular police be put in charge of the town."[57] Such requests proliferated, demonstrating that, while the elite initially attempted to maintain their position as the masters and directors of the familia in the face of disorder, their attempts were failing. As the elites' traditional resources diminished, and as preexisting circulations of exchange were thereby disrupted, the unconscious masses proved unwilling to bend to the meanings the elite made of them. In short, the situation, people, events, and happenings to which the elites' schemas referred were repeatedly resistant. The elite domesticated tutelage in accordance with their preexisting schemas, but in the social field their schemas faced a recurrent recalcitrance.

Tutelary Politics and Recalcitrance from Above

The social disorder did not mean that Muñoz Rivera and his party were ousted from their seats of official power. Given the restrictions on suffrage and officeholding, the Federals still staffed the municipal governments. Therefore, even as their schemas faced recalcitrance in the social field, they still enjoyed some of the political control they had had during Spanish rule. Furthermore, they pinned much hope on the future. Having narrated tutelage as a movement toward autonomía, they were still expecting tutelary rule to grant all power and privileges to their party, a development that might in turn enable them to reassert their grip over the familia. But on this count, another problem emerged. As the American officials had their own designs and understandings of the situation, the elite soon faced recalcitrance in the political field just as they were facing it in the social field.

The trouble began in the municipalities. Initially, military officials had given municipal governments some autonomy to cultivate consent from the local elite while also providing them experience in democratic self-government.[58] As seen in chapter 2, the Federals dominating municipalities interpreted this autonomy as a move toward autonomía and so allowed corruption and conducted party-based patronage just as they had done during the Autonomic Regime. But as tutelary occupation proceeded onward, American officials became determined to halt such practices. They insisted on giving "lessons" in "conducting the affairs of . . . municipalities impartially . . . without regard to party politics" and in carrying out the duties of office "based upon principles of administration and honest differences in opinion."[59] Accordingly, American authorities took some new steps to intensify political education. One involved appointing members of the minority party (Barbosa's Republican Party) to vacant seats on municipal councils. The idea was "to secure minority representation and to check the abuse of political power in municipal administration."[60] Another involved consolidating some of the smaller municipalities into singular entities. One goal here was to reduce the number of municipal offices that had typically served as a resource for political patronage.[61] Furthermore, when American authorities distributed funds to municipalities for infrastructural projects, they did not privilege Federal districts. To give a "lesson" in bipartisanship, they insisted that the few districts where Republicans held municipal seats should receive funds too. Finally, authorities conducted new investigations of municipal finances. Treasurer Willoughby wrote home: "I am determined to investigate all of the financial affairs . . . and if possible put a stop to the mismanagement and dishonesty that is rampant."[62]

All of these steps threatened the Federals' political power. Most critically, though, they likewise threatened their cultural structures. The Federals had narrated tutelage as a movement toward autonomía and thereby classified autonomía to mean municipal autonomy, but the Americans' assertions of control over municipalities violated the narrative. At the same time, the Federals had classified their party as the sole representative of the people. They had therefore predicted that their party would receive all patronage resources rather than having to share them with the so-called minority party. But the Americans' attempt to induce bipartisan cooperation undermined this expectation as well.

To worsen the matter, American authorities began an assault upon the Federal Party's powers at the central level. General Brooke had initially installed Muñoz and his councilors to high office, but as the latter persisted in their party-based corruption, Brooke's successors decided to dismantle the Federals' high posts. General Guy Henry replaced Brooke and abolished the

Federals' positions, declaring that they were "not compatible with American methods and progress."[63] He later explained to Washington: "When I arrived here I found an insular cabinet, which one person, Mr. [Muñoz] Rivera, controlled, the other secretaries being under him. I allowed the system to continue until I found it was wrong and did not accomplish the purpose intended — honest administration."[64] This had serious consequence for the Federal leaders. In place of the cabinet, General Henry instituted four heads of departments, each independent of the other and all directly answerable to the military governor. Muñoz Rivera and his fellow Federal leaders were therefore reduced to appendages. Their status as directors was officially squashed.

The situation continued to deteriorate after civil government was instituted. First, the Foraker Act passed by Congress in 1900 called for a civil government headed by a composite body known as the Executive Council, which was to include a civil governor-general and other councillors with an American majority. President McKinley appointed Charles H. Allen as governor. Thus, rumors that Muñoz would be appointed as governor proved to be just that — rumors. Second, while the Americans appointed a handful of Puerto Ricans (including Muñoz and a couple of other Federal leaders) to fill remaining council seats, they also appointed leading members of the minority party, the Republicans. Again, the goal was to teach the Puerto Ricans "bipartisan" cooperation.[65] Things worsened further as the Executive Council proceeded with its first line of business. According to the Foraker Act, the Council was to divide the island into seven electoral districts for the first elections for the House of Delegates. As council members began their work, the Americans on the Council proposed a plan that, according to the Federals, gave a clear advantage to the Republican Party. The Federals were indignant and devised their own plan that tipped the scale in their favor. "[Muñoz] Rivera had his own way in the island [previously]," explained Governor Allen to Elihu Root on the Federals' plan, "and although [Muñoz] Rivera's agents are thus employed everywhere, he still will be satisfied with nothing less than turning over the whole island to him." In response, Allen and the other American members used their veto power to reject the Federals' plan.[66]

In the Americans' narratives, all of these moves were simply part of political education. But for Muñoz and his Federal Party, the moves were entirely unforeseen. By domesticating tutelage and narrating it as a movement toward autonomía, the Federals had classified themselves as the government party and the Americans as akin to Sagasta during the Autonomic regime. They predicted that tutelage would grant their party a privileged place. But it was antithetical to these classifications for the Americans to dismantle the Autonomic Cabinet and fill vacant municipal seats with members of a so-called minority party. It was also contrary to their preexisting assumptions for the Americans to reject their plans for electoral districts, intervene in municipal affairs, and annex municipalities. The predictions registered by the elites' domestication were thereby invalidated; their cultural structures faced recalcitrance.

The Federals first responded to this recalcitrance by continuing to employ their prior narratives and schemas. For example, when Muñoz learned that the military rulers were intervening into municipal affairs, and that patronage resources were not being channeled solely to the municipal districts where his party dominated alone, he responded by declaring that the interventions were an affront to the president of the United States. "In the island there are things happening that the President of the Republic would surely not approve of. Various officials of the army inhibit the development of municipal life; they seek to intervene in all the affairs; create insoluble difficulties and give occasion to a profound anxiety."[67] Muñoz protested as if it was in the inherent nature of American-styled government to leave local governments completely alone, without intervention at all — as if President McKinley would be as offended as Mateo Sagasta would have been. Relatedly, when municipal councils learned of the Americans' plan to disincorporate and consolidate some municipalities, they sent many letters of complaint to American officials and even to President McKinley. They claimed that it was a threat to "Gobierno Autonómico," a "violent trespass, assailing our natural and political rights, which no democratic government should retrench."[68] The Federals' newspapers registered additional protests. One editorial began by evoking a fondness for Sagasta's regime: "[Under the Autonomic government] we were ourselves responsible for our decrees, and we framed them with the utmost prudence, but also with an independence which was neither questioned nor curtailed by the metropolis. In a word, self-government was unfolding itself without obstacle and Puerto Rico was beginning to feel herself mistress of her present and of her future." The editorial proceeded to script

American tutelage not as a movement toward autonomy but as retrogression: "When the historic edifice of the colonies, crowned by the gift of autonomía, disappeared, destroyed by your squadrons, all the hopes of their people turned to that other edifice which was to be erected on the broad basis of a democracy which is the astonishment of the world [i.e., the United States]. Even the most pessimistic believes that in no case or under no pretext would it [the United States] curtail the liberties conferred by the former ruler."[69]

The Federals did not only write letters and editorials. When General Henry announced the dissolution of the insular cabinet, Muñoz and his fellow cabinet members swiftly resigned. They justified their resignation by stating that the dissolution implied that "the North American system had not been implanted here in all its grand and perfect amplitude."[70] Muñoz later clarified that the "motive for our resignation" was to affirm that "Puerto Rico should maintain its autonomía, the autonomía we were enjoying when the [American] occupation began."[71] Later, the Americans tried to temper Muñoz's criticisms by appointing Muñoz and his friends to the Executive Council, but after the gerrymandering affair, when the Federals' plan for electoral districts was rejected, Muñoz Rivera and his colleagues resigned yet again. Muñoz cabled the President: "The plan adopted is unfair to the federal party, which is in the majority in this island. . . . We feel it is our duty to protest against the present administration in this island so long as we are unjustly treated.[72]

The sense of injustice guiding the Federals' resignations should be clear: the Federals reassessed the situation, dug into their preexisting repertoire, and reframed their earlier categorization of tutelage. They had initially taken the Americans' discourse and tutelary structures to mean that they would be granted eventual autonomía, but they now classified it as a reenactment of the pre-Autonomic days when conservative Spanish rulers had consistently favored the Spanish political party, the Incondicionales, to the detriment of Muñoz's party. That is, they adjusted their classification of the Americans as akin to Sagasta and reclassified them as akin to the conservative Spanish rulers who had supported a minority party unrepresentative of the familia. Fittingly, the Federals referred to the Republicans as the "new incondicionales" and asserted that American support of them was "the knock of death to autonomía."[73] They accused the Republicans of obtaining "an unjust protection and support like that which Spain gave to its incondicional servitors" and argued that the Americans' support of the Republicans encouraged the "unconscious masses" to violently attack them.[74] This was a renewed classification, even as it was structured by the elites' prior schemas. Initially, the Federals had predicted that the American officials were like the liberal Spanish rulers, such as Sagasta. But as they faced recalcitrance, they shifted their classification and equated the American rulers with the conservative Spanish rulers in the pre-Autonomic days; that is, the pre-Sagasta Spanish rulers who had favored the minority party.

Fittingly, amid their complaints, the Federals resorted to a tactic that they had used on conservative Spanish rulers during the pre-Autonomic period. They declared retraimiento, stating that their party would abstain from the upcoming House of Delegates elections. This was a direct outcome of the Federals' new assessment of the tutelary situation, even as it reflected a continued employment of prior cultural schemas. It was a call for a "justice," a demand that the regime stop favoring the putative minority party, cease state centralization, and restore lost privileges. It was an attempt by the Federals to win some sympathy from the U.S. government and, hopefully, extract concessions.[75] Accordingly, as the Federals declared retraimiento, rumors circulated that Muñoz Rivera was trying to align the Federals with the Democratic Party in the States, just as he had aligned his Autonomist Party with Sagasta's liberal party in Madrid.[76] If the Republican Party in the United States, led by President McKinley, was not the proper liberal party that would grant them autonomía, perhaps the Democratic Party was.[77] All of this shows that the Federals continued to draw upon their prior cultural schemas to make sense of their dire situation. At the same time, they registered a new prediction: if the American rulers were akin to the Spanish rulers in the pre-Autonomic days, they would respond to retraimiento as the Spanish rulers had—that is, by granting concessions. But here the Federals ran into recurrent recalcitrance. As it turns out, the American officials were not the same as the Spanish rulers of old, either the liberal Sagasta types or the conservatives. Rather than taking the Federals' retraimiento as a dignified acceptable protest, they took it as violent contempt for the United States.[78] They also took it as further evidence that the Puerto Ricans were locked in a "rudimentary stage of political development." The Federals' retraimiento, wrote Governor Allen "simply show[s] how incapable they are of self-government."[79] The party's refusal to participate in the elections was "a personal foible at variance with every view of American politics."[80] The Federals were merely "crying like children."[81] In the end, the American officials ignored the Federals' electoral abstention and proceeded with business as usual.[82]

The use of retraimiento in this context had an unintended consequence. With the Federals' abstention, the Republicans won all of the seats in the House of Delegates. The Federals, rather than receiving concessions as their renewed classification had predicted, were locked out of state power completely.[83] As the administrator Rowe observed, "it did not occur to them [the Federals] that the position they had taken placed them at the mercy of the Republican party."[84] And at the mercy of their rivals they were. Having shut themselves out from both the House of Delegates and the Executive Council, and only controlling the municipal governments, they stood powerless as the Americans continued to intensify political education and intervene in local affairs. And Americans on the Council and the Republicans in the House of Delegates stripped the Federals' municipal powers further. They passed new legislation that put local taxation in the hands of the central government. They also dismantled municipal police forces which the Federals had once controlled, thereby putting into the hands of the American central authorities "where it could be administered in a non-political manner."[85] For the Federals, all was lost.

True, the Federals had been marginalized from the center of power during Spanish rule too. The conservative Spanish regime had favored the Incondicional Party, leaving the Federals (at that time the Autonomists) with few spoils of office. Still, even in that scenario, the Federals had at least had the support of the gran familia. They had been locked out of state power, but they had still enjoyed social and political power from their clients. They had been able to use retraimiento as a tactic of last resort. The problem was that now, as U.S. rule proceeded, they had none of this. The Federals were locked out of central state power; the disorder and violence that reigned across the island signaled a threat to their self-classification as the majority party and the benevolent directors of the familia; and the so-called unconscious masses were not acting unconsciously. And retraimiento, a tactic that followed from the Federals' renarration of tutelage, failed completely. The American rulers proved themselves irreducible to the Sagasta type, but by rejecting retraimiento they also proved themselves irreducible to the conservative Spanish type. The issue for the Federals, then, was more than a loss of power. It was an unprecedented breakdown in their previously institutionalized cultural patterns. Nothing about the elites' preexisting schemas and narratives worked as before. The predictions registered by their meaning-making activities were repeatedly invalidated in practice. This was a radical resistance to the elites' schemas — a convergent and recurrent recalcitrance.

Could things have been otherwise? Was such a radical resistance to meaning making the only possible fate of culture in the tutelage empire? A look at what happened in the Philippines offers a contrast.

VALIDATION IN THE PHILIPPINES

Like their Puerto Rican counterparts, the Filipino elite also registered predictions as they domesticated tutelage into their preexisting cultural order. In the political field, they expected the Americans to lay down the conditions for their own kind of self-government. As they categorized it, tutelary colonialism would insert them into the state so that they could act as the directors of their society. American officials on high would act as benevolent patrons, giving them the room and resources to fulfill their self-proclaimed role as the directing class. Presumably, this was the "obligation" the Americans had contracted with them. Furthermore, in the social field, the Filipino elite predicted certain relationships with their clients. Classifying themselves as the benevolent directors of their society, they tacitly predicted that they would have the resources to do so. Patrons are patrons only in relation to clients, and one needs surplus to have clients in the first place.

While the Filipino and Puerto Rican elite alike had registered predictions by domesticating tutelage, however, the Filipino elites' schemas faced a very different fate than those of their Puerto Rican counterparts. While the latter's schemas faced recalcitrance in both the social and political field, the Filipino elite faced it only in the political field. Even then, recalcitrance was fleeting at best. Ultimately, rather than seeing their predictions repeatedly resisted, the Filipino elite saw their schemas validated. This difference was due to two factors: (1) the particularity of the Filipino elites' economy, hence the persistence of preexisting social relations and (2) the content of the elites' schemas in relation to the tutelage project as it unfolded in time.

It is useful to begin by discussing the unfolding of the tutelage project. For as occupation proceeded into the postwar period, the American authorities introduced new policies, institutional arrangements, and collaborative strategies that paralleled those in Puerto Rico. First, the transition to civil rule served to centralize power in the hands of American authorities. By the Organic Act of Congress, legislation was left to the Philippine Commission. While a handful of Filipinos had been appointed to serve the commission, American appointees outnumbered them, and the governor-general and head of the Commission was an American.[86] Furthermore, the major executive agencies were put into the hands of American appointees. The Executive Bureau, the Bureau of Audits, the Department of the Interior, the Department of Commerce and Police, the Department of Finance and Justice, the Department of Public Instruction — these were all headed by Americans appointed by the governor-general.

The American authorities also restricted the power of local governments and intensified political education, just as did their counterparts in Puerto Rico. Part of the goal was to tame the elites' ostensible "corruption." The commission appointed Americans to the provincial boards and gave them supervisory powers. The boards consisted of, among other posts, a provincial governor, a treasurer, and a provincial supervisor (in charge of public works), but the commission decided to ensure that American agents were appointed as treasurers.[87] The commission also gave the American treasurers the right to appoint municipal treasurers below them, thereby taking the power of appointment away from Filipino municipal mayors. Furthermore, in order to facilitate "a much-needed lesson [to be] taught to the municipal officials," the commission gave the treasurers the power to audit municipal finances and regulate local ordinances.[88] Finally, the commission tightened surveillance over local officials. Besides watching over municipal finances, American officials on the provincial boards were supposed to keep an eye on both the Filipino governor beside them and municipal officials beneath them. Along with the Filipino provincial governor, they were required to make periodic inspections of the municipalities and report wrongdoings on the part of officials. And to top it all, the system of surveillance was centralized in the Executive Bureau. The bureau was charged with receiving complaints about corruption from field officers and facilitating the trial and punishment of suspects.[89]

Another similarity has to do with strategies of rule and patterns of party collaboration. As we have seen, the Federal Party leaders in Puerto Rico, by narrating tutelage as a movement toward autonomía, expected to secure privileged patronage relations with the American authorities. Filipino ilustrados in and around Manila hoped for similar relations. On the one hand, the Federalista Party (the "party of peace," not to be confused with the Federal Party in Puerto Rico), had already been formed by a small handful of ilustrados. The ilustrados had initially supported American rule, and in return the Americans appointed some of them to the Philippine Commission. On the other hand, those ilustrados who had not initially surrendered lost out on these appointments. When they finally surrendered, they tried to form new parties to make up for the loss. Countless parties therefore emerged. Considered more "nationalist" than the Federalistas, they included the Partido Conservador, the Partido Democrata, the Partido Liberal, the Partido Independencia, and various incarnations of the Partido Nacionalista. As the historian Ruby Paredes has shown, the goal of these parties was to secure patronage from the center. Governor Taft noted that the new parties wanted "sanction" from the American regime so that party leaders could "go to the people in the provinces and towns . . . and solicit support with the statement that the Government has recognized the party."[90]

Yet, just as the Federals in Puerto Rico were denied party privileges, so too were these nationalist parties in the Philippines. When one of the earliest parties, the Partido Conservador, approached the American rulers for recognition, they got the cold shoulder. They first went to the Philippine Commission, but the Commission was intractable, reporting that they were "too busy to receive them."[91] They then approached General MacArthur and presented their platform to him. As the platform did little else than proclaim the loyalty of the party to the American regime, MacArthur's response was hardly amenable. He replied curtly: "It is assumed that all parties are loyal to the fundamental idea of American sovereignty." MacArthur then delved into a lecture about how parties need the approval not of rulers, but rather of the people. "Free government," he said, "is submission to the declared government *and* acceptance of . . . the declared views of the majority."[92]

The same thing happened in 1902 to the Partido Democrata. The leaders of this party wrote to Taft requesting recognition for their platform. Taft responded with a letter that stated that it was all very fine that Filipinos form parties, but he could not grant them "official recognition and sanction." As Taft later told Elihu Root, his response made the party leaders "very mad and angry."[93] Other parties likewise approached Taft, but they, too, got the cold shoulder.[94] To make matters worse, these alternative political parties did not have the opportunity to have representation in a national legislative assembly. While the American officials had initially announced that a legislative assembly would be established, they deferred its establishment in these early years. In 1901, Commissioner Moses told despondent ilustrados in Manila that "it would be premature" to have a legislative assembly right away.[95]

All of these developments proved disappointing to the elite. As seen in chapter 3, some ilustrados in Manila had surrendered to American rule in the hope that the archipelago would be granted the status of "independence under an American protectorate" — a status that would mean a state of perfected razón between the Philippines and America. But the Organic Act turned tutelage into something else altogether: a situation wherein the Filipino elite had precious few powers in the central state. American authorities flatly rejected any talk of "independence under an American protectorate." Taft wrote to Pedro Paterno, one of the ilustrados who had advocated protectorate status: "No one having any authority to speak for the United States has ever said one word justifying the belief that such a protectorate will be established. It is impossible."[96] The rejection of patronage to nationalist parties was also disappointing. The elite had scripted tutelage as a movement toward perfect razón, wherein the American officials and Filipino elite would have reciprocal relations of exchange, and whereby the American officials would give the elites the political freedom to cultivate clientele in their districts. But by centralizing the state and favoring only a few Federalistas, the Americans acted to the contrary. Fittingly, many of the displaced elites in Manila began registering complaints in their newspaper organs. An editorial in *El Renacimiento* complained:

> It has always been said that we are to be instructed in the arts, methods and practices of self government. Very well. The proposition is not only plausible, but also in accordance with the principle that the sons of Washington have not come to oppress us, but to convert us into a free people. The ac-

tual American administration — and this fact is undeniable — has fittingly granted many Filipinos positions in the civil government of the archipelago in its various arms and manifestations. . . . But ask ourselves: is this sufficient enough for the Filipinos to be perfected in the art of self-government [*gobierno propio*]? Why isn't it intended to grant full freedom to the Filipinos within the executive body? Why are some of the heads of the diverse Departments of the government of the islands not given to Filipinos of known capacity?[97]

Another editorial complained about the Federalistas' appointments to the commission: "A large portion of the Filipino people feel that these three Filipinos have been selected and are kept on the commission because they serve the purpose of making it appear that the republic of the United States is not arbitrarily governing a subject people but is giving them a large share in directing their own affairs."[98] The editorial complained further about the control exercised by Americans on the provincial boards: "There can be said even less to sustain the proposition that the provincial governors govern their provinces. . . . a treasurer and a supervisor really direct the actions and policy of the governor."[99] All the while, these and many other editorials registered demands for a national legislative assembly.

There was disappointment on yet another register. This had to do with patronage and patronage resources for local governments. By domesticating tutelage, local officials had expected to cultivate patron-client ties with the American authorities in the state center. They would give their support to American tutelage while, in turn, the Americans would give them resources to dole out to their clients. We have seen this in chapter 3, but the following entry from the journal of administrator Cameron Forbes is further indication: "Sunday, October 23. Found a package for me which, when unrolled, proved to be a pair of beautiful *patates* or woven mats such as people sleep on here. These were sent by Governor Sanz of Romblon, who had called on me several times. A fine, fierce looking mestizo with long black moustaches and pompadour hair. His gift would be a little more welcome if the mail had not just brought a request for a coast guard boat to be assigned to his province."[100] In "calling on" Forbes several times, Governor Sanz initiated a preexisting patron-client schema. If an official had wished to initiate an exchange with a higher official, the protagonist had to first establish direct contact and secure a one-to-one relationship. The relationship secured, the official typically offered tokens of exchange in hopes of a sufficient return. When there had been such a return, a series of reciprocal exchanges ensued. When not, there was no expectation for future exchanges.[101] Accordingly, since Forbes was a member of the Philippine Commission, the body that held a monopoly over central state power (and, therefore, over the distribution of resources to local governments), Governor Sanz tried to initiate a series of exchanges with him — beginning, in this case, with the receipt of a new boat.

Forbes noted many similar incidents in his journal. Local officials from across the provinces consistently asked for resources outside the channels that the Americans deemed proper. For example, when news spread that Forbes had been allotted some moneys for infrastructural works, provincial officials asked for their share. Forbes wrote: "The P500,000 which I have in many hands to be allotted to the different provinces is eagerly sought for, and each day some delegation from a province comes in and gives excellent reasons why they should have more than their fair share."[102] Local officials also expected control over resources. For instance, while the provincial governments in the Philippines had been put in charge of spending for public works, municipal-level officials sometimes asked from Forbes that they be put in charge themselves. "One thing all the presidentes [municipal mayors] of all the towns have asked for," observed Forbes in his journal, "is the right to spend provincial funds for public works instead of having the province spend them. It is natural that they should want the handling of more money and patronage, hence power, but unwise that they should have it until they have demonstrated their ability to use it well by making good results with the municipal funds they have."[103]

Such expectations for patronage resources from the state center were not unlike the expectations of the Puerto Rican elite — the elite in both colonies had classified the Americans as patrons who would give them local resources for patronage. Yet, as in Puerto Rico, the American officials in the Philippines did not always behave in accordance with the classification. On the one hand, officials indeed provided some resources to local governments in both colonies. In Puerto Rico, the military regime distributed some funds for developmental projects and, while the economic crisis meant that the government was strapped financially, the civil administrators later were able to fare better, securing loans for municipalities to build schools, roads, and other infrastructure.[104] Similarly, in the Philippines, American officials lent or gave funds to local governments, typically totaling nearly 20 percent of the insular governments' budget.[105] On the other hand, the Americans' actions in both colonies did not fully accord with the elites' expectations. While American officials gave resources to local governments, they gave them only as they saw fit. As we have seen, American authorities in Puerto Rico did not give Federal districts a monopoly over patronage and instead gave resources to Republican districts as well. Similarly, in the Philippines, the American officials gave some resources to local governments but doled them out unevenly. While Forbes distributed some funds, for instance, he denied Governor Sanz's request for a boat. He also denied many other requests. The result was a palpable disappointment. When Taft, having been previously promoted from governor of the Philippines to secretary of war, returned from the United States on an investigative trip in 1905, he received letters from local officials conveying their unfulfilled hopes: "On a visit you made to this province while you were Governor-General of the Philippines, you promised us, in a speech delivered here, two very important public works. . . . So far, nothing has been done, and it is for this reason that I make bold to address you, in the name of the people who have honored me with election to office, to request that your promises be fulfilled."[106]

In short, the Americans' policies, collaborative strategies, and actions were similar in the two colonies. While the elite in both colonies expected local autonomy, American authorities did not always provide it. And while the elite in both colonies classified Americans as patrons, American officials did not always meet the classification. As in Puerto Rico, the Filipino elites' schemas faced some initial recalcitrance. So what was the difference between the two cases?

Difference in the Social Field: The Philippine Economy and Validation

The first difference has to do with the socioeconomic field. In the Philippines, there was a remarkable historical continuity with the social configurations obtained previously during late Spanish rule. Unlike Puerto Rico, there was no large-scale economic crisis that disrupted preexisting patron-client relations. This is not to say that all was well in the Philippine economy. Due in part to the Philippine-American War, there were some problems. Some sectors of the export economy, such as the sugar sector, saw a decrease in production during this period.[107] Furthermore, many areas of the archipelago had been adversely affected by ecological disasters emerging in the immediate aftermath of the war. Locusts and rinderpests led to a decrease in the carabao (oxen) population critical for cultivation and transportation, while cholera and malaria epidemics broke out in some communities.[108]

Still, these problems did not pose a serious threat to the export economy as a whole, despite the war that raged in parts of the countryside. While certain agricultural sectors like sugar suffered in the first years of U.S. rule, others did not. In fact, demand for all Philippine products except for sugar remained high in the world market. Export values steadily increased through 1910 and, consequently, production increased too.[109] Even the value of sugar increased in this period, and production levels slowly climbed back to the levels evident during late Spanish rule.[110] In 1902, executive secretary Luke Fergusson reported with cheer: "I was informed by many of the older citizens that, within their recollection, there was never a time in the history of the islands when they were enjoying so much prosperity as they are at present."[111] Governor Wright added two years later: "The purchasing power of the people, so far from decreasing, is gradually increasing."[112] If anything, agricultural problems were restricted to the first years of American civil rule, 1900 to 1902. To take one example, close to half of annual reports by the provincial governors for the years 1901 to 1903 noted problems with agricultural production. By 1905, the proportion of governors' reports complaining about such problems declined to one-fifth.[113]

The question, then, is whether the agricultural problems in the immediate postwar period adversely effected the Filipino elites' traditional base of socioeconomic power and, hence, preexisting circulations of social exchange. Due to four features of the Philippine economy that together distinguished it from Puerto Rico, the answer is no. First, the Filipino elite were not dependent upon a single export crop. By the 1870s, tobacco, abaca, and sugar, as well as minor products like coconuts and coconut products, indigo, and dyewood, were all being cultivated and catered to the world market.[114] Second, the markets for Philippine products were not tied to the Spanish empire as was Puerto Rican coffee. Products went everywhere from England to Canada,

TABLE I Merchant and Landed Political Elite

	Puerto Rico	Philippines
Landed Only	38 (90.5%)	39 (65%)
Landed + Merchant	4 (9.5%)	21 (35%)
Total	42 (100%)	60 (100%)

China to Japan.[115] Third, unlike in Puerto Rico, Spanish capital did not dominate finance and circulation in the Philippines. Spanish financiers were notoriously absent, and foreign merchants from other parts of the world were minor players. Instead, the Filipino elite often financed their own production, which meant that in times of economic downturn, they were indebted to no one but themselves and had their own surplus for further savings or investment (table 1). Finally, agricultural production in the islands was less dependent upon export than Puerto Rico. At the onset of American rule, more than 60 percent of total acreage was devoted to export crops, while in the Philippines only 40 percent was for export. The rest was devoted to immediate local consumption.[116]

These factors helped even the sugar elite in the Philippines. The elite did not lose land, and, with their own capital and the variety of export opportunities, they simply shifted their resources to other crops (such as the profitable hemp).[117] Furthermore, the areas not dependent upon distressed crops like sugar, but which did in fact experience short-term crises (like the loss of carabao due to rinderpest and other epidemics), were also able to sustain themselves. Due to the features of the Philippine socioeconomic system just noted, the Filipino elite still had resources to dole out to their clients. Exemplary here is the report of the provincial governor of Capiz on how food shortages and epidemics after the war were managed:

> The work done by the provincial officials towards rousing the public spirit and encouraging the pueblos to combine against the evil by planting alimentary tubercles, maize, cacao coffee, cocoa-nut trees, hemp and tobacco, is beginning to have its effect. . . . In the work of relieving the sickness which prevailed in this province and of staving off famine . . . committees [have been] formed for the purpose of distributing food and of succoring the poor and sick. In the gardens of this government house,

dinners were supplied every day to about six hundred persons, who came in from the remote pueblos hungry and faint — and this for three consecutive months.[118]

Notably, the Filipinos undertook these activities without the financial aid of the American authorities. Unlike the Puerto Rican elite, they did not need any.

It followed that while the Puerto Rican elite complained about their lack of capital and various economic problems to the Americans, and as they complained about moral breakdown, social disorder, riotous mobs, and violence from below, the Filipino elite were relatively complacent. Provincial governors consistently reported on the "tranquillity," "peace," and "harmony" in their districts. "If the inhabitants of this province could pride themselves on anything," reported one governor, "it would be of their unspeakable love for peace, good order, and labor; of their unbreakable adhesion and respect to the constituted government."[119] Furthermore, none of the editorials of the elites' major newspaper organ, *El Renacimiento*, complained about social disorder, violence, or even crime of any kind. A few mentioned the problems of *bandolerismo* and *ladrones* (bandits), but these problems had been typical of the Spanish period, and there were no expressions in the editorials of direct threat to the elites' position.[120] Nor did provincial governors, when they reported on such matters, convey a sense of novel threat. While Governor Epifanio Santos of Nueva Ecija, for instance, reported that there had been "a band of evil persons" who tried to create "public disorder," Santos did not then express shock. To the contrary, he scripted the incidents as continuous with the past.[121]

The relative continuity in social relations made for a very different situation than in Puerto Rico. While the Puerto Rican elite saw their predictions in the social field invalidated due to the breakdown of patron-client relations, the Filipino elite saw their schemas affirmed. As the elite classified themselves as the directors and bearers of razón, looking after the well-being of their communities, and as they thereby predicted a continuation of patronage resources and patron-client relations, their predictions were ultimately proven true. Fittingly, while the Puerto Rican elite complained about the unprecedented social disorder, the Filipino elite continually classified themselves as benevolent directors in full control of their clientele. Claro Pascual Sevilla, governor of Bataan, noted the peace and order in his province and then attributed it to the "intelligence" of the Filipino officials.

I have also observed that all of the employees, insular, provincial, and municipal . . . comply with their duties with good sense, judgment and intelligence, and the tranquility of the province is due to this valuable combination in connection with the ability of the people to understand, and their earnest efforts to adapt themselves to the new institutions that the Government of the United States has given them in the ample autonomy which they enjoy in municipal and provincial government. These conditions have firmly established a state of peace and order that neither the public disasters which for years have afflicted the province nor any other causes have been able to shake, and it is this spirit which has operated greatly to diminish all sorts of crimes and conflicts so frequent and inevitable during the calamitous periods of transition.[122]

Similarly, when the Filipino governors reported upon conditions in their respective areas, they continued to employ patron-client idioms to fashion themselves and their relations with their subjects. In his 1906 report, Governor Jayme of Occidental Negros stated that the "former friction" of the war period has "been followed by currents of mutual regard and confraternity, arising from the wisdom of their rulers and the good sense of the inhabitants."[123] Governor Paras of Tayabas claimed that in his province there has been "complete peace, the result of the sensible conduct of these people and of their mutual regard for one another and the authorities." One governor, after asserting his subjects' "love" of government, culled references to ancient philosophy: "The love of the government as constituted is as spontaneous as the gushing of waters from a fountain. 'What should a man do to be exceedingly loved?' asked Alexander of one of the 10 Indian philosophers, famous for readiness and succinctness in answers, of whom he was making trial, and whose answers if judged unwise would condemn the answered to death, 'He must be very powerful,' said he, 'without making himself too much feared.' "[124] Other Governors were less eloquent, but nonetheless equally complacent. Governor Villamor of Abra reported that in his district, "the authorities and the people have a mutual respect and regard for each other." Governor Manuel Quezon of Tayabas added that in his province, "the common people live happy and satisfied [under] the directing class . . . there is perfect accord between the rich and the poor."[125]

Schemas of Patronage and Validation in the Political Field

There was another difference between the contexts of elite meaning making in Puerto Rico and the Philippines. This had to do with the political field: while the Puerto Rican elites' schemas in the political field faced repeated recalcitrance, the Filipino elites' schemas faced a limited recalcitrance. Their predictions did not prove true initially, but they were affirmed in the end. The reason does not lie solely in the American officials' ruling strategies or the trajectory of political education. As seen, the strategies and the overall trajectory were similar. In both colonies, American authorities restricted the power of local governments while sporadically providing resources to them. They also maintained ultimate control over the central state and engaged in patterns of party-based collaboration in the state center. In both colonies, authorities finally instituted a national legislative assembly. The difference between the two cases lies not in these factors alone but in combination with the particular cultural schemas at play. Tutelage unfolded similarly in the two colonies, but the elites' schemas — and hence the specific predictions they registered of tutelage — were not so similar.

In both Puerto Rico and the Philippines, the elites' cultural structures involved patron-clientelism. Their schemas of self-government involved patronage between the imperial ruler and the elite, and between the elite and the so-called masses. But the schemas of patron-clientelism had different valences. In Puerto Rico, the elites' schemas contained a *party-based* element of patronage. For the Puerto Rican elite, self-government meant autonomía, which in turn meant the rule of the so-called majority party (the Federals). At the same time, the Puerto Rican elites' schemas led to particular predictions: the American officials, like the liberal Spanish rulers before, would favor the majority party, give them patronage resources, and give them full power over the state. The Filipino elites' schemas were different. Because party politics had not been institutionalized during Spanish rule, the Filipino elites' schemas did not equate self-government with single-party rule or single-party patronage. Their schemas classified self-government as involving patronage, *but not party-based patronage.* American officials would give the elite some resources — regardless of whether or not the organizational channel of these practices followed party lines; and they would give leaders among the elite political power, regardless of what party those leaders came from. In this sense, the Puerto Rican elites' predictions were narrower than those registered by their Filipino counterparts, hence their expectations were higher.

These different schemas, along with the different predictions that followed from them, thereby faced different fates as tutelage proceeded — even as tutelage proceeded similarly in the two colonies. Consider, first, the issue of patronage and local governments. As we have seen, the American officials in both colonies sometimes granted patronage resources to local officials, even as they did not always do so. In Puerto Rico, this inconsistency was antithetical to the elites' predictions, because the elite there had predicted resources to flow along party lines just as they had done so during the period of autonomía under Sagasta. That is, the districts controlled by the Federal Party would be granted all resources while the few districts controlled by the Republicans, or the so-called minority party, would get nothing. Accordingly, when the American officials granted resources to Republican districts, even if they also gave some to Federal districts, the Federal Party protested vehemently. The American officials were acting against the principles of single-party rule, hence acting contrary to the prediction that they would bring autonomía. On the other hand, because the Filipino elite did not predict resources to flow along party lines, the inconsistency of the Americans' patronage did not have the same meaning. As long as the Americans provided resources to local governments, regardless of which local governments or political party received them, the American officials fit into the elites' classification of them as patrons providing surplus. Local officials therefore expressed disappointment when their municipality did not consistently receive resources, but they did not resign. Instead they waited in anticipation, registering their hope that their districts would finally get some resources. When the American officials did provide resources, local officials responded with affirmation. The municipal council in the town of San Pedro constructed an arch bearing an inscription that favorably compared American rule to Spanish rule:

The Americans gave us
Many schools and liberty;
What did the friar give us?
Darkness and inability.

Similarly, after Forbes provided infrastructural resources to local governments, local officials in turn offered their approbation by naming roads and bridges after him. As Forbes recorded in his journal: "The total list, as I remember, is the Forbes Park in Baguio . . . the polo field in Manila, and I am told a street in Manila; a bridge in Negros; a bridge in Iloilo; and a bridge in Cebu."[126]

Consider, too, the elites' predictions of political representation and power in the state center. In both cases, the elite predicted that political power would eventually devolve and the American officials would act as patrons to leading political elites. In neither colony did this happen at first. In Puerto Rico, the Federals hoped to obtain a privileged place in the state center, but the American officials also gave the minority party some representation. The Federals then met this initial recalcitrance by carrying out their party-based tactic of retraimiento — they boycotted the elections for the First House of Delegates. There was a parallel to this in the Philippines. As we have seen, American officials first rejected the efforts of nationalist Manila-based ilustrados to secure a privileged position in the state center through their newly formed political parties, and instead kept a few members of the small Federalista Party in the high positions of state. As a result, the displaced ilustrados protested, complaining that tutelage was not leading toward the kind of "self-government" they had imagined. This displacement was similar to that in Puerto Rico, but there was a critical difference. When the Federals in Puerto Rico enacted retraimiento, they had registered a new prediction: the American authorities would concede to the protest and restore the party's lost privileges. In contrast, the Filipino elites' complaints did not predict party privileges, they only predicted that some power would be devolved. They demanded that more participation be given to Filipinos than that which had already been granted. Nor did the Filipino elite have a party-based tactic of retraimiento. They rather confined their complaints to the press while waiting for American authorities to devolve power.

It followed that the institution of the national legislative assembly in the two colonies resonated very differently to the elite. In Puerto Rico, when the American officials established the House of Delegates and refused to concede to the Federals' retraimiento, the elites' predictions were further invalidated. The Puerto Rican elite had first predicted party-based patronage, and the

Americans' actions resisted the classification. Then, by conceding to the Federals' retraimiento, the Americans proved to be recalcitrant yet again. In short, the establishment of the House of Delegates served to make recurrent recalcitrance in Puerto Rico. In the Philippines, however, the establishment of the Philippine Assembly had the opposite effect. Displaced ilustrados had complained about the lack of representation, and they demanded more of it. The announcement in 1906 that the assembly would be instituted met the demand. Indeed, without a party-based tactic of retraimiento, the Filipino elite did not abstain in the elections. They participated fully. In fact, the displaced ilustrados who had previously seen their parties go unrecognized by American authorities won seats in the new Assembly (e.g., Pedro Paterno, Macario Adriatico, Vicente de Vera, Leon Guerrero, Alberto Barretto, and Jose de la Viña). Further, many of the provincial governors and officials who had complained about U.S. intervention into local affairs also participated in the elections, and they too won seats in the assembly. Out of the eighty delegates, at least fifty-four came from prior positions in the local governments.[127]

In contrast to what happened in Puerto Rico, then, the establishment of the Philippine Assembly served to affirm the predictions the Filipino elite had registered. By domesticating tutelage, the Filipino elite had predicted that American rule would be a movement toward self-government, propping the elite into the higher rungs of power and thereby fulfilling the "obligations" American authorities had presumably contracted. The establishment of the assembly fulfilled this prediction. It affirmed the classification of the Americans as the Filipinos' grand patrons, thereby realizing the law of razón between the Americans and the Filipino people.

How do we know the national assembly resonated in this way? Consider the difference in response. In Puerto Rico, after the House of Delegates was instituted, the Federals vehemently protested the event, charging the Americans with not realizing autonomía. Conversely, the Filipino elite were full of praise. Filipino officials across the island sent many letters of approbation to Governor Taft after the assembly was announced. Municipal officials in Luzon wrote that, by granting the assembly, "the democratic liberality and generosity of the Great American Nation" had been revealed. The governor of Batangas wrote that the people of his province offer "their adhesion and profound gratitude for the inauguration of the Assembly." A municipal official in Laguna declared that the people of his town were "enthusiastically and gratefully joyful for the opening of the first Philippine Assembly" and that they wished to send their "cordial welcome" to Taft "to whom the Philippines owe this transcendental step in the road towards self-government."[128] Furthermore, and perhaps most tellingly, the very first action taken by the delegates after the inauguration of the assembly was to compose a message to President Roosevelt. The message read, in true patron-client form: "Resolved, by the . . . Philippine Assembly, That on behalf and on behalf of the people of the Philippine Islands they convey, and do hereby convey, to the President of the United States, and through him to the Congress and the people of the United States, their *profound sentiments of gratitude and high appreciation* of the signal concession made to the people of the Islands."[129] From such discourse, in sharp contrast to the protests and disappointment in Puerto Rico, the difference between the two cases is clear. Unlike in Puerto Rico, the Filipino elites' particular predictions and the unfolding of tutelary occupation happily coincided.

THE TURNING POINT REVIEWED

As tutelage unfolded, what changed in each colony, and how did the changes differ between the colonies? The answer does not lie in the elites' interests, incentives, or goals. Throughout this period these were continuous. Nor does the difference lie in the tutelage project itself. As we have just seen, while the tutelage project changed over time in each colony, those changes were similar in the two colonies. The answer instead lies in the convergence of crisis conditions and the particular schemas at stake. The combination of these factors differentially validated the elites' schemas (table 2). In Puerto Rico, the socioeconomic crisis and the elites' particular party-based schemas — in relation to the Americans' policies and strategies — made for a convergent and recurrent recalcitrance. The elite drew upon their preexisting schemas to make meaning of the tutelage situation, but those schemas were repeatedly invalidated from all the fields they referred to. In both the social and political field, the predictions the elite registered by their meaning making were invalidated. And while the elite at first responded by renarrating American rule, the new predictions were also invalidated. As tutelage proceeded, neither the "unconscious masses" nor the American officials acted as the elites'

TABLE 2 Differences between Puerto Rican and Filipino Elite Contexts, ca. 1901–1907

Factor/Event	Puerto Rico	Philippines
State centralization as U.S. rule proceeded	Yes	Yes
Establishment of national assembly (Philippine Assembly; House of Delegates)	Yes	Yes
Collaborative Patterns: American officials reject party privileges/ patronage while also providing intermittent patronage resources to local governments	Yes	Yes
Social patron-clientelism part of meaning of self-government?	Yes	Yes
Party patron-clientelism part of meaning of self-government?	Yes	No
Socioeconomic crisis	Yes	No
EFFECT UPON SCHEMAS	Recalcitrance	Validation

schemas had implicitly predicted, and tutelage as a whole did not follow the elites' autonomía narrative. The Filipino elites' schemas faced a different fate. While the Filipino elite also domesticated tutelage in accordance with their preexisting schemas, those schemas did not face a convergent and recurrent recalcitrance. As social relations in the Philippines persisted as before, the elites' predictions about relationships between the directing class and the "directed class" were validated in the social field. And while the elites' schemas faced some initial recalcitrance in the political field, the recalcitrance was fleeting at best. Because single-party patronage had not been part of the elites' institutionalized schemas of self-government, the Americans' policies and collaborative strategies — which were similar to those in Puerto Rico — ultimately affirmed the elites' narratives and classifications. In the end, the Filipino elites' schemas were validated.

Recognizing this emergent difference is critical for our story. As we will see, it is because of this difference that the initial domestication gave way to two different forms of cultural transformation.

Chapter 5

DIVERGENT PATHS

The elite in both Puerto Rico and the Philippines initially domesticated tutelage, thereby registering implicit predictions about it. But due to differences between socioeconomic conditions and the elites' patronage schemas, their respective predictions were differentially validated. What happened as a result? Here we will see that the differential validation pushed the initially similar cultural paths in different directions. In Puerto Rico, recalcitrance compelled the elite to problematize the situation as they had done before. As their predictions were repeatedly invalidated, the elite questioned the schemas that had guided those predictions in the first place. Then, in accordance with this questioning, they stopped domesticating tutelage. Rather than paying selective attention to the Americans' tutelary texts and messages, they opened themselves up to them, seeking them out and learning more about them. In short, they expanded their cultural repertoire. Conversely, the continued validation of the Filipino elites' schemas led to a continued domestication. American officials continued to preach their own ideas and ideals of what democratic self-government meant, but because the elites' schemas were repeatedly validated, those schemas remained the most available, familiar, and retrievable. Therefore, rather than learning new schemas, the Filipino elite continued to employ their preexisting ones to make meaning.

To better see this divergence, let us begin in Puerto Rico, where all was not well for the Federal Party.

The Federal Party faced both socioeconomic and political troubles by the first year of civil rule. First, due to the economic crisis, patron-client relations had begun to break down; consequently, the Federals were visited by unprecedented social disruption and violence. Second, American authorities assaulted their municipal autonomy, marginalized them from the state center, and seemingly favored their rivals, the minority Republican Party. These troubles posed a serious threat to the elites' preexisting power but, just as importantly, they invalidated their predictions of how tutelage would unfold and how people around them would act. Their clients, the so-called unconscious masses, did not act as docile clients, American officials did not behave like Prime Minister Sagasta, and, in all, tutelage was not leading to autonomía as the elite had previously experienced it. The Federals first responded by adjusting their initial understandings in accordance with prior signifying patterns. Retraimiento was a manifestation of this adjustment: the Federals reclassified the American authorities as akin to conservative Spanish rulers who had previously threatened autonomía by favoring the minority party. Yet this classification was not validated either. The American authorities refused to recognize retraimiento and proceeded to institute the House of Delegates without granting concessions. Therefore, recalcitrance was not only convergent—coming from all sides at once—it was also recurrent: it happened over and over again. Nothing about the elites' previously institutionalized schemas worked as they had before; their cultural repertoire had been exhausted.

So what did the Federals do in this situation? As we will now see, the first thing they did was *problematize* their situation. Due to recalcitrance, they questioned everything that they had not questioned before. As colonial authorities had repeatedly failed to conform the Spanish type of ruler, the elite questioned the meanings they had made of them; as the "unconscious masses" simultaneously proved unwilling to bend to the elites' claims to be the legitimate "directing class," the elite questioned exactly how the unconscious masses should be regulated. This problematization was no small matter. It signaled the end of domestication and opened up the path toward repertoire expansion.

A defining characteristic of problematization is that social actors engage in "reflective and interpretive work": they recognize that the situation is novel and that something new must be done about it.[1] This is exactly what the Federals did after the failure of retraimiento. In June 1901, the leaders of the Federal Party called on Governor Allen and paid him a visit at the Fortaleza.[2] Previously the Federals had been carrying out retraimiento — criticizing the regime, demanding recognition of their *dignidad*, and awaiting political concessions. But at the meeting, the Federals shifted their approach. They informed Governor Allen that their party had a new program, and that they would "cooperate with the Governor in whatever way benefits the country." The Federals had decided to disavow retraimiento. Rather than abstaining from colonial politics, they would cooperate with the government and participate in future elections. "The moment has come to stop small disputes," they told Allen, "and all men of good will should unite to help the good government."[3]

This disavowal of retraimiento is remarkable. Previously, the Federals had not had to do such a thing. During Spanish rule, they had ended retraimiento only *after* they had received concessions from the regime. Before they had decided to meet with Allen, the Federals had been vigorously defending their decision to use retraimiento. Yet, taking a swift turn, they disavowed it. The *New York Sun* wryly remarked: "The members of the Federal party who were previously tenacious opponents of the administration have been changed into supporters of its politics."[4]

Why did the Federals take this unprecedented step of disavowing retraimiento? Part of the reason lies in the brute facts of disorder and political displacement, which lent a new urgency to their situation. As retraimiento had failed to provide concessions to the Federals, and as the Republicans took the House of Delegates while protests from below continued, the Federals decided a new line of action was necessary. To be sure, before their meeting with Allen, the Federals held meetings at which they produced a new manifesto. The manifesto stated that the "policy of abstention" had served to let the Republicans take the House while also encouraging "the persecution of the federal element of the population," the "disturbances of the public peace . . . in which the Federals have always been the victims," and "our deplorable social and moral conditions."[5] The Federals thus acknowledged that the failure of retraimiento had not had its intended effect; they accordingly dropped it. "The Federal party," their manifesto stated, "has changed its policy of opposition, softening it, weakening it, and carrying it to the utmost extreme of mildness, because its leaders considered that *no other conduct is possible* to avoid the ferocious attacks of which the federals were made the victims."[6] The manifesto declared further: "The federal party will attempt to remedy these evils . . . it will change its policy of retraimiento for a more expansive one."[7]

Still, the brute fact of disorder and displacement was not determining in itself. Also critical was the fact that disorder and displacement had served to invalidate the elites' classification of themselves and those around them. It was this invalidation that compelled the disavowal of retraimiento. Administrator Leo Rowe intimated this in his discussion of retraimiento's failure: "The Federal party was taught a lesson which it is not apt soon to forget, viz., that active participation in the political life of a country is not only the right but the obligation of any party organization, and that this obligation cannot be disregarded with impunity."[8] While it is not necessarily the case that the Federals learned this particular "lesson," it is the case that, due to the repeated invalidation of their predictions, the Federals questioned the cultural assumptions that had guided those predictions in the first place.

First, the failure of retraimiento demonstrated once and for all that the American rulers were not of the type the elite had assumed. It is not simply that the Federals acknowledged the failure of retraimiento, it is also that they acknowledged that it had failed exactly because the American authorities were not of the type they had assumed. After the disavowal, one Puerto Rican official approached Mr. Garrison, the American auditor, and said: "Mr. Garrison, you do not seem to care whether a man is a Federal, a Republican, or what he is, whether he has a pull or whether has not, whether is white or black; all you want to know is whether his claim is right, fair, and just. We are not accustomed to that kind of dealing."[9] Herminio Diaz, among those who had visited Governor Allen, explained that retraimiento "had not produced the intended result" because "American politics *does not understand it.*" Diaz warned his colleagues as the next House elections approached: "Retraimiento, used before and if repeated today, would only carry with it, as in the past, our complete abandonment of the Puerto Rican legislature, the only body where the sacred interests we should defend can be aired."[10]

Second, the invalidation of the elites' predictions also compelled the Federals to question their own image. As the Federals learned that retraimiento was not something that Americans "understand," they likewise questioned the understandings the American officials had had of them. For instance, in response to retraimiento, authorities proclaimed that the Federals were "un-American" and "anti-American." But after the Federals disavowed retraimiento, they countered the charge. They changed their name from the Federal Party to the American Federal Party and declared they would participate in the 1902 elections.[11] The change was clearly motivated by their recent reckoning. As party leader Santiago Palmer, in a letter to President Roosevelt, explained: "The American Federal party had thought for a moment of abstaining from casting their votes, as it did in 1900, *but fearing that such a step might be construed as an unpatriotic act,* we resolved to go to the polls."[12] Governor Hunt added in his corresponding letter to Roosevelt: "In order to avoid the criticism they must have felt would be made if they again refrained from participating in elections . . . [the Federals] concluded to go to the polls, and did so."[13] Therefore, as the 1902 elections approached, Federal leaders urged their *co-religionarios*: "Deposit your sacred votes on the 4th of November, retraimiento is impossible."[14] Recognizing that the American authorities were not of the type they had assumed, they insisted: "there is no more remedy" but to "take to the polls."[15] Fittingly, the Federals never again abstained from electoral politics during American rule. They had indeed learned a "lesson."

In short, while the brute fact of disorder and displacement compelled the elite to do something about their ailing situation, the fact that they disavowed retraimiento followed from recalcitrance. Disorder and displacement did not matter in and of themselves, they mattered because they served to disrupt the elites' cultural assumptions. In accordance with this disruption, the Federals questioned their classifications. In turn, this problematization led to another significant outcome. Not only did it compel the elite to disavow retraimiento, it also compelled them to take an entirely new line of action. The Federal leadership announced the new line of action in their manifesto. They declared that, besides participating in future elections, they would begin a campaign of commentary and complaint, speaking directly to American authorities and expressing their views to them. They avowed to lend "arms of advice and persuasion," speaking the "voice of truth" to them: "The federal party will . . . change its policy for a more expansive one, and . . . make [American authorities] hear the disinterested voice of truth, the voice of the endangered interests of the country, and point out to him the road by which the tranquility and the moral and material welfare, which are indispensable to the happiness of the island, can be attained. This is at present the sole aspiration of the party." The goal of this new approach, then, was to compel the American authorities to act — to do something about the distressing conditions of the island: "Our directors do not propose anything else but making observations to the Government about matters of administration and policies; and they hope that as they are just, they will be heard. In this consists, then, the change of our politics; that is, from the old retraimiento to a rapprochement with the government in order that with this counsel it will be able to modify its methods."[16]

In the immediate postretraimiento period, the Federals did what they said they would do. Still locked out of the state center, but commanding the majority of municipalities still, they used "arms of advice and persuasion." They presented their observations and opinions, shared their assessments of happenings and events, and offered solutions. They posted grievances, made appeals, and wrote letters. They also aimed their discourse at the American public more widely.[17] A closer look at this new tactic to replace retraimiento now merits attention; it will disclose that recalcitrance not only compelled a shift in tactic but also led the Federals to cease domesticating tutelage and instead expand their repertoire.

Listening and Persuading

What exactly was this new campaign of commentary and complaint about? In certain regards, the campaign was not entirely novel. The Federals' publicly stated goals remained the same as ever. Throughout the period, the Federals asserted that they still wanted to stop the dominance of the Republicans and the disorder posed by the "unconscious masses." They also stated that they still wanted economic aid, autonomía, and eventual statehood in the Union. Furthermore, registering commentary and complaint was something the political elite had always done. During Spanish rule, the elite had registered complaints to rulers, and retraimiento itself had been a kind of complaint as well as commentary. Their postretraimiento campaign was very similar, especially in the sense that it was directed toward American executive authorities. The Federals registered complaints with the governor, other officials in the executive department, and even President Roosevelt. For this very reason, in fact, the American officials took the Federals' campaign as retrograde and hapless. Administrator Willis Sweet saw it as a legacy of the elites' Spanish political education, by which the Puerto Rican people had been "taught to appeal to the administrative or executive officer in all of their troubles." In Sweet's view, the problem was that the Puerto Ricans were relying upon "the old habit of appealing to the Governor for interference" rather than doing what good American citizens should do: register complaints through formal channels in the courts or bureaucracies.[18]

On the other hand, the Federals' postretraimiento campaign was indeed novel. If the Federals deployed an "old habit" of appealing to executive authorities, they put that habit to new use, retooling their prior skills and competencies and reorienting themselves to the Americans' stream of discourse. This happened precisely because their prior predictions had been invalidated. As they questioned their cultural assumptions about the American authorities and their own self-image, they also sought to learn more about who the American authorities were, what they had to say, and how they might better deal with them.

Consider the first manifestation of the postretraimiento approach. It came in the form of a letter to Governor Hunt, who had taken office not long after the Federals had issued their new manifesto.[19] The letter contained the same grievances as before, pinpointing the problems of disorder and displacement that had first motivated retraimiento. It complained about the "acts of savagery" committed against them, taking special note of the "riotous mob" that had paraded through San Juan and transfigured Muñoz Rivera into a loca. The letter also blamed the Republican Party for supporting the disorder, asserting that the Republican appointments to the San Juan council "encouraged" it.[20] What is novel about the letter, however, is that it began by referencing Governor Hunt's own discourse, in this case his inaugural address. In that address, Hunt had reiterated the same tutelary themes of his predecessors. He had said that U.S. rule was about giving "object lessons . . . to educate, to impart lessons of self-help, and to permanently build up a government according to the highest standards of American republican institutions." He had stressed that political officials should conduct office with "impartiality" and "faithfully administer the law"; that "the truest patriot" is one who "never falters in his respect for the law, who raises his voice to counsel quiet obedience to it." He had also preached against personalism, patronage, and party conflict: "Let me earnestly beg you to remember that political differences ought to be based upon measures rather than upon personal prejudices; that it is the duty of every citizen to practice tolerance toward his neighbor and to respect his opinions though different from his own."[21] Hunt had even referred to some particular happenings at the time. Alluding to the Federals' previous retraimiento, he asserted: "No permanent good is accomplished by hasty resignations or by keeping alive political feuds, or by refraining from participation." Aware of the social disorder that had erupted, Hunt had further suggested that government should be "a government of law and not of the sword." He then concluded: "The past may be crowded with sorrows; it is no time or place to dwell upon them. We now live under the institutions of America . . . where Washington, Lincoln, Garfield, and McKinley stand as exemplars of American citizenship."[22]

From the Federals' letter to Hunt, it appears that they had paid meticulous attention to his speech.[23] The letter began by quoting the speech directly: "To His Excellency the Civil Governor. In your inaugural address you . . . declare: 'Life and property are guaranteed by this government of the law, not of the sword.' Well, then, your Excellency: it is necessary that these words shall not remain a mere figure of speech, or a vain promise, which time will prove to be such; but that they be translated into acts, which shall put an end to the doubts that pessimistic breasts may harbor." After then complaining about the "riotous mob" and the Republicans' support of it, the letter concluded by referring to the governor's speech again:

> If the words used by your Excellency in your address . . . reflect faithfully our Excellency's intentions, the people of San Juan and of the whole country hope that you will execute justice, and that the author of the lawless acts [in San Juan] will be punished. But if impunity once more protects these acts of lawlessness, let not your Excellency doubt that the shameful scenes

of last year will be repeated. . . . And the words, "Life and property are guaranteed by this government of law, not of the sword," instead of a solemn promise will be a miserable falsehood, which will steep in the profoundest pessimism the souls of all honorable persons. It is the part of your Excellency's government to prove that order, justice and liberty are not conventional phrases in the countries protected by the American flag.[24]

The novelty here is twofold. First, even though the letter complained about some of the things that had compelled retraimiento, the goal of the letter was not the same. Retraimiento was an attempt to regain lost political resources and obtain political favor, but the Federals in their letter did not ask for these things. Instead, they simply tried to persuade the governor to do something about the violence and disorder on his own volition, urging him to stop it on his own accord. Second, the *content* of the letter was different than before. The Federals urged Hunt to stop disorder and displacement, which was the same goal of retraimiento, but rather than expecting retraimiento to effectively communicate through a silent indignation, the Federals appealed to Hunt's own discourse. They made close and consistent references to Hunt's speech, quoting it directly. In other words, they tried to persuade the governor *by holding him up to his own standard*: his stated ideal that government should be a "government of law" and that citizens should always "respect the law." "Your Excellency," the letter pleaded, "it is necessary that these words shall not remain a mere figure of speech, or a vain promise . . . but that they be translated into acts."

This novel mode of persuasion was repeated throughout the Federals' postretraimiento campaign of commentary and complaint. For instance, when the Federals heard rumors that a new municipal police force was to be created in the Republican-controlled city of San Juan, they wrote another letter to Hunt in hopes of persuading Hunt to prevent it. The letter complained that municipal police force had been previously "employed to aid the organized mobs in their attacks against the Federals." It then referred to Hunt's discourse. Just as Hunt had urged the Puerto Rican people to be tolerant of "opinions though different from his own," the letter stated: "The only goal of the Republicans is to create a body of armed men who attack citizens whose opinions different from their own."[25] In yet another letter, the Federals complained that a Republican justice of the peace in Caguas had been harassing the Federals. The letter then asked Hunt to order an investigation, and it did so by referring to Hunt's discourse. Just as Hunt had urged local officials not to use their official powers as "political tools," the letter complained that the municipal police in Caguas had become a "political coterie . . . serving as *the tools of a political party*." Just as Hunt had stressed that courts should "administer the law with absolute impartiality" and "without regard to party politics," the letter stated that "the Court [of Caguas] is practically a Republican Club since it is always full of Republicans; the Federals are always arrested and accused, Republicans are never accused." Finally, as if paraphrasing Governor Hunt's contention that adherence to "good laws" means "successful self-government," the Federals' letter concluded: "There is nothing more censurable or that will make a honorable people more indignant than having just and wise laws be converted into the instruments of politicians."[26]

We can now better understand the Federals' new approach, and how recalcitrance had led to it. Because the Federals could no longer rely on traditional resources to stop displacement and disorder themselves, they tried to persuade the authorities to handle it on their own accord. And because the Federals had learned that retraimiento would not persuade the American authorities to act (because the American authorities were not of the type they had assumed), they adopted a different line of action: they appropriated the Americans' own standards to better persuade them. The Federals listened carefully to and then seized the Americans' own discourse of government and politics, thus trying to persuade authorities and the authorities' own discursive terms. It is as if, recognizing that retraimiento was something that American politics "does not understand," the Federals tried to appeal to that which the American rulers might better understand, or what the Federals must have assumed that the American rulers would better understand: the Americans' own utterances.

A look at the entirety of the Federals' discourse in this period further reveals this new approach. As Hunt had stated that officials should act with "impartiality," the Federals asked him to remove appointed Republican officials who had used the police for partisan ends on the same grounds. "You can be vindicated," said one letter, "with acts of impartiality. Begin by removing Fajardo and Egozcue [two appointed Republican mayors] of their offices."[27]

As Hunt had stated that government should be a "government of law," the Federals visited the Governor at his office and told him that the Federals were "anxious for prosperity and the rule of law."[28] One letter even offered detailed references to the municipal code, despite the fact that the municipal law had long been ignored by the Federals. The letter recounted incidents in which the Republican-controlled police force had harassed Federal Party members with the use of firearms and then reiterated sections 9 and 10 of article XVII of the municipal code, which clarified the proper situations in which firearms could be used. The letter concluded: "Honorable Governor, oh that this article of the law be complied with!"[29]

The Federals' other complaints were similar. Some referred to the details of the Foraker Act, which had called for the executive council to draw up an electoral plan for the House of Delegates. This was the act that had led to the gerrymandering in favor of the Republicans, the result of which was the Federals' indignant retraimiento. But the Federals, rather than employing retraimiento to protest, instead referred to the details of the Foraker Act itself, claiming that the electoral plan passed by Americans violated section 28. The letter complained: "The federal party asked THAT THE LAW SHOULD BE FULFILLED: that the island should be divided WITH ALL THE EQUALITY POSSIBLE."[30] If the Americans did not understand retraimiento, would they not understand the very laws they had formulated and imposed? The Federals also made references to key figures in American politics. Governors had often made such references; Governor Hunt's statement on the "institutions of America" and "Washington, Lincoln, Garfield, and McKinley" is but one example among many.[31] But the Federals took these references with new seriousness. Two months after Hunt's speech, they criticized Governor Allen and the gerrymandering affair by holding Allen's actions up to the ideals of George Washington: "Governor Allen . . . seems to have proposed to himself not only [the defeat of the Federal party in the elections] but also its exter-mination, forgetting and acting contrary to those wise counsels of Wash-ington recorded in his Farewell Address to the People of the United States, at the termination of his second Presidential period, that rulers should avoid the dangers of party spirit carried to excess."[32] Would not the Americans be persuaded by the venerable words of their own political thinkers and tradition?

True, the Federals had always heard what the Americans said, wrote, and distributed. As seen in chapter 2, the Federals had heard the Americans state that tutelage would give them "autonomy" and eventual "self-government." But as the Federals had assumed that the Americans were like the Spanish rulers of old, they had also assumed that the Americans were not saying anything new. The new tactic was different, exactly because the Federals had previously faced recalcitrance and had thereby questioned their assumptions. If the Americans were not like the Spanish rulers of old, what exactly were they like? If the Americans did not "understand" retraimiento, what exactly did they understand? If retraimiento was "un-American" and "unpatriotic," what precisely did it mean to be an American and patriotic? In short, recalcitrance led to problematization, which in turn led to a new approach that involved a novel process of learning.

Cultural Learning and Repertoire Expansion

Cultural learning is already evident in the examples already discussed — the Federals listened meticulously to Governor Hunt's speech so as to better persuade him. But the process is also evident in various other sources. Consider the Federals' main party organ, *La Democracia*. Amid domestication, *La Democracia* had not offered articles or commentary on the full breadth of the American officials' speeches, legal codes, or the Foraker Act. Both before and during retraimiento, it had reproduced some speeches and laws, but it had paid bare attention to their details, offering little commentary. This followed from cultural constraint — as the Federals made meaning of tutelage in accordance with their prior schemas, they paid selective attention to the Americans' texts and messages.[33] But after the disavowal of retraimiento, *La Democracia* carried editorials and articles offering detailed commentary on the Americans' discourse to register complaints about American rule. A sample of articles from *La Democracia* discloses the process. As table 3 shows, the proportion of articles that either (a) explicitly quoted a speech, circular, memo, or report by an American official or (b) referred to a specific section of a legal code increased over time. The very titles of the editorials signal this heightened attention: "Mr. Hunt's Address"; "Speech of Governor Hunt at the breakfast in San Juan"; "Speech of Mr. Hunt at the Regional Federation Meeting"; "A Report of the ex-Governor"; "The Speech of the

TABLE 3 *La Democracia:* Quotes and References to American Discourse
(Speeches, Memos, Laws)

Year	No. (out of 24)	Percentage
1899	4	17
1900	3	13
1901*	13	54
1902	11	46
1903	18	75
1904	14	58
1905	13	54

Source: *La Democracia*, two editorials per month, randomly selected
*1901: Year Federals disavow retraimiento (July)

Governor: Good Impressions."[34] Furthermore, the heightened attention began in 1901, when the party disavowed retraimiento. This suggests that it was only after the Federals had faced convergent and recurrent recalcitrance that they sought to learn more about the Americans' meanings.

Another index of the learning process comes from correspondence between municipal officials and American authorities. During the first years of American rule, 1898–1900, letters to American officials from municipal officials typically welcomed American occupation and expressed their hope for autonomía. Then, as the American authorities began to intervene into municipal affairs, letters complained about the threats to "Autonomic Government" that the interventions posed. But after 1901, when the Federal Party disavowed retraimiento, the discourse changed. Foremost, it expressed an unprecedented concern over the details of municipal laws and regulations. Local officials inquired: Can special sessions of the municipal council be held to finish up matters such as the municipal budget? Should the municipal mayor sit as the presiding officer at council meetings with the right to vote? Can the municipal council appoint officers besides those designated by law, such as clerks, gardeners, or street cleaners? Can municipal governments entrust to private contractors infrastructural work if the work amounts only to $2–$10? Whereas local officials had previously ignored the law and hired partisans for infrastructural projects, they now sought permission to hire private contractors for work totaling $10, or asked if it was within the law to appoint gardeners. Whereas municipal mayors had been subjecting the municipal governments to single-party rule — blurring legislative and executive functions — they now worried about whether they could vote in council meetings. After problematizing the situation and disavowing retraimiento, the Federals became obsessed about legal and procedural minutiae, whereas they had not been before. They sought to better understand the laws that the Americans had passed but to which they had previously paid selective attention.[35]

The extent to which the Federals paid attention to the Americans' discourse was thus new after convergent and recurrent recalcitrance. But also important is the *content* of what they received — exactly *what* they heard and read in the Americans' discourse. The elite paid heightened attention, but with a specific purpose due to convergent and recurrent recalcitrance. To persuade the Americans to act on disorder and political displacement, the Federals thus had to discover what the Americans themselves had to say about disorder and displacement. For example, as the Federals tried to persuade Hunt to stop disorder and stop granting favors to the Republicans, they seized upon the particular aspects of Hunt's discourse that referred to the same issue. Rather than simply seizing and then domesticating phrases like *self-government*, the Federals seized Hunt's specific statement that "life and property are guaranteed by this government of law, not of the sword." Similarly, rather than complaining that the Republicans were incondicionales, a minority party receiving unjust favor, they seized Hunt's utterance on impartiality and party politics. In short, it was in relation to the particular features of convergent and recurrent recalcitrance that the Federals listened. Because the American officials did not act as party-based patrons, the Federals sought to discover what American political thinkers had to say about political parties, thereby finding and rearticulating George Washington's statement that rulers should "avoid the dangers of party spirit carried to excess." Similarly, because American officials did not grant electoral favors like Sagasta had, the Federals sought to discover what the Foraker Act had to say about electoral districts. As the Federals' claims to political authority based upon the "directing class" were invalidated in the social field, they sought to learn what the Americans had to say about political authority. What did the municipal code, for instance, have to say that might help persuade the American authorities to stop Republican abuses of police power that in turn contributed to social disorder?

A book by the prominent party leader and friend of Muñoz Rivera Cayetano Coll Cuchí, offers a condensed look at this learning process. The book, *La Ley Foraker*, was written in 1903 and dealt exclusively with the Foraker Act. This is notable in itself, for the act had been instituted in 1900, when the Federals were in the midst of domesticating tutelage. The fact that Coll Cuchí decided to study it and write a book about it three years later suggests that it was only after convergent and recurrent recalcitrance that he felt compelled to return to it. Specifically, he attacked the Foraker Act with close attention to its various sections, showing that the happenings of the previous years went against the act's rules, that American occupation failed to live up to the law's own stated standards, and that the act itself violated American traditions.

Coll Cuchí especially seized upon section 17 of the act. This was the section that had given the president the right to appoint the governor and the Executive Council and the council the right to set up the electoral districts for the House elections and to legislate for the island. This was the section, then, that had served to help to displace the Federals from the center power and uproot their municipal autonomy. It was the section that had caused so much recalcitrance from above.[36] Coll Cuchí analyzed this section and then discussed American political thinkers (the ones whom Governor Hunt had referred to in his speech). He read and discussed Jefferson's *Notes on Virginia*, various writings of John Adams, the Constitution of Massachusetts, James Madison, and the Federalist Papers. What he found is the claim, stated by Jefferson — whom Coll Cuchí quotes directly — that "the concentration of [legislative and executive] powers in the same hands is precisely the sole definition of a despotic government." Coll Cuchí then compared this to section 17, which concentrated the legislature and the executive functions of the colonial government, and exclaimed that the Foraker Act is "an affront to democratic principles." The Foraker Act violated America's own "Republican doctrines" and was thereby "an offense to the memory of the fathers of the American Constitution."[37]

The labor of learning evidenced in Coll Cuchí's book later bore fruit. In 1905, municipal officials penned a letter to the United States Congress asking for an amendment to the Foraker Act. They asked that legislative functions be removed from the Executive Council and be vested in the House and a new elective Senate. The justification was precise: "In opposition to the most simple principles of political law obtaining . . . under a representative system, *such as that of your own country*, the legislative and executive powers are merged in the executive council. . . . For that reason we . . . appeal to you for assistance."[38]

In short, convergent and recurrent recalcitrance set the Federals along a path toward repertoire expansion. Because their predictions were invalidated, the Federals questioned the assumptions that had guided those predictions in the first place. Then, in accordance with the reckoning, they adopted a novel approach to American authorities. True, the approach was narrowly motivated: the Federals simply aimed to persuade the Americans to act. But unlike retraimiento — which had also been an attempt to persuade the Americans to act — the new approach involved cultural learning. Because the Federals had questioned their previous assumptions due to recalcitrance, they learned that the American officials were not of the type they had presumed, and so they tried to better understand the Americans' own understandings. As they had faced social disorder from below, their prior schemas on authority and political relations were invalidated, so they specifically sought to understand the Americans' own understandings on how the "masses" should be regulated. The result was critical. Whereas the elite had previously dissociated a "government of law" and "rational politics" from proper governance and authority (instead relying upon party-based or patronage authority), they now learned that these were part of the Americans' scheme. And whereas they had previously equated self-government with autonomía and had equated both with a concentration of legislative and executive powers in the hands of a party or jefe, they now learned that their powers were to be separated. Even American officials were impressed. The insular secretary noted, after receiving the inquiries from Federal officials on the specifications of the municipal code: the "Porto Ricans [*sic*] are fast-grasping the theory of representative government."[39] The Federals, rather than remaining dupes of inherited cultural structures, adopted new ones.

But do not colonized elites everywhere internalize and deploy the categories imposed by their rulers? Some argue that, yes, colonial elites inevitably learn the idioms of the colonizer, not least to resist power by the same terms power imposes.[40] But the foregoing analysis of the Puerto Rican elites' reception over time unsettles this assumption. The Puerto Rican elite did not at first learn and employ the Americans' idioms. They did so only after their predictions of tutelage repeatedly proved untrue from all sides at once. Just as importantly, a comparison with the Filipino elites' reception below will further affirm the claim. We will see that the Filipino elite indeed "resisted" colonial power, but they did so through terms very different than those that the Americans imposed. We will also see that this difference in turn depended on differences between the validation of the elites' schemas.

THE PHILIPPINES: DOMESTICATING DISAPPOINTMENT

The Puerto Rican elite ceased domestication and opened themselves up to tutelary messages, but how did the Filipino elite respond to the messages? Something of an answer can be found by examining the Filipino elites' discourse in one period in particular: the period before 1906, when the commission finally announced that the Philippine Assembly would be established. As seen in the previous chapter, this was the period when the Filipino elite became disappointed with the progress of American occupation. The elite had predicted that they would obtain control over the state and that American authorities would act as patrons to local governments, but American authorities did not always meet the expectation: they centralized the state, rejected attempts by Manila-based ilustrados to secure privileged positions for their political parties, and failed to consistently provide patronage resources. The period is worth examining, therefore, because it is comparable to the post-retraimiento period in Puerto Rico. In both colonies, the elite faced some disappointment; their political interests were not realized. In both cases, too, the elite had an incentive to do something about the situation. As authorities centralized the state, the elite in both colonies faced the threat of losing political power and a turn away from more self-government. Fittingly, after first facing political disappointment, the Filipino elite did what their Puerto Rican counterparts did: they began a campaign of protest and persuasion. The Manila ilustrados, who had failed to receive official favor for their parties, turned their labors toward political propaganda in the press, and their editorials were increasingly critical of occupation (table 4). Furthermore, the disappointed Manila ilustrados formed new political associations aimed at mobilizing forces across the archipelago. Provincial elites joined in the effort

TABLE 4 Philippine Newspaper Complaints about American Tutelage, 1903–1906

Year	No. Editorials Complaining (Total Editorials Analyzed)	Percent Editorials Complaining
1903	2 (21)	9.5%
1904	9 (23)	39%
1905	11 (22)	50%
1906	15 (24)	62.5%

Source: *El Renacimiento* (random sample, two editorials per month, 1903–5; incomplete due to unavailability of newspaper issues)

and, together, they registered yet more complaints about tutelage. They demanded more political representation and tried to convince the American authorities that they should receive it.[41] If we were to find a process of cultural learning in the Philippines, we would most likely find it here — *before* the elite had received the final benefit of the Philippine Assembly.

On the other hand, despite these similarities between the two cases, there was a difference. As seen in the previous chapter, while the Filipino elite before the establishment of the assembly had faced some recalcitrance, that recalcitrance was limited. First, because the Filipinos' resource base was strong and because, therefore, socioeconomic patron-client relations persisted as before, the elites' self-identification as the "directing class" in the social field was affirmed. Unlike in Puerto Rico, recalcitrance in the Philippines was not convergent: the Filipino elite faced some resistance to their schemas in the political field, but their schemas in the social field were validated. Furthermore, even recalcitrance in the political field was limited. Because the Filipino elite did not have party-based schemas of what self-government involved, recalcitrance was not recurrent. The American authorities did not always act as patrons providing resources, but in relationship to the particular predictions the elite registered, they sometimes did. Unlike in Puerto Rico, the elites' schemas were validated. The American authorities were proved to be patrons indeed, and — like all patrons — they had their favorites.

We will now find that the validation of the elites' schemas in turn affected how the elite received the Americans' imposed signs. While the Puerto Rican elite scrutinized and learned the Americans' meanings, the Filipino elite persisted in employing their own. Even as the Filipino elite complained about tutelage, and even as they tried to persuade the Americans to change the direction of tutelage and help them realize their goals, they did not question their assumptions nor learn the Americans' signifying patterns. Rather than expanding their repertoire, the Filipino elite continued to domesticate what the American authorities offered to them.

The Discourse of Disappointment

One of the notable features of the Filipino elites' critical discourse in this period is that it was personalized. As the Manila-based elite failed to realize their political goals and win official favor, and as the elite everywhere witnessed the centralization of the colonial state, they targeted particular U.S. officials and placed blame on them. A key target was Luke Wright, who had replaced William Taft as governor-general in 1903 and whose regime coincided with increasing centralization. For example, at a luncheon of Filipino governors and visiting American dignitaries, some officials overheard the Filipino governors attacking Wright directly. One provincial governor, Arsenio Cruz Herrera, made "some very loud remarks" indicating "hostility to Governor-General Wright." Cruz Herrera gave a "running-fire talk all through the meal," producing a "harangue" against Wright and "at times getting to his feet." He complained that Wright, and other officials of Wright's regime, "did not sympathize with the Filipinos" and that this was "reflected in many of the laws passed [by Wright]." He concluded that due to Wright, "the present government here has lost the confidence of the Filipinos."[42]

Such criticism of Wright was widespread. Editorials in a leading Manila newspaper, *El Renacimiento*, constantly attacked him, claiming that while Taft's regime had inspired "confidence" among the Filipinos, Wright's regime had brought only "discontent."[43] This hostility toward Wright is not unlike the Puerto Ricans' hostility toward American officials in Puerto Rico. As the Puerto Ricans initially faced recalcitrance, they sometimes targeted the American governors as the source of the problem. But there was an important difference. The Puerto Rican elite targeted and criticized particular officials by employing the very standards of politics and authority articulated by the American rulers themselves. They blamed rulers for not upholding a "government of law" and for not acting in the interests of "tolerance" and "respect." The Filipinos' criticisms were not of this sort.

Witness a brief exchange between the Filipino elite and the American community in Manila, occurring at the height of centralization. Americans in Manila had been shrugging off the Filipinos' discontent with Wright's regime, asserting that their discontent was merely the expression of the Filipinos' own "character and attitude." *El Renacimiento* offered a counterpoint, contending that the problem was not with the Filipinos but with the regime and its personnel:

> To say that the success of American politics in the Philippines depends almost exclusively on the character and the attitude of the people of the Islands is to discard other factors, the most important probably being: the know-how [*pericia*] or the tact of the ruler. There exist two elements whose forces should converge for that success . . . : the people and the government, the one that obeys and the one that commands. Not all the failures of colonial politics . . . should be attributed to the inhabitants of the governed country. At times — and history does not lie in this — the failure arises [from the] little experience and *habilidad* (skill/ability) of the governors. It is not just, then, to make the success dependent purely on the people. It is necessary that both elements or factors come together to a true joining of forces.[44]

Unlike the idioms the Puerto Rican elite employed amid their criticisms, there is nothing novel about the idioms employed in this editorial. The categories instead reach back to late Spanish rule, when the elite had attacked the Spanish administration for being bad patrons, claiming that colonial problems were due to the Spanish rulers' own inabilities, not the Filipinos'.[45] Indeed, the editorial above employed these schemas to defend the Filipinos' criticisms of Wright. Wright's regime was failing not because of the Filipinos, but because of Wright's lack of "know-how," "skill" and "tact." Wright was a bad token of the same old type, an incapable patron like the bad patrons during Spanish rule.

Such classifications of Wright are evident across the Filipino elites' discourse. For instance, when Governor Wright and other officials visited Sorsogon province, a local official by the name of Jose de Vera gave a speech in which he first noted the Filipinos' discontent with Wright's centralizing regime and expressed the Filipinos' "desire to find the best solutions to their problems." Vera then affirmed the Filipinos' hope in U.S. rule but qualified it by stating:

> [Our] faith and confidence would be stronger and more robust when you solve, with the self-denial and altruism of a redeemer, the problems in which are presented conflicts of interests between both peoples. . . . In this situation respective to both peoples, the position of the United States is the more delicate one. . . . A small error committed, a *mala inteligencia* that guides actions . . . these are exploitable and exploited reasons for the discontented native . . . to accuse the Noble American Nation, of prostituting its sacred mission which has been taken up upon coming to the Philippines and retaining it.[46]

Vera justified the Filipinos' discontent by stating that it arose only when rulers show a *mala inteligencia*. Again, this was not a novel classification, nor was it an appropriation of the Americans' own categories. Whenever Spanish rulers had deviated from the ideals of razón, the elite had responded by claiming that the rulers were showing a skewed or "obtuse" intelligence as opposed to good rulers who had intelligence and showed "rectitude" (i.e., those who adhered to the dictates of razón). Vera drew upon this very same opposition to make meanings of American rule and express discontent with it.

Newspaper editorials at the time also drew upon preexisting signifying patterns. They asserted that the Filipinos had a *desconfianza* (lack of confidence) with the regime, the very same term they had used to register their disappointment with Spanish rule. They also asserted that the desconfianza was due to the "lack of inteligencia between the governors and governed."[47] Razón was not realized. Other discourse opposed Governor Wright and his regime to Governor Taft, again employing the same schema. If Wright was a bad patron, Taft was the paradigmatic one — as was Taft's superior, President McKinley, who had first laid out the tutelary policy. Cruz Herrera ended his diatribe against Governor Wright by stating that "the American people's intentions were recognized by the Filipinos as good, but that they were not to be realized here with men not in sympathy with the instructions of McKinley and with the policy inaugurated by Taft."[48] Similarly, editorials in *El Renacimiento* complained that the Filipinos had lost their confidence in the regime primarily because of Wright's actions and character, over and against Taft's.

The discontent among Filipinos "is no doubt due to the difference in point of view and methods between the former and present governor [i.e., Taft and Wright]."[49] Taft's regime and his policy thus appear as an exemplary of reciprocity between ruler and ruled; Wright's appears as a deviation.

Even the Manila-based ilustrados who had initially failed to obtain official recognition for their political parties classified Taft as the ideal patron. Pascual Poblete had failed to get recognition for his Nationalist Party, but he nonetheless published articles in his *El Grito del Pueblo* praising Taft. The articles classified Taft as the Filipinos' "most beloved friend," who deserved "sincere affection and respect," because Taft "has demonstrated his inteligencia in governing the people."[50] Similarly, when Taft departed for the United States in December 1903, *El Grito* bid him farewell as a client to a patron: "The inhabitants of the islands hope that, given the love that Mr. Taft has always demonstrated for the progress and well-being of these islands, he will return as soon as possible, where seven million hearts reserve for him sincere and everlasting gratitude."[51]

Another previously disappointed ilustrado, Pedro Paterno, offered similar approbation. Paterno published a short story about Taft in his newspaper, *La Patria*, which scripted him as a benevolent "genius." The story related that the author had had a brief encounter with Lapu, "the great Prophet" and famed native chief who had killed Ferdinand Magellan in the sixteenth century. The author had entered the "traditional cave of Lapu" in search of Lapu's wisdom. After reciting "the magic words" to conjure Lapu, Lapu then appeared to speak about "the governmental work of the wise Mr. Taft":

> Lapu said: Taft is a genius whose elevated judgment cannot be appreciated by you. . . . he came to the Philippines as Commissioner and become governor and an excellent governor. His artistic work should be viewed like a great oil painting, from only one point of view; [but] Taft was not allowed to complete his work which would have been like a piece of sculpture to be seen from every side. The work of the wise Taft is but a beginning whose conclusion you have not been able to see, as he has been proposed as a member of the Supreme Court and has become Secretary of War. But notwithstanding its incompleteness, the work of Taft is great. . . . Time and liberty are necessary in order to judge Taft's governing genius. It should be remembered that the man was obliged to leave his artistic work incomplete.

The story concluded by appealing to the reader: "Intelligent reader, we have not the space to record all that we heard in that cave . . . but we do not wish to close without stating that we departed from that mysterious place with high hopes, confiding in the Honorable Taft."[52]

Not all of the Filipino elite shared Paterno's references to Lapu, but they did share Paterno's praises of Taft. Felipe Meniamis, a Filipino bureaucrat in the civil service board, informed his superiors about many speeches made by prominent Filipinos that make evident the fact that "Governor Taft is the idol of the natives."[53] Mrs. Campbell Dauncey remarked in her memoirs that Filipinos in Iloilo saw Taft as "a sort of patron saint, rivaling Dr. Rizal" and expected "all blessings to spring up miraculously in his footsteps."[54] Commissioner Bernard Moses recorded (perhaps with a tinge of envy) that the "prominent Filipinos" consistently referred to Taft as their "protector," expressing an attitude that was "of apparently genuine regard and affection."[55]

Rather than suspending their prior models, the Filipino elite continually used them to make meanings of the changing field. Disappointed and even disillusioned with the regime, they nonetheless domesticated it all, classifying their problems as the work of incapable patrons. But did they continue to domesticate tutelary messages as well?

Appropriate Appropriations

The Filipinos did not completely ignore the Americans' discourse in this period. To the contrary, beset by political disappointments and the prospect of further political centralization, they lent it some attention. Like their Puerto Rican counterparts, they even commented on the Americans' speeches and, at times, appropriated keywords and phrases. Not surprisingly, the elite most often paid heed to Taft's discourse, the words of the model patron.

The process had begun soon after the announcement that Wright would succeed Taft as governor. After the announcement, a number of articles in the elites' press began making references to speeches that Taft had previously given in Manila and Iloilo. In relation to Taft's other speeches, there was nothing especially remarkable about these two speeches. They simply reiterated tutelary themes. Taft stated, for example, that "the United States is here for the purpose of preserving 'the Philippines for Filipinos' for their benefit, for their elevation, for their civilization."[56] But the speeches were in fact peculiar because they were pitched at American settlers and foreign business-men. In this context, Taft did not just reiterate the tutelage policy, he de-fended it. American settlers and foreign residents had been hostile toward tutelage, asserting that the United States should keep the islands forever and should not bother training Filipinos for self-government. Taft used his speeches to argue back.[57] He later explained to his brother at home: "While I was in Iloilo I took occasion to say in a speech . . . that we were running the Government for the benefit of the Filipinos; that it was their country, and that people who came here and were disappointed at its being so run did not have to stay. This created a great howl among the extreme Americans and the foreigners."[58]

While Taft had directed his speeches at Americans and Europeans, and while it caused a "howl" among them, the Filipino press also seized them. They especially seized his phrase "the Philippines for Filipinos." One edi-torial used it to protest centralization:

> We have experienced many deceptions, many wounds. . . . The better offices should not be reserved for the sons of the metropolis. We have been working and continue to work so that all possible participation in the different arms of the administration are given to us. . . . Upon the flutter-ing, then, of that flag, upon unfurling that banner which Mr. Taft main-tained exactly in Iloilo, we work, not animated by arrogance, but out of the belief that this region is for those who have inhabited it since prehistoric times, and that it will be "the Philippines for filipinos."[59]

The editorial indicates a process parallel to the process contemporaneously unfolding in Puerto Rico. Just as the Puerto Rican elite seized the Americans' discourse in the postretraimiento period, so too did this editorial turn to Taft's discourse to symbolically register state centralization and rally against it. Indeed, the editorial pinpointed one of the major causes of political dis-appointment (that Americans were being favored at the highest positions of the colonial state) and then used Taft's phrase as a standard to assess and criticize it. "We work out of the belief that this region . . . will be 'the Philippines for filipinos.'"

Other editorials in many newspapers also evoked the phrase amid criti-cisms of Wright's regime. It became a rallying cry. One editorial referred to it as "our flag of the fight" and "our sacred motto."[60] Throughout the archi-pelago, in fact, Filipinos evoked it. American residents complained that Taft's phrase, which they saw as a "childish slogan," had become "immensely popu-lar" among locals.[61] An army officer stationed outside Iloilo remarked that even schoolchildren were uttering it.[62] "The phrase got about everywhere," noted Mrs. Dauncey.[63]

Still, if the Filipinos' appropriation of Taft's utterance shows a parallel with the Puerto Ricans' appropriations, exactly *which* utterances they appropriated were different. This is critical. The Puerto Ricans seized the Americans' utterances about a "government of law," "rational politics," and "tolerance" for other political parties. These elements cut to the heart of what govern-ment meant and how it should have been conducted. The Puerto Rican elite seized them because their schemas in the social field had been invalidated. In contrast, the Filipinos seized only Taft's specific statement, "the Philippines for Filipinos." They did not, seize, for example, Taft's inaugural address, whereby Taft had stressed that the Filipinos needed to be tutored in "meth-ods of free and honest government" and had warned against the "spoils sys-tem" and the use of "official position for private ends."[64] Nor did the Filipino elite refer to the other aspects of Taft's speeches at Iloilo and Manila besides "the Philippines for Filipinos." In fact, at those speeches, Taft had said many things. He criticized the "evils of 'caciquism,'" stressed that "the real and highest object of all modern liberal governments" is "respect for personal rights and individual liberty," and warned that Filipino officials "have much to learn in the matter of exercising only the authority conferred by law upon them."[65] Americans present at the Iloilo speech therefore wrote that the speech "gave them [the Filipinos present] some good lessons on the failure to work for the elevation of the masses and the aristocratic class-feeling in the islands."[66] Yet the Filipino elite paid little mind to these elements of the discourse. Amid the entire stream of Taft's utterances, they responded to and appropriated only Taft's phrase "the Philippines for Filipinos."

This is critical because, unlike the other aspects of Taft's speeches, or of tutelary discourse generally, the utterance "the Philippines for Filipinos" did not disrupt the Filipinos' prior meanings. It was simply a statement about tutelage and the direction it should take. It is as if the continued validation of the Filipinos' models meant that the Filipinos, unlike the Puerto Ricans, did not seek new ways of classifying government or new meanings of political authority. Their preexisting models validated as ever, the only aspects of the Americans' discourse that resonated with them were those that were appropriate to their particular situation of political disappointment. They seized the Americans' discourse to hold the Americans up to their own standards, but as they did not face convergent recalcitrance, they only seized the standards which referred to political centralization while remaining impervious to the Americans' talk about the "rule of the majority," "honesty and efficiency in government," or "law and order."[67] They appropriated the Americans' discourse, but what they appropriated was suitable for the continued validation of their cultural structures.

Persuading Power

Admittedly, the foregoing discourse was not aimed at American officials. It was a dialogue among the Filipino elite themselves. It might be the case, then, that the Filipino elite consciously refused to discuss the Americans' models. After all, publicly disseminating those models might have threatened the elites' own political standing and undermined their self-fashioned status as the "directing class." Were the Filipino elite cultural entrepreneurs, strategically choosing *not* to disseminate the Americans' models, even though they may have fully received them? Was their selective appropriation of American discourse a hidden transcript, a calculated domestication prompted by utility maximization?[68]

To test the hypothesis, we can turn to the elites' discourse, pitched directly at American officials. We have seen how the Puerto Rican elite redeployed the Americans' categories and schemas of government as they tried to persuade the Americans to meet their demands. The question is whether the Filipino elite did the same. After all, the Filipino elite, like the Puerto Rican counterparts, also wanted the Americans to grant them more self-government. Did the Filipinos try to persuade the Americans by using the Americans' own schemas, only to then repress those schemas in their public discourse?

Consider the elites' correspondence with Taft. When Taft made a brief sojourn back to Washington, and when he later returned to the Philippines, he received multiple letters from Manila and provincial officials. This was after ilustrados had failed to get their platforms recognized by Taft, and just as the regime began to intervene into local affairs. We might expect, then, that the Filipinos wrote to Taft to register their disappointment. But they did not. Instead they employed patron-client discourse to register loyalty and deference. Francisco Morales of Bulacan wrote: "Your return to these Islands I presume will bring to [the islands] a new age of prosperity and happiness. Therefore a true lover of his country can but send you more respectful welcome as I do now. . . . I am always unconditionally at your orders."[69] Macario Favila of Pangasinan wrote similarly: "In the name of the inhabitants of Pangasinan and in that of the Provincial officials, I beg you will be pleased to extend to the Honorable Governor Taft on his return to the Capital our cordial welcome with the expression of homage of our respect and consideration."[70] Even Pascual Poblete, who had failed to get his party's platform recognized, framed his letter to Taft through clientelistic idioms. He lent to Taft his "immense gratitude and sincere respect," adding that his peers send "the homage of their absolute adhesion and unconditional loyalty." "Long Live the United States of America! Long Live the Philippines! Long live Mr. Taft, the true friend of the Filipino people and the intrepid defender of the rights [*derechos*] of these Islands!"[71]

When Taft left the Philippines in 1903 to become the new secretary of war, he received yet more letters. These letters are especially informative for our purposes. As the new secretary of war, Taft was put in charge of all colonial affairs. If anyone in Washington would help remedy the Filipinos' situation, it was Taft, and the elite were fully cognizant of Taft's newly assigned place in the imperial hierarchy. Moses noted that the Filipinos looked upon Taft "as the man who stands between them and the re-establishment of absolute rule."[72] But again, the elite did not redeploy the Americans' own discourse. While they indeed urged him to help them deal with centralization, they did not employ novel idioms. The letter from Aniceto Clarin, governor of Bohol, is exemplary. He asked Taft to help the Filipinos, but he just referred to him as a "loving father."

> I, and with me all persons who know you personally or through your acts, which have been decidedly for the best of the Filipino people, greatly deplore your unexpected departure from these Islands for the home land. You are now going away from us Filipinos, who expected our future happiness and salvation from your noble and generous disposition and from

your fatherly care; but I, and with me the true Filipinos, am confident that you will not forget or desert us, notwithstanding the great distance which separates these Islands from their sovereign country. On the contrary, we hope that in the high position you will occupy at the side of the Honorable President of the great republic and the powers which regulate Philippine matters, you will like a loving father remember the faithful inhabitants of the Philippine Islands, and will no doubt not grudge your protection and assistance to the poor children which you are leaving in these Islands, plunged into sadness upon seeing their kind, clement and beloved Governor General go away from them.[73]

Such flowery and flattering discourse might make us skeptical about Clarins's sincerity. But other elites used the very same categories, and the "sincerity" of the discourse is not at stake here.[74] At stake is the discourse itself, which, unlike the Puerto Ricans' discourse, drew upon the elites' previously institutionalized schemas.

Taft was not the only American whom the elite tried to persuade. They also tried to persuade American statesmen. These attempts came to the fore in 1905, when a party of U.S. congressmen and other dignitaries visited the archipelago. The goal of the visiting party was to investigate conditions in the Philippines by collecting information and gathering opinions, and the Filipino elite responded in force. Municipal councils, provincial officials, and various political associations in the Manila area wrote collective petitions. Prominent Filipino officials gave speeches at events held in the visiting party's honor, and many others spoke at public hearings held by the congressmen. This discourse is especially opportune for our purposes. First, the visit occurred at the height of centralization. Wright had been in office for two years, and the Filipinos had already begun their criticisms of his regime. This, then, was one of the first opportunities for the Filipino elite as a whole to speak directly to their colonial masters, express their dissatisfaction with tutelary rule, and make formal demands. In fact, at the head of the visiting party was Taft himself. Taft had told the Filipinos when he left the islands, "til I come again," and alas, he had returned.[75] This was a prime opportunity for the Filipinos to hold the United States to Taft's promise of "the Philippines for Filipinos" and to ask for more self-government. Furthermore, the Filipinos were prepared. They knew about the visit long before its occurrence and had time to reflect upon what they would do and say. They were well aware that their fitness would be on display. Before the visit, *El Renacimiento* beseeched: "But let us by all means attempt that the members of Congress obtain a true conception of these islands and their inhabitants, a correct and exact idea of our intellectual status, our social conditions and concepts, for . . . in these humble huts beneath the rough dress and skin browned by the sun, may be found a good people, upright, capable and anxious to be correctly appreciated and understood by the great American people."[76] On the day the visitors landed, another editorial warned: "The leaders of American politics which have come among us this day . . . have come . . . to study . . . the real sentiments and most urgent needs of the people of these islands. . . . Let not therefore the honorable members of Congress allow themselves to be misled by first impressions."[77]

The visit therefore constituted a situation not unlike the situation in Puerto Rico, where the elite vowed to make the Americans "hear the disinterested voice of truth." It is also similar in that the Filipino elite had a new incentive to try to persuade the Americans to realize their goals. Like their Puerto Rican counterparts, Manila-based ilustrados were locked out of the state center, and local officials did not have representation in the Philippine Assembly (for at this time, the assembly had not yet been set up). Still, the elites' efforts did not involve appropriating the Americans' political models. Consider the petitions from provincial officials to the visiting party. Some of these did not even ask for political reforms and instead asked Congress to enact policies that would help them accumulate more wealth (e.g., the suspension of the land tax or reduction on export taxes). They framed these economic demands by familiar idioms of patronage and gratitude, rehearsing the classification of U.S. rule as an "obligation" contracted between Filipinos and Americans: "We beseech you in the name of the province of Cagayan to inform the chief magistrate of our great country, the U.S. of America, upon your return there of our gratitude and of our hopes awakened by your visit, of the affection of this people towards him and of our confidence that he will lead us to our moral and material advancement."[78]

Other petitions and requests from provincial officials did in fact make demands for political reform. A petition from the council of Balayan in Batangas not only asked for economic concessions, it also asked for the immediate establishment of a national assembly, "greater participation in public employments by Filipinos," and "independence with the protection of the North American government." But even as the petition made these political demands, it employed preexisting classifications of political relations. The petition first employed patron-client idioms, expressing its "profound gratitude in advance" for the "favor" of reading and considering the petition. It then justified its political demands by saying: "The stability of a government rests, according to our own experience, on good and adequate laws together with good and capable rulers [*gobernantes buenos y aptos*], without which lack of governmental equilibrium [*desequilibrium*] follows or else general lack of confidence. In view of this principle and to the end that the Filipino heart may be more and more inspired with a confidence in the rectitude [*rectitud*] and sincerity of the aims of the North American government, [we] hereby ask for [the foregoing concessions]." Rather than drawing upon American models of governance, this petition drew upon the Filipinos' own preexisting models. It placed the responsibility for government on the capacity of rulers and made appeals to the rulers' sincerity and "rectitude" — the very category by which the elite classified good rulers who bore razón. It also emphasized that without such rulership, there would be a "lack of equilibrium," another category by which the elite had classified good relations between patrons and clients. Accordingly, the petition ended by promising to maintain the Filipino side of the mutual exchange between the Philippines and the United States, offering its "adhesion" to the American regime if the United States granted the Filipinos' political demands.[79]

The pattern is evident in all of the petitions, requests, and demands made by the Filipinos during the visit. On the one hand, they all tried to persuade the American visitors to grant them not only economic measures that would enhance agricultural production and wealth, but also political measures that would increase the Filipinos' political control and give them more participation in self-government. On the other hand, unlike the Puerto Rican elite, they did not appropriate the Americans' models, concepts, or classifications in their efforts at persuasion. Sometimes they simply made their demands by appealing to the fact that, without them, the Filipinos would not have sufficient participation in political affairs. These made no reference to American models at all.[80] Other demands were framed by references to the "obligation" that the Americans had contracted with the Filipinos. The claim was that the

United States had to fulfill its end of mutual exchange. For example, one petition asked for greater Filipino participation in government and stated: "The American people by taking upon themselves the tutelage of this Archipelago by virtue of the protocol signed in Paris, took upon themselves the obligation of aiding the Filipino people in the establishment of a stable government in these Islands. They can not exempt themselves from this responsibility."[81] Juan Sumulong, a provincial official from Rizal, used the same idioms in a speech he gave before the visiting congressmen:

> We have contracted debts of gratitude with this legislative body [the U.S. Congress], and particularly those members . . . who have been motivated by a true care of our prosperity and interests. We hope that the benefits that we have received from Congress will not be the last ones, and we trust that your experience during this visit, and the resolutions you pass afterwards, will produce reasons for a renewed gratitude toward you. . . . For our part, we will work here so that the Filipinos have more confidence [*confianza*] in the intentions of America.[82]

One petition took its appeals even further than this. The petition was written by twenty-two prominent Filipinos from the Manila area (many of whom had previously failed to get their party platforms recognized), who then presented it to the congressmen during public hearings held in Manila. The petition asked for "independence under an American protectorate" and stated that the Filipinos deserved this because they were already capable of self-government. It then justified the request on the following grounds:

> The political condition of a country principally depends upon the degree of governableness of its people. The more governable the popular masses are the better the political condition of the country. When a people such as the Filipinos give signal evidence of their capacity to obey during a period of over three hundred years . . . it must be granted . . . that they possess the art of government. . . . If the Philippine archipelago has a governable *popular mass* called upon to obey and a *directing class* charged with the duty of governing, it is in condition to govern itself. These factors . . . are the only two by which to determine the political capacity of a country; an entity that knows how to govern, the directing class, and an entity that knows how to obey, the popular masses.[83]

The petitioners went further to say that a division between a directing class and the popular masses would not be tyrannical; rather it would lead to a state of "justice." Explicitly countering the claim that self-government should not be granted because "the ignorant people would be exploited by the intelligent Filipinos," the petition claimed:

> If the country [the Philippines] should have ruled its own destinies, far from being tyrannical — according to the scruples of some people — the government established would have been a model of justice, for neither the culture of the directing class is great enough to impose obedience in a tyrannical sense nor is the culture of the popular masses so wanting as to allow themselves to be tyrannized. It is only where there is positive want of equilibrium between the culture of one class and the ignorance of another that a government is able to tyrannize a people, which condition does not exist in the Philippines.[84]

Not surprisingly, the petition had the opposite effect for which it was intended. While aimed at convincing the Americans that the Filipinos were fit for self-government, it was received by the Americans as yet more affirmation that the Filipinos were not fit. Taft himself later derided the petition. Appalled at the "candor" with which the Filipinos spoke of directing classes, he referred to it as an example of the elites' tyrannical orientation and hence their need for American tutelage. He added: "One important difficulty with the reasoning of the petitioners is in the premise that the small educated class knows how to govern. They need quite as much training in popular government in order to exercise power moderately, justly, wisely and effectively as the common people need of education to make them realize what their rights are under a popular government."[85]

The congressmen present at the hearings were also unmoved, if not altogether incredulous. After the petition was presented, one of the congressmen further questioned Vicente Lukban, a signer of the petition. The congressman was especially curious about the so-called directing class referred to in the petition.

Representative Grosvenor: If it will not trouble the gentleman, I would like to ask him a question. The document to which he refers and a copy of which I have here, and which will be put into the record, refers to two classes, the directing class or class which knows how to govern, and the obeying class or class which knows how to obey. I would like to ask him to which class he belongs.

Señor Lukban: We would not wish to answer that question ourselves because we might perhaps in answering it be considered as immodest and lacking in the humbleness of spirit which we should show, but the mere fact that we have come to this Marble Hall to take part in this discussion would indicate that we consider ourselves, although we do say it, as a part of the directing class. [Laughter].

Representative Grosvenor: Well, that answer could have been put in much fewer words.

Representative Cooper: "Does the speaker think that a republic founded upon [directing and directed] classes such as he proposes can endure? No Answer.[86]

Lukban tried to be "modest" (as he put it), but he remained impervious to the lines of the questioning, paying little mind to the congressmen's incredulity. The record shows that Lukban gave "no answer" to the question and instead dove into an oratory complaining that American officials received a higher salary than did Filipino officials. The response of the senators was recorded by Forbes, who wrote in his journal later that evening: "These fool [Filipino] politicians here bring arguments to show that the Americans are not doing the right thing and incidentally display an absolute ignorance of the real object of the measures they criticize and also of fundamental principles of democracy and of civilization. It was a picture to see the faces of the [American] Senators as these orators progressed."[87] As the Filipino elite continued to domesticate the tutelage situation, the American officials continued to be condescending.

DIVERGENCE EXPLAINED

Studies of local responses to colonialism implicitly run between two poles. On one end, some insist upon the colonized's ability to absorb the ideas and artifacts imposed by foreign intrusion without detriment to their preexisting meaning structures. These works disclose processes of indigenization by which local peoples receive things in terms of their preexisting cultural order, thereby reproducing that order. Other studies, by contrast, insist that colonized peoples quickly adopt what the colonizers offer and thereby expand their cultural repertoire. Charging former studies with "culturology," these works suggest that colonial subjects should not be seen as cultural dupes, forever constrained to reproduce their inherited meaning system. Instead, colonized subjects are better seen as agentic actors capable of casting it off entirely, not least in an effort to better realize their goals.[88] Yet in Puerto Rico and the Philippines, we see both sides of the contested coin. The Puerto Rican elite stopped domesticating tutelage and questioned their cultural assumptions. The constraints of their previously institutionalized cultural system were lifted, and the elite accordingly sought out and learned new meanings. The Filipino elite followed a different path. Even as they complained about the regime and tried to persuade the American authorities to grant them more "self-government" before the establishment of the assembly, the elite continued to employ their previously institutionalized schemas, making sense of their political disappointment in terms of their own preexisting signifying patterns. The possible turning point from domestication to repertoire expansion was thereby averted. The Filipino elite did not heighten their attention to and learn the Americans' meanings, they rather paid selective attention to them just as they had before. While their Puerto Rican counterparts opened themselves up to tutelage, the Filipino elite continued to domesticate it.

Putting both of these processes into comparative light enables us to consider *why* they occurred, where case-specific studies of one or another outcome occlude this question. Why did the Puerto Rican elite expand their repertoire while the Filipino elite did not? The answer does not lie in looking at what happened from the top down. In both colonies, American authorities took the very same steps in the same sequence — intensifying political education and centralizing the state, collaborating with a handful of elites in the center while dismissing others, and establishing a national assembly. Nor does the answer lie in the elites' preferences or incentive structures.[89] On the one hand, the idea that interests and incentive structures mattered is intuitively attractive. After all, retraimiento's failure in Puerto Rico served to displace the Federals from the center of state power. They therefore had an enhanced incentive to adopt the Americans' meanings and regain what they had lost. On the other hand, this cannot explain why the Filipino elite failed to expand their repertoire. The Filipino elite faced a similar situation to that faced by the Federals in Puerto Rico. Before the establishment of the national assembly, they too had been displaced from the center of state power, so they too had an incentive to learn about and deploy the Americans' signs. But they did not. This divergence defies the predictions of an instrumentalist approach to culture.

Did the fact of social disorder and protest in Puerto Rico make for a difference in incentives? True, social disorder was present in Puerto Rico while absent in the Philippines. This could have signaled to the Puerto Rican elite (as opposed to their Filipino counterparts) that their prior schemas were a liability—the unconscious masses would not accept them and vote them out of office. But the problem with this argument is that, while the Puerto Rican elite faced protests from below, those protests did not in fact change incentives. Restrictions on the suffrage meant that the unconscious masses could not vote. Besides, the Federals continued to control municipal posts.[90] Furthermore, while the comparative lack of social disorder in the Philippines might have meant that the Filipino elite had precious little incentive to disavow their schemas, the Filipino elite nonetheless had an incentive to disavow them when trying to persuade the American authorities to grant them independence (as the elite themselves noted). We would then expect a bifurcated cultural outcome in the Philippines to match the bifurcated incentive structure. We would expect the elite to deploy their preexisting schemas when talking to the directed classes while, at the same time, employing the Americans' schemas when talking to the Americans (not least to convince them they were capable of self-government, hence capable of independence). Yet this code switching did not happen. As we have seen, even in the elites' private correspondences with American authorities, they continued to employ their preexisting cultural schemas and narratives of razón when trying to persuade them to help.

The elites' cultural paths diverged not because of interests, incentives, or ruling strategies, but rather because of the differential validation of their schemas. In Puerto Rico, the economic crisis led to a social crisis: the so-called unconscious masses defied the meanings attributed to them by the elite. Furthermore, the conjuncture of the elites' particular party-oriented schemas and the intensification of political education meant that the Americans did not act like the party-based patrons the elite had assumed them to be. The elites' predictions faced recurrent recalcitrance from all sides at once; the very schemas by which they had domesticated tutelage were invalidated. This invalidation was important not because it changed incentives, but because it disrupted the elites' assumptions. The invalidation of their predictions compelled the elite to question the schemas that had guided those predictions in the first place. If the American authorities were not like the Spanish rulers of old, what exactly were they like, and how can we best deal with them? If the "unconscious masses" were not "unconscious," how should political authority regulate them? Recalcitrance thereby set the elite along a distinct cultural path. It compelled the Puerto Rican elite to problematize the situation, adopt a new approach to American authorities in accordance with the reckoning, and thereby expand their cultural repertoire — learning about the Americans' discourse where they had previously domesticated it.

The Puerto Rican elites' repertoire expansion shows that colonized subjects can indeed cast off the constraints of their previously institutionalized cultural system, but only when the predictions registered by that system are repeatedly invalidated from all sides at once. The comparison with the Philippines offers affirmation of this claim. The Filipino elite also domesticated tutelage, thereby registering predictions about it and others around them. But due to their stronger economic base and the lack of party-based schemas, their predictions were validated as tutelage proceeded. The elite had classified the American authorities as better patrons than the Spanish, and the Americans affirmed the classification. The elite had classified themselves as the directing class, and their resource base facilitated the categorization. This validation therefore led to a path different from Puerto Rico. Even before the establishment of the assembly, when the nationalist elite had an incentive to learn about the American authorities' meanings so as to better persuade them (just like their Puerto Rican counterparts), they did not adopt a new tactic of persuasion and initiate cultural learning. They did not question their assumptions of themselves, the "masses," or the American authorities, because the contingent validation of their schemas meant that everything confirmed what they had already presumed. In terms of the meanings the elite made, nothing was broken, so nothing needed to be fixed. As the predictions registered by their schemas contingently proved true, those schemas remained the most familiar and available. Thus the elite continued to employ them, effecting a continued domestication of all the messages and meanings that the Americans offered up.

In brief, due to the differential validation of schemas, the elites' initially similar cultural paths diverged. It is now time to see exactly where those paths ended up.

Chapter 6

STRUCTURAL TRANSFORMATION IN PUERTO RICO

You would see a lot of good things if you went to Porto Rico — good roads, prosperous plantations, children singing the Star Spangled Banner. You will see another thing. You will see a people in a peaceful revolution, fighting by constitutional methods, *by American methods*, for what they believe is right.

REGIS POST, FORMER SECRETARY OF PUERTO RICO, ADDRESSING THE LAKE MOHONK CONFERENCE, 1909

The Puerto Rican people should take from the American people all that is good.... We americanize ourselves by legality, by justice, by liberty.

JOSE AUGUSTÍN APONTE, MEMBER OF THE PUERTO RICAN UNION PARTY, 1908

Close to four years after the Americans had first arrived, the Puerto Rican elite sought out and learned new political meanings. As their prior cultural schemas had been repeatedly invalidated on all fronts, they questioned their assumptions and expanded their repertoire. But in itself, repertoire expansion did not constitute a structural transformation in political culture. The elite may have learned new meanings and models, but they might have then restricted the use of those meanings and models to specific situations, employing them here and there while at other times resorting to their prior schemas. A structural transformation would involve more than this.

It would involve the consistent and repeated use of the new cultural structures. It would mean that cultural users publicly and routinely employ new signifying patterns in and for the same referential fields, using them in sustained practice. Preexisting cultural structures would then be marginalized and replaced, disappearing from social use. At most they would remain as latent capacities, rarely if ever conjured. In either case, prior schemas would be forsaken for new oppositions and contrasts, new categories and narratives, new models and meanings. This would be a true structural transformation in political culture.

This chapter shows that such a structural transformation occurred in Puerto Rico as tutelage proceeded into its latter years. The same Puerto Rican elites who first domesticated tutelage and then expanded their repertoire in the postretraimiento period not only used the new cultural structures to speak to American officials.[1] They also used them as they spoke to each other and to their compatriots. Furthermore, they put newly learned cultural structures into practice, deploying them to make sense of and guide their conduct. The transformation was profound. The Puerto Rican elite refashioned themselves, their own behavior and relations with others, and the very character of colonial politics. American authorities were not lost on the transformation. "It is remarkable," noted the governor in 1907, "how rapidly the people of Porto Rico have grasped the forms and meaning of the American system of government."[2]

This structural transformation in the elites' culture has gone unnoticed in existing studies of elite politics during this period.[3] The goal of this chapter is to fill the gap. In so doing, we will reach an understanding of structural transformation as a particular form of change. We will also come to a richer understanding of how and why it happened in the first place.

TRANSFORMATION IN DISCOURSE

We have seen that the repeated and convergent invalidation of the Puerto Rican elites' schemas compelled them to question their assumptions, learn more about the Americans' schemas, and then use the Americans' own discourse to try to persuade them to act. But exactly how did this new tactic, part and parcel of repertoire expansion, give way to a structural transformation? Part of the answer lies in the Federals' short-term goals. On the one hand, the social disorder and violence against the Federals subsided. The American authorities responded positively to the Federals' complaints about violence and, concerned about the violence themselves, they made sure that the insular police cracked down on it whenever possible.[4] On the other hand, the Federals still remained locked out of the state center. Having learned their lesson that the American authorities would not bend to retraimiento, they indeed participated in the 1902 elections for the House of Delegates, but they fared poorly. During the elections, the Republicans used their appointed powers to ward off a possible Federal victory, employing the familiar tactics of intimidation, party violence, and patronage. Furthermore, the Americans' moves toward centralization and their appointment of Republicans to fill vacant municipal seats seemed to signal that the Republicans were the new government party—or so feared the Federals. "The Republicans throughout the island believed that the Administration was on their side," reported administrator Sweet, "and the Federals believed the story, because their own leaders told them so."[5] The result was that the Republicans again captured about half of the seats in the House, with the Federals having only the rest.[6] The Federals were dismayed. They feared that the rise of the Republicans, if continued unabated, would eventually serve to "declare the death of the Federal party."[7]

The Federals' short-term goal, then, was to win back political posts and restore some of their lost power. To do so, they began a campaign of criticizing the Republicans, hoping to delegitimize their rise. They also hoped to delegitimize the American regime; for, in their view, the putative support given by the regime to the Republicans was part of the reason the Republicans had been able to rise to power in the first place. "Not a day passes," complained the Republicans' newspaper organ, "when a violent and irritating attack on the Republicans appears in the Federal press."[8] "It seems," wrote one Republican leader," that there is a campaign to show that [we] are not capable of leading municipal life."[9]

Yet realizing this goal of winning back power is only part of the answer. The Federals had long sought to regain political power, and they had long criticized the American regime and the Republican party to do so. After the American authorities had first dismantled their privileges, they had attacked the Republicans for being a "minority" party that did not truly represent the will of the familia. They had likewise attacked the regime for presumably lending its support to the Republicans and for thereby undermining autonomía. This is what retraimiento had been about in the first place, and the discourse was a continuation of the criticisms the Federals had registered against the Incondicionales during Spanish rule. It was not new for the Federals to be displaced from power and to want to regain it. Nor was it new to criticize opponents and ruling authorities to do so. The pursuit of short-term goals and the incentives for criticizing opponents had long existed, but structural transformation had not. Therefore, in itself, the pursuit of interests cannot explain why structural transformation occurred at the particular time it did.

The key instead has to do with recalcitrance. As convergent and recurrent recalcitrance had compelled the Federals to question their assumptions, learn the Americans' schemas, and thereby expand their repertoire, the Federals had become armed with new tools. They became equipped with new schemas on governance, politics, and conduct learned and appropriated from the Americans' tutelary discourse. The key to structural transformation, then, is that the Federals pursued familiar goals in this postretramiento period indeed, but recalcitrance and the subsequent process of cultural learning meant that they now had novel schemas to achieve those familiar goals. The shift from domestication to repertoire expansion to structural transformation was a path-dependent process determined by the fact of recalcitrance rather than by the naked pursuit of political power.

Going Public

To see how this process worked, witness first the Federals' public discourse in the postretraimiento period. We have already seen that, in their correspondences with American authorities, the Federals spoke back to American authorities in the Americans' own terms. They learned and then used the Americans' schemas to speak to colonial authorities in their private correspondences. But this practice also gave way to another: the Federals did not simply use the new schemas to complain to American authorities, they also used the new schemas to talk to their peers and colleagues around the island. In this way, rather than restricting the use of the newly learned schemas to particular sites, the Federals put the new meanings and models into public circulation.

The process began as the Federals produced articles and editorials in their major press organs complaining about social disorder. The disorder had subsided, but the Federals could not forget it. Just as they had done in their private letters to American authorities, they reframed social disorder and violence as violations of the Americans' own uttered standards. One editorial seized speeches given by Governor Hunt, in which Hunt had preached against social violence by stressing that "liberty and license are not the same." The editorial used this speech to accuse Governor Hunt of himself encouraging the social disorder: "It is sad to see that a man who has such a clear concept of what 'liberty' is has permitted and cooperated with 'license.' "[10] Another editorial accused the Republicans for instigating violence against Federals in some towns. The editorial then declared: "And [all of this] even as Mr. Hunt in his speeches speaks of the obligatory cliché of progress, of prosperity, and of culture that we have reached and of the guarantees that exist for the security of property and persons!"[11]

The Federals also used the Americans' signifying patterns to publicly criticize the favor that the administration lent to the Republicans. Rather than appealing to autonomía and its associated categories, they complained that the favor violated the Americans' own standards of "rational politics" and impartiality. One editorial complained that the administration had granted loans to Republican districts. This was a typical complaint, and previously the Federals had registered it by claiming that the Republicans were a "minority" party who did not deserve such loans. But this editorial did not employ such categories; instead it referred to Governor Hunt's inauguration speech. After decrying the loans given to Republicans, it exclaimed: "Mr. Hunt has said that his government will be one of justice and impartiality. We want this to be demonstrated."[12] Another criticized the American treasurer, Mr. Solomon, for putatively rejecting the budgets passed by Federal-controlled municipalities while approving those passed by Republican municipalities. "We call the attention of the honorable civil governor and the Treasurer of Puerto Rico to ensure such infringements upon the law, *serving the interests of a political party*, are avoided, while the insular Treasury pays a good salary to Mr. Solomon for a public office which should have *absolute respect to the Law*."[13]

These kinds of criticisms proliferated throughout the Federals' public campaign. Attacking the Republicans, editorials asked their readers: "Had not

Mr. Hunt said in his [inaugural] message of September: 'we now live under the institutions of America, where Government is of the people, by the people, and for the people?"[14] Reviewing Governor Hunt's term of office at the end of his tenure, *La Democracía* claimed that Hunt "acted in every way contrary to his [inauguration] speech" by permitting "the laws to be violated in favor of a party"; by letting the municipal police become "an auxiliary arm of the party to the point that the police acted partially"; and for giving power to "a clique of politicians who are not working for the interests of the country but are only in search of public employment."[15]

The change in the Federals' discourse is remarkable. Whereas they had previously complained about the regime and the Republicans by employing their familiar schemas of autonomía or claims about "minority" parties, they now complained by measuring all events and happenings to the Americans' own standards. The pattern is palpable. If there is a felt dissatisfaction or felt threat to one's interests, see what the American authorities might have to say about it. If a Republican Party member instigates violence, what would the Americans say? If the regime favors the Republicans, what in the Americans' discourse might prove that the favor should not be continued? The Federals' campaign thereby put new cultural structures into place — insinuating them into public discourse where they had not been before and marginalizing preexisting schemas in the process.

A closer look at the Federals' discourse reveals the stark transformation. Consider an editorial that attacked Mateo Fajardo, the Republican mayor of Mayaguez. The editorial reported that Fajardo had been suspected of fraud by the Americans. It then urged that Fajardo be removed: "When a person called upon to be an example of administrative morality is the first to trample upon the law and abuse his office by robbing the state, that person cannot justifiably continue to hold his post, because he has lost all prestige before the citizens and loses confidence that the government has put in him." The editorial also referred to a report made by Samuel Friedman, the investigator of the treasury office. The report claimed that when the Americans tried to investigate Fajardo's activities further, the police of the city refused to help them. Friedman reported that the police stated that they "were not willing to persecute or detain Mr. Fajardo." In response, the editorial exclaimed:

These phrases reveal an inconceivable anarchy; they show an impunity in favor of an alcalde that even the president of the United States does not enjoy, who . . . remains under the action of justice as the most plain citizen. . . . The police [force] of Mayaguez has said: "We are not willing to persecute nor detain the alcalde." What police is this that in such a way understands its duties? What guarantee can be given to the citizens and to justice? What anarchy is this that Mateo Fajardo has introduced to Mayaguez? And the governor, will he consent to this contempt of such magnitude?

Mr. Fajardo should not continue exercising his authority, while above him weighs the accusation of defrauding the State. If not, it would be immoral. *He should be suspended until his innocence shines through the sword of the law.* He is unable, day by day, to represent the government with dignity. And the police [force], which frankly declares that it is only at the service of the person of Sr. Fajardo, while the people pay for them to watch over order and the interests of the citizens, should be expelled. The immorality in administration that corrodes us . . . has to stop *in order that the law is real in this American land.*

We do not know what the governor will think of these scandals which the city of Mayaguez presents. We are only of the opinion that a government such as ours should not shelter nor tolerate such immoralities.[16]

What is novel is that the editorial did not discredit mayor Fajardo on the grounds that he was a member of a minority party. It did not complain that he was an Incondicionale or Republican Party member who unjustly held his position by virtue of favor received from rulers above. It rather discredited him by holding his actions up to the legal-rational models of governance that the Americans had been articulating. Just as Hunt had said in his address that officials should "faithfully administer the law," the editorial complained that Fajardo was "trampling upon the law" and that he should be upheld to the "sword of the law." The criticisms thereby effected a new signifying pattern. It is not that governmental officials are illegitimate when they are unduly appointed and do not represent the people; they are illegitimate when they violate the law.

This transformation in the Federals' discourse was not isolated to complaints about Fajardo. The Federals consistently held up the Republicans to

TABLE 5 Editorials in *La Democracía* Criticizing the Republican Party, 1900–1905
Source: *La Democracía*, two editorials per month

	(1) All Editorials: Percentage Mentioning the Republican Party	(2) All Editorials: Percentage that Refer to the Republican Party and Criticize their Violations of the Law	(3) Editorials Mentioning the Republicans: Percentage that Criticize their Violations of the Law
1900*	58	0	0
1901**	67	8	38
1902	71	29	41
1903	46	42	91
1904***	71	25	35
1905****	25	29	100

*Year of retraimiento
**Year when Federals disavow retraimiento (July)
***Year when Federals, as the Union Party, win the elections for House delegates; Republicans decline in membership and influence
****First year Union Party holds House of Delegates

the Americans' models of law and impartiality, even though they had not held themselves up to them before. One editorial referred to the municipal code to show that the Republican mayor in San Juan, by creating offices for his friends and followers, was in "clear violation of the law." It then equated such violations as "corruption most repugnant," thereby classifying corruption in legal-rational terms just as the American authorities did.[17] The new discourse also classified single-party dominance as "tyrannical" just as the American officials did. One editorial complained about the Republicans' use of the courts for partisan ends and then asserted: "To create district courts which obey . . . the leaders of their political party and not the mandates of the civil or penal code is the height of tyranny."[18]

A random sample of editorials in *La Democracía* from 1900 to 1905 indexes the extent of the new discourse. The sample shows an increasing concern over the Republicans during the Federals' retraimiento period (table 5, column 1). It also shows an increase in the use of legal-rational idioms to criticize the

Republicans (column 2). None of the sampled editorials that mentioned the Republicans in 1898 and 1899 made references to legal standards. Nor did any in 1900, when the Federals initiated retraimiento. Instead, when these editorials referred to the Republican Party, they asserted that the Republicans were like the incondicionales, unjustly receiving the support of Governor Allen. But the references to violations of legal rationality increased thereafter. Indeed, in 1900, none of the editorials that mentioned the Republican Party used legal-rational idioms. But by 1905, any time there was a mention of the Republicans there was also a criticism of illegal activities (column 3). Evidently, the Federals became adept at incorporating the Americans' standards of legal rationality into their public discourse, all the while marginalizing their own preexisting ones.[19]

Self-Reconstruction

Criticism of rivals is one thing. Self-criticism is another. The Federals did both: not only did they hold the Republicans up to new signifying patterns, they also held themselves up to them. Again, the Federals' discourse is revealing. For instance, when the Americans did in fact investigate Mayor Fajardo, the Americans' newspaper the *San Juan News* praised the governor for trying to stop the "spread of corruption in politics" and then articulated typical tutelary discourse: "We [the *San Juan News*] are here to encourage very worthy causes and oppose every wrong. We will not lend our assistance to protect wrong-doing [i.e., corrupt officials], it matters not where it may be found. If Federal officeholders go wrong we are as quick to censure them and ask for their prosecution just as we are in dealing with Republican officials."[20] The Federals' organ, *La Democracía*, responded affirmatively to this article. It reproduced the article verbatim and then tacked to it at the end: "We are in full agreement."[21] The Federals thus deferred to the Americans' own discourse, concurring that they were not outside of the law either. They insinuated that rational politics was a standard to which everyone should adhere, including themselves. *La Democracía* put it explicitly in its discussion of Republican corruption: "You [the Republicans] have governed until now with the sword and fraud; we will govern with order and with honor."[22]

The Federals also classified themselves and their own actions in terms of the Americans' models of interparty tolerance. One editorial first quoted

Governor Hunt's speech, in which Hunt had said that "political differences ought to be based upon measures rather than upon personal prejudices . . . it is the duty of every citizen to practice tolerance toward his neighbor and to respect his opinions though different from his own." After quoting this, the editorial asserted:

> Mr. Hunt makes an appeal to the political parties which seems to us very fitting, and which we sincerely hope may serve as a lesson to our opponents. And it is that more respect shall be paid to the individual; since political agreements ought to be based rather on established facts than on personal prejudices: it being the duty of every citizen to respect the opinions of every other, no matter how far they may differ from his own. This counsel to make politics a matter rather of ideas than of persons is now practiced by the federal party.[23]

The Federals even disavowed their models of patronage and favor amid their criticisms of the regime and the Republicans. "Our party does not ask . . . privileges of any kind,"[24] they said. "The Federal party neither asks nor desires that unjust favors shall be granted to it, it asks and it will always ask that government shall seek the support of honorable men."[25] They thereby classified winning favor and reaping the spoils of office as illegitimate. In fact, in response to Hunt's inauguration speech, one editorial proclaimed:

> The Federal party does not aspire to bureaucratic posts, to live off public employment or favors. The Republicans remain in those posts, and their ineptitude will end by annulling themselves for all public office. Have no fear, then, Mr. Hunt that the federal party will get themselves in with the government and ask of him injustices nor to try to weigh the balance of the law in its favor. That has been the goal of the republican party, not the Federals, always respectful of law.[26]

But if the Federals fashioned themselves through the new signifying patterns, would not their prior meanings of self-government and democracy have been transformed at the same time? To be sure, consider the only editorial from *La Democracía* that tried to define "democracy" in the new context. The editorial was published after the Federals had disavowed retraimiento and as they had begun to incorporate the Americans' models in their own discourse. It began by laying down a broad definition of democracy: "Democracy, as the etymological structure of the word suggests, is the rule of people deciding their own destinies." The editorial then asserted: "But the spirit of democracy is not only found in that formula. Something larger, something more sublime than the rule of the people is necessary to constitute the sacred word, democracy. . . . GOOD [*bien*] is the supreme foundation of democracy." After making this rather elusive claim, the editorial complained about the social disorder and the Republicans' domination of the state:

> Governmental despotism has arisen . . . making the state an instrument of shame, turning liberty into slavery, law into myth, and right into bloody mockery. In the name of democracy the greatest outrages have been committed and lies, pernicious and beheading beliefs have infiltrated the popular arena, in detriment not only to democracy but also to public morals. . . . Meanwhile the democratic ideal has died assassinated by republicans' disorder; falling with it liberty, peace, order and morality. The stick and the sword have been lifted over ideas; the bad over the good; and brutal despotism over democracy. And in this context of evil and anarchy, of swords and sticks, the people cannot be free, prosperous nor happy.

The editorial explicitly equated democracy with "law," which it in turn equated with "public morals." The "democratic ideal," the editorial claimed, has fallen, and so too has "liberty, peace, order, and morality." The editorial then suggested what "true democracy" means:

> Do the people want to be happy, prosperous, and free? Very little is needed to make it so: Educate yourself in the sane practice of true democracy. . . . Respect and consecrate freedom of thought, loving other men as yourself, even though they may hold the most opposed theories and political or religious beliefs. Demand from rulers the faithful compliance with the Law, and from the judges the strict legal administration of Justice. All that constitutes the practice of the GOOD, which is also the practice of DEMOCRACY.[27]

We must recall that the other explicit definition of democracy before U.S. rule had also been published in *La Democracía*. Titled "The Democratic Doctrine," it had been written by the Federals' leader, Muñoz Rivera, and defined democracy as a state in which a jefe rules the collectivity which votes for him and whose conscience, will, and desires the jefe interprets and condenses. But the new editorial suppressed these categories. There is no recourse to old concepts for thinking about democracy. There is no mention of a jefe condensing or interpreting the will of the "unconscious masses," no implication of single-party rule and patronage, no conjuring of the categories that the Federals were disavowing in their public discourse. Instead, the editorial redefined democracy altogether. Incorporating the categories that the Federals seized from the Americans due after experiencing recalcitrance, the editorial classified democracy in terms of respect for "opposed theories and political or religious beliefs," "faithful compliance with the Law," and "the strict legal administration of Justice."

As democracy was reclassified, so too were the procedures for enacting it. Consider a Federal Party circular, distributed by the Federal subcommittee of Arecibo, addressed to the "Federal Farmers of Arecibo." It warned against Republican attempts at vote buying:

> It has come to the attention of this [Federal] subcommittee that some individuals of the . . . Republican Party have been through the district offering farmers oxen, cows, carts, etc. in exchange for a vote in favor of the Republican Party. . . . No Puerto Rican of honor and shame should accept this disgraceful contract, [it] is an insult for those who accept it and a vile trick by those who propose it. Countrymen of the district of Arecibo! *No man of honor sells his vote, the most precious gift of free men.*[28]

While this circular might not be surprising, considering that the Federals had much to gain from stopping the Republicans' electoral bribery, it nonetheless marks a transformation. After all, the Federals themselves had been engaging in vote-buying themselves amid their domestication. Further, the circular did not say that the farmers should accept bribes from their own party members and not from Republicans. To the contrary, the circular put value on the sanctity of the ballot itself, rather than on party affiliation. It was homologous with the Americans' discourse about voting, classifying the ballot as a "precious gift" not to be debauched.[29] It classified the ballot, in other words, with an abstract and external object, something that worked upon people and their actions rather than the other way around. An editorial titled "The Vote," circulated before the 1904 elections, made this equation explicit:

What is the vote? Your personage; your face, your thoughts, your conscience, your sentiment, your soul. And can it be bought or sold? The hand that buys it is dishonor, but more miserable and dishonored is the hand that sells it. [The vote] should signify with honor and dignity your noble aspiration of citizenship. You should transmit through it your conscience, your homage to the patria, your honor of being a man, your Puerto Rican sentiments. The vote will honor you if you honor it.[30]

The Federals also disavowed their concept of elections as a display of party power and intimidation. Party leaders still scripted electoral politics as a "battle," as they had before, but in the new discourse they scripted it as a battle of ideas and principles that had to be conducted with restraint. An editorial in *La Democracia* proclaimed: "The political parties fight to obtain victory in the elections, developing their ideas, combating their adversaries only with the arms of reason, and persisting day after day in working for their country. This cannot be diminished by trying to denigrate persons. [The parties should] educate the people in clear and sane principles."[31] Another editorial even disavowed the old metaphor of political parties as military organizations, suggesting that party members should no longer submit their thoughts and bodies to the party jefe–cum–military general. The editorial was titled "Discipline":

"Discipline." Here is a word which is much abused in the political parties, above all when those parties are not based in honor and justice. Some believe that this discipline has to be identical to that which is used in military organizations, where, rather than by thought [*pensaimiento*], it is necessary to work as a unanimous force of will toward a determined end, attained by absolute moral and material obedience, without adhering to reason nor logical criteria but to the commands of a Jefe who assumes in himself all the responsibilities of the work which is charged to him. Members are commanded and it is necessary to obey. This is discipline. Military discipline. But *political discipline* is another thing. A political group is not constituted like a military body. . . . the political goal is not the military goal. In the army the conscience of those who obey is excluded, only [the conscience of] those who command and assume the right to think [matters]. In politics it is assumed that each citizen has a conscience of their own ideas and by the solidarity of these ideas come political parties. Politics is . . . the science of good government [*la ciencia de buen gobierno*] and it is not assumed that those to whom that good government extends will be simple machines without judgment, without will, who throw themselves to defend an ideal unknown by them.[32]

Muñoz Rivera himself used this discourse in his campaign speech: "Go to the ballot box calmly without prejudices or bastard passions. The same moderation which is shown in political debate . . . must be affirmed in the elections, because we, by reflection and temperament . . . respect the word of law."[33]

The transformation in the meaning of democracy and self-government is most clearly seen in the governmental forms that the Puerto Ricans associated with them after experiencing recalcitrance. As discussed in chapter 5, the Federals referred to the Americans' own traditions and declared the Foraker Act to be an "affront to democratic principles."[34] The Federals then concluded that the Foraker Act should be fixed so as to separate legislative and executive functions, primarily by adding a new elective Senate.[35] The Federals continued with these demands throughout the period, writing public petitions that they then sent to Congress. One party leader wrote: "What do the people of Puerto Rico really want? Self-government. If the people of the United States wish to submit us to a proof of 100 years before making us either a state or an independent nation, let them at least grant us an elective senate appointed by our people."[36] Prior meanings were thus transformed. Whereas the Federals had previously equated "self-government" with the Autonomic regime (which had concentrated powers), and whereas they had previously asked for "self-government" from the Americans according to that Autonomic model, they now asked for a separation of powers and equated it with self-government. As one petition pleaded after demanding a separate Senate: "We desire the opportunity, heretofore denied to us, to show that we are now capable of self-government."[37]

In sum, the Federals effected a profound transformation in their discourse and meaning structures. But why did it occur? As seen, the Federals were precisely motivated. They wanted to discredit the regime and its supporters while heralding themselves as the true bearers of democracía. But these goals were not new. The Federals had pursued the same goals before. What differed, and what led to the transformation, was the convergence of these short-term goals with recalcitrance. Because their schemas had been repeatedly invalidated from all sides, the Federals had questioned their prior schemas and learned new ones, thereby expanding their repertoire. This therefore gave the elite new schemas by which to make meaning of their opponents, of themselves, and of politics and governance more broadly. The Federals aimed to realize familiar goals, but to do so they employed the new cultural means they had learned. And as they did so, they repeatedly employed previously foreign signifying patterns while marginalizing their preexisting ones from the sphere of use.

CODES OF CONDUCT

Still, it is one thing to reclassify the governmental and political world through public discourse. It is another to deploy those classificatory schemes in practice. If the Federals constructed patronage, interparty violence and intolerance, the concentration of powers, and disregard for law as antithetical to good self-government, what about their behavior? Did they employ the new meanings and models as guides for political and governmental conduct? To obtain an answer we can analyze political conduct over time. The period under scrutiny begins in 1902; that is, after the Federals had disavowed retraimiento but still dominated municipal governments. There was a brief period in which the Federals did not control all of the municipal governments in the island (ca. late 1902 and 1903), but things changed thereafter. In 1904, the Federal Party changed its name to the Union Party. The party then emerged victorious in the elections and dominated the municipal governments for the next decade.[38] For tracking the Federals' conduct over time, we would do well to analyze what happened in this period.

An analysis of the period after 1904, when the Federals-as-Unionists emerged victorious, is especially opportune for analytical purposes. On the one hand, the victory for the Unionists was a vindication of the elites' earlier efforts; it was a moment when the elites' power was finally regained. "What can be said after such a splendid victory?" wrote one party member to his colleague. "We should close our lips, raise our eyes to the sky, and pray to God that, for the good of the Patria, never again will the Republicans occupy the seats."[39] Yet, because of this regaining of power, the victory signaled a certain repetition of the past. Putatively, the Unionists became the new government party, just as they had been during late Spanish rule and as they had believed themselves to be at the onset of U.S. rule.[40] The question is whether they acted as such. Even after they finally realized their short-term goal of regaining political power, and after they had presumably become the new government party, did they resort to their prior codes of conduct, speaking the Americans' schemas in discourse but not employing them to guide their political activities? If so, we could easily attribute the elites' change as a temporary one.

Yet this did not happen. Rather than resorting to practices of the past, the party radically altered its conduct in accordance with the new meanings made. As seen, before 1902, the American authorities had complained that the Federal officials used municipal finances for narrow partisan purposes rather than for "good city administration" — attending to "sewers, paved streets, electric lights, fire protection, and efficient police service."[41] This was a symptom of domestication: local officials had been completely "unaware" that attending to public works was "one of their essential functions" because they presumed their role was to cultivate patronage.[42] Yet after the disavowal of retraimiento, the Americans began to notice that municipal finances were being used in the proper manner. "We feel encouraged at the progress," reported the governor. "Municipal budgets are made with better regard to incomes; municipal officials take more interest in public business affairs."[43] This improvement was due not to the fact that the effects of the 1899 hurricane had worn off, but to the Puerto Rican officials' own agency. Governor Hunt declared that municipal improvements had come about because of the "manner in which municipal functionaries discharge the duties intrusted [sic] to them." The insular secretary added that the municipal officials "have displayed a keen desire . . . to distinguish himself by economizing and administering the town effectively," such that "the municipal governments are working much more smoothly and harmoniously than at any time heretofore."[44]

This attention to "economizing" rather than party patronage or "private" purposes continued over the next few years. The insular treasurer noticed that the fraudulent activities and illegal taxes diminished significantly after 1902.[45] The governor summarized in 1905: "Municipal administrations are every year becoming more accustomed to their duties and more familiar with the needs and resources of their towns. . . . As a whole the municipal administrations show a desire to carry on the affairs of their towns on a sound

business-like basis, and an inefficient administration has become the exception on the island."[46] The transformation in conduct proceeded even after the
Union Party had won the municipal seats in 1904. The insular secretary
reported that "No other country . . . can show equal progress in respect to the
administration of local affairs to that accomplished by Porto Rico [*sic*] during
this brief period of five or six years."[47] He continued his praise:

> Almost complete success [in local affairs] has been obtained, until today
> the government of municipalities compare — in respect to the logical dele-
> gation of powers and imposition of responsibilities; in meeting the funda-
> mental problems of democracy, the combination of administrative effi-
> ciency with popular control; in securing a return for sacrifice made in the
> way of payment of contributions [taxes]; in honesty and . . . in efficiency
> of administration — with that of municipalities in almost any state of the
> Union. The accomplishment of this result is one . . . in which the munici-
> palities themselves can take legitimate pride.[48]

American authorities throughout the period registered similar observations: "An improvement is to be noted in the condition of the municipalities
throughout the island, and the experience of the past six years is beginning to
show results . . . in the greater efficiency of the administrative officers."[49]
"The condition of the municipalities in general throughout the island is better than at any time since the establishment of civil government."[50] Local
officials even stopped abusing their authority. The secretary reported that
complaints from American field agents "relating to the abuse of authority . . .
have been very much reduced."[51] He later commended the "comparative
freedom of these local governments from graft and from the control of private interests."[52]

There were also changes in electoral practice. One indicator of this is
quantitative. While the Americans did not keep detailed numeric data on
electoral corruption, they did count the number of ballots rendered void due
to corruption. They did this for the mayoral elections of 1899 and 1906, and
for the elections for commissioner to the United States for 1908. The data are
imperfect, but it offers the best possible insights into the elites' conduct over
time. It also suggests a significant change in conduct.[53] As seen in table 6,
from 1899 to 1908, there was a decrease in the percentages of void ballots (of

total votes cast). Strikingly, the percentage of void ballots decreased even as the actual number of voters increased. Even though the possibility for corruption rose as the electorate expanded, the number of void ballots declined.

Admittedly, these figures are not conclusive in themselves.[54] But qualitative evidence corroborates the numbers. Consider the observations made by Americans like Willis Sweet. Sweet had first served as an administrator in the regime; later, in 1906, he set up and edited his own English/Spanish newspaper, the *Porto Rico Review/Revista de Puerto Rico*. The newspaper often carried field reports on elections, which serve as a good source of information, not least because the newspaper was politicized. Sweet and his newspaper had been critical of the Puerto Rican political elite, so we would expect that if the elite had conducted electoral corruption, Sweet's newspaper would have disclosed it. But an analysis of the newspaper shows that the elites' major parties did not in fact engage in corruption during the later elections.

During the 1910 and 1912 elections, for example, rumors circulated among resident Americans that the Union Party was engaging in bribery, just as the Federals had done in the 1899 elections. These rumors came from visiting American reporters and observers. One such observer, the writer William Boyce, contended: "At an election [in Puerto Rico] I heard of, the price of a vote was $3. The voters received a pair of shoes worth $2 and a hat worth $1. Looking from a hotel balcony at the election crowd, the new white straw hats stood out among the dingy, discolored ones like daisies thickly scattered in a field of brown. One firm was said to have had orders for $600 worth of merchandise the day before the election."[55] On the one hand, it is true that the Union Party collected money for electoral campaigns. A letter sent by the Union leadership to local partisans asked that "persons who pecuniary situation permits send forty dollars or more" to Union headquarters, while "other party members send ten dollars or more."[56] On the other hand, Sweet's analysis suggested that the money was not in fact used for bribes.[57] Sweet concluded that the rumors circulated by the likes of Boyce, noted above, were false: "They [the Unionists] are spending some money, there is no doubt about that, but we do not accept the theory that men like Mr. Georgetti [wealthy and prominent Unionist leader] are deliberately corrupting the ballot. They spend money, of course, but not . . . in buying voters." Sweet also said that "money is always spent in politics" but "there was never any danger

TABLE 6 Protested and Void Ballots, Puerto Rico, 1899–1908

Election	Total No.	Percentage*
1899 Mayoral	471	.91
1906 Mayoral	157,868	.76
1908 Commissioner	158,134	.51

Source: Puerto Rico Board of Elections (1908)
*Percentage is based on number protested and void ballots of total votes cast.

of these young men [the Unionists] corrupting the ballot if they could." Sweet even took a trip throughout the island during the election period of 1910 to observe things firsthand. He concluded again that rumors of corruption were false. After his investigation into politics in the town of Coamo, he reported that "Men are not bought and sold [there]."[58] In the town of Juana Diaz, he found that "Juana Diaz is beyond the reach of schemers or vote-buyers." He also found that although Juana Diaz was a "hotbed of political controversy," and while the "[electoral struggle] has been bitter in the extreme," "the struggle is one of those earnest battles of men, wherein the principle at stake develops the best that is in the people, and victory is sought by appeals to reason rather than to brawls and personal conflicts."[59]

Other American observations (published in the annual reports of the governor, the secretary, and the attorney general) concur with Sweet's discoveries. While reports published by the American administration from 1899 to 1904 are filled with complaints and notes about bribery, fraud, and partisan violence, subsequent reports fail to mention such practices. In fact, these reports replace earlier complaints of corruption and violence with laudatory commentaries on electoral conduct. "I am glad to say," reported the governor after the 1904 elections, "that much improvement was shown over conditions in prior elections, and throughout the [electoral] campaign no serious disturbances occurred in any part of the island. The registration days and election day passed off without a single case of disorder."[60] The secretary added: "On the whole, this election may be considered to have been fairer and carried off with less disturbance than any previous election in the island of Porto Rico."[61] This was the electoral year when the Unionists first entered the scene: if they were the government party, they surely did not act like it.

Reports on later elections show the same trend. For the 1906 elections: "The registration and election passed off with absolutely no disturbance of any kind, and the general feeling was that they had been fairly and correctly conducted."[62] For 1908: "The elections . . . took place with almost complete absence of friction or of criticism or complaint by either party of the manner in which the law had been administered. There can be no doubt that the elections were held with absolute honesty and fairness."[63] Reports of elections thereafter made no mention at all of violence or corruption. Instead, the insular secretary was full of praise:

> The manner in which the elections were conducted, the respect shown by all citizens, not only for the law, but for the rights of other citizens, and the peace and order which prevailed all through the island on election day constitute the best evidence for those who are watching with interest and anxiety the progress of the Porto Ricans on the road toward complete self-government, that the people of the island are fully prepared for the use of the ballot, and for the establishment in the island of a form of government conducted by the Porto Ricans under their responsibility.[64]

These reports were published and public, and therefore must be viewed with some suspicion. But the reports and observations filed in the office of the secretary concur with the published reports. As in the published reports, American observers reported various incidents of corruption and violence from 1899 to 1902, but after 1902 these negative reports decline, and later records reveal no instances of corruption or violence.[65] Amassed with the quantitative evidence noted earlier, the lesson is clear: as the elite changed their conduct in office, so too did they change their electoral conduct.

DEMONSTRATING DISCIPLINE

Still, the political elites' changed conduct might not be surprising. After all, American authorities had taken proactive measures to discipline and punish corruption, setting up a system of surveillance to squash the "personal politics" and "bribery" that had marked earlier years. By this system, they had begun to put guilty officials to trial.[66] They had also instituted the Australian ballot system, adopted by progressive reformers in the United States, which made for tighter supervision over electoral conduct. We might therefore wonder: was the changed conduct simply due to the magic of disciplinary power?

It is not the case that the Puerto Ricans responded mechanically to imposed structures of surveillance and punishment. We have already seen that the municipal officials took active interest in improving the financial condition of the municipalities. They "displayed a *keen desire*" to distinguish themselves, thereby "economizing and administering the town effectively." These officials had not previously been held and tried for corruption, so their changed conduct could not be said to be the result of direct discipline upon their bodies. True, the changed conduct might have been the result of their *fear* of punishment rather than its application. This is how the panopticon works after all. Or as rational choice theories of action might suggest, the new disciplinary mechanisms posed sanctions that made the cost of adhering to old practices too high.[67] But the evidence belies these explanations. If the fear of punishment were at stake, the local officials did not have to display the kind of energy and zeal the Americans attributed to them. If they feared sanctions, they could have simply fulfilled their functions without trying to "distinguish" themselves or without showing a "keen desire."

The elite showed such keen desire — indeed, so much so that they later imposed disciplinary measures upon themselves. After the Federal Party had adopted its postretraimiento approach, municipal officials actively sought out more information on legal codes. As seen in chapter 5, this was part of their attempt to learn more about the Americans and their ways. Whereas municipal officials had previous paid selective attention to the codes, they wrote letters inquiring about the minuscule details of municipal codes and regulations dictating proper conduct. This process continued throughout the period, concomitant with the elites' transformation in political conduct; and the officials did not ask only about regulations or codes which might have led to punishment. They asked whether it was proper for municipal councils to hold special sessions on the budget, whether the mayor should sit as the presiding officer at council meetings, or whether municipal councils could hire gardeners and clerks if those posts were not designated by law. Furthermore, when formulating their own municipal ordinances, local officials soon came to consult the American secretary in the insular government for advice — a practice which the secretary took to be "gratifying" because it showed how eager the officials were to work with, and within, the terms of American governance.[68]

Rather than following the unconscious mechanics of discipline, the elites allowed their changed conduct to be guided by the new meanings they made. That is, the new models of conduct the elite learned were not organized *in* unconscious practice, they were put *into* practice by the agents. For example, one leader of the Union Party holding the mayorship in Mayaguez directly urged his fellow councillors to adhere to the new standards the party had deployed in discourse. In his inaugural speech, he preached against interparty violence and the suppression of minority opinions:

> I hope that my beloved fellow citizens will not forget my sincere declarations and, whether Unionists or Republicans or Federationists, black, white, rich or poor, look in all these men, not as those who come here with hearts swollen of bastard passions or personal hate, wielding ignoble arms of injustice, but look in them as good amigos . . . who feel inspired by the spirit of the good [*bien*] to labor incessantly with the instruments of love, good faith and enthusiasm. All that we should demand from our beloved fellow citizens is support for our honored conduct and help, always inspired in the most high democracy and liberty, in the most absolute order, and in true love to the people of Mayaguez in general.[69]

This official also suggested that there should be an "inspector general" to keep an objective eye on the mayoral position and the councilors. The inspector would "combat all lack of compliance to ordinances." "Immorality and neglect," he added, "should be reprimanded and extirpated with a strong hand and without prejudice, applied where they are found. Morality is the oil that engineers should apply to the municipal machine and all of its dependent parts and all of its circuits."[70] His colleague preached similarly: "We are animated by both a great love and a great hate. By that love, we proclaim the legality of our right, the unity of right and respect to Law; by that hate, we fight all abuses, coercion, and violations."[71]

Consider, too, the elites' approach to elections. As opposed to the early years of occupation, the elite did not treat American supervision of elections as a hindrance or impediment, seeking to relegate corrupt electoral activities to an imagined space outside panoptic view. To the contrary, they *requested* surveillance. For the 1904 elections, for example, Union leaders visited the governor and urged him to ensure electoral propriety. They asked for his assurance that the elections would be conducted "with the greatest possible legality and the complete impartiality of the Government."[72] In addition, as Election Day approached, party members sent telegrams to the governors' office requesting strict policing of the balloting process. Then, after the polling booths closed without scandal, the Unionists praised the police. "I heard one of their orators," noted an American observer, "call for three cheers for the police." Add this to the elites' calls for interparty tolerance and respect for the ballot, and it is not surprising that the 1904 elections were "the first at which no disturbance was reported at any polls."[73] Even later, after the Unionists had won the 1906 elections, party members showed little tolerance for corruption. When rumors circulated that there had been electoral fraud, *La Democracía* declared: "We ask the Hon. Governor and the Hon. Attorney [of Puerto Rico] that they investigate these accusations to uphold the prestige of the law."[74]

The Puerto Ricans' changed conduct was thus shaped by the new cultural models they learned, adopted, and imposed upon themselves. The motivation was precise: they wanted to change their image. To be sure, when the Federals criticized the Republicans and preached against corruption and "respect for law," they framed it as a matter of their "reputation." "We advise ourselves and our correligionarios," said one editorial, "not to commit the same error; as we have said, it would damage not only their interests but also their reputation. . . . We should demonstrate greater energy in the fulfillment of our duties in regards to the respect and reverence to the laws."[75] More specifically, the elite wanted to change their image before the United States. Just as the Federals had learned that retraimiento would not work on the Americans, so too had they come to understand that their prior conduct would do little other than demonstrate that Puerto Ricans were incapable of self-government. "If from your official position you labor for the good of the country," they beseeched to the Republicans, "you will make noble and just those aspirations. But your scandals have brought discredit to the Puerto Ricans in the United States, and with the result that now the press of that country judges us in a way unfavorable and stigmatizes us as poor administrators, inept, uncivilized and little."[76] Corruption would then impede the goal of achieving statehood. "We should demonstrate," said one party manifesto, "that while our adversaries [the Republicans] do not know how to conduct ourselves as true Americans, we Federals have enough to show that citizenship agrees with us."[77]

The elites' changed electoral conduct was especially oriented toward the goal of demonstrating fitness. During a campaign speech, Muñoz Rivera told his partisans and opponents alike: "The elections approach, and it is necessary that all Puerto Ricans, having in view the supreme interests of the country, put its effort in . . . a solemn and ordered demonstration of our culture and civil abilities. On this point, as in many others that effect public habits, the American people is a model people. All the divisions cease when the elections open. And the law shines in all its integrity, always realized with honest and clear intentions, never violated by anyone."[78] A circular distributed by the Unionist Party leadership on the eve of the 1910 elections made the same point, just in more detail:

> Dear Countrymen: The complaints which reach official spheres and the directive centers of the political parties with regard to intransigent actions . . . invite the leadership amicably to call the attention of the Unionist local authorities to the necessity of demonstrating, with the eloquence of deeds, that the Union of Porto Rico never seeks through intolerance the triumph of its ideas and its men. The undersigned *well knows that the accusation of incapacity for self-government*, made against the Puerto Ricans, is absolutely gratuitous; but it is indispensable that *we should relieve our accusers of even a pretext for formulating it*. One of the most beautiful demonstrations of political education is found in the respect shown the ideas and rights of adversaries . . . the elections of 1910 should signify a backward step in the hard-won road to the conquest of our legitimate rights. It rests upon the people, and especially upon the local [party] authorities, to . . . exercise their rights with all tenacity, with all energy, and with all enthusiasm, but with the respect which we owe to the rights of others, and without putting in the way of the adversaries illegitimate obstacles against the propaganda of their principles and the defense of their ideals. The Union of Puerto Rico being a party of order and an association of patriots, the leadership felt no inconvenience in assuring the Honorable Governor, in its name, that the local Unionist authorities, without exception, would fulfill the duties which their office and patriotism impose upon them.[79]

Fittingly, after the election, the party's press organs took pride that the elections had been scandal-free and that their electoral conduct would demonstrate their capacity for self-government to the American people: "The insular government can [now] say to the American administration that here, in this small and beautiful island, the right [to vote] is exercised and the duty is fulfilled by men putting in their actions an overwhelming energy, marching toward serene and tranquil ideals, paying homage to justice and neither disturbing nor wanting to disturb public order."[80] By their dutiful conduct and respect for law and order, claimed another editorial, "we attain the respect and esteem of the American people."[81] Party leader Jose Augustín Aponte added: "The Puerto Rican people should take from the American people all that is good . . . for its own organism. The unionists have given that example in the last elections: *we Americanize ourselves by legality, by justice, by liberty*."[82]

Perhaps nowhere is the elites' attempt to demonstrate fitness seen more clearly than in the activities of the Union Party in the House of Delegates. The Union entry into the House marked the first time that the old leaders of the Autonomist and Federal parties held national office for a prolonged period under U.S. rule, and they were determined to use the House to codify their newfound models. For one thing, the Unionists explicitly rejected any notions that they were the new government party. Soon after the party's entrance into the House, an editorial in *La Democracía* declared that it would not seek favor from the Americans; it then added a subtle critique of colonialism's contradictions: "We have said that we are not a governmental party, because here in this island there is no power for the political parties."[83] Furthermore, the new Union delegates declared that their tenure should serve to reconstitute the Puerto Ricans' image before the metropolitan public. "It is necessary," declared one Union leader, "to show the government and the people of the [American] republic that, having been given in the House of Delegates an instrument for intervention into the regime of the island, we know how to use it, always with prudence and moderation, but also with firmness."[84] In addition, the party stressed that the goal of their labors in the House would be to adopt legislation that served "to adapt the country to the models which, in the American Union, have served for bringing extraordinary progress."[85]

The Unionists' legislation followed. The legislation they introduced was guided by the political models they had been upholding in discourse and conduct. In fact, some of the surveillance measures that might otherwise explain the elites' changed conduct were initiated by the Unionist legislators. In the first year, Unionist delegates introduced a new electoral law: the very first electoral law ever initiated by Puerto Ricans themselves.[86] The law retained the Australian ballot that the Americans had previously introduced, but it added new features aimed at uprooting corruption. It called for more detailed registration lists to prevent fraud, more electoral inspectors representing each of the major parties, more polling clerks, and so on.[87] American officials admitted: the new law was "absolutely bipartisan in character . . . eliminating the advantage which accrued the party which had a majority of the electoral officials."[88] The executive secretary praised it: "There are few, if any countries offering conditions anything like those obtaining in Porto Rico [sic], possessing a general election law under which the people can as honestly and fearlessly express their wishes at the polls."[89]

The House also introduced legislation regarding the municipalities. Control over municipalities by the American regime had been a sore point for the elite, and the House accordingly made some moves to remedy it and restore some lost municipal power. But their bills nonetheless sought to restore lost municipal power along American lines. One of their earliest proposals was to change the municipal system to a county system modeled directly after the county system in the United States. The county bill called for the centralization of certain municipal functions into seven county district boards. Never before had the Puerto Ricans called for such a system. As we have seen, they had rather insisted on full municipal "autonomy" to shore up patronage power, such as the kind of local autonomy established under the Autonomic regime. But with their county proposal, which centralized rather than devolved key municipal functions, the Unionists equated both "self-government" and "autonomy" with the Americans' county system. "The 'self-government' that we ask for Puerto Rico has to be for all the institutions of the country," asserted delegate Jose de Diego, "[therefore] the autonomy of the municipalities is necessary, and because of this we have proposed the Law of Counties."[90] To this Diego added that the law, while originating from the Unionists, was not "unionista, but impartial."[91] Diego's colleague Matienzo Cintrón put it simply: "The form of counties for ruling local life is Anglo-Saxon, and undoubtedly is a superior evolution of municipalities within the principle of decentralized power."[92]

The county bill was rejected by some American members of the Executive Council. While some of them fully supported it (and had suggested it in the first place), others feared that the proposed system was far too complicated to work effectively.[93] The irony was not lost on the Unionists: "It is curious that the men who have come to us, speaking for six years about Americanism, today try to impede the only law . . . that would be truly American."[94] But party leaders were not dismayed. They returned to the drawing board with a more simple system for municipal governments that nonetheless retained the spirit of the county system. It called for strict financial accounting and spending, introduced measures to ensure a separation of powers between the local executive and legislative branches, and dictated that grievances against local governments had to be sent to the attorney general's office.[95] Thus, whereas previously the Americans had complained about the Puerto Ricans' "old habit" of appealing to the executive authorities, the new law changed all that by the Puerto Ricans' own initiative. The Americans were impressed. It was a recognition on the part of the Puerto Ricans that "their protection is in the courts . . . against any illegal or arbitrary act on the part of a municipal administration." The insular secretary added how "remarkable" it was that the Puerto Ricans "have rapidly learned to recognize the separation which exists between the legislative, judicial, and administrative branches of the government."[96]

The Unionists even passed a stricter civil service law. The law was drawn from the law in the United States and was expressly aimed at ensuring that public jobs went to the most capable people rather than "those who had provided services during the elections. . . . With this law will die the seed of political favoritism and only those that have the capacity for it will receive the employment."[97] Again the Americans were impressed, so much so that the governor later made a favorable comparison of the elites' activity to legislation in the United States: "The members of the assembly labored faithfully and zealously to solve the problems presented to them for the best interests of the island. Their work will compare favorably with that of any State or Territorial legislature on the continent of the United States. . . . The work of the assembly deserves the highest praise and demonstrates the encouraging progress that has been made during the past few years in this branch of governmental work."[98] As the elite changed their meaning system and conduct, so too did American authorities alter their initial views of their ability for democratic self-government.

This chapter has shown a remarkable shift. Whereas the Puerto Rican elite initially domesticated tutelage and reproduced their prior cultural system, they radically transformed it in the end. They abjured prior cultural meanings and models and adopted previously foreign ones. They then put the new schemas to use in their discourse and to guide their conduct. The motivation was precise. The elite wanted to demonstrate their fitness for self-government. As the Unionists in the house declared: "Our primary mission is self-government, which is also the principal objective of our conduct."[99] They wanted such self-government in the form of full statehood in the American Union. Jose de Diego declared that he felt himself "an American, a good American" and that "American principles, American laws and American ways of thinking and doing, should be adopted."[100] House delegate Jose Augustín added: "We want Americanization, if that brings to us progress and culture; the expansion of our commerce and the development of our industry. We want Americanization, and with it self-government."[101]

In this sense, an instrumentalist theory of culture would be affirmed. The Americans' meanings and models served as a strategic resource for the elite to better realize their goals. Still, an instrumentalist theory of culture is not sufficient to understand the shift from the domestication to structural transformation. Ever since the beginning of U.S. occupation, the Puerto Rican elite had asked for self-government in the form of statehood. They had always been aware that the Americans were observing them. The interests and incentives for transformation had long been there. But at that time the elites' discourse and conduct was very different. As we have seen, they were guided by the elites' preexisting schemas. Therefore, while the Americans' meanings and models had always been available as a strategic resource, the elite did not always avail themselves of the opportunity. Due to the constraints of their previously institutionalized cultural structures, the elite did not even recognize a difference between theirs and the American rulers' meanings in the first place.

The cause of structural transformation lies not in incentives but in convergent and recurrent recalcitrance in conjunction with the elites' preexisting goals. The elite had extended their prior cultural structures, but the implicit predictions registered by those structures had not proven true. They extended them again and again, yet resistance to their predictions persisted. It was only under these conditions that the Puerto Rican elite sought and learned new cultural structures, retrieving them from the Americans' tutelary discourse. It was only after the constraints of culture were lifted due to the invalidation of their previously institutionalized schemas that the elite questioned their assumptions, rethought the meanings they had made, and then expanded their repertoire. And it was only then that the elite used the newly learned signifying patterns repeatedly, publicly, and in all sites to better realize their goals. The path from domestication to structural transformation was lit not by interests or incentives alone, but rather by the repeated and convergent recalcitrance to the elites' schemas — the very schemas by which the elite had set foot on the path in the first place.

If recalcitrance was indeed the key, however, it would follow that continued validation would have led the elite along a different cultural path, one ending up at a different place besides structural transformation. We will now see that this hypothetical scenario was reality in the Philippines.

Chapter 7

CULTURAL REVALUATION IN THE PHILIPPINES

While the repeated invalidation of the Puerto Rican elites' schemas opened up the path toward structural transformation, the validation of the Filipino elites' schemas led to a different process. As seen in chapter 5, the Filipino elite did not expand their repertoire. They continued to classify the American officials as patrons, fashion themselves to be the "directing class," and narrate tutelage as a matter of razón. Accordingly, while the Filipino elite indeed heard the Americans' messages, they continued to employ their own preexisting schemas to make meaning of them. But is this to say that cultural reproduction continued as well? As the elite continued to domesticate tutelage, were their schemas interminably reproduced at the same time? In this chapter, we will see that as the Filipino elite employed their prior cultural structures as tutelage proceeded, those cultural structures were indeed reproduced, but they were also *revalued*. That is, as the elite continued to draw upon familiar signifying patterns to engage tutelage due to the validation of their predictions, they simultaneously complicated those patterns. This was a cultural change, but it was different from structural transformation in Puerto Rico. It was a change that occurred within an overarching continuity, and a continuity that occurred as change. Rather than abjuring their prior cultural structures, the Filipino elite repeatedly used them; they also modified, elaborated, and extended those schemas in the process.[1] Exactly how did this happen?

CONTINUITY IN DIFFERENCE: DOMESTICATING DISCIPLINE

In chapter 5 we saw that the Filipino elite continued to employ their previously institutionalized schemas to make sense of the Americans' tutelary messages. The American authorities preached about legal rationality as the basis for proper conduct; they preached about the "evils of caciquism," the need for "impartial" politics, and the methods of "free and honest government," but the elite continued to find old meanings in all of it. This continued domestication was due to two factors: first, the strong economic base of the elite and the related persistence of preexisting social relations; second, the conjuncture of the elites' particular schemas and the unfolding of tutelary occupation on the ground. These factors served to validate the elites' schemas and thereby make for a continued domestication of the Americans' tutelary messages.

It should be clear, however, that the validation of the elites' schemas did not mean everything about the Filipino elites' world was the same as it had been before. It is only to say that the predictions registered by the elites' schemas were validated in time. Some change surely happened during American rule. In fact, tutelary colonialism brought a number of alterations in the elites' world, particularly in the political field. First, unlike before, the Filipinos were allowed to hold elective provincial offices. During Spanish rule, these offices had been held by appointed Spanish officials. Filipinos had held positions only at the municipal level. During American rule, though, the Filipino elite were given more official powers than before, and their powers were more extensive. Not only did they hold municipal posts, they were also put into provincial positions, thereby ruling over wider domains. Second, the Americans inaugurated the Philippine Assembly. There had not been an insular (or national) assembly during Spanish rule, and while the Malolos regime had had a similar assembly, it had not been regularized. By contrast, American rule enabled the Filipinos to hold national legislative seats for a sustained period. This further extended the domain over which the directing class ruled. The final important change was that American officials put an emphasis on undoing political corruption to a degree that the Spanish authorities had not. As seen in chapter 4, American authorities intensified their efforts in surveillance and punishment. The Executive Bureau was put in charge of investigating corruption and trying cases, and over time its work steadily increased. In 1903, for instance, the bureau filed close to 150 cases. By 1910, the number of filed cases more than doubled. "Practically all the time of three lawyers in the executive bureau," complained Worcester, "is taken up in examining evidence and reports of administrative investigations of charges against municipal officials."[2] Furthermore, the American governor-general retained the right to remove local officials if found guilty of impropriety, and the governor often put the privilege to use. "Much of my time now," wrote Forbes in 1909, "is taken hearing the evidence in cases of maladministration in the municipalities. I have the power to remove any office and disqualify him from holding any office, and everyday I either suspend or remove and often disqualify several."[3]

In light of these changes, American rule was a new game entirely. But what is remarkable is that, despite the foregoing changes, the Filipinos continued to engage offices and elections in familiar ways. Just as they continued to domesticate the Americans' messages due to the repeated validation of their schemas, so too did they continue to engage tutelary institutions by employing those schemas. This is worth investigating further.

The continuity in the elites' conduct is partly disclosed in data collected by the Executive Bureau. The data runs from 1903 onward, referring to cases filed against local officials suspected of corruption and the number of officials actually found guilty.[4] As noted already, the Executive Bureau increased its work over time and filed more and more cases. But the data shows that there was a contemporaneous increase in the number of officials actually found guilty of corruption. Cases filed correlated with numbers of found guilty (see figure 2). Of course, the increase in guilty verdicts may have less to do with an actual increase in corruption than an increase in the bureau's activity. The correlation between cases filed and guilty verdicts suggests this. But the correlation also suggests that, at the very least, corruption did not subside over time. If anything, corruption was probably more endemic than the data suggests, for the data refers only to those instances of corruption that the bureau was able to uncover.

Qualitative evidence affirms that corruption proceeded unabated. While American reports on Puerto Rico praised the Puerto Ricans for "grasping"

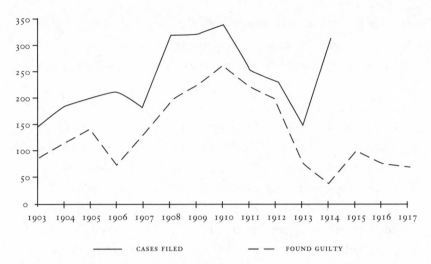

FIGURE 2 Political Corruption in the Philippines, 1903–1917 (Municipal Officials)*
SOURCE: *Report of the Philippine Commission* 1904–1918.
*List of Charges: "Neglect of Duty," "Abuse of Authority," "Violation of Election Laws," "Malversation, etc.," "Extortion, etc.," "Bribery, etc.," "Crimes of Violence," "Slander," "Bad Habits, etc.," "Forgery, etc.," "Ignorance, etc.," "Interference with Religious Affairs," "Larceny, etc.," "Others"

American ideas and "methods," and while they stood amazed at the decrease in corrupt activities, contemporaneous reports on the Philippines disclosed continued corruption. Secretary of War Dickinson investigated both Puerto Rico and the Philippines in 1910 to find that, in the Philippines, "caciquism, i.e. local 'bossism,' is just as potential now as ever."[5] Investigative commissions traveling throughout the archipelago in the 1920s found that "caciquism" and "corruption" were "seething" in nearly every province.[6] While these reports were published and public (and are therefore worthy of skepticism), even personal journals and memos circulating within the regime reveal the same thing. Years after the bureau intensified its activities, for example, the chief of the law division filed an internal memo on a problem that had vexed the regime since the beginning — "illegal taxation" and "voluntary contributions." The report found that such practices were persistent and widespread, "more or less general throughout the islands."[7] In response, the authorities issued memos to local officials condemning the practice, but, as the law division complained, the practice persisted nonetheless.[8]

American authorities also found a range of associated "abuses of power" across the island. They found that local officials continued to use the police force as their own personal henchmen, that they exercised influence over local Filipino courts through patronage, and that they continued to employ office for what Taft called their own "private emolument."[9] Authorities also found that local officials continued to use patronage to cultivate and sustain their networks of personal exchange. "When there is a native in authority," lamented Forbes in 1905, "he usually has some one perfectly unsuited whom he wants to promote. Usually a pariente [relative]."[10] Six years later, in 1911, Forbes found that this remained to be the case, concluding that the Filipino officials "haven't wakened up to the fact that a new order of things is in effect."[11] Even the new provincial offices became sites for political corruption. Though the provincial seats were new, Filipino officials practiced them as they had practiced municipal offices, using them as nodal points in local circulations of exchange and acting as if they were grand patrons to their districts in disregard for formal law:

> The provincial governor is regarded by a large proportion of the people of his province . . . as a personal guide, philosopher, and friend. To him go his followers for advice regarding family and business affairs, to get a relative out of jail, or to ask for jobs for themselves or their *parientes*. The governor's authority is still thought of as having no limit, and he is often besought to intervene in judicial matters and otherwise to exert arbitrary power in behalf of faithful supporters and their friends.[12]

In turn, provincial governors received loyalty and deference from their clients, personally commanding services of all kinds from them. Forbes discovered that provincial governors were able to command the labor of municipal officials in their districts, recording with astonishment: "At Barcelona there was a fine school building without a roof, as the [municipal councillors] couldn't be persuaded to do anything. [The Governor of Albay] went over there himself and stood over the . . . municipal council for four days while they . . . built the roof with their own hands and free of charge."[13]

The Filipino elite also continued to engage the new elections as if they were not really new at all. Reports in the *Manila Times*, the main American-run newspaper of the time, are suggestive, confirming the consistent complaints about electoral conduct in the American officials' reports (table 7). In

TABLE 7 Newspaper Analysis of Electoral Corruption, 1902–1916

Year	No. of Articles Analyzed	No. Mentioning Corruption
1902	12	6 (50%)
1906	14	11 (78%)
1912	16	6 (38%)
1916	25	16 (64%)
Total	67	39 (58%)

Source: *Manila Times*

1902, half of the articles from field reporters that discussed elections also mentioned corruption. This proportion is the same that the Executive Bureau estimated for the same year: the bureau reported corruption in "about one-half of the municipal elections."[14] For the next electoral periods, the proportion of articles referring to corruption increased with only one instance of decrease (in 1912).[15]

Other data are affirmative. In 1907, the Executive Bureau began to report the number of electoral contests and allegations of corruption demanding investigation. Electoral "contests" are those elections in which the outcome was questionable due to violations of the law; "allegations" refer to charges of corruption in elections where the outcome of the election would not be changed by a guilty verdict. The bureau does not offer percentages or disaggregate information, it gives only the total number. But the raw numbers can be used for a longitudinal analysis because, after 1907, the total number of elections for each year was the same (all municipal, provincial, and national elections). The data confirm that corruption persisted (table 8). In fact, from 1909 to 1919 the raw number of contested elections that demanded investigation doubled. Unlike Puerto Rico, the increase roughly correlates with the increase in registered voters (figure 3).

What the Americans called "corruption" thus persisted in the Philippines. The fact that reports from American authorities on Puerto Rico were filled with praise, while the same types of reports from American authorities on the Philippines (often, as in the case of Dickinson's report, from the exact same authorities who reported on Puerto Rico) continued to find corruption is a critical index of the difference. But if so-called corruption indeed continued

TABLE 8   Election Contests and Allegations of Electoral Irregularities, Philippines,
1907–1919

Year	Contested Elections	Allegations	Total
1907	211	missing	incomplete data
1909	223	166	389
1912	451	183	634
1919	467	473	940

Source: "Reports of the Executive Bureau," in *Annual Reports of the Philippine Commission* (1907–12) and *Annual Reports of the Governor-General of the Philippine Islands* (1912–19).

in the Philippines, what about the new institutions and mechanisms of discipline that authorities imposed? Did not these have an effect of abating the elites' practices? Surely, the Filipino officials were not unaware of the disciplinary mechanisms. Forbes recorded in his diary that provincial officials sometimes suspended their corruption when placed under the "direct supervision" of an American field agent. Therefore, "wherever supervision was relaxed, the old order of things [would] immediately crop up again."[16] Taft claimed that some municipal officials sometimes felt "restraint" from abusing their power due to "fear of inspection by the central government and its prosecution."[17] At least some Filipino officials, then, had a sense that corruption was not acceptable. In fact, Filipino officials themselves sometimes registered charges of corruption. The Executive Bureau received charges not only from American field agents but also from Filipino officials against *other* Filipino officials.[18]

Still, the evidence suggests that discipline and punishment did not have a widespread, sustained, or consistent effect, and in this sense the situation remained very different from Puerto Rico. First, while Forbes found that some local officials suspended their corrupt activities when in the presence of Americans, he also found that many local officials continued to act as if their corruption was perfectly acceptable. In 1905, for instance, Forbes had complained that the officials tried to use their power to grant positions to friends, family, and followers. Four years later, when Forbes assumed the position of governor-general, he was dismayed to find the persistence of the practice while noting that most local officials conveyed little shame about it. Forbes

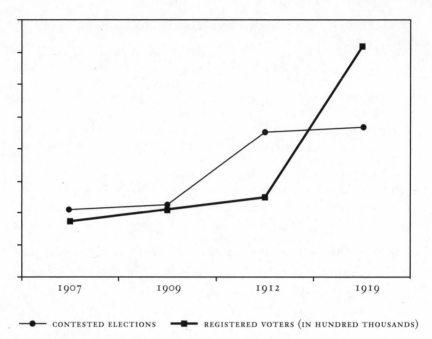

FIGURE 3 Electoral Protests and Number of Registered Voters, Philippines*
SOURCE: Table 8 and RPC 1910: 54; Forbes 1928: 2:118.
*"Electoral Protests" = total electoral contests

recorded that one provincial governor wanted his brother appointed to a recently vacated gubernatorial post. The provincial governor was "very insistent about my giving that brother a job he was unfit for merely on the ground he was his brother, considering that a qualification rather than a disqualification." Forbes was also appalled to find that other forms of corruption persisted and that "there is no public opinion against it."[19] Other observers found that "the use of public office for purpose of bribery and graft is very general . . . and is in no public sense a dishonorable thing. Graft is almost a prerequisite of office."[20] Similarly, Taft complained that when local officials restrained themselves from corruption at all, it had little to do with the "fear of condemnation by the public opinion of the local community . . . even if the official is to seek re-election."[21] Again, the contrast with reports on Puerto Rico is remarkable, suggesting thereby a real continuity in local elite conduct.

The charges of corruption registered to the Executive Bureau by Filipino officials are further indicative. The Bureau reported that Filipino officials registered charges against other officials, but it also noted that, upon investigating the charges, the charges were legally unsound. "The natives of these islands, especially those of the half-blood [i.e., mestizos]," wrote the secretary of the bureau, "are by nature contentious . . . and a preliminary inquiry usually shows the charges preferred to be groundless."[22] The bureau did not say more on the matter, but this discovery is suggestive in itself. To say that a charge was groundless was another way of saying that it did not have a basis in the Americans' legal and administrative codes. That is, the Filipinos were either unaware of the legal codes or were operating from a different code altogether, one that eluded what the Americans called corruption. A look at the available evidence suggests the latter rather than the former.

Consider one such "groundless" case in 1913, fifteen years into tutelary rule. In that year, the governor of Capiz registered charges against Filipino Justices of the Peace (JPS). The governor's complaint was that when he visited the JPS, they had failed to "salute" him, even though his "visits were frequently announced."[23] Of course, this was hardly corruption as the Americans defined it, which is why the Executive Bureau dealt with the complaint by a letter stating: "The theoretical principles of democracy prevailing under this government do not require such courtesies as a matter of law."[24] But in local conception, giving a salute was much more than a matter of courtesy. During Spanish rule, so-called courtesies such as salutes were ways of showing deference and respect. They were not unlike the decorations and orders of nobility bestowed upon officials during the Spanish and Malolos regimes — signs that the recipient bore razón. Thus, not to offer such salutes or tokens of deference was to suggest that the official did not bear razón. In local meanings, this would be a serious offense indeed.

Consider another charge of corruption. The charge was registered in 1907 in the city of Iloilo by a man named Quintin Salas. The accused was Benito Lopez, the governor of Iloilo province. Salas accused Governor Lopez of corruption because Lopez had "failed to satisfy the expectations of Salas." Specifically, according to Salas, Governor Lopez owed him a "debt of gratitude," but Lopez had not paid his debt.[25] This, too, is suggestive. A "debt of gratitude," translated into Tagalog as *utang na loób*, referred to a clientelistic debt. It meant that one had to reciprocate so that the exchange would be mutual. Salas's accusation that governor Lopez owed him a debt of gratitude but had "failed to satisfy" was in this sense an accusation that Governor Lopez had violated the law of razón.

These cases reveal that the Filipino elite continued to classify corruption as they had before: as a violation not of formal legal codes but of the natural law of mutual exchange, the law of razón. "Every practice contrary to . . . reason [*razón*] and truth," Apolinario Mabini had said in the 1890s, "is properly an abuse, that is to say a corrupt practice, since it corrupts society."[26] A Tagalog civics text written in 1905 further attests to the persistence of this meaning of corruption. In his *Mga Katuiran ng Filipino* (*The Reason/Right of the Filipinos*), Lopez wrote:[27]

> If any leader does not know how to give to his subjects, one can bring an action against him to a higher leader on account of his shortcomings or one can shout to all so that everyone can unite toward overthrowing him from this position or replacing him with someone who knows how to respect his subjects, and if the highest leader fails to satisfy he should defend and clarify to himself and to all the law [*katwiran*] that he violates in order to make everyone understand his mistake, because law [*katwiran*] is the freedom that is not only made into a duty, but the real cleansing of the people.[28]

Lopez claimed that a leader who deserves to be removed from office is one who "fails to satisfy." This is similar to the term that Quintin Salas had used when charging the provincial governor with corruption: the governor had incurred a "debt of gratitude" but then "failed to satisfy." In this scheme, a patron was a bad patron when he violated the tenets of mutual exchange, and on this ground should be removed from office.

This meaning is further disclosed in Lopez's claim that a leader who deserves to be removed from office is one who violates *katwiran*. Translated into English, this term meant "law," but it does not translate exactly as the "law" that includes official legal codes, or secular and manmade law such as the kind that the Americans instituted. Had Lopez wished to conjure this meaning of law, he might have used instead the words *batas* or *kautusan* instead of *katwiran*, signifiers that also referred to law at the time. But Lopez instead used the signifier *katwiran*, which made for an important difference. *Katwiran* meant "law," but it translated more precisely into something else. In popular folk idioms at the time, as Ileto shows, *katwiran* referred to the "light" or "straight path" which an upright political leader must follow, as opposed to the evil and deceitful path taken by those who do not adhere to mutual help and exchange.[29] And as we have seen in chapter 3, *katwiran* also translated into Spanish as *razón*.[30] Lopez thereby suggested that, by following the "straight path," by adhering to katwiran/razón, a political official would bring happiness and satisfaction to his people, just as a patron would bring happiness and satisfaction to his clients. And as long as the official adhered to katwiran/razón, and therefore as long as the official satisfied the people, the official should stay in office, regardless of whether or not the official violated formal legal codes.

In short, the validation of the elites' predictions not only led the elite to continually employ their prior schemas to receive the Americans' messages (as seen in chapter 5); it also led the elite to continually employ those prior schemas to also engage the new forms and mechanisms of political education. What the Americans called "corruption" thereby persisted as before — if only because, for the Filipino elite, it was not quite corruption. While the American authorities classified corruption as transgressions of legal-rational codes, of a lack of self-restraint and self-discipline, the elite classified it as a matter of salutes and razón, of debts incurred and not paid back, of bad patrons who did not satisfy. Contra Foucault, and in stark contrast to what happened in Puerto Rico, even the mechanisms and modalities of discipline were domesticated, rendered meaningful by local schemes.[31]

CONTINUITY *BY* DIFFERENCE: CULTURE REVALUED

We can now approach an understanding of cultural revaluation. On the one hand, as seen above, the elite persisted in employing their previously institutionalized cultural schemas, in both discourse and political conduct. On the other hand, the continued usage of prior schemas happened in a changed context: tutelage brought new institutional forms. The elite employed validated schemas, but in a changed field of referents. This led to a certain kind of cultural change. As the elite employed their prior schemas in the new context, they revalued them to meet the exigencies of the new context. Revaluation happened not in spite of the changes but through them. This revaluation can be traced by examining the elites' activities in two specific sites: (a) elections for provincial and national positions, and (b) the Philippine Assembly. As these sites were the major political-institutional changes initiated by tutelary colonialism, it is fitting that they are also the sites wherein revaluation can be seen.

Provincial and National Elections

Consider first the electoral field. As noted, elections continued to be marked by so-called corrupt practices as tutelage proceeded. Bribery, electoral fraud, and factional violence persisted — guided by schemas classifying politics into patrons and clients, good rulers and bad rulers, and different factions and networks of exchange (thus guided by classifications of who could be intimidated, threatened, or treated as objects of violence). These schemas of conduct had been forged and employed during Spanish rule, when elections had taken place at the municipal level. It is therefore puzzling that electoral corruption persisted during U.S. rule, for elections during U.S. rule were entirely new when compared to Spanish rule. First, American officials added new rules to prevent electoral corruption. The electoral law supplemented the existing Australian ballot system by adding yet more features to "forbid . . . acts of intimidation and corruption as manifestly strike at the root of our electoral system."[32] For example, to prevent fraud, registry lists had to be kept in triplicate, and to prevent intimidation, incumbent municipal or provincial officials could not run for the same office again.[33] Such rules had not existed during Spanish occupation, and when they did exist they were rarely if ever heeded.[34]

Another innovation was that elections during U.S. rule took place at an unprecedented spatial scale. Rather than occurring only within the municipality, they covered the entire province or assembly district, exceeding traditional municipal boundaries. Therefore, the elections entailed a new level of impersonalism. During municipal elections, candidates had benefited from long-standing personal relations with most of the electorate. In some municipalities there had been only twenty-three qualified voters; at most there were two hundred.[35] "Everybody knows everybody else in these towns," reported one American agent. There was "an intimacy of acquaintance" during elections.[36] This intimacy surely facilitated schemas of mutual exchange and the practical use of preexisting patron-client networks, but for provincial and national elections, such "intimacy of acquaintance" was not possible. In order to win office, candidates had to win votes from electors across multiple municipalities, securing the support of people with whom they had not had personal direct relations. True, personalized exchange with voters was still manageable to a certain extent, given the fact that the electorate was restricted to wealthier and educated residents. Until 1907, the electorate for provincial elections consisted only of municipal councilors and mayors (presidentes), such that there were sometimes only five hundred voters. Still, after 1907 the voting base was expanded to include not only local officials but also all prior officials, the literate, or those who met certain property and tax requirements.[37] This extended the scope of electoral action far beyond the Filipino elites' previous experience.

In short, provincial and national elections during U.S. rule were a new game entirely. Given the new game, the so-called bribery, personal intimidation, factionalism, and fraud conducted during municipal elections would appear to have been much more difficult to carry out. Prior schemas of conduct, rooted in face-to-face patronage with voters, faced clear impediments. Still, what is most curious is that the Filipino elite continued in all such practices despite the new scale and scope. As noted earlier, the conduct evident during municipal elections was also carried out for national and provincial elections, and corruption increased with the expansion of the electorate. How was this possible? How did schemas of personalized exchange persist in this new context? It is here where we can see revaluation.

Consider the following confidential report on the 1912 elections for provincial governor in Bulacan. The report was made by an American officer of the constabulary force who witnessed the election first hand:

> The election in the province of Bulakan [sic], where I went to view it near at hand, clearly demonstrated to me the need for a severe lesson. . . . The voters who lined up in front of the polling places, and before entering the booth, each carried a written ballot on which appeared the names of the candidates for whom they were going to vote so that the election inspectors could copy those ballots, but unfortunately instead of copying those ballots the inspectors wrote on the official ballots the names of the candidates they wanted, the result being that the men elected were not elected

by the will of the voters but were candidates of the inspectors. In each election precinct . . . [Teodoro] Sandiko [one of the candidates] had at least one inspector and in some precincts in addition to the inspector he had even the secretary of the Board of Inspectors and that is the reason why the members of the Sandiko faction are always elected . . . all this is due to the fact that the inspectors were bought before the election. Francisco Mendoza [rival candidate] also made use of this method and in [the town of] Bocaue, where that candidate had only a few voters obtained by paying their personal *cedulas* [taxes], he got a majority of the votes because he had bought two inspectors, one in each precinct, and each of these two inspectors were worth more than sixty votes.[38]

The officer stated that "this occurred in all the towns which I visited," from Mindoro to Pangasinan to Rizal. Others reported that it happened across the archipelago, over and over again. In some instances, the bribed election inspectors did more than change the names on the ballots, they also prevented voters of opposite factions from casting their votes. They also stuffed ballot boxes, or simply added votes from thin air when the verbal tallying was too close for their comfort.[39] It was a "system of corruption that staggers one," Forbes wrote in his journal.[40]

The Filipino elite had always conducted bribery during municipal elections. It was a manifestation of personalized exchange between patrons and clients; in this case between candidates and electors. But as seen in the foregoing reports, bribery during provincial elections was somewhat different. Rather than occurring as a series of exchanges between candidates and voters, it happened between candidates and election *inspectors*. Candidates, rather than cultivating personalized relations of exchange with the expanded electorate, simply cultivated personalized relations with the new key people in the electoral process. The inspectors, not the voters, were "bought before the election."

The example discloses a twofold process constituting revaluation. On the one hand, there was cultural continuity. The schema employed to engage provincial elections was the same as before — as ever, patrons sought clients to help win elections. Furthermore, the use of the schema also had the same effect of domestication. In the Americans' plan, the election inspectors were supposed to be objective and nonpartisan, "performing their duties under the

Election Law without prejudice or favor toward any person, candidate, party, society, or religious sect," but the Filipino elite indigenized the new structure by turning the inspectors into clients.[41] This thereby cut at the heart of the "gr-r-eat Austr-r-ralian ballot system" (as some Americans joked), and vulgarized "the real purpose for which [the Australian law] was instituted."[42] On the other hand, these continuities were concomitant with and made possible by a certain change. To meet the new spatial scope of elections, the Filipino elite employed preexisting schemas of personalized exchange by refocusing them to special sites. That is, they strategically refocused the schema to encompass not voters but election inspectors. This was a *new* use of a prior schema. The old schema encompassed new people in new structural slots (e.g., inspectors), but in practice the new people were nonetheless classified by old categories and oppositions, as clients of a patron.[43] This was a continuity that unfolded as a change, and a change that unfolded as continuity. The elites' patron-client schemas were revalued.

The same process, however occurring through different means, is noticeable in the gubernatorial campaign of Benito Lopez of Iloilo, a prominent urban merchant and attorney from a landowning family. The beginning of Lopez's campaign involved the same practices that had marked campaigns for municipal elections: Lopez held a series of social gatherings at his house with municipal officials (the voters in this case) from his immediate area, and then offered favors to the municipal officials in return for their vote. But then, to reach out to municipal officials and voters in distant locales, Lopez elaborated by employing a friend to help him. Lopez offered the friend legal services in return for the help, thereby turning him into a client. He then gave the new client 500 pesos, which was to be "divided in the different towns" by the client. The new client, in other words, was to bribe voters himself on Lopez's behalf. Lopez also instructed him to send other municipal councilors to his house, where he held yet more banquets and offered favors in return for their vote. He collected the names of his guests on cards of paper so that "he might have a remembrance of them and know whom to thank if he won" — that is, so he could recall whom he had bribed.[44]

This case further shows revaluation of patron-client schemas. Lopez did not suppress a patron-client schema when he campaigned, he extended it in new ways. To reach a distant and impersonal electorate, Lopez hired a client who in turn acted as a middleman. Lopez thereby established a relationship of exchange with this particular person, and in turn the person established a direct series of exchanges with voters. Personalized exchange remained the key schema. The only difference is that the schema was extended to encompass more and more people and create a larger following than before, constituting a larger translocal network of exchanges. Patrons were still patrons, clients were still clients. It is just that the patron-client cluster was turned into a patron-client pyramid.

This was common during the new elections, which is exactly how the so-called bribery evident in municipal elections also happened during provincial and national assembly elections. Candidates, for example, held illicit gatherings and "costly entertainments" at their home, just as candidates had done so for municipal elections previously; the only difference was that candidates used middlemen to cart in potential voters from distant localities. The voters were brought in from near and far, arriving in carriages, horses and, later, automobiles.[45] Their votes were then bought. During the provincial elections in Rizal, votes were reportedly going for 5 pesos apiece.[46] In addition, middlemen used their candidates' money to pay taxes of potential voters so that people otherwise disqualified from voting could vote for the middleman's candidate. As before, then, candidates who could not even read or write registered to vote, which explains why, in one election for the Philippine Assembly, a reporter from the *Manila Times* saw some voters "trembling" as they wrote the names of their candidates on the ballot. When the ballots were later read aloud, nonsense words like "balacayo-Ten you" were heard, as was another word which sounded strangely like "Buffalo Bill."[47]

The revaluation of the elites' prior schemas in these ways carried new dynamics that nonetheless followed from the old. For example, given the new spatial scope, candidates could not always rely on granting personal favors to the countless new clients voting for them, and they therefore had to use money. Money had been exchanged during municipal elections, but with the provincial and assembly elections, it became all the more important. American agents were shocked by "the amount of money expended by the candidates in making their several campaigns." The result for some candidates was unprecedented financial trouble. One candidate had to mortgage his home to secure the necessary funds, "and the morning after election found himself beaten and bankrupt."[48] Another had to sell at least 312 hectares of land worth 50,585 pesos over the course of 1901 to 1908 to keep his gubernatorial campaigns going.[49] Furthermore, even when candidates promised personal favors and not only money to secure clients, this itself caused new trouble given the new scale. Eager to initiate exchanges with new voters, candidates made promises they could not keep. In 1906, "in each municipality not less than six to twenty different persons were promised the appointment of justice of the peace and the notary public," and "one or more from nearly every municipality was promised the fat plum of provincial secretary, even though the vacancy in that position was by no means a certainty."[50]

It followed that intense competition, intimidation, and violence persisted as before, but on an expanded scale. Benito Lopez, for instance, instructed his middleman to tell those who did not want to partake of his bribes that he would prosecute and jail them. For this, Lopez promised to use his brothers, all attorneys whom "everybody feared."[51] Similarly, Mary Fee observed that the governor of her province jailed members of the opposing factions before election day.[52] Administrator Forbes added that the jails in Cebu were used "for election purposes" only — "Nothing showed up maladministration more quickly than a study of the jails, and I never missed a chance to go in [during my inspection tours] and look at them."[53] As the *Manila Times* put it: "The aspirants for local office in the provinces . . . have friends to serve and enemies to punish."[54] This intimidation (compelled by the refusal to engage in reciprocal exchange) thus led to violence. In Bulacan, voters who "refused to vote as instructed by the agents of one of the candidates for Governor" were "chastised with a club and a small riot resulted."[55] A decade later, in 1912, similar incidents were reported across the islands, leading observers to conclude: "Political rivalry has too often amounted to violent hostility."[56] As schemas of personalized exchange persisted by their revaluation, so too did their concomitant opposite — the dark side of idealized reciprocity.

If the elites' previously institutionalized schemas persisted by being extended in new ways, there was also a related dynamic: the elites' prior categories were elaborated upon. Preexisting signifying patterns were continuously used, but they were internally complicated to render alterations in the field meaningful. This is seen in the use of middlemen. Soon after the first series of provincial and national elections, American observers noticed that new political actors, whom the Americans referred to as "campaign managers," populated the political field. According to reports, these were the "friends" of candidates who busied themselves "getting out the vote."[57] These actors had not been present for municipal elections; logically so because they were necessary only for the provincial and national elections, and they were the very middlemen whom we see in the cases above. A classic study by Mary Hollsteiner found that the Filipino elite called these new characters *líders*. The translation of this term into English is "leader," but in local terms it meant someone who "[is paid] by candidates with favors which can in turn be distributed to his followers." Not surprisingly, Hollsteiner dates the emergence of these characters to the American period.[58] New categories thereby emerged but they followed from preexisting cultural structures.

This categorical elaboration is further seen in the proliferation of political parties for the provincial and national assembly elections. In the early years of U.S. rule, the dominant party was the Federal Party, but neither that party nor any other was important for municipal elections. Candidates were merely members of the municipality's various factions and clans — representatives of one or other patron-client cluster in the town — and party labels were not needed. But as candidates extended their local circulations of exchange at the municipal level to meet the expanded spatial scope of the new elections, so too did the local factions at the municipal level extend. Through middlemen and the new forms of bribery, patron-client clusters in one town were connected to clusters in other towns to form patron-client pyramids. The pyramids were then given names. They became political parties, and the name of the party was used to distinguish between them.

In the town of Taal, for instance, two leading families had dominated politics during late Spanish rule: the Agoncillo and the Marella/Villavicencio families. Extended kin of these families then competed for municipal offices during early American rule, but for the Philippine Assembly elections in 1907, they expanded their influence using middlemen to encompass surrounding towns. The Agoncillo faction, joining with other local families, became the party called Bando Ibaba, referring to their influence in the southern region of the province (*Ibaba* meaning "below"). The Marella/Villavicencio faction extended their influence to the north to became the Bando Ilaya (literally, the "upper band").[59] Similarly, in Pampanga, the two major candidates ran under different party names, but in actuality they represented two different factions that had previously operated only at the municipal level.[60] In Cavite, gubernatorial candidate Leonardo Osorio ran under the party umbrella of the Nacionalista Party after he and an already existing Nacionalista member agreed to join forces. The Nacionalista member had already cultivated strong translocal ties and offered his campaign machine to Osorio for a "considerable sum." In this way, Osorio joined the party.[61] Furthermore, Hollsteiner found that one municipal official joined the Progressista Party in 1906 only because "he owed a debt of gratitude to them [the leaders of the party]." He owed an utang na loób.[62] It is not surprising, therefore, that political parties besides the Federal Party proliferated the scene only after the Americans had introduced Provincial and National Assembly elections.[63] Nor is it surprising that the new parties did not differ significantly in policy or platform. As they were loosely formed pyramids effected by new translocal exchanges, they centered around the candidate/leader of the party. "Political parties based on opposing principles of government have not yet crystallized," noted the executive secretary, "so that politics and the personality of the politicians are indistinguishable."[64] In short, as patron-client schemas were extended or refocused in practice, so too were new categories elaborated upon in the process. New categories emerged to refer to new things — middlemen and líders, the Progressista Party, the Bando Ibaba, and so on — but the new categories were simply logical extensions of preexisting cultural structures.

The Philippine Assembly

The foregoing processes constituting revaluation during elections are also evident in the elites' new Philippine Assembly. As seen in chapter 4, the Philippine Assembly served to validate the elites' classification of the American officials as true patrons realizing razón. The elite therefore extended to the officials their debt of gratitude. But as the inauguration of the assembly validated the elites' schemas, so too did the elite engage the assembly by revaluing those schemas. To see this, it is helpful to first situate the new assembly in relation to the elites' historical experience.

Like the elections just discussed, the inauguration of the Philippine Assembly marked a significant change in the elites' world. Before American rule, there not had been such an assembly. The Congress of the Malolos regime had been a wartime congress, primarily devoted to writing the Philippine Constitution. By contrast, the assembly during American rule offered Filipinos the first chance to participate in national legislation for an extended period, and in direct engagement with American officials. True, by the Malolos government, the Filipino elite had developed categories for national legislative activity. Mabini classified the Malolos legislature as a site for the bearers of razón. While all branches of state would guide the "social body" (the web of mutual and interlocking personal exchanges constituting society), the legislative branch was to "guide and direct" the others. It was the "intellect" of the social body; it alone could ensure "the greatness of society and the well-being of its members."[65] But because the legislature was not instituted for a sustained period, we have yet to see how the assembly as the institutional site for razón could have actually worked in a peacetime setting.

The issue is a curious one indeed. Local officials had scripted themselves as bearers of razón. They had classified themselves as the patrons of their districts, initiating and sustaining the mutual exchanges by their "intelligence," paternalistically and personally attending to the directed classes in their respective localities. But in the context of the new Philippine Assembly —whose jurisdiction covered the entire country, and not just one municipality or province— how could such classifications of rulers, and such personalized relationships with clients, actually work? Assemblymen, unlike municipal officials before, were responsible for multiple municipalities, each populated by people with whom they did not have personalized relations. Surely this expanded scope of governmental action would have posed limits to the realization of razón.

In addition, the American authorities intended the Philippine Assembly to be another key site for political education, thus a site in which prior meanings and modes of conduct would be erased and replaced. Taft claimed that the assembly was to be "the most important step" in tutelage, a critical stage in the Filipinos' political development.[66] It would force Filipino assemblymen to formulate legislation under the Americans' guiding hand, giving them "a most valuable education" in the "science and practice of popular representative government." One of the things the assemblymen were to learn, for example, was the principle of formulating and legislating with "sane judgement," informed by "practical information."[67] This meant basing legislation upon national statistics. Bills were to be based upon expert knowledge and objective facts — using information from the recently finished census — to constitute what the Americans called "intelligent legislative action."[68] All appropriation bills were to take the treasury into strict account, and bills for infrastructural development were give funds to local governments when and where they were most needed. The Americans hoped that most money should go to districts where roads were too short for comfort, or where they were in a "disgraceful condition" and in need of repair.[69] Governor Forbes himself maintained various lists and figures, all laying out budgets and expenses, highlighting where roads and other infrastructure were necessary, and projecting "progress" over time. Accordingly, at the inauguration ceremonies in 1907, the American officials gave speeches stressing that the assemblymen should "legislate wisely" in the "onward march of civilization." They laid out various economic and social statistics from the census, highlighting the need for infrastructural development and suggesting where, when, and how central funds should be spent.[70]

The assembly was novel. Yet, from the beginning, there were signs that it might not be so novel, and that its educating function might not be realized. At the inauguration ceremony, after the American officials had made their speeches, the Right Reverend Jorge Barlin (the first Filipino Bishop after the Spanish had been ousted) gave an invocation. The invocation intimated a model for legislative action very different from the one the Americans had just offered:

> To Thee, O Most High Creator, omnipotent, sole King great and most terrible, who reignest with eternal majesty over the universe . . . as the one Lord God, who created it with Thy power . . . to Thee, Word of God on Highest, in whom the light of intelligence exists from eternity . . . to Thee, Fount of Wisdom, whose currents are eternal commandments, from right and from justice, for man and for States . . . to Thee, O Father of Light, from whom cometh every perfect gift . . . to Thee, by whom rulers govern with wisdom, and law-givers decree just laws, and the princes and the heads of peoples command good things, and the judges administer justice; we invoke Thee to-day, in the great day of our history, in the day when the Filipino people . . . come together for the first time to deliberate over their future destinies. *Shower on their noble representatives the abundance of Thy*

gifts, light on their intelligence, firmness on their will, rectitude, nobility . . . so that they may decree what will be good and useful for the people, that which will contribute to their greatest happiness and greatness, which will make them walk always in the path of true human progress, to the glorious summits of sound liberty.[71]

Pedro Paterno, the man who had asked that "decorations and orders of nobility" be given to local officials, heard these words. He had been elected to the assembly. So too had a number of former Malolos officials, some of the ilustrados who presented their justification for self-government to the 1905 visiting party, and former municipal and provincial officials.[72] We can imagine, then, how these assemblymen must have basked in Bishop Barlin's words. They must have sat proudly hearing his claims about their "intelligence," "rectitude," and "nobility"; about how God sanctions them to do "what will be good and useful for the people"; about how God will give them the light of razón/katwiran by which to "walk always in the path of true human progress." They must have taken it as an acknowledgment of the privileged status which they had been claiming for themselves; an approbation of their self-fashionings as the bearers of razón. Perhaps this is why the assemblymen stood up and gave victorious applause to Barlin's invocation. It was "the first time," wrote Forbes, "I ever heard a prayer clapped."[73]

We cannot hastily conclude that the elite classified themselves or the assembly in this way. But at least two sources suggest that Barlin's invocation was indeed taken in the light of razón. Consider first an essay by Macario Adriatico (former provincial governor who was then elected to the assembly). In 1917, Adriatico published an essay that employed the discourse of directing classes and popular masses exactly. He referred to Filipino officials as "the directing class," and the title of his essay was "Our Directing Class, or the Aristocracy of the Intellect." He also reiterated the notion, raised at the 1905 hearings with U.S. congressmen (see chapter 5), that the existence of this directing class was not a liability for good government. It would not, for example, lead to "tyranny" in the Philippines because "There would be no clashing of interest [between the directing class and popular masses]. On the contrary there would be mutual dependence among the several elements of which [society] is composed." Adriatico then used the same classification to talk about the Philippine Assembly. "There rarely happens anything in which the beneficent influence of the intellectual element, that is, the directing class, cannot be observed. . . . There is hardly any provincial governor or municipal president who is not an intellectual person, and the intervention of the directing class is most evident and patent in our Assembly."[74] Notably, Adriatico uttered this statement ten years after the assembly had been first inaugurated. Apparently, the new spatial scope of the assembly in practice had not disrupted prior classificatory schemes.

Adriatico was not alone in domesticating the assembly. A passage in Honorio Lopez's civics text, *Marunong ng Pamahalá sa sariling Bayan* ("Wise Administration of Our Country"), published in 1915, referred to the assembly in this way:

> *Question.* what are the duties of all deputies [in the assembly]?
>
> *Answer.* To make laws and represent the people for the good of all. The responsibility [*kautangang*] that should be fulfilled by all representatives [*kinatawan*] is to express the sentiments of the people that they represent and they are the first to know what is good for their fellowmen. Honor [*karangalan*] is necessary for the deputy.[75]

Lopez stressed that the assemblymen "are the first to know what is good for their fellowmen" and that they should "represent the people for the good of all," an idea that situates the legislator as the privileged bearer of razón. Only the legislators know what is best, and therefore only they can "represent" the people. Moreover, Lopez used the word *kinatawan* for "representative," a word which conjures the social body that Mabini had discussed previously. It is derived from *katawan*, meaning the "body," such that the literal translation of *kinatawan* becomes "one who 'does' the body." The implication was that assembly members enact and animate the body and give it life, just as Mabini had said they should.

The categories employed by both Adriatico and Lopez further affirm what we have seen in chapter 5. The elite continually employed their prior schemas rather than seeking out new ones—in this case to render the new assembly meaningful. But a closer examination of the assembly adds something more. It shows that as the Filipino elite continually used their prior schemas, they modified them. Indeed, to meet the new scope of the assembly, the elite further complicated their prior cultural structures. They did so, first of all, by extending them to a national scale, creating patron-client pyramids covering the entire archipelago. This is seen if we examine the assembly's legislation. On the one hand, much of the legislation passed by the assemblymen in the first three years was oriented toward securing funds to build roads, schools, irrigation works, and so on.[76] This pleased the American officials, who were eager to see infrastructural development. On the other hand, the assembly did not only pass bills to build roads and schools, they also passed bills that aimed to control appointments to the bureaucracy; to enable provinces to remit, suspend, or postpone land taxes; to audit the accounts of the (American) Insular Auditor; and, in general, to secure various powers of controlling and distributing resources. The assembly even tried to secure money for seemingly ridiculous purposes, such as when they passed a bill providing 34,000 pesos to send a delegate to the International Navigation Conference in St. Petersburg. The bill was ridiculous, because by the time the bill had been passed, it was too late for the delegate to attend the conference.[77]

It is as if the assemblymen did what the American administrators before 1907 had refused to do: offer surplus to local officials. Occupying the central seat of power previously monopolized by the American commissioners, the assemblymen tried to distribute resources down to the local level so as to engage in mutual exchange with local politicians. Indeed, assemblymen were already locked into mutual exchanges with many local officials: that was what the corruption and bribery during elections was all about.[78] The assemblymen had come into office through votes delivered to them by local officials; they were therefore indebted to those officials. Their legislation was aimed at meeting the debts — call it pork barreling.[79] The assemblymen acted if as they were bearers of razón, just as local officials did for their districts, engaging in "mutual exchange" and "mutual help." The only difference was that they engaged in such reciprocal exchange with provincial and municipal officials, not commoners. Thus, the schema of razón was reconcentrated and extended outward at once. It was reconcentrated on local officials and, as the local officials were distributed across the islands, it was extended outward at the same time to cover the spatial scope of the entire nation.

But then, if the elite were exchanging only with local officials, razón was not exactly razón. According to preexisting discourse, the enactment of razón by the legislature should serve and ensure "the greatness of society and the well-being of its members." Pork barreling, such as seen in the assemblymen's legislation, hardly served such an end. The assembly passed legislation beneficial to themselves and to their network of friends below, but not to commoners. How did such intra-elite patronage serve society and its members as a whole? More specifically, how could Honorio Lopez claim, as he did in his 1915 civics text, that the duty of the assemblymen was to "make laws and represent the people *for the good of all*?" How could the elite still boast, as Macario Adriatico did, that the assemblymen, as the directing class, ensured the "mutual dependence" and mutual exchange between social elements?

In elite conception and practice, more was going on than pork barreling. Return to the assembly's legislation. As we have seen, the assembly passed bills that provided infrastructural funds to give to local governments. But it should also be noted that those bills were also structured so as to give local officials autonomy to decide precisely where those funds should go (e.g., to roads or to schools), without consent or supervision from above. These provisions brushed against the Americans' plans for legislation, for the Americans wanted infrastructural funds to be earmarked based on statistical data. The Bureau of Public Works counted the school-age population and compared it with the number of school seats in each province, measured road mileage province by province, and tabulated which roads needed repair by counting the number of wheels which passed over each road, and so on. Assemblymen, as part of their political education, were supposed to have used this data when crafting their bills.[80] But contrary to that political rationality, the assembly produced legislation such that local officials and local officials alone should determine where the funds could go. Bill no. 559 sought to quadruple the amount of funds spent on local infrastructural projects, but made it so that those funds could be spent by local officials without the direction of the Bureau of Public Works. Bills no. 505 and 660 of the second legislature sought to place the supervision of public works administration strictly in the hands of a provincial official not responsible to the dictates of the Bureau of Public Works.[81] As Speaker of the Assembly Manuel Quezon said, the goal was to "grant the provinces autonomy in the expenditure of their funds."[82]

So zealous were the assemblymen in these efforts that they often legislated for large public works projects "without due regard to the available balances in the treasury."[83] They also passed a range of other bills that gave complete autonomy to local officials, such as bills which placed education in control of municipal boards, allowed municipal councils to fill their own vacancies, gave municipal presidentes (mayors) the right to appoint police in barrios and rural areas, take away the supervising controls of the provincial treasurer, and so on.[84]

All of that is suggestive. As we have seen in chapter 3, local officials used the surpluses they accrued in office to carry out personalized exchange between themselves and the so-called popular masses in their respective locales. They used public funds in the treasury, or otherwise collected tribute, then expended those funds as they saw fit. The assemblymen were aware of these practices. Over half of them had served in local governments themselves. In a sense, then, the assembly's legislation was surely a kind of pork barreling, but it was more specifically a way of enabling and ensuring the local operations of razón. Through their legislation, the assemblymen provided local officials with surpluses, and the autonomy to use those surpluses as they saw fit, and the local officials in turn inserted those surpluses into local circulations of mutual exchange. The assemblymen tried to create the conditions under which razón could best function, allowing personalized exchange at the local level to be realized and perpetuated further. This was a new logic of social regulation, but it was structured by familiar schemas.

The Filipino elites' explicit discourse indeed conceptualized their legislative activity in this way. Adriatico referred to the assembly as "the nerve center of modern society . . . the meeting place of the men of privileged intelligence, because just as the health of the individual depends largely upon the proper organization of his nervous system, so does the welfare of a people almost always depend upon the proper organization of its legislative power."[85] Thereby activating Mabini's classification of the legislature as the site of the intellect/razón, Adriatico fashioned the assemblymen as "the men of privileged intelligence," and he imagined the assembly itself as the "nerve center" (i.e., the brain) of the body. In short, he classified the assembly as the center through which the multiplicity of nerves in the body are organized and processed, the organ of the body that facilitates and regulates the nervous system of exchanges. The assembly was the nodal point of interconnected circuits of idealized reciprocity, the site through which the circuits of exchanges in society were processed and regulated.

This was how the assembly functioned in practice. Into the assembly came votes and supports from officials at the lower level of the state; out of it came surpluses to the local officials in return. Those surpluses were then placed into local circulations of "mutual dependence" and "mutual exchange" by the local officials, ostensibly to realize the people's "welfare." In effect, the assemblymen, unable to carry out the terms of razón through personalized relations with the people, created a new patron-client pyramid, one extending across and melted into the hierarchical structure of the colonial state itself. By such practice, they classified themselves and their actions as serving the benefit of all. By ensuring that the natural law of mutual exchanges in the social body was realized to its fullest, the elite also claimed that they were securing "the greatness of society and the well-being of its members." They claimed, as speaker of the house Manuel Quezon did, that "the record made by the Philippine Assembly, as a legislative body, shows conclusively that its foremost interest is to promote the welfare, uplifting, and liberty of the masses."[86]

This respatialization of exchange relations in practice, however, also brought with it categorical elaboration. By classifying themselves as the ultimate bearers of razón, and by creating a patron-client pyramid extending across the national level, the legislators created a new categorical hierarchy. At the top of the hierarchy were themselves, the assemblymen or national legislators. Adriatico therefore claimed that while local officials and assemblymen together constituted the directing class, the assemblymen were of a higher strata. The assembly, he said, is where "the cream of the intellectual element of each province or district is gathered."[87] Similarly, Pedro Paterno, in his 1910 civics text, referred to the individual assemblyman as an *hombre de estado*, literally a "man of state." Such a man of state "sees far and procures well-being [*bienestar*], not only for the present but for the distant future," while, lower on the scale, local officials attended to "the necessities of the moment."[88] Honorio Lopez referred to the assemblymen as the *kinatawan*, which means, as we have seen, "one who enacts or 'does' the body," one who gives life to its nervous system of exchanges. Lopez had not used that term to refer to the local officials, and fittingly so, for by the cultural structure extended (and then categorically elaborated), only the assemblymen had the privilege of enacting the social body through their regulations of razón.

Such categorical elaboration is seen further in a parallel term that Honorio

Lopez used to refer to the assemblymen. He called them the *makapangyari-han*. Lopez had not used that term in his 1905 text to refer to the local officials, and in fact the term is not found in dictionaries before the inaugura-tion of the assembly.[89] What was the meaning of this term?

Makapangyarihan derives from the word *kapangyarihan*, a word that had been used before in the Philippines to refer to "power." But as John Sidel's rich analysis of the term shows, *kapangyarihan* as power had long referred to a specific kind of power: "the spiritual substance which animates the universe and [which] is often concentrated in certain power-full beings and objects."[90] Leaders of villages in pre-Hispanic and early Hispanic times — the *datus* — were believed to have had access to such power. Through "supernatural feats and bravery in battle," or through the "provision of sumptuous feasts," the datus showed that they had the prowess to access *kapangyarihan*, which meant that they had the privileged ability to secure surpluses from outside of the community and then distribute it in the community for benefit of the village. As Rafael (1993b) intimates in his discussion of these practices, only one who could access *kapangyarihan* could successfully initiate war and trade with other villages and bring back its booty — booty which one then distributed to the villagers to initiate personalized exchanges with them and, in effect, natu-ralize oneself as a village leader.[91] Uses of the word at the time of American occupation connoted something similar. During the revolution, generals and commanders wore special amulets that putatively lent them the cosmologi-cal power of *kapangyarihan*. Wearing the amulets, the general or leader of the troop was supposed to have the power to magically deflect bullets and blows. As Ileto notes, General Aguinaldo was known for channeling this kind of power.[92]

Makapangyarihan, the new word used by Lopez to refer to assemblymen, therefore translated more precisely as "one in power" or "one who has access to power." In referring to assemblymen as such, Lopez scripted legislators as the modern embodiment of barangay leaders from the past, and the political embodiment of revolutionary leaders who could deflect bullets. The term connoted that assemblymen had privileged access to outside surpluses which could be distributed locally. In fact, informed by a new Filipino historiogra-phy which (re)invented precolonial villages as Tagalog kingdoms embodying justice and the protection of rights, the assemblymen in the American period expressly tried to show their historical continuity with the datus of the past.[93]

Adriatico scripted himself and the directing class as the modern embodiment of the datu precisely. "Our directing class," he says, "has derived its gifts of government from the past, because the chronicles tell us that in the infancy of our people, the directing class. . . . was nothing but a best friend [the datu] of the *barangays* [villages]." He asserted further: "Through the Legislature . . . it [the directing class] has achieved the preservation of order, the development of education, the improvement of roads, bridges, and public buildings, the introduction of sanitary or hygienic measures, the creation of a National Bank, the establishment of irrigation systems, the revision of the codes . . . the nationalization of railroad, and the adoption of measures of all kinds for the welfare of the community."[94]

Adriatico classified assemblymen as the ones who introduced new infrastructural developments to their local communities by their privileged access to the state center, just as the datus of before had brought in surpluses attained through their access to the cosmos/outside power (the kapangyarihan). The colonial state itself, in this meaning, was the new source of kapangyarihan which only the assemblymen — the makapangyarihan — could access and use to initiate mutual exchange. Fittingly, one of the Tagalog words used today to refer to the national state is *kapangyarihan*. Typically associated with pork barreling, the term specifically refers to the surplus in Manila from which assembly members draw and by which they provide resources to their local districts.[95] As Sidel notes, "*Kapangyarihan* still constitutes an essential basis for the legitimation of powerful individuals' authority in Philippine society."[96] Accordingly, this equation between the national state and kapangyarihan was first made during the American period, after the establishment of the Philippine Assembly.

REPRODUCTION AND REVALUATION IN CONTEXT

This chapter has shown that as the Filipino elite engaged tutelary offices and elections, they continued to extend their preexisting cultural structures. As they domesticated the Americans' tutelary discourse, so too did they continue to domesticate the institutional forms of political education. Yet the continued use of those prior cultural structures also brought with it an alteration in the structures. This was a cultural change indeed. The elites' political culture was not exactly the same as before. Prior cultural models of conduct were re-spatialized as the field itself was respatialized; schemas of exchange reached

TABLE 9 Paths of Meaning-Making

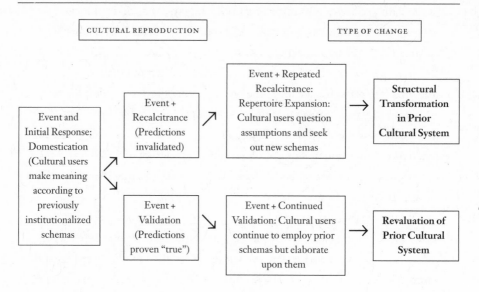

| CULTURAL REPRODUCTION | | | TYPE OF CHANGE |

beyond the immediate locality, outward and upward, or they were put to new use at new focal points in the electoral process, concentrated to specific people and sites. New categories and terms emerged, just as new things, structures, and people emerged in the new referential field. The makapangyarihan, the hombres de estado, the "cream of the intellectual element," and the kinatawan populated political discourse where they had not previously; while líders and middlemen emerged in electoral discourse where such categories had not been articulated in earlier days.

The change cannot be overlooked, but neither can its particularity. Cultural change occurred, but it was a change that unfolded as continuity, and a continuity that unfolded as change. While cultural structures were complicated, the overarching system of parallels and contrasts in the cultural system remained. Categories like the makapangyarihan, the hombres de estado, the "cream of the intellectual element," and the kinatawan surfaced indeed—as did líders and middlemen—but all of them remained subcategories within larger ones, delimited by the same overarching parallels and contrast as before. The makapangyarihan were still part of the directing class as opposed to the popular masses, *líders* and *middlemen* still referred to clients of patrons, and political parties were still patron-client networks. While schemas of personalized exchange were refocused to particular people and sites, or expanded to encompass larger spatial scales, they were still schemas of personalized exchange fashioned as mutual — in opposition to the use of force or the failure to pay a debt owed. Unlike in Puerto Rico, the elites' preexisting categories and schemas were refocused, extended, and elaborated upon, but they were not disavowed.

Existing scholarship on the Philippines has already intimated that the first decade of American occupation did not bring a radical transformation in the elites' political culture and conduct. It thereby suggests that cultural reproduction was the hallmark of American rule. But this conventional wisdom must be elaborated. First, reproduction did happen, but it also happened as change. It is not as if a deeply engrained Filipino culture persisted. Reckoning revaluation enables us to capture reproduction while also recognizing it as a form of change. Second, the fact that reproduction-as-revaluation occurred raises the question of *why* it occurred. This is a question that existing studies have not sufficiently addressed. By putting the Philippines into a comparative frame, our analysis offers an answer. The explanation does not lie in an essential Filipino culture, it rather lies in the contingent validation of the elites' schemas. In contrast to the Puerto Rican elite, the Filipino elites' resource base was much stronger during American occupation, so the social relations by which the elite had previously forged their cultural schemas persisted as before. The elites' self-classification as the directing class was affirmed in practice. Furthermore, unlike those of the Puerto Rican elite, the Filipino elites' schemas of self-government did not involve political parties, so the Americans' ruling strategies did not undermine the predictions the elite had made of them. The elites' predictions of tutelage — registered by their initial domesticating activities — were thereby affirmed. Their schemas were reinstitutionalized in time, so those schemas remained the most available, familiar, and retrievable. The result was that the elite never questioned those schemas and instead continued to use them to make meaning, thereby remaining impervious to tutelage's lessons. The only difference from before was that they modified and elaborated upon the schemas in the process, thereby meeting the political changes wrought by tutelage (even if those changes did not bring recalcitrance). Due to the affirmation of the elites' predictions conjoined with shifts in the political field, everything happened as if nothing had changed — and everything changed as if nothing had happened.

RETURNING TO CULTURE

Exploring the cultural dimensions of tutelary colonialism in Puerto Rico and the Philippines, we have seen that tutelage entailed exercises in cultural power. American officials employed signs to win hearts and minds while striving to manage, manipulate, and marginalize meanings they did not prefer. We have also seen the limits to this power. The elite in both Puerto Rico and the Philippines accepted tutelage's signs, but only as they domesticated them, thereby reproducing their preexisting cultural system. We have further seen that this initial domestication eventually gave way to different forms of change. In Puerto Rico, the elite questioned their initial assumptions, expanded their repertoire, and effected a structural transformation. By contrast, the Filipino elite continued to domesticate tutelage while revaluing their prior schemas at the same time. To illuminate all of these dynamics, this book has elaborated upon an approach to culture that apprehends it as a semiotic system-in-practice. Rather than conceiving of culture as subjective values or beliefs, a strategic resource, or an easily malleable substance molded by states from the top down, we have analyzed culture as a systematic repertoire of schemas, narratives, and classificatory codes that agents use to make meaning of the world, render the world intelligible, and navigate their way through it.

It is time now to review, clarify, and elaborate. We will return, first, to the question raised at the outset. What was the role of culture in tutelary colonialism?

CULTURE AND TUTELARY COLONIALISM

In some ways, inquiring into the role of culture in colonialism harkens back to traditional studies of the Philippine-U.S. colonial encounter. These studies examined culture, but they treated it in structural-functional terms. They therefore saw tutelage as a manifestation of American values and democratic beliefs and suggested, by implication, that tutelage was an exceptional imperial project reflecting America's supposedly "exceptional" political culture and "national character."[1] Subsequent scholarship has rightly pointed out the deficiencies of this approach. Speaking of culture as values is to run into essentialism. It is to presume a coherent "American culture" and problematically portray U.S. rule as uniquely benign. One alternative has been to shift the focus and disclose the violent and exploitative character of tutelary rule, thereby disavowing questions of "culture" altogether. Other scholarship, part and parcel of postcolonial analyses, has disclosed the racialized categories underwriting tutelage (reframing culture as "colonial discourse") or the ways in which the presumably static and coherent "American culture" was reworked by the colonial experience itself.[2] This alternative work therefore offers new ways of rethinking tutelary colonialism and critiquing its presumed exceptionalism.

This book joins the critical spirit of this latter work but its goals have been slightly different, if not more humble. Rather than eschewing an analysis of culture or reorienting our focus to the culture of the metropole (or the "discourse" of the colonizers), it has tried to wrestle back a place for examining culture and meaning without carrying the problematic conceptual baggage of traditional scholarship. By treating culture as a matter of cultural structures and meaning making, for example, we have seen that tutelage was indeed shaped by culture. It was not shaped, however, by a cohesive or essential "American culture" (as if such a thing can be pinned down at all). Rather, tutelage was shaped by the particular meanings the American officials made, and these meanings were in turn drawn from the officials' specific experiences and institutional location. This is why, for example, American colonial officials decried the local elites' "corruption" even as political corruption marked

American politics at home. By their particular progressive movement schemas, they classified corruption as antithetical to the culture of liberal democracy.[3] Furthermore, by examining culture as a semiotic system-*in-practice*, we have seen how culture was not just a matter of discourse among colonizers but a matter of signs and meanings deployed by American authorities on the ground to represent the legitimacy of their rule to colonized subjects, cultivate consent, and win hearts and minds. This examination has yielded fresh insights into why the tutelage project was enacted in the first place. American officials landed upon the idea of democratization and tutelage toward self-government only by reckoning that the Puerto Rican and Filipino elite had themselves demanded such things from Spain. American authorities proclaimed a project in democratic tutelage partly in an effort to legitimate rule to the elite, and the fact that they employed those particular signs and symbols was partly determined by what American officials discerned in the elites' own demands. This recasts conventional wisdom on the supposedly exceptional character of America's liberal imperialism. Tutelage was not a reflection of America's unique anticolonial and democratic beliefs but partly the product of the unique demands registered by the Puerto Rican and Filipino elite. If American empire was exceptional at all, it was due more to the exceptional demands of the local elite than to the exceptional character of America's deep traditions or beliefs.[4]

If our analysis of the colonial officials' schemas and use of signs has helped recast traditional understandings of exceptionalism, it has also opened up the space for examining local reception. Looking beyond the categories and classifications of the colonizer, we have examined the meaning-making activities of the Puerto Rican and Filipino elite. What did the elite make of tutelage and its attendant exercises in cultural power? How did they receive the signs of tutelary rule? Extant scholarship overlooks this issue at its own peril. Traditional case studies have indeed tracked elite "response" to American intrusion, but they reduce it to a matter of stimulus-reaction, digging for the subjective values that dictated the elites' conduct or the calculations of utility that underpinned their acceptance or rejection of rule. By overlooking meaning *making*, these studies fall prey to the American officials' own presumption that the elite spoke of things like self-government, democracy, liberty, and rights without truly understanding their content. "The passwords in [the

Puerto Rican elite] camp," argues Edward Berbusse, "were often converted into verbal dogmas that were honored but not too closely scrutinized for meaning. Into such phrases as 'freedom' and 'self-government,' 'popular sovereignty' . . . they poured a content of enthusiasm."[5] Alternatively, by examining signifying patterns and meaning making, we have seen that the elites' "enthusiasm" did not replace semiotic content. When the elite spoke of democracy and related things, they were not ignorantly hurling "verbal dogmas" devoid of meaning but rather articulating their own particular meanings that scholars have not detected.

Probing these meaning-making processes has been fruitful in another way. By tracing them, we have been able to ascertain why the elite accepted tutelary rule but not its lessons, how they resisted occupation in effect but not necessarily in motivation, and how exercises in cultural power were effective on one level but only as they failed on other levels. In this, our analysis has been informed by innovative scholarship that has already disclosed the ways in which subject populations around the world localized, appropriated, or otherwise resisted the imposed artifacts of colonial rule. As Emily Rosenberg summarizes: "The tools of empire — from professional expertise to military hardware, to products of daily consumption, to gender norms — may be exported and even sometimes acquired. But how they are reshaped and then used by local cultures may be a 'different story altogether.'"[6] Still, the preceding chapters have also extended this work in several respects. First, while extant studies offer thick descriptions of localization, indigenization, or appropriation, they have yet to explain *why* these processes occur. By their case-specific focus, the causal mechanisms pinpointed in extant work have remained either implicit or, at best, untested by the rigor of comparison. Furthermore, while extant studies have traced the ways in which local populations may resist, indigenize, or domesticate imposed things, they have yet to show whether or not these practices can give way to local transformation. If, as Rosenberg notes above, foreign things are "reshaped . . . by local cultures," how might foreign things in turn reshape the local cultures they enter? Is the domestication of foreign elements during colonialism interminable? When, if ever, might it lead to cultural transformation?[7]

Exceptional works on colonial encounters around the world have indeed addressed cultural transformation, but their limits invoke the need for a critical transcendence as well. Consider Sahlins's study of the Hawaiians' encounter with Captain Cook. This study is notable because it attempts to track cultural reproduction and transformation in one and the same frame. Sahlins shows that when the Hawaiians received Captain Cook, they rendered him meaningful by their preexisting categories. But this same process of indigenization later led to change. Sahlins calls it the "functional revaluation of categories" — the "old names that are still on everyone's lips acquire connotations that are far removed from their original meaning."[8] Still, if Sahlins finally offers an analysis of how reproduction can lead to change, the type of change he pinpoints is particular. Revaluation happens behind people's backs. This is why Sahlins calls revaluation a "functional" revaluation: schemas change by their *function* in the new field, not by social actors directly seeking out new meanings or lines of conduct.[9] Furthermore, functional revaluation does not involve the adoption of new cultural structures to replace preexisting ones. Overarching signifying patterns of parallel and opposition persist, they are just complexified. It is therefore fitting that critics have charged Sahlins's study as a form of "culturology" — a portrayal of cultural users as unagentic dupes of their given meaning system. Apparently, people are forever programmed by inherited cultural structures and, even in the face of novel events, they are incapable of learning new models, actively constructing new meanings, or altering their scripts of action. In Sahlins's model, the most people can do is extend prior cultural schemas to unwittingly effect their revaluation. Revaluation as change still manifests cultural constraint.[10]

We have seen that revaluation did happen in the Philippines as tutelage proceeded, but we have also seen that, in Puerto Rico, a different form of change occurred. The Puerto Rican elite did not remix or revalue their prior cultural repertoire, they expanded it by learning the Americans' schemas. They then put the new cultural schemas to use, marginalizing their prior schemas in the process. This offers a significant complication to Sahlins's seminal study and the debates over agency or culturology that have followed from it. Foremost, it suggests that we should consider different *forms of cultural change*. It also suggests that, rather than arguing about whether the colonized are ever "agentic" or not, we should consider the different *types of agency* associated with these different forms of change. After all, even though revaluation occurred in the Philippines behind the elites' backs, it was not as if the elite lacked agency. They helped effect revaluation by creatively modifying their schemas in the face of tutelage's new institutional arrangements. Compared with structural transformation, therefore, we see not a lack of agency but a different type. Revaluation involves improvisations upon given schemas; structural transformation involves seeking out and learning new ones.[11] The larger lesson is as follows. Rather than universalizing theory — trying to determine whether cultural users *always* improvise their given schemas or always learn new ones, whether they are *always* cultural dupes or *always* bearers of "bourgeois rationality" (as Sahlins puts it) — we might fare better to probe the conditions under which one or the other might occur.[12]

UNDERSTANDING REPRODUCTION AND TRANSFORMATION(S)

Here arises the final issue we have addressed. What accounts for these different forms of change? More to the point: why did the elites' initially similar paths diverge toward two different types of cultural transformation? On its face, this question might not warrant curiosity. After all, there were vast differences between Puerto Rico and the Philippines that we might intuitively muster to account for elites' cultural paths. The Philippines was a large archipelago of disparate islands; Puerto Rico was smaller. Racial, cultural, ethnic, and linguistic lines were likewise different. In Puerto Rico, the history of slavery had led to the establishment of Afro-Caribbean groups that in turn mingled with natives and creoles to create an overarching racial and cultural spectrum. That spectrum was in turn organized into a larger hierarchy across the small island, led at the top by a Spanish mestizo and creole elite. In the Philippines, various hierarchies intermingled along ethnic, linguistic, and cultural lines, in part articulating with geography, and the elite's background was largely Chinese or Spanish mestizo rather than criollo. All of these differences — and many more — are no doubt real. Our goal in comparison is not to deny them, nor has it been to treat Puerto Rico and the Philippines as if they were exactly similar. The question is not whether there were differences between the two countries and histories but which ones — if any at all — matter for helping us explain the elites' cultural trajectories.

In terms of the differences just noted, we can easily see that they do not get us too far for meeting our task of explanation. After all, in the first ten years of

U.S. rule, these differences were comparably constant over time, yet the elites' cultural paths were not. The elite in both colonies domesticated, then their trajectories diverged. The shift from domestication to different forms of change, therefore, cannot be due to the aforementioned *constant* differences between the colonies. It would even be difficult to refer to geographical differences to account for the elites' cultural paths. The disparate Philippine geography, for example, did not impede the transmission of the Americans' meanings to the elite. As American authorities in the Philippines tightened their surveillance to undo "corruption," they assigned American authorities to each of the provinces, which then oversaw the political elites' conduct while offering direct "lessons" to them (chapters 5 and 7). This made the cultural transmission of the Americans' meanings and models comparable to transmission in Puerto Rico. If anything, the assignment of agents to the local level in the Philippines might have made transmission across spaces there even more possible than in Puerto Rico, because in spite of Puerto Rico's smaller size, American authorities there were not appointed to the local level, they were instead confined to San Juan. Nor did geographical complexity in the Philippines impede transmission among the Filipino elite. Colonial state formation helped overcome spatial differences between the elite through forums such as provincial governors' meetings in the capital and the Philippine Assembly. The elite newspapers and journals that proliferated in the period facilitated an imagined community and a forum for discursive exchange (chapter 4). This does not mean that the elite as a whole became homogeneous or shared the exact same political interests. Elite factions and intra-elite disputes over sectoral interests persisted. It does mean, however, that the elite were given new platforms, spaces, and mediums to interact and communicate with each other despite the archipelago's disparate geography.

The fact of the Philippine-American War is also a potentially critical difference to consider. While so-called insurgents in the Philippines resisted American occupation by force, the Puerto Rican elite were more receptive to American sovereignty. But again, exactly whether and how the war accounts for the elites' complex and shifting cultural paths is the key question. In fact, it would be difficult to account for the elites' paths by reference to the war alone. War was absent in Puerto Rico, but American authorities enacted a tutelage project similar to that in the Philippines; and, most importantly, the

Puerto Rican elite initially domesticated tutelage just like their Filipino counterparts. If the fact of war somehow affected the elite trajectories, we would be obliged to find a war in *both* cases to account for the elites' initially similar cultural trajectories. Over time is another matter. Did the war in the Philippines have long-term repercussions that somehow shaped the fact that the Filipino elites' path diverged from that of their Puerto Rican counterparts? Conventional wisdom might propose that the war compelled American authorities to engage in collaborative patterns with the local Filipino elite that in turn prevented the proper inculcation of tutelary "lessons." Out of fear that the elites' anger might respark revolutionary sentiment, American authorities lightened the lessons. But as we have seen, compared with Puerto Rico, the Americans' ruling strategies and patterns of collaboration in the Philippines, despite the war, were similar enough to not make this factor a determining one. Tutelary controls, mechanisms of discipline, and collaborative patterns with political parties and elites unfolded similarly in the two colonies (chapters 4 and 7).

Looking beyond these intuitive accounts, we have turned to explicit theories, some of which underlie the intuitive hypotheses. Yet these theories have not sufficed either. Treating culture as deep values and beliefs that are congruent or incongruent with those of tutelage matches intuitive accounts that would point to linguistic, ethnic, racial, or cultural differences between the two colonies, but we have seen that the values approach does not meet our task of explanation. It could not account for why the elite in *both* colonies domesticated tutelage, despite any differences between them in political cultural values or orientations. An adjustment of the theory would posit that the Puerto Rican elite did not in fact have values more congruent with tutelage and that they were more akin to those of the Filipino elite. Domestication in both colonies could then be explained as a clash of incommensurable values, beliefs, and norms. But the problem with this modification is twofold. First, if the Puerto Rican elites' values were akin to the Filipino elites' values, in the sense that both of the elites' values were "incongruent" with tutelage, why did the Puerto Rican elite at first welcome American occupation without resisting it? The values approach cannot account for this. In the approach, values determine meanings and hence conduct — therefore the Puerto Rican elite should have responded to tutelage just like their Filipino counterparts. Second, if the Puerto Rican elites' values were dysfunctional with tutelage, why and how did they transform their culture *during* tutelage? Such a change is inconceivable in the values approach, which can explain change only by referring to a shift in cohorts. As we have seen, though, such a cohort shift did not happen.

An alternative explanation has come from studies that emphasize culture's strategic and instrumentalist uses. This approach has wide resonance in the social sciences. It also has affinities with the notion in some sectors of cultural sociology that culture should be seen as a tool kit from which people pick and choose as they pursue their goals.[13] On the one hand, we have seen that the elite in both colonies used culture to realize their interests. On the other hand, we have also seen that an emphasis on culture's strategic uses alone is insufficient for explaining the elites' cultural trajectories. It cannot explain, for instance, why the elite domesticated tutelage and thus failed to employ the meanings that would have best served their goals. The Puerto Rican elite wanted statehood, and they sought to convince the Americans of their capacity for it. They had an interest in and incentives for learning, using, and performing the Americans' meanings of what self-government entailed. Nonetheless, during the first years of rule, they did not do this. Furthermore, even the Filipino elite had an incentive to learn the Americans' meanings. While their goal was eventual independence rather than statehood, they could have learned and used the Americans' meanings to achieve it. As they themselves asserted, if they demonstrated their fitness for self-government, they could convince the American authorities to grant them eventual independence. But the elite did not do this.

The strategic uses approach might remedy these problems treating culture as a matter of imperfect "information" or "knowledge" that poses a "constraint upon the equilibrium path."[14] As David Laitin puts it, culture has two faces: it can be a constraint (as when certain symbols become "hegemonic"), and it can be a "strategic resource. The hegemonic side of culture implies that "certain cultural calculations are not made . . . even if they could yield added utility," while the other side means that people are "instrumental in using culture to gain wealth and power."[15] This extension of the rational choice approach might then explain domestication — the elites' preexisting cultural system was hegemonic, thereby preventing them from adopting the best second-order strategy for realizing their first-order goal. That is, the elite domesticated tutelage rather than adopting the Americans' meanings because their hegemonic culture meant that they lacked the proper "information" or "knowledge." But this extension runs into two further problems. First, once we admit the issue of information or knowledge, we have already gone far beyond the confines of the strategic uses model of action.[16] Second, even if we stretch the instrumentalist approach and its reference to hegemony, information, or knowledge to account for domestication, the stretched theory cannot then account for why domestication gave way to transformation. The Puerto Rican elite stopped domestication and learned the Americans' meanings — thereby acquiring new "information." The Filipino elite did not. Instrumentalist theories — even with a modified emphasis upon information, knowledge, or hegemonic culture — cannot explain this, because these theories have yet to reveal how hegemonic constraints might be lifted or how repertoires might be expanded. As proponents of theory themselves admit, an analysis of utility works best as an explanatory framework only when information and knowledge are held *constant*. In our cases, it is exactly the *shift* in the elites' knowledge and information through repertoire expansion that demands explanation. People realize their goals by employing their existing cultural tool kits, and they are thus constrained. But when do they ever *expand* their tool kit to thus achieve old goals by new cultural means? When are the "constraints along the equilibrium path" lifted?[17]

A final approach had us look beyond calculations of utility in people's heads (and the values in their hearts) to instead consider the role of political institutions, colonial policies, and ruling strategies — culture from the top down. This consideration is fitting. Some scholarship on U.S. colonialism implicitly conjures it — perhaps because a focus upon culture from the top down effectively displaces blame from the colonized's "culture" to the colonizer. In this view, if tutelage in the Philippines failed to insinuate liberal democracy, it was because the project itself contained inherent contradictions — an argument that parallels the argument that the Philippine-American War led to a loosening of tutelary effort. As Paredes argues about the Philippines:

> The whole American effort to develop democracy was flawed by an organic contradiction. The inhabitants of a colony are subjects, not citizens; power flows downwards from the metropole. . . . Any attempt at the devel-

opment of democratic institutions in circumstances so constitutionally antithetical to their prosperity can only produce a distorted experience for the colonized. . . . Not only are institutions distorted but political leadership is compromised. Elections and public service do not create titans legendary for their bold, commanding leadership, but pygmies stunted by the constraints of collaboration. . . . Unprotected by any constitutional liberties . . . native politicians are forced to operate within assigned political boundaries and, more importantly, to curry favor with colonial officials to win their patronage. Denied the luxury of integrity and independence, native leaders quickly learn a duplicitous political craft of manipulation and dissimulation.[18]

We have seen that tutelage was inherently contradictory, but we have also seen that a focus upon its contradictions or upon ruling strategies is not sufficient to explain the elites' cultural paths. American authorities in Puerto Rico enacted the same colonial project as that in the Philippines, operating by the same "interlocking coercive relationships" and patterns of collaboration. In both colonies, American officials shifted their ruling conduct in the same direction. In both, they intensified political education, instituted new control over local governments, and constructed a national legislative assembly — collaborating with certain parties while denying the privileges of others. It follows that these similarities, hence a focus upon culture from the top down, cannot explain the elites' divergent trajectories on the ground.[19]

Our alternative has been to summon a different strand of theorizing in the social sciences and to approach culture as a semiotic system-in-practice. Rather than looking at the congruence or incongruence of values, interests, and incentives, or the Americans' ruling strategies, this approach urged us to consider the constraints posed by institutionalized culture upon the elites' meaning-making activity. It then alerted us to the possibility that the elites' cultural paths diverged because of the relative validation of the elites' cultural schemas — that is, whether the predictions registered by the elites' semiotic practices were proven true by contingent happenings and events on the ground.

The comparative method by which we have reached this approach is worth clarifying. Traditional comparative studies employ either John Stuart Mill's "method of agreement" or his "method of difference."[20] Our method has been different because our goal has been different. The goal has been not only to explain why the elite in both colonies domesticated tutelage, nor only to explain two different forms of change. The goal has been to explain cultural *trajectories* — paths of meaning making over time. We have had to explain why two paths that started at the same point later diverged. This has therefore involved putting the methods of agreement and difference into sequence so as to capture beginning points, turning points, and end points. In other words, we have employed not only a comparative sociology but also a comparative-*historical* sociology that tracks meanings in motion, turning points, and processes in time. Through this historical-comparative analysis, we have been able to induce a better explanation for the elites' cultural paths.[21]

First, to explain domestication, we worked from a method of agreement. Why did the elite in *both* colonies make meaning of tutelage in terms of their preexisting cultural system, thereby reproducing that system while remaining impervious to tutelage's "lessons"? Differences between the two cases cannot explain the similarity in outcome. Only similarities can. Thus, the elites' different goals and interests, their different socialization and background (or "values"), and underlying conditions in which American occupation began (peace in Puerto Rico vs. war in the Philippines; relative elite cohesion or homogeneity) do not provide an answer. Instead, we have found that the elite in both colonies had already had particular schemas on what democratic self-government meant, how it should be conducted, and how it should be realized. Before American rule, these schemas had been fixed in practice and thereby institutionalized. Therefore, the elite in both colonies domesticated tutelage because of the constraints of their previously institutionalized cultural system. As the elite in both colonies already had their own preexisting cultural schemas on democratic self-government, they were constrained to employ those schemas as they constructed meaning. As those schemas had been institutionalized, they were the most available and familiar to the elite. Therefore, the elite first conjured them as they made meaning of tutelage.

Note that this happened in both Puerto Rico and the Philippines, regardless of differences between them. It happened regardless of which cultural schemas provided added utility, regardless of the elites' subjective values, and regardless of whether colonial occupation began with war. Note, too, how this explanation differs from traditional understandings of colonialism as a "clash of cultures." Our investigation shows that while there were indeed cultural differences between occupier and occupied, these differences were not about cultural essences. They did not lie in the depth of cultural values but rather in different histories of culture's institutionalization. We cannot say, therefore, that the elite made the meanings they did because of what their "values" and "norms" told them to do but rather because their particular history had posed constraint by making some schemas more available, familiar, and retrievable than others. The elite conducted themselves as they did not because of their timeless or essential culture, but rather because the schemas they employed enabled the elite to make meaning of the world and thereby act in it.[22]

To explain the divergence in the elites' cultural paths, we shifted the analytic method accordingly. As the elites' paths differed over time, we have looked for emergent differences between the cases rather than similarities. This is why a focus upon cohorts and their values, or interests and incentives, does not suffice. These factors were constant over time. It is also why a focus upon the Americans' ruling strategies cannot help. They were similar across the colonies and shifted over time in the same direction. We have seen instead that the emergent difference had to do with whether or not the elites' schemas faced recalcitrance; that is, whether the predictions they registered of tutelage by their initial domestication proved true. In turn, this depended upon differences between the two colonies in: (1) emergent crisis conditions and shifting social relations; (2) the content of the elites' schemas in relation to shifts in the American officials' tutelary strategies. These two differences then set off different processes in the two colonies that ended as different forms of cultural transformation.

On the one hand, in Puerto Rico, the economic crisis and the elites' party-based schemas meant that tutelary rule did not meet the predictions registered by the elites' domesticating activity. The economic crisis meant that the actions of the so-called unconscious masses did not fit into the elites' characterization of them; the elites' party-based schemas meant that as the American officials engaged in patterns of party collaboration, political education did not lead to the kind of single-party rule which the elite had predicted. These events were important not because they altered incentive structures, but because they consistently disrupted the elites' assumptions. The elites' cultural meanings — the very meanings by which they had domesticated rule in the first place — were invalidated from all sides, and even as the elite at first responded by extending their prior meanings (i.e., carrying out retraimiento), those meanings faced recalcitrance, too. The result was that the elite problematized the schemas that had guided those predictions in the first place. They questioned their assumptions about themselves and their clients, the American officials, and tutelage as a whole, and thereby sought to learn more by paying heightened attention to the authorities' tutelage discourse. Further, the elite put the newly learned models to use, deploying them to better realize their goals while marginalizing their prior schemas in the process. In this way, domestication gave way to structural transformation.

Alternatively, as tutelage proceeded in the Philippines, the elites' predictions were validated in practice. Because the elite did not face an economic crisis or a breakdown in preexisting patron-client relations, and because the elite did not have single-party schemas on democratic self-government, tutelage met their expectations and affirmed their cultural assumptions. Thus, rather than questioning the schemas that had guided those assumptions, the Filipino elite continued to employ them to make meaning. They therefore continued to pay selective attention to the Americans' discourse, seizing only upon specific terms like "The Philippines for Filipinos," while employing their familiar schemas to guide their conduct. In short, as their schemas were validated, those schemas remained the most available, familiar, and retrievable. The elite therefore continued to employ them. The only difference from before was that, as the elite continued to use their prior cultural structures to make meaning and engage tutelary forms, they modified those structures in the process. Tutelage introduced new things — from a national assembly to provincial offices and elections — but as the introduction of those things did not invalidate the elites' predictions, the elite simply complicated or refocused their prior schemas to meet them. Domestication gave way to revaluation.

Note that this part of the story does not involve neglecting the first. We cannot forsake the explanation of domestication for the explanation of divergence. They are two moments in the same overarching process of meaning making. The prior institutionalization of schemas posed constraint upon the elites' reception to tutelage, thereby leading to domestication. But by that very constraint, the elite registered particular predictions of tutelage rather than others, thereby putting their schemas at certain risks. In Puerto Rico, crisis conditions and the particular schemas at play (in conjunction with the Americans' ruling strategies) converged to realize those risks. Conversely, in the Philippines, socioeconomic continuity and the elites' different schemas on patronage and democracy meant that the risks were averted; their predictions were affirmed. In this sense, the divergence in the elites' cultural trajectories happened not in spite of domestication but through the schemas, and hence the predictions, that domestication entailed.

Some clarification is warranted. Why not just assert that structural transformation happened in Puerto Rico because patron-client relations were disrupted by the economic crisis, and that structural transformation did not happen in the Philippines because there was patron-client continuity? Why do we need to examine signifying patterns, meaning making, and recalcitrance at all in order to understand the divergence? The problem is that pinpointing a breakdown in patron-client relations does not tell us how or why the event led to outcome. Indeed, while rational choice theories would suggest that the breakdown mattered because it changed incentive structures, which in turn shape cultural outcomes, we have seen that this was not the case. True, the breakdown in patron-clientelism likely gave the elite a new incentive to act, but the particular action they took was not determined by the brute fact of the breakdown nor by the presumably new incentive. Rather, the breakdown in patron-client relations mattered because it posed repeated recalcitrance, and it posed repeated recalcitrance only by virtue of schemas by which the elite rendered the event meaningful. That is, patron-client relations were at stake only because they the elites' cultural schemas on democracy and self-government referred to them. Had the elites' political schemas not included reference to patron-client relations, the breakdown of those relations might not have posed recalcitrance at all.

Two points follow. First, treating culture as a semiotic system-in-practice is not an appurtenance to the explanation but essential for it. Without understanding signifying patterns, meaning making, and the particular predictions that followed, we would not have been able to discover why the breakdown in patron-client relations mattered. Rather than a critical realist explanation, we would have been left with a positivist correlation. This means, second, that our model does not fall into a strictly "materialist" explanation, but neither does it fall into a cultural interpretivism or reduce outcomes to "discourse." Recalcitrance, the key explanatory factor in our story, is neither an "idealist"/discursive nor a "materialist" phenomenon. It refers to the *conjuncture* between culture and the world — the relationship obtained between signifying patterns and the people, events or happenings referred thereby. To locate cultural change either in cultural or "discursive" logics on the one hand, or in the brute reality of the material world on the other, would not suffice. It is the relationship between them that matters.[23]

The analysis thereby yields a larger model that is as processual as the phenomenon under scrutiny. It specifies paths of meaning making; it explains starting points, turning points, and end points at once. It thereby facilitates an understanding of constraint, reproduction, and change, cultural systems and different types of cultural transformation. If we wanted to be schematic we could boil the model down to simple steps. First, when cultural users initially make meaning, they do so by using previously institutionalized tales and types — hence the tales and types most familiar and available to them. In turn, the meanings thereby made serve to guide users' conduct, their relationships with others in the world, and how they pursue their goals. Second, by making these meanings, cultural users register particular predictions of the world, yet the world does not have to conform to the predictions registered. When the world does conform, previously institutionalized schemas are validated and reinstitutionalized. Thus social actors will continue to use them, even as they might modify them to meet the exigencies of novel events. In other words, when culture's predictions prove true, people reproduce their culture while revaluing it in the process. On the other hand, if the world proves repeatedly recalcitrant to the meanings made, a different path is opened up: cultural users will question the schemas that guided those predictions and seek new ways of classifying, narrating, and engaging the world around them. They will thereby expand their cultural repertoire and open up the path toward structural transformation.[24]

The implication for existing treatments of "culture" in the social sciences is worth noting. For decades, "culture" has been analyzed in the shadow of structural functionalism and its inherent troubles. Of course, historical anthropologists have long moved beyond structural functionalism to theorize culture in new innovative ways. But other social scientists — especially in sociology and political science — have opted instead to overlook culture altogether. At most, they have chosen to treat culture as strategic instruments or as an effect of activities from the top down. This choice has been rightly motivated. Treating culture as subjective values and beliefs, or even as a "system," fell prey to cultural essentialism, portrayed actors as cultural dopes (forever doomed to enact "the system" or live by their deeply ingrained "values"), and precluded an analysis of transformation. To study strategic utility or powerful states rather than meanings and meaning systems has therefore appeared a fruitful alternative to these traps. But in the event, analyses of meaning and meaning systems have fallen by the wayside — relegated to subfields in sociology or political science that have been forced to incessantly argue for the importance of "culture" as a causal "variable."[25] Our analysis offers a different way out. It suggests that we should not reject cultural analysis on the grounds that it necessarily implies essentialism, a lack of agency, or interminable cultural reproduction. It rather suggests that we can analyze cultural systems and meanings, if only we consider culture as a semiotic system-in-practice and thereby take seriously how meanings are made, remade, or even abjured depending on institutional constraint, culture's predictions, and recalcitrance.

LOOKING BEYOND

Yet all of this is in the abstract. The concrete limitations of our examination merit reconsideration. As noted in the introduction, colonialism everywhere was a multifaceted process that had effects on several registers at once. Diverse groups betwixt and between the ossified categories "colonizer" and "colonized" were involved in it. While this book has many conceits, it does not and cannot purport to capture all of these complexities. It has tracked not all colonized groups but only the political elites subjected to "practical political education." Filipino or Puerto Rican immigrants to the United States, peasants in the countryside or workers in Manila, cosmopolitan writers and intellectuals outside of the political elite — all of these groups and how they engaged colonialism is outside our scope. Nor, by the same token, has this book tracked all of colonialism's cultural effects or cultural transformations on all registers of colonial society. It has rather focused upon how the political elite received the meanings, models, and practical templates that American authorities associated with their idealized vision of liberal democracy and whether transformation occurred along those lines specifically. Racial ideologies, colonial and anticolonial nationalism, schemas regarding gender relations — these and other elements have not been our key focus, and other studies might better explore transformations at these levels.[26]

If this book does not address all of the actors that played a part in colonialism, however, and if it has overlooked other registers of culture and cultural change to more narrowly examine the impact of the Americans' meanings and models on liberal democracy, this is not because the latter have higher value a priori. It is only because tutelary colonialism itself valued them and made them a critical dimension of American rule. As noted from the beginning, this book has aimed to apprehend tutelary colonialism's cultural power and its effects. Discourses of democracy, political office, ballots, and electoral conduct were inextricably tied to tutelary colonialism's exercises in power. They constituted some of the key elements that the grandiose tutelage project wittingly tried to impose and which colonial power deliberately put into play. They were the things that American authorities idealized, that authorities deployed to win hearts and minds, and that authorities used as measures of colonial power's success. They were therefore the things with which the colonized elite were forced to deal (and as seen, the elite dealt with them indeed, however according to their own distinct cultural lights). To focus only upon the impact of tutelary colonialism's educating efforts at the political level might be narrow, but to overlook them is to elide critical dimensions of America's exercises in colonial power.

At any rate, the concentrated focus and comparison of the preceding chapters has significant implications for studies of U.S. colonialism, Puerto Rico, and the Philippines. On the one hand, this book has drawn heavily upon extant studies. Historians and area scholars have long labored in the archives, providing important insights and information that enable the present study. This book has added its own primary sources, but it nonetheless stands upon and synthesizes the labors of existing scholarship. On the other hand, authors of the existing scholarship have not yet put their findings into comparative relief, remaining focused instead upon one or another colony. One of this book's conceits is that a comparative frame facilitates new interpretations while problematizing the theories of culture upon which many existing studies implicitly rely. Consider conventional works on the Philippines. Working from an implicit structural-functional approach to culture, these works have long discussed presumably "Filipino" cultural values like utang na loób or *hiya* (shame) typically associated with patron-client "norms." They have also suggested that such values persisted throughout U.S. rule. Our examination does not contradict the overarching point of this scholarship. We have seen that idioms of utang na loób and patron-client practices were an integral part of the Filipino elites' meaning system, and that cultural reproduction did happen in the Philippines (even though it later happened as revaluation). In fact, Philippine scholars uncomfortable with structural functionalism's shadow have not rejected claims about Filipino values or reproduction either. Ileto's brilliant study accepts that the elite and the populace were "linked" through debt relations and utang na loób, and his analysis does not deny that cultural reproduction happened. It rather rejects the presumption that such values and their reproduction necessarily led to "harmony" and "equilibrium" in Philippine society.[27] Our investigation joins this critique but adds a series of others. First, while it does not invalidate the claim that cultural reproduction happened in the Philippines, it rejects the structural-functionalist *characterization* of it. It was not that essential Filipino values and norms were reproduced during the first decade of U.S. rule; it is rather that particular signifying patterns were reproduced and later revalued. Second, our analysis rejects the conventional *explanation* for reproduction. To explain cultural reproduction, existing scholarship has tautologically referred to the values themselves. If the elites' presumably deep values were reproduced during U.S. rule, it must have been because their values were deep and hence durable. If they were deep and durable, they must have been reproduced.[28] But the case-specific focus of these studies means that their causal claims have not been put to a falsifiable test. As extant scholarship has focused only upon a case of cultural reproduction (the Philippines) rather than comparing it to a case of structural transformation (Puerto Rico), it has readily fallen prey to structural functionalism's tautological and "culturalist" explanation. Without a sustained comparative analysis, it has been far too easy to fall into the trap of cultural essentialism, attributing all that happened to a presumably deep and durable "Filipino culture." It has therefore been tempting to imply that the Filipinos got what they deserved from U.S. rule.[29]

Our comparative analysis offers a better explanation. By comparing Puerto

Rico and the Philippines, we have learned that the elites' political culture was reproduced during American occupation due to the elites' strong economic base (and hence the persistence of social relations), along with the conjuncture between the elites' schemas and the Americans' tutelage project. These factors served to continually validate the elites' predictions, thereby making the elites' schemas continually familiar, available, and retrievable, and in turn setting the elite on the distinct path of continued domestication and revaluation. The Filipino elite engaged tutelage in terms of razón, but they did not do so because their "culture" told them to. They rather did so because the razón schema had been previously institutionalized and was therefore rendered most familiar, available, and retrievable to the elite. The schema persisted during tutelage not because it was deeply engrained in the elites' hearts, but because it was reinstitutionalized due to the contingent affirmation of its implicit predictions by the things, people, and events the schema referred. It follows that we can no longer claim that cultural reproduction happened because of the Filipinos' deep and timeless "culture." We must rather recognize that sometimes cultural schemas are resisted by the world they refer to, sometimes they are not.[30]

None of this is to imply that reproduction-as-revaluation continued indefinitely in the Philippines. Because our focus has been on how a single cohort dealt with the transition from Spanish to American rule and the subsequent influx of American meanings, our analysis has been restricted to the initial decade and a half of U.S. occupation. What happened afterward in the Philippines (or in Puerto Rico) is an open question. It might be the case that certain individuals of later generations beyond the first decade and a half of occupation in the Philippines became more adept at adopting, and perhaps manipulating, American schemas.[31] It might also be that case that, in Puerto Rico, preexisting discourses and practices of patronage and the familia later resurfaced in elaborated form. Even if they were marginalized during the first decade of U.S. rule, they might have remained silently stored in the cultural archive, to be conjured at a later time. These possibilities remain open; to presume that our analysis of the first decade and a half of U.S. rule can answer them is to transgress one of the main points of our study: that culture is about meanings in motion and hence open to change over time. Still, even if our analysis cannot explain what happened later in the two colonies, it does have some implications for understanding other periods and processes. After all, the different forms of change in Puerto Rico and the Philippines meant that certain schemas were employed and instituted, thereby registering new predictions of how the world would respond. To understand what happened after the period of revaluation in the Philippines or structural transformation in Puerto Rico, therefore, we might explore whether those new predictions were validated or not. In this sense, while the substantive content of our analysis has been narrow, its analytical implications are potentially more broad.

To return to the final issue: might our analysis also say something more broadly about debates on American imperialism in the twenty-first century, with its attempts to occupy foreign societies and transform them along America's idealized, fantastical lines? These debates rage on. Some claim that foreign occupation always leads to an interminable clash of values. Empire necessarily fails because of motivated resistance against it or incommensurable cultural differences. Others claim that empire can be successful, as long as benign Americans tout the proper will and commitment. Empire works depending on the agency of the imperialist. Our analysis offers some different insights on these issues. Note first that the processes we have found exceed extant categorizations. Between successful transformation or inevitable culture clash, between easy acceptance and valiant resistance, we have seen a range of other possibilities. Domestication, for example, was not a clash of values, nor was it a matter of witting resistance. It was rooted in differences in interpretation that neither colonizer nor colonized recognized. This differential interpretation might have been unmotivated and unintended, but in any case it posed serious trouble for American authorities. While the authorities in Puerto Rico were initially complacent because the elite warmly accepted occupation, the elite, by domesticating tutelage's signs (the very signs that had helped to secure consent in the first place), unwittingly produced an ostensible corruption and electoral violence that served to disrupt the state machinery and strike the American authorities with fear. If existing scholarship on "culture clash" overlooks the possibility for domestication at its own peril, so too do American occupiers who fail to reckon the polyvalence of the signs they utter.[32]

Some might take this point to suggest that American imperialists need only be *better* imperialists if they want to effect change (perhaps they should study semiotics). This leads to the other side of the debate. According to proponents of empire, colonialism can indeed be successful. It can effectively refashion and transform ruled societies on the rulers' own terms; it takes only the proper will and concerted commitment.[33] This argument strikingly parallels theories of culture that treat it from a top-down, state-centered perspective. It also parallels historiographical arguments that American colonialism "failed" in the Philippines because of the American authorities' own shortcomings. Yet our illumination of American rule in Puerto Rico and the Philippines complicates this view as well. First, even if colonial rulers muster all the will possible, even if they try to employ signs and symbols to win hearts and minds, and even if they manipulate interests and incentives or shift their strategies due to contingencies on the ground, they cannot easily transform local meaning systems from the top down. Domestication and reproduction, transformation and revaluation — all of these things happened in America's early overseas empire, but they did not happen under conditions that were willed by anyone in particular. Second, even when transformation along the Americans' projected lines did occur — as in Puerto Rico — it was not a happy outcome. After learning the Americans' meanings and models, the Puerto Rican elite turned them against their rulers. Indignant and rightly confrontational, their resistance increased rather than decreased in proportion to the structural transformation that occurred. To be sure, it was only as tutelary rule proceeded onward in the first decade of the twentieth century that calls for national independence in Puerto Rico became more and more palpable. Just as some among the political elite appropriated American discourses of democracy, they also grew more and more nationalist if not "anti-American" altogether, and this set the precedent for later national independence movements carrying out "terrorist" activities against the United States.[34] "Americanization" might have happened effectively in Puerto Rico, but it simply brought with it new dilemmas, contradictions, and tensions that were far beyond the scopes and hopes of the imperialists' ostensible goodwill. In America's earliest empire, ostensible success also meant a terrible failure.

APPENDIX: BIO-DATA

APPENDIX REFERENCES

I first constructed a list of Filipino and Puerto Rican political officials and party leaders from 1898 to 1910. The lists of officials are incomplete but relatively systematic, coming in the form of official registers, reports, lists, electoral results, and so on. I then collected biographical information. This information comes from lists of merchants, professionals (e.g., from lawyers' associations), and landowners in specific industries; commercial guides on businessmen; municipal histories; and, for the Philippines, Cullinane 1989. For Puerto Rico, data were collected by Angel Quintero-Rivera of the University of Puerto Rico (who graciously shared his unpublished data). Other sources provided systematic comparative data: Jackson 1906 for the Philippines and Jackson 1910 for Puerto Rico. Other sources are Blanch 1894; Choudons 1911; *Gaceta Oficial de Puerto Rico*; Goberino de Philippines 1898; Gobierno de Puerto Rico 1897; Government of Porto Rico, Bureau of Property Taxes, "Comparative Statistical Report of Sugar Manufactured in Porto Rico from the Crops of 1908, 1909, 1910, 1911" (USNA, BIA, RG 350, box 16, 126-14); T. Kalaw 1913; Magalhaes 1898; Official Gazette of the Philippines; Secretary of Porto Rico, *Porto Rico Register* (1900, 1901, 1903, 1910); Tuohy 1908; U.S. Bureau of Insular Affairs, "Coffee Exporters of Porto Rico" (USNA, BIA, RG 350, box 16, 126-14); U.S. Bureau of Insular Affairs, "Result of the Elections of February 3, 1902" (USNA, BIA, RG 350, box 293, 2710-26); U.S. Bureau of Insular Affairs, "Statement Showing, by provinces, the names and political affiliations of all the elected Assemblymen, Provincial Governors, and Third Members of the Provincial Board," Nov. 2, 1909 (USNA, RG 350, BIA box 605, 10265-38); U.S. Bureau of Manufacturers, "List of Sugar Factories in Porto Rico," July 7, 1909 (USNA, RG 126, file 9-8-20); and Dean Worcester, "Personal and Police History of Deputies to First Filipino Assembly" (WPC, Documents and Papers 1834–1915, vol. 1, item 18).

TABLE 10 U.S. Colonial Officials

Experience	Puerto Rico	Philippines
Business	7	10
Politician	21	20
Law	36	40
Expert/Academic	36	30
Total	100%	100%
	(N=14)	(N=10)

Sources: Jackson 1906, 1910; *Register of Porto Rico* 1901, 1903. Those who served in both colonies counted once for each colony. Counts represent listed occupations.

Business = listed in primary source as "business man"

Politician = elected office

Lawyer = professional lawyer, judge

Expert = university professor, bureaucrat with PhD

TABLE 11 Puerto Rican and Filipino Political Elite, Decade of Birth

Born in	Puerto Rico	Philippines
1840s	15	3
1850s	19	25
1860s	33	35
1870s	26	35
1880s	7	3
Total	100% (N=27)	100% (N=148)

TABLE 12 Previous Office-Holding Experience of Political Elite

	Philippines	Puerto Rico
Office Held During Spanish Rule	53	60
No Office Holding Evident	47	40
Total	100% (N=158)	100% (N=166)

Source: *Guía Oficial* of 1897 (Puerto Rico) and 1898 (Philippines)

TABLE 13 Socioeconomic Class: Puerto Rican and Philippine Political Elite

	Philippines	Puerto Rico
Land (%)	61	48
Merchant (%)	4	22
Professional (%)	35	31
Total	100% (N=159)	100% (N=116)

"Land" = landed only and/or landed + other (merchant, professional)
"Merchant" = merchant only
"Professional" = professional only

TABLE 14 Place of Education: Puerto Rican and Philippine Political Elite

	Puerto Rico	Philippines
Within Colony Only (%)	42	86
Abroad (%)	58	14
Total	100% (N=66*)	100% (N=146)

*Thirteen educated in United States

NOTES

INTRODUCTION: COLONIALISM AND CULTURE IN THE AMERICAN EMPIRE

1. Taft to Root, Aug. 18, 1900, ERP, folder T.
2. USMG 1899: 1:342.
3. Davis to J. Bird, June 1, 1899, AGPR, FF, GC, PP, Caja 181.
4. Root 1917: 265.
5. Lowenthal 1991; Smith 1994.
6. See Brewer 1990 for an overview.
7. Guha 1997: 4.
8. Quoted in Rothbard 1958: 115.
9. Robinson 1972; Engels and Marks 1994.
10. Vincent 1988: 149; Ranger 1983.
11. Comaroff and Comaroff 1991; Cooper 1992.
12. Mitchell 1991: 34–35, ix; see also Prakash 1999; Scott 1999.
13. See Fanon 1965: 37–42.
14. See also Comaroff and Comaroff 1991: 4; Merry 2000: 6. These studies do not use the term *cultural power*; I here adduce their insights.
15. Besides the classics (LaFeber 1963; Williams 1969), see also Deitz 1986, Caban 1999, and Ayala 1999 on American economic interests in Puerto Rico.
16. Seminal works here include Kaplan and Pease 1993. See also Thompson 2002 and Vergara 1995, and especially, on American officials' "orientalism," Ileto 1999.
17. Ileto 1995; Warwick Anderson 1995; Rafael 1993a.
18. Ileto 1995 and 1999 and B. Anderson 1995 show that sanitation and health systems constituted regimes of power. As we will see in chapter 1, the tutelage project and its program of "political education" constituted a regime of power too.

19. Willoughby 1909a: 166.

20. Ferguson 2004: 29; Ignatieff 2003.

21. Mitchell 1991: xi; cf. Dirks 1992. The same approach to resistance, which occurs only on the colonizers' terms, is seen in the literature on collaborating elites. Presumably, the elite always already played the anticolonial "game" based upon prior processes of cultural colonization, while other actors, such as subaltern peasant groups, were not so culturally colonized. See Guha 1997: 210, cf. Joseph 1998: 13.

22. The literature on conversion is massive, but see especially Comaroff and Comaroff 1991 and 1997, and see Todorov 1984.

23. Findlay 1998: 161.

24. Ileto 1979; Rafael 1993a.

25. Pratt 1992: 6.

26. Merry 2000: 30.

27. Bhabha 1994.

28. Burke 1997: 208,

29. On critical realism, see Steinmetz 1998.

30. Gleeck 1976: 29; Lande 1965; also see Wells 1969 on Puerto Rico.

31. The point of this "values" approach was to wrestle the concept away from previous anthropological definitions, which treated culture as "ways of life" and defined everything as culture and analytically to distinguish culture as a particular system distinct from other systems, e.g., the economic or the psychological.

32. Almond and Verba 1965; Pye and Verba 1965. While structural functionalism as a general theory has long dissipated, its approach to culture remains in various forms in the social sciences today. See Huntington 1997; Inglehart 1990; Turner 1995; for a review, see Jackman and Miller 1997.

33. Merry 2000: 28.

34. Geertz 1973; see Laitin 1986: 16; and see Taylor 1985.

35. On the cultural turn, see Bonnell and Hunt 1999; cf. Suny 2002.

36. Ortner 1997: 6.

37. Marcus 1997: 96; Suny 2002: 1486.

38. Geertz (1990: 331) admitted this problem himself.

39. In a seminal essay, Geertz theorized change in structural-functional fashion — that is, as a matter of "correspondence" between systems (1971: 142–69) — but he later abandoned the approach on his admitted claim that "correspondence" was a meaningless concept (Aronoff 1993: 5).

40. Johnson 1997: 9. Important works in this tradition include Cohen 1974 in anthropology and Laitin 1986 in political science. See also the essays in *APSA-CP Newsletter* 8, no. 2 (1997), Chong 2003, and reviews by Julia Adams (1999) and Barbara Geddes (1995).

41. Dennis Chong (2003), for example, argues that people change their values and beliefs when new laws or reference groups impose sanctions that make the cost of adhering to old values and beliefs too high.

42. Mamdani 1996; W. Miles 1994.

43. Laitin 1985: 103.

44. See Caban 1999: 162–97; Quintero-Rivera 1974; Cubano-Iguina 1988.

45. On the Filipino elites' economic interests, see Fast and Richardson 1979. On the elite as oligarchs and caciques, see Ileto's trenchant critique (1999).

46. Paredes 1988.

47. See Giddens 1986, Bourdieu 1977, and their articulation by Sewell 1992. In anthropology, see Dirks 2001; Ohnuki-Tierney 1991; Ortner 1991, 1994; Rosaldo 1989: 91–143; and Sahlins 1981. On the "new cultural sociology," see Alexander and Smith 1993; Kane 1991, 1997; Lamont and Thévenot 2000; Sewell 1999; P. Smith 1998; Somers 1995; and Swidler 2001. In political science, see Wedeen 2002. On the cross-disciplinary "cultural turn," see Bonnell and Hunt 1999.

48. On narratives, see Somers and Gibson 1994; Steinmetz 1992; on scenarios, schemas, and scripts, see Cole 1996: 125–29; DiMaggio 1997; Ortner 1991; Sewell 1992.

49. Lamont and Thévenot 2000; Swidler 2001.

50. Sahlins 1985; Sewell 1999: 47; cf. Swidler 2001.

51. Ortner 1997: 8.

52. Wedeen 2002.

53. Olick and Levy 1997; Sewell 1992: 20. "People act on the basis of preferences and toward desired goals," notes Suny (2002: 1494), "but the preferences, goals and strategies are provided and given meaning within a cultural system."

54. Cf. other notions of constraint, e.g., Chong 2000: 3.

55. See Ann Swidler's "settled lives" (2001). Exactly why and how some cultural structures become institutionalized rather than others is a contingent matter. What is important is that, at any given time, the fact of prior institutionalization poses further constraint upon meaning making.

56. While alternative models surely persist, floating around or stored in the archive of culture, they are less familiar, and so cultural users will be less likely to first turn to them to render the world meaningful (Swidler 2001). It also follows that different social groups even within the same society will be more familiar with some schemas than with others. As different groups are located in different institutional nodes in a society, they will also have different cultural kits, even as those tool kits together constitute an overarching system.

57. Ortner 1997: 9.

58. The officials typically moved up the colonial state hierarchy and moved between the colonies.

59. The three types were often intertwined. Officials who had previously served as elected political officials at home had also had experience in law, and some of the officials who came from universities had served on expert commissions or had worked in state bureaucracies dealing in social statistics.

60. Taft 1908: 24.

61. Pomeroy 1944.

62. In discussing the Philippines, I focus my analysis on the groups whom the Americans referred to as the "Christianized" populations, as opposed to highlanders and southern Moros, whom the Americans excluded from the tutelary process.

63. Kaye 1903: 168; May 1980: 46. For discussions of these elites, see, for Puerto Rico, Bernabe 1996, Nazaro Velasco 1996, Quintero Rivera 1981, 1988. For the Philippines, see Cullinane 1989, McCoy 1993, Owen 1971, Paredes 1988, and Paredes 1990.

64. On elite formation and state formation in the Philippines, see B. Anderson 1995. Later, I discuss differences between the Puerto Rican and Filipino elite in more detail.

65. To maintain a clear focus throughout the study, I devote most attention to the dominant political elites in each country rather than the alternative party members.

66. I restrict the concerted focus to the period before 1912. By that time, a new cohort had begun to take over, and the first generation of "students" retired. Also, in 1912, democratic tutelage was lessened in the Philippines due to taking of the presidency by the Democrats.

67. Cullinane 1989: 270, 310–11; May 1980: 189–90.

68. These percentages are an underestimate. To find previous officeholding experience and make the data comparable, I was able to use only one source: the 1897 *Guía Oficial* for Puerto Rico (a Spanish government publication containing a list of all officials of Spanish rule for the year 1897); for the Philippines the *Guía Oficial* for 1898 (previous issues are not available in the archives). It is most likely that there were many more officials during U.S. rule who had also held office during Spanish rule, just that they were not holding office during the years listed in these issues of the *Guía Oficial*.

69. There is obviously a long history of cultural contact before U.S. arrival. My analysis does not claim that the Puerto Ricans and Filipinos were passive and pristine natives. All my analysis claims is that the elite had articulated certain political meanings before U.S. rule, and I study one moment of cultural contact in a larger infinite history.

70. Dietz 1986: 57–58; Director Census of Porto Rico 1900: 95–96; Quintero-Rivera 1980: 106–7.

71. U.S. Bureau of the Census 1905: 2:78, 102.

72. On Puerto Rico, see Bergad 1978, Picó 1995: 95; on the Philippines, see esp. McCoy and deJesus 1982.

73. If anything, the data underestimates the number of landholders, for it is likely that the political elite had more land than available sources suggest. But at any rate, it is clear that the political elite in both colonies reflected the landed and agrarian structure of their societies.

74. Jackson 1906; 1910. Also see Quintero-Rivera 1981 and local genealogies and histories (e.g., Gaudier Texidor 1957; Limon de Arce 1938).

1. TUTELARY COLONIALISM AND CULTURAL POWER

1. SJN, May 2, 1903, 3.

2. Luke Wright to Bishop Federick Z. Rooker, Bishop of Jaro, May 6, 1904 (CE, 1, 3.18, "1904, May"). For similar response in Puerto Rico to critics, see Willoughby 1905: 18.

3. George Davis to J. Bird, June 1, 1899 (AGPR, FF, GC, PP, Caja 181).

4. May 1980: 16–17; Karnow 1989.

5. Forbes, journal, Aug. 16, 1904, 1:41 (WCF, fms AM 1365); see also Moses, "Philippine Diary," part 5, Nov. 6, 1901 (BM).

6. *Congressional Record*, Jan. 9, 1900, 704.

7. See especially Kramer 2006.

8. On Lamarck, see Stocking 1968: 247.

9. E. Ross 1901: 67. For a further analysis of these different types of racial discourses and their application to American colonies across the empire, see Go 2004.

10. Root to Lowell, Feb. 11, 1904 (USNA, RG 350, file 364-62, entry 5); USWD 1899a: 26.

11. Rowe 1904a: 39.

12. Carroll 1899a: 262.

13. G. Davis 1900: 73.

14. USWD 1899a: 26.

15. USPC 1900: 1:81.

16. Taft to Henry Hoyt, Sept. 8, 1900 (CE, 1, 1.16).

17. Quotes combined from Taft in Taft 1908: 24 and U.S. Congress 1903: 1:86.

18. USMG 1899: 1:342.

19. Taft in U.S. Congress 1903: 1:90.

20. Taft quoted in Stanley 1974: 65. It followed that critics of tutelage worked from the idea that the colonized, because of biology, blood, and stock, could never learn the ways of self-government. See Burch 1902: 94.

21. Cameron Forbes passed the time on his journey from San Francisco to Manila reading stacks of papers on European empires; and Bernard Moses responded positively to Horace Fisher's book, *Principles of Colonial Administration* (1899),

which covered the European experience and highlighted its nascent efforts in the civilizing mission (Moses, "Philippine Diary," part 1, July 21, 1900 [BM]).

22. Burgess, quoted in J. Pratt 1936: 8; Giddings 1898: 601.

23. W. Wilson 1901; Moses 1905.

24. W. Wilson 1901: 292, 296, 297–98.

25. On connections between discourses of groups at home and abroad, see Amoroso 2003 and Kramer 2006. For divergences in views between the military and civilian officials, see Go 2004.

26. Buenker 1988; Rodgers 1982. Scholars have yet to draw out the full connections between progressivism at home and empire abroad, but for suggestive insights, see Abinales 2003, Adas 1998, and Gillete 1973.

27. W. Wilson 1887: 209–10; on political science, administration, and progressivism, see Frisch 1982.

28. Advocacy associations such as the National Municipal League, founded in 1894, bore the stamp of the new administrative science and thus joined academic thought with political activism.

29. Jacobson 2000: 193; Hyslop 1899: 470, 473.

30. W. Wilson 1901: 292. Notably, Woodrow Wilson had made his claims about reform at home and tutelage abroad shortly after he had given his maiden political speech in Baltimore — a speech at which he shared the platform with Theodore Roosevelt and made pleas for municipal reform (Frisch 1982: 301–4).

31. Beveridge 1907: 3, 14; his speech from 1900 reproduced on ibid, 10.

32. Hyslop 1899: 481.

33. These included, for the Philippines, Dean Worcester, professor at Michigan; Jacob Schurman (president of Cornell); and Bernard Moses, professor at Berkeley; for Puerto Rico, Henry Carroll, who had previously directed a religious census, and Leo Rowe, who had been part and parcel of the new science of government with Frank Goodnow, Wilson, and others and had helped draft the founding document of the National Municipal League. Furthermore, whenever key policy issues arose during the course of rule, the colonial administrations typically turned to academic expertise. For instance, when the regimes first broached the question of economic policy for the colonies, they turned to the preeminent economist James Conant.

34. For Root's views, see Root 1907. Root had initially started as a boss lawyer but eventually became a key progressive reformer within the Republican Party (Jessup 1938: 228–30).

35. Brownell and Sickle 1973: 173–74.

36. Both Taft and governor William Hunt in Puerto Rico had gone to Yale, class of 1878 (Osborne 1904: 4759). Other officials in Puerto Rico with Progressivist credentials included William F. Willoughby, Jacob Hollander, and Samuel Lindsay, all of whom were professors and had served in city-level commissions and/or served as experts in federal agencies.

37. Forbes 1928; GPR 1902: 57.

38. For a further clarification and elaboration of this theme in the context of America's wider empire, see Go 2007.

39. D. Williams 1913: 60–61.

40. USPC 1900: 90.

41. Schurman to John Hay, June 3, 1899 (MP, ser. 1, r. 7).

42. USPC 1900: 90.

43. Ibid.: 83.

44. Ibid.

45. Telegram to Guy Henry, March 11, 1899 (MP, reel 6, ser. 1).

46. Brig. Gen. U.S. Volunteers to Commanding Officer, U.S. Troops, Oct. 11, 1898 (RG 395, Entry 5875, "Aguadilla letters rec'd").

47. Rowe 1904b: 143–44.

48. Carroll 1899b: 7.

49. Ibid.: 55–56.

50. Ibid.: 260, 58.

51. USWD 1899a: 28. Similar recommendations are seen in USMG 1899: 1:342. Some officials suggested that statehood was something that "they have a right ultimately to expect" (G. Davis 1900: 75).

52. USPC 1900: 1:83–85.

53. Ibid.: 1:82.

54. Ibid.: 1:109, 1:120; Philippine Commission to Elihu Root, Aug. 21, 1900 (MP, reel 31, ser. 3).

55. USPC 1900: 1:101.

56. Buenker 1988; Ross 1984: 757; Wiebe 1995. For a broader discussion on the particularity of liberal democracy, see Parekh 1993.

57. R. M. Taylor 1971: 1:68.

58. Forbes, journal, Aug. 17, 1904, 1:43, (WCF); Forbes to H. L. Higginson, Sept. 2, 1904 (WCF, "Philippine Data: Political," 1:10); R. M. Taylor 1971: 1:68, 120–21.

59. USWD 1899a: 26.

60. Willoughby 1909b: 419.

61. Taft 1908: 7–8; USWD 1902: 116.

62. Platt 1901: 148.

63. Willoughby 1909a: 162.

64. At the time, this notion of liberal democracy was only emerging into its current form in the United States (Buenker 1988; Ross 1984: 757).

65. Woods quoted in Jacobson 2000: 186, Willoughby 1909a: 162; report of second Philippine Commission, quoted in Willoughby 1905: 187–88.

66. GPR 1905: 40–41. See also USSC 1902: 1:51.

67. As Robert Wiebe (1995: 40) puts it: "Free individuals formed democratic communities, democratic communities sustained free individuals."

68. Foucault, Burchell, Gordon, and Miller 1991.

69. Root 1907: 10–11. Wilson distinguished American democracy from its British predecessor precisely on this point. As opposed to the British, says Wilson "we printed the *SELF* [in self-government] large and the *government* small in every administrative arrangement we made and that is still our attitude and preference." For Wilson, this meant that "authority" in modern America is "nowhere gathered or organized into a single commanding force." Instead it derives from the "moderate and sensible discipline which makes free men good citizens" (W. Wilson 1901: 295–96; orig. capitalization and emphasis).

70. Willoughby 1909a: 161–62.

71. USPC 1901: 1:20; Roosevelt to Charles Eliot, April 4, 1904 (Roosevelt and Morison 1951: 4:769).

72. Willoughby (1909b: 419).

73. R. M. Taylor 1971: 1:68; Root 1917: 289; Sweet 1906: 13–14.

74. Sweet 1906: 13–14; Wilson in Worcester 1928: 2:972.

75. USWD 1902: 19–20, orig. Spanish version Rivero Méndez 1922: 210–11.

76. Miles 1911: 299, 301. See also, for the Americans—cognizance of Puerto Rican demands for democracy, James Wilson to J. G. Gilmore, July 30, 1898 (RG 108, v. 189: 190).

77. See report of Davis, USMG 1899: 1:322.

78. There were also other proclamations of similar character in this period (see Forbes 1928: 2:429–30, 2:437–38; USPC 1901: 1:119–21.

79. USPC 1900: 1:3–4.

80. Moses, diary, part 1, July 16, 1900 (BM).

81. G. Davis 1898: 329; quote from J. Wilson 1912: 2:453.

82. E. Ross to Asst. Adj-Gen, Regular Brigade, Aug. 16, 1898 (USNA, RG 108, v. 190); Herrmann 1907: 42; quote from Guy Henry to W. McKinley, April 8, 1899 (MP, reel 6, ser. 1).

83. USPC 1900: 1:178; Taft to George Davis, May 14, 1901 (WHT, ser. 3, r. 42).

84. Roosevelt 1968: 87.

85. Rafael 1993a; Salman 1995.

86. Foucault 1979: 136; 1990. David Scott (1995) clarifies the distinction between discipline and "colonial governmentality." Some scholars on the Philippines have emphasized the disciplinary nature of U.S. colonial rule (Rafael 1993; Salman 1995), but here I stress the governmental aspect that has been overlooked.

87. Taft, quoted in Alfonso 1969: 243; Burch 1902.

88. Taft 1908: 24.

89. Fowles 1910: 47.

90. GPR 1901: 418.

91. "Address of the Governor to the Alcaldes and Municipal Judges of Porto Rico . . . July 13, 1910" (USNA, RG 350, entry 1069-5).

92. Recorded in D. Williams 1913: 192, 236.

93. PRH, Jan. 18, 1902.

94. USPC 1903: 2:902.

95. Quoted in Willoughby 1905: 126–27.

96. USPC 1905: 1:353–54; Forbes 1928: 1:535.

97. Director Census of Porto Rico 1900: 190; GPR 1902: 84.

98. Root 1907: 19.

99. Taft 1908.

100. Willoughby 1905: 15.

101. Davis to Root, Oct. 14, 1899 (ERP, container no. 3, 1899, D-H).

102. Taft, quoted in MT, Jan. 31, 1901, 1; Worcester, quoted in May 1980: 42.

103. USPC 1900: 92–93.

104. Believing that the vast majority of the population was too "ignorant" to vote, the Americans initially restricted the suffrage to the wealthier and educated. The idea was to extend the suffrage later, as long the Puerto Ricans and Filipinos proved fit.

105. PRR, July 23, 1910, 7; March 13, 1907, press release of Philippine Commission on Act 1582 (USNA, BIA, RG 350, entry 10265-18).

106. See Cullinane 1971 for the best discussion of these state structures.

107. Taft to Henry M. Hoyt, Sept. 8, 1900 (CE, I, 1.16, "1900 September").

108. Willoughby 1905: 16; Willoughby 1909a: 166.

109. Taft 1908: 26.

110. USWD 1899e: 27. During the early stages of U.S. rule, the particular political form that such full self-government was eventually to take was undetermined. In fact, in regards to both colonies, the Americans initially left open the possibility for either statehood or national independence, though later it became clear to most policy makers that the Philippines should not become a fully fledged state in the Union, due to racial fears from groups in the south and elsewhere.

111. Forbes 1928: 1:98. George Marvin, a lower-level official in Puerto Rico, claimed similarly that tutelage would induce the "Americanization of a Latin community" (1903: 649).

2. DOMESTICATING TUTELAGE IN PUERTO RICO

1. Henry to McKinley, Aug. 14, 1898 (MP, reel 4, ser. 1).

2. Oliver 1901: 104, 121.

3. Garcia 1989: 123–24; Negrón Portillo 1997; Picó 1987, chap. 6.

4. LD, March 24, 1899; LD, April 29, 1900, 2; Pubill 1900: 87, Cancel 1998: 47; José Lorenzo Casalduc to Miles, Aug. 31, 1898 (RG 108, v. 191, 1315-16).

5. LD, Feb. 3, 1899, 2.

6. Nieves 1898: 110–11.

7. Mayor San German to General Schwan, Aug. (n.d.) 1898 (USNA, RG 395, entry 5943).

8. Henry to McKinley, Aug. 15, 1898 (MP, reel 4, ser. 1).

9. R. Davis 1898: 319, 329. See also Herrmann 1907: 32.

10. Carr 1984: 32; see also Alegria 1972.

11. Díaz-Quiñones 1999: 188; Luis García 2000; Santiago-Valles 1994.

12. See, for example, Dietz 1986.

13. The elite "found 'civilized' Spanish imperial origins perfectly compatible with the new reality of the New American empire" (Díaz-Quiñones 1999: 188).

14. Valle 1907: 567; Pumarada O'Neill 1990: 51.

15. Bergad 1983: 205–6.

16. Carroll 1899b: 507; see also 151, 332, 336–39.

17. Once Spain decided upon exit, Madrid set high tariffs on Puerto Rican goods, while Cuba, declaring its independence from Spain, quadrupled its import fee. See Bergad 1983, appendix 1; Dietz 1986: 99–100.

18. LD, Jan. 27, 1899, 2; Feb 27, 1899, 2, see also Bergad 1983: 207.

19. See interviews in Carroll 1899b: 768, 782; also LD, Jan. 28, 1899, 1, and Muñoz Rivera 1899.

20. Larringa quoted in Azel Ames to President McKinley, Feb. 7, 1900 (USNA, BIA, RG 350, entry 719-23); also U.S. Congress 1904: 385.

21. Ibid.: 338–39.

22. USWD 1902: 30.

23. GPR 1901: 420, 431; USWD 1902: 30. These kinds of declarations went on repeatedly and publicly, and they circulated widely (see esp. OGPR; Frances Gallart 1998: 132; J. Wilson 1912: 454–56).

24. As noted in the previous chapter, such corruption also marked American politics at home. But by virtue of that very fact rather than in spite of it, the elites' conduct marked the kinds of practices which American colonial officials classified as antithetical to their Progressive-era models of proper self-government — and which, accordingly, they repeatedly warned against.

25. Boyce 1914: 91; Van Buren 1905: 127. My point is not to say that the elites' practices were inferior to American "democracy." After all, corruption prevailed in the United States at the time too. The point rather is that the elites' practices were deemed by some Americans (particularly those associated with the Progressive movement) to be inferior.

26. G. Davis to E. Root, Oct. 14, 1899 (ERP, container no. 3, 1899, D-H); Guy Henry to W. McKinley, Jan. 23, 1899 (MP, reel 4, ser. 1).

27. G. Davis 1900: 102; OGPR, Dec. 17, 1898, 1.

28. From first quote to last in order: LD, Nov. 24, 1898, 2; LD, Jan. 27, 1899, 2.

29. LD, Nov. 17, 1898, 2; LD, Dec. 6, 1898, 2.

30. Thus, the distinct "origins" of the elites' political culture is not at stake here. Nor do I presume that the elites' "culture" was static. The point is to track a series of

signifying patterns at a specific period in time, while recognizing a larger history of formation and external influence.

31. Implicit in my discussion of "patron-clientelism" that patron-client relations play out at different registers homologously (e.g., social, economic, political; Scott 1972).

32. On these relationships, see Baralt 1999: 86; Bergad 1983: 133; Buitrago Ortiz 1976: 27–28, 40–42; Buitrago Ortiz 1982; Dietz 1986: 40; Picó 1981: 197–98, 203–4; Picó 1985; Wolf 1956.

33. Wells 1969: 34–35; Quintero Rivera 1980: 107; Wolf 1956: 195; Mayol Alcover 1974: 158–59.

34. From the novel *La Charca* by Manuel Zeno Gandía, quoted in Findlay 1999: 58.

35. Buitrago Ortiz 1982: 167–8, 171–2; Díaz Hernández 1983: 39–40; Picó 1993: 66; USWD 1899b: 81.

36. Bergad 1983: 150–51; also Buitrago Ortiz 1982: 62; Picó 1993: 42–43.

37. Normandía Ayala 1984: 19–21; Pubill 1900: 63–73, 80; Wolf 1956: 195. On renouncing salaries, see, e.g., LD, July 26, 1896, 3.

38. USWD 1899c: 36; Secretary of State to George Davis, May 17, 1899 (AGPR, FF, Gob-Munic., box 110, file 3142); Carroll 1899b: 19.

39. E. Wilson 1905: 56–57.

40. See Phelan 1960 on "flexible" bureaucracies; on exchange and political patronage see Cubano-Iguina 1988–89 and Buitrago Ortiz 1982: 146–48; on law, see Carroll 1899b: 19; E. Wilson 1905: 56; USWD 1902: 249. Distressed laborers and poorer groups rarely if ever took their issues to the courts, and the courts were controlled by officials and allied landed families anyway.

41. E.S.L. 1898: 7.

42. On Isabela, see Barceló Miller 1979: 67–68; on Mayaguez, see Gaudier Texidor 1957; on Utuado, see Picó 1993: 43 and Ramos 1946.

43. Mayol Alcover 1974: 126; Buitrago Ortiz 1982: 154–55.

44. The rise in coffee production was enabled by the expansion of cultivated acreage, hence the subsumption of more tenant-clients.

45. Some Puerto Ricans were merchants, but the Spaniards clearly dominated the lines of circulation Cubano-Iguina 1988–89; Dietz 1986: 29–30. Picó 1993: 42–43 notes that as long as the coffee economy remained intact, relations between the Puerto Rican landowners and the Spanish merchants remained amicable.

46. Barceló Miller 1984: 55–57; Limon de Arce 1938: 405.

47. Brau 1956: 177, 181, 186, 356, 358–59. Brau applied the same conception to relations between merchant and landlord. For more on Brau's thought, see Garcia 1989: 23 and Quintero Rivera 1988.

48. See Quintero Rivera 1981: 24, 1988: 47–48, 199–200. Also see Diego 1890: 41; LD, Jan. 26, 1898, 2, and Findlay 1999: 57–59.

49. LD, April 5, 1897, 2; see also Díaz Soler and Matienzo Cintrón 1960: 125; and Cubano Iguina 1998: 654.

50. Cepeda 1888: 10.

51. Ibid.: 16.

52. LD, April 24, 1896, 2; Cubano-Iguina 1998: 652.

53. LD, April 24, 1896, 2; LD, Feb. 20, 1897, 2.

54. Quoted in Cubano-Iguina 1998: 651.

55. LD, Jan. 26, 1898, 2.

56. Quoted in Cubano-Iguina 1998: 644n40.

57. Brau 1973: 125.

58. LD, May 22, 1893, reprinted in Muñoz Rivera 1960: 152.

59. Muñoz Rivera 1960: 152–53.

60. Diego 1890: 63.

61. Ibid.: 41–42.

62. Cepeda 1888: 7.

63. Domínguez 1887: 24.

64. Muñoz Rivera quoted in Cruz Monclova 1964: III, 3, 316–17.

65. Coll y Toste to W. H. Hunt, Nov. 30, 1902, 2 (USNA, Secretary of the Interior Office, RG 48, M824, Roll #2); Díaz Soler 1960: 592, 692–93; SJN May 2, 1903, 3; Wells 1969: 58; Carroll 1899b: 600.

66. BG 1971: I, 1, 16; Cubano-Iguina 1995: 410.

67. Cepeda 1888: 77–80; also LD, April, 3, 1897: 3.

68. LD, Feb. 17, 1897, 2; Muñoz Rivera quoted in Arana-Soto 1974: 82.

69. Muñoz Rivera in LD, April 9, 1896, quoted in Cubano-Iguina 1998: 652. On the autonomists' discourse and campaigns, see Partido Liberal Comité Provincial 1897: 1–2; LD, April 3, 1897, 2; May 24, 1897, 3.

70. LD, March 13, 1897, 2; see also Cubano-Iguina 1998: 655.

71. Cepeda 1988: 75.

72. Ibid. For this conception of elections across different parts of Latin America, see Morse 1989: 102–3. On the equation between elections and "representation," see Guerra 1994.

73. USWD 1899c: 36.

74. Cepeda 1888: 27, 37.

75. BG 1971: I, 1, doc. no. 24, 172.

76. Cepeda 1888: 39–40.

77. Juan del Valle to FD, March 8, 1897 FDG, I, IX, 3

78. BG 1971: I, 1, 16; Cubano-Iguina 1995: 410. On the uses of retraimiento, see Kidder 1965: 150.

79. BHPR 13, no. 2: 96.

80. Negrón Portillo 1990: 20–21.

81. S. del Valle Atiles to Federico Degetau, Oct. 14, 1897 (FDG, 2, 1, 30).

82. Carroll 1899b: 344; see also Cubano Iguina 1995: 414; Negron-Portillo 1990: 49–50.

83. These activities are described in the following primary and secondary accounts: Bayron Toro 1977: 105–8; BG 1979: I, 1, 24; Burgos Malave 1997: 204; Carroll 1899b: 342, 792; Cruz Monclova 1962: III, 3, 477; Diaz Soler 1994: 705; Paco del Valle to Federico Degetau, March 28, 1898 (FDG 2, II, 30); "Report of Republican Committee on Insular Affairs" (AGPR, FF, GC, box 68, file unnumbered); USWD 1902: 11.

84. Burgos-Malave 1997: 205–12; Negrón Portillo 1980: 137–38; Picó 1993: 198–99; "Report of Republican Committee on Insular Affairs" (AGPR, FF, GC, box 68, file unnumbered).

85. Pedro to Federico Degetau, Jan. 13, 1898 (FDG 2, II, 5); Francisco del Valle to Federico Degetau, Jan. 17, 1898 (FDG 2, II, 7).

86. Coll Cuchí 1972: 178.

87. Maj. Gen James Wilson to Brig. Gen. J. G. Gilmore, July 30, 1898 (RG 108, v. 189, 190).

88. "Yauco (P.R.) E.U.de América. July 29 de 1898. El Alcalde, Franciso Mejía," in Rivero Méndez 1922: 218.

89. Ibid.: 674.

90. "Acta de . . . Fajardo" in memoirs of López Giménez 1998: 85–86. Other council discourse in BHPR 6, no. 1: 58; "Munic. Council of Cabo Rojo" Aug. 14, 1898 (USNA, RG 395, entry 5858); Rivero Méndez 1922: 675–79, 218.

91. Rivero Méndez 1922: 409; my italics.

92. LD, Sept. 19, 1899, 2.

93. "Al Pueblo de Puerto Rico: Manifesto," in Fernández Méndez 1975: 1:45–46.

94. Nieves 1898: 11.

95. This idea, part and parcel of Spanish ideologies of republicanism, had been used by liberal Spanish elite across the country as an important ideological basis for opposition to Isabel II in the revolution of 1868. It was then appropriated by Puerto Ricans as they demanded the autonomic regime in the 1890s.

96. LD, Oct. 5, 1899, 2. Quiñones in GPR 1900: 417.

97. LD, Aug. 5, 1899, 2; also March 29, 1899.

98. The origins of this equation between Spanish federalism and U.S. federalism could be traced back to the views of the Liberal-Autonomist party, whose platforms for autonomy were most likely inspired by a localized understanding of the U.S. federalist system. This is suggested but not elaborated upon in Guillermety 1995: 123.

99. LD, June 15, 1899, 2.

100. This view may have been due also to the fact that the United States had annexed Hawaii and was contemplating its incorporation as a State.

101. LD, March 29, 1899, 2, capitalization original.

102. L. Muñoz Rivera to E. Root, Aug. 14, 1899 (USNA, BIA, RG 350, entry 168-17).

103. LD, Oct. 7, 1899, 2; also LD, Dec. 10, 1898, 2.

104. U.S. Congress 1904: 382–83; also Carroll 1899b: 800.

105. BHPR 8, no. 6: 356–57.

106. For a related theoretical discussion of "selective attention" by cultural sociologists, see DiMaggio 1997.

107. Willoughby 1909b: 421.

108. Rowe 1904a: 145; GPR 1901: 341; Willoughby 1909b: 419. Reports of these activities are many and do not only include Americans' accounts; Barbosa's party members also reported on them (E. Gonzalez to Governor-General, Feb. 5, 1900, AGPR/FF/GC-181; EP, Sept. 8, 1899, 2).

109. Edward Lee to secretary of Puerto Rico, July 16, 1900 (AGPR, FF, GC, Gob., Informes, box 69, file 480).

110. For the American authorities, these appointments were meant to smooth the transition to U.S. rule and achieve collaboration. "They understand clearly," Brooke wrote to President McKinley about the new appointees, "that this is a military government and that their collaboration will be of great value to me; in fact, without it, and because of their knowledge of [civil] affairs, I could not do without their services" (Brooke to H. C. Corbin, Oct. 24, 1898, quoted in Rosario Natal 1975: 259).

111. GPR 1902: 78; also Davis 1900: 54; Willoughby 1905: 126; 1909b: 421; 1910: 78.

112. Alonzo Gray, 1st Lt., 5th Cavalry to Adjutant General, Sept. 15, 1899 (USNA, RG 395-5908); Willoughby 1909b: 420–21; 1910: 78, 86.

113. Rowe 1904a: 145; Willoughby 1910: 431.

114. GPR 1901: 341; see also USWD 1902: 109 and GPR 1902: 76.

115. Willoughby 1909b: 419, 421; also Rowe 1904a: 146; Brig. General of the U.S. Volunteers to Secretary of PR, July 10, 1899 (AGPR, FF, GC, Gob., Munic., box 72, file 10466); Capt. Bishop to Adjutant General, July 5, 1899 (AGPR, FF, GC, PP, box 181, file 4693); Myer to Battle, Nov. 26, 1899 (USNA, RG 395, entry 5928).

116. Willoughby 1910: 77, 127.

117. Resident of Quebradillas to Secretary of Interior, June 2, 1899 (in USNA, BIA, RG 350, entry 719-2). The Americans then had to issue a circular ordering: "No man is to be refused employment, or is to be employed, on account of his belonging to a political party" (Director of Public Works, June 2, 1899, USNA, BIA, RG 350, entry 719-1); LD, Feb. 25, 1899, 2.

118. Wilson 1905: 60; Rowe 1904b: 60.

119. OGPR, Dec. 14, 1898, 1; see also Henry to Adjutant-General, Jan. 15, 1899 (USNA, RG 350, entry 168). Muñoz was not just deviously manipulating his power.

120. EP, Jan. 14, 1900, 2.

121. Coll Cuchí 1972: 94

122. Bishop to Adjutant General, July 5, 1899 (AGPR, FF, GC, PP, box 181, file 4693); Brig. General of the U.S. Volunteers to Secretary of PR, July 10, 1899 (AGPR, FF, GC, Gob., Munic., box 72, file 10466); Capt. Casey to Adjunct General, June 7, 1899 (AGPR, FF, GC, Gob., Munic., box 181, file 2751).

123. Quoted in Berbusse 1966: 105; see also Myer to Battle, Nov. 26, 1899, reporting on discussion with a Federal Party member (USNA, RG 395, entry 5928). Also see GPR 1901: 103.

124. P. Guash to Brooke, Dec. 1, 1898, AGPR/FF/GC/PP, box 181; U.S. Senate 1900: 59.

125. U.S. Congress 1904: 222.

126. GPR 1901: 20–21.

127. General Orders, no. 160, Oct. 12, 1899 (USNA, BIA, RG 350, entry 1286-2).

128. "Ex Parte: In the matter of Thomas Vasquez, Petitioner. Ex Parte: In the matter of José Juan Vidal, et al., Petitioners" (unpublished ms., 1900, UPRL); Report of Captain Vance in USWD DCIA 1900: 6–7.

129. USWD 1902: 112.

130. Wilson 1905: 99; LD, Feb. 28, 1905, 6; USWD 1902: 272.

131. Quote from USWD 1902: 272.

132. Acevedo, et al., to Secretary of State, Oct. 15, 1902 (AGPR/FF/GC, PP, Caja 181); Palmer to Roosevelt, Nov. 5, 1902 (USNA, RG 48, film #824-2); USWD 1902: 272.

133. LD, Sept. 15, 1899, 2.

134. E. Wilson 1905: 74; GPR 1901: 46.

135. Garcia to Governor, Nov. 4, 1902 (AGPR, FF, GC, Judicial, Tribunales, file 2306); see also Federal Committee to Governor, Oct. 25, 1900 (AGPR, FF/GC/PP, box 181, file 787); Gregorio Duran to Governor, Oct. 25, 1902 (AGPR, FF, GC, Judicial, Tribunales, file 2306); Rowe 1904b: 147–48; USWD 1902: 112.

136. Ricardo to Governor, Nov. 7, 1900 AGPR, FF/GC/PP/box 181; Silverstrini de Pacheo 1980: 34.

137. Rowe 1904b: 147–48; see also Alcalde of Aguadilla to Secretary of Puerto Rico, Oct. 15, 1902 AGPR, FF/GC/PP, box 181, file 787; SJN, Sept. 21, 1900, 2; Negrón Portillo 1990: 172; Independent, Oct. 18, 1900, 2479; Hunt to Secretary of the Interior (USNA, RG 48, file #284, roll 2, 10–13).

138. Rowe 1904b: 147–48.

139. Pagan 1959: 60; A.H. Lambert to Secretary of PR in AGPR, FF/GC/PP/box 181, file 1460.

140. GPR 1901: 18–20.

141. Davis to Root, Oct. 14, 1899 (ERP, container no. 3: 1899, D-H); Rowe 1904b: 155.

142. USWD 1902: 30.

143. Rowe 1904b: 155.

144. USMG 1899: 322.

145. Colton to Clarence R. Edwards, Nov. 22, 1911 (USNA, RG 350; entry 1286-23).

146. Nor can domestication be explained from the top down; that is, by want of the Americans' efforts. The American authorities had made their narratives, meanings, and models clear.

3. WINNING HEARTS AND MINDS IN THE PHILIPPINES

1. Wolff 1991: 10.

2. USMG 1899: 4; Golay 1998: 52, 65; Ninkovich 2001: 51.

3. Quoted in Weinberg 1935: 283. Officially the war lasted from 1899, when the first shots were fired, until General Aguinaldo was captured and the Malolos regime was disassembled in 1901 (Stanley 1974: 51).

4. The literature is large, but for review, see Velasco Shao and Francia 2002.

5. Otis 1900: 2906.

6. Quoted in Brands 1992: 58.

7. Historians have tracked the elites' religious orientations and visions of nationhood and race (see, e.g., Aguilar 1998; Rafael 1993c), but the elites' schemes on democratic self-government or associated concepts like rights, freedom, or liberty have not been fully examined. Exceptional works include Majul 1967 and 1996.

8. Again, as in chapter 2, an analysis of the "origins" of the elites' political culture is not my task. After all, once we talk about origins, we are forced into an infinite regress that is obliged to track the origins of the origins. My point is rather to abstract a meaning system as evidenced in the elites' discourse and conduct at a specific moment in time, analyzing it for its own internal patterns while acknowledging that it was only one small moment in a larger process of formation and transcultural influence. Nor do I aim to presume a single "Filipino culture." I am speaking here only of what a handful of Filipino elites said and did.

9. Larkin 1972: 83; Echauz 1894: 45; Aguilar 1998: 145; Kerkvliet 1977: 6–7; Fegan 1982: 95–96. I cannot discuss the complexity of different forms of agricultural production across the archipelago. I here abstract shared elements from the different systems. For an overview see the essays in McCoy and de Jesus (1982).

10. Kerkvliet 1977: 6.

11. On utang na loób, criticisms of the scholarly uses and abuses of the idiom have emerged (Bennagen 1985; Gonzales 1982), for scholars have typically treated utang na loób as an essential and transhistorical "Filipino value." Other scholars, however, avoid these essentialisms and have treated the practices associated with utang na loób as historically forged and politically charged (Rafael 1993: 124–26; Ileto 1979). This is the approach I adopt here. Specifically, I treat it as indicative of the kind of schemas that guided elite practice, without presuming that they constituted essential, subjective values or norms.

12. Kerkvliet 1977: 9–11.

13. Robles 1969: 64, 67.

14. Foreman 1906: 224; quote from Montero y Vidal 1886: 163; also see Corpuz 1957: 69.

15. Robles 1969: 69; on these activities, see also Bankoff 1992; Corpuz 1957: 111, and Sidel 1993: 116.

16. Altamirano y Salcedo 1902: 8; Alvarez 1887: 307; Corpuz 1957: 114; Foreman 1906: 222–23; Montero y Vidal 1886: 163.

17. Alvarez 1887: 307, 318; Borromeo 1973: 127; Larkin 1972: 93; May 1980: 54; Robles 1969: 85, 240.

18. On taxation and tribute, see Blair and Robertson 1903: xxxvi, 286; on buwis, see Aguilar 1998: 66–67, 75, 214n21; Noceda and Salucar 1860: 62, and Forbes 1928: 1:259–60.

19. Robles 1969: 281–87.

20. This logic of elections can be discerned from existing secondary studies and primary descriptions of elections. See Alvarez 1887; Jesus 1978; May 1988.

21. Alvarez 1887: 318.

22. Jesus 1978: 152–53; May 1988: 33–34.

23. Steinberg 1967: 7–9 summarizes the vast literature that discusses these community and exchange logics.

24. In Tagalog, this logic was rendered categorically as a distinction between the "ins" and "outs," or loób and labas (Alejo et al. 1996).

25. Mabini was revered by nearly all groups, and he later served as a key adviser to the revolutionary government at Malolos. For the best overview on Mabini, see Majul 1996.

26. Mabini 1931: 2:22–23, 2:68.

27. The similarities between the thought of Adam Smith and Mabini are surely there, but Mabini's discussion of "mutual exchange" for the realization of need is irreducible to economistic readings of Smith. For Mabini, mutual exchange was the basis of morality.

28. Mabini 1931: 2:68.

29. As quoted in T. Kalaw 1956: 73.

30. Mabini 1931: 2:23. This discourse of exchange, debt, and reciprocity in part drew from Christian ideologies with which the Filipino elite were familiar. Many of the ilustrados had been educated in Catholic schools. But the discourse was also grounded in lived experience, rather than being only ideological or cosmological.

31. Mabini 1931: 1:105, 2:22; Majul 1996: 236.

32. Mabini 1931: 2:23.

33. Retana 1892: 207.

34. From the first public petition reigstered against the "friarocracy" in Retana 1892:

207, 217–18. On the movement, see Fajardo 1998: 342. See also Candido García, "Official communication entering complaint against the priest of his village," Jan. 17, 1888, Manila (Newberry Library, Ayer ms. 1351).

35. Rios reproduced in Taylor 1971: 1:148.

36. Speech of M. H. del Pilar in T. Kalaw 1956: 33–34. Of course, to speak of the Philippines as something that had existed when Legaspi first arrived was itself an invention; the point is that the ilustrados did not see it that way.

37. *La Solidaridad*, March 31, 1895. Pilar called this "the civilising procedure" — "the exchange of products for the material, and the exchange of ideas for the moral" (*La Solidaridad*, Jan. 31, 1895).

38. *La Solidaridad*, March 31, 1895.

39. *La Solidaridad*, Jan. 15, 1895.

40. See the word entries in Laktaw 1965. The term *delicadeza* to further describe a good ruler is related: this was the word that Hispanicized Filipinos used to refer to that "special intuitive sense" involved in forging successful patron-client relationships (Paredes 1988: 50).

41. Taylor 1971: 1:148, exhibit 22. Even conservative Filipinos arguing against either reform or revolution used the same cultural structure, but they stressed that Spain was in fact fulfilling their obligations. See, for instance, Buencamino's discourse in ibid., 1:153, exhibit 23.

42. *La Solidaridad*, Jan. 15, 1895.

43. *La Solidaridad*, Aug. 31, 1895.

44. Mabini 1931: 2:23.

45. Ibid.: 1:104.

46. HR, Oct. 2, 1898. See also HR, Oct. 23, 1898, 3, and Nov. 6, 1898, 2.

47. Ileto 1979: 86–87.

48. Mabini 1931: 2:23–24.

49. Jacinto reprinted in Santos Cristóbal 1918: 424.

50. Mabini 1931: 2:68.

51. "Speech of Emilio Aguinaldo," Aug. 3, 1898, in Taylor 1971: 3:185, exhibit 86.

52. Jacinto in Santos Cristóbal 1918: 425, 427.

53. Mabini 1931: 1:104; see also Taylor 1971: 3:142–43.

54. Alvarez 1887: 318.

55. Quoted in Santos 1918: 949–50.

56. Mabini 1931: 2:24.

57. Taylor 1971: 3:142; see also HR, Sept. 28, 1898, 2.

58. Alvarez 1992: 346. See also *La Republica Filipina*, Sept. 15, 1898, 3.

59. Taylor 1971: 3:104, exhibit 28.

60. Mabini 1931: 2:23.

61. Ibid.: 69.

62. Calderon 1919: 474. See also Rizal 1922: 282; Aguinaldo in Taylor 1971: 3:185, exhibit 86; HR, Oct. 2, 1898, 1.

63. Taylor 1971: 3:113–16, exhibit 35; 157, 273.

64. HR, Oct. 2, 1898, 17.

65. Taylor 1971: 3:60, exhibit 59; the revolutionary flag is referred to in "Proclamation of the Independence of the Filipino People," 3:105, exhibit 28.

66. HR, Jan. 1, 1899. Even the nonrevolutionaries recognized and shared in the meanings. The debate between revolutionaries and nonrevolutionaries was a contest over the meaning of *structure*.

67. USPC 1900: 1:3–4.

68. USPC 1900: 1:6; Schurman to J. Hay, April 13, 1899 (MP, ser. 1, r. 6). Local newspapers acknowledged the proclamation, as far down as the central southern island of Cebu. See, e.g., *La Justicia*, April 16, 1899.

69. USPC 1900: 1:6. Worcester, diary, May 26, 1899 (WPC, Documents and Papers, vol. 16).

70. The dissenters included the more aristocratic and conservative elites who had joined the revolution against Spain only at its tail end (Golay 1998: 50, see also Agoncillo 1960).

71. USSC 1902: part 3, 2630; May 1979: 553; Owen 1979; Totanes 1990: 488–89.

72. "Poblete's Peace Rally," Nov. 17, 1901 (CE, 1, folder 1.25, Nov.–Dec. 1901).

73. Ignacio Villamor quoted in Scott 1986: 168.

74. "Interview . . ." enclosure in William H. Taft to Elihu Root, Dec. 14, 1900 (ERP, container 164, "Special Correspondence, 1900–1902").

75. Out of the sixteen provincial governors, ten had been military officers of the republic; two had been members of the Malolos Congress; and one had been a journalist for the republic's revolutionary journals.

76. Quezon 1946: 88.

77. Pardo de Tavera 1901: 162, 163.

78. Filipinos may have also surrendered at that time because revolutionaries sensed that Aguinaldo was already weakened by the U.S. military, which is partly why Aguinaldo was captured. Nonetheless, the data combined with the testimonies presented here at least show that the establishment of local governments with Filipino participation played a key part.

79. D. Williams 1913: 66.

80. USPC 1900: 1:100–3; from Cebu, see *La Justicia*, April 16, 1899, and June 25, 1899; Paterno 1900. Ruby Paredes 1990 notes that the concept of "independence under an American protectorate" was used interchangeably with "autonomy"; she has also hinted at some of the particularities of the meaning of the concept, though I elaborate the meaning here in greater detail.

81. USSC 1902: part 1, 341–42. See also Forbes 1928: 2:387n1.

82. The Americans later suppressed talk of it (declaring it agitational and treasonous), and thus the historical record on the Filipinos' direct discourse about it is sparse. The best we can do is piece together disparate elements and commentaries, sometimes by the American officials.

83. USSC 1902: part 1, 739.

84. Forbes, journal, Aug. 9, 1904, 1:51 (WCF, handwritten journal, ms# AM 1365).

85. USSC 1902: part 4, 128; see also part 5, 237.

86. REN, Feb. 27, 1903, 1. Elite demands for education, infrastructure, and so on are seen in REN, Nov. 17, 1903; USPC 1900: 2:422; *El Grito*, Oct. 9, 1903, and Philippine Commission, Executive Minutes, Dec. 21, 1900, 198–99 (Doe Library, University of California, Berkeley).

87. Untitled newspaper clipping from Moses, diary, part 2, Feb. 18, 1901, (BM).

88. Quotes of speech combined from two sources: James LeRoy, travelogue, May 1, 1901 (James A. LeRoy Papers, Bentley Historical Library) and *La Paz*, May 5, 1901 (clipping from Moses, diary, part 4, Aug. 23, 1901 [BM]).

89. "Interview . . ." Taft to Root, Dec. 14, 1900 (ERP, container 164, "Special Correspondence, 1900–1902," held in folder Oct. 1901).

90. F. Buencamino to W. H. Taft, Nov. 1, 1900, in Paredes 1980: 217.

91. MT, April 12, 1901, 1. See also Paterno 1900: 8. Moses, diary, part 3, May 13, 1901 (BM).

92. USPC 1901: 1:78; also MT July 5, 1901, 4.

93. Forbes, journal, Aug. 19, 1904 1:47 (WCF); see also Paredes 1990: 214.

94. MT, March 18, 1902, 3. See also USSC 1902: part 3, 2278. Even those hesitant to lay down their arms used the same cultural structure. In their discourse, the Americans would not fulfill their obligations; American occupation would merely reproduce Spanish rule. The Americans were but different tokens of the same patronage type. See "Faustino," May 2, 1899 (MP, ser 1, r. 6); *La Justicia*, April 16, 1899; Mojares 1999: 24, Worcester, diary, May 26, 1899 (WPC, Documents and Papers, vol. 16); Schurman to John Hay, June 3, 1899 (MP, ser. 1, r. 7); Pardo de Tavera 1901: 161–62. See also Ileto 1979, on peasant-based revolutionary movements, and Rafael 1993a, on urban workers in Manila.

95. Newspaper clipping from MT in Moses, diary, part 2, Feb. 18, 1901 (BM); see also Worcester, WPC, Documents and Papers, vol. 1, entry for Feb. 12, 1901.

96. Taft to Henry M. Hoyt, March 6, 1901 (CE, 1, 1.21).

97. USPC 1900: 2:2.

98. Ibid.: 2:50–51.

99. Ibid.: 2:51, emphasis added.

100. Taft to Root, July 14, 1900 (ERP, container no. 164); also USSC 1902: part 1, 51.

101. Taft 1908: 31; see also USPC 1900: 1:182–83 and USSC 1902: part 1, 61.

102. USPC 1900: 2:51.

103. Ibid.: 2:52.

104. USPC 1900: 2:23, 2:67; see also the responses of Torres, Alberto Barretto, and others, 2:188, 2L371.

105. Quoted in Forbes 1928: 2:497.

106. USPC 1900: 2:72.

107. Taft quoted in MT, Jan. 31, 1901, 1.

108. USWD 1901: 1:21. Gobernadorcillos were renamed mayors or presidentes and made elective, and Filipinos were also allowed to hold provincial posts (USWD 1900a: 474–89).

109. Moses 1908: 127–28.

110. Taft 1908: 34.

111. USPC 1901: 1:40; see also USPC 1904: 1:83–84.

112. D. Williams 1913: 260. See also Forbes 1928: 1:154–55; "Memorandum of the Chief of Law Division, regarding voluntary contributions" (WPC, Documents and Papers, vol. 1, item 26); Cullinane 1971: 32–33.

113. USWD 1901: 1:20. On the various practices see USPC 1901: 40; USWD 1901: 1:20–21; USPC 1904: 1:84.

114. Forbes quoted in Cullinane 1971: 32; also USPC 1914: 14.

115. Forbes 1928: 1:158–59.

116. Forbes, journal, Dec. 3, 1904, 1:116 (WCF, ms# AM 1365).

117. "Memorandum of the Chief of Law Division."

118. May 1980: 54; USPC 1910: 83.

119. Bernard Moses, diary, part 7, Dec. 14, 1901 (BM); see also USPC 1904: 1:85.

120. Forbes, journal, Aug. 19, 1904, 1:52 (WCF, fms AM 1365).

121. Forbes to Henry Higginson, Sept. 2, 1904; Forbes, journal, 1:10 (WCF).

122. Williams 1913: 284.

123. Ibid.

124. Report of Aguedo Agbayani, Gov. of Ilocos Norte, Jan. 11, 1902, in USSC 1902: part 2, 459–60, emphasis added.

125. REN, Oct. 1, 1903, 1.

126. Fee 1910: 14.

127. Freer 1906: 19.

128. Ibid.: 19.

129. USPC 1904: 1:37.

130. MT, Nov. 30, 1903, 1.

131. MT, Jan. 22, 1904, 4.

132. MT, Nov. 30, 1903, 1; Dec. 16, 1903, 1; MT Jan. 31, 1906, 4.

133. USPC 1907: 1:166; USPC 1904: 1:368; 1906: 34–35; MT Dec. 7, 1905, 5. See also Meimban 1997: 214–16.

134. USPC 1907: 1:166, 1:368; MT, Feb. 8, 1906, 4.

135. MT Jan 10, 1907, 10; USPC 1904: 1:368; 1905: 1:35; MT, Nov. 30, 1903, 1.

136. USPC 1905: 1:34–36; USPC 1904: 1:368; see also MT, Oct. 1, 1906, 2; Oct. 2, 1906, 4, and Jan. 7, 1907.

137. USPC 1905: 1:33–34. See also USPC 1904: 1:315. It is likely that much more corruption went undiscovered, but even the reported proportion is high. During the high phase of corruption in the United States, from 1789 through 1916, less than 2 percent of all Congressional elections were contested due to bribery and intimidation (J. Baker 1998: 214).

138. USPC 1904: 1:37.

4. BEYOND CULTURAL REPRODUCTION

1. Stern 1998: 53.

2. Fox 1985; Obeyeskere 1992.

3. GPR 1907; Hartzell 1909: 172; Post 1909: 184.

4. Knowledge of Spanish, in fact, had been one of the office-holding requirements during Spanish rule, and this set the basis for holding office during American rule.

5. On the Filipino political elite and the connections they developed with each other over time, see Cullinane 1971.

6. As critics note, therefore, structural-functionalist approaches lack "coherent explanations of what can change culture *even among fully socialized adults*" (Rogowski 1997: 15; emphasis added).

7. See especially Chong 2002.

8. "The elections and offices set up by the Americans did not serve to create good democratic political leaders," because of the fact of colonialism and the ruling strategies of collaboration (Paredes 1988: 65). See also the essays in Owen 1971.

9. A related difference might have to do with the relative availability of the Americans' models. Given the geographical dispersion of the Philippine archipelago, for example, we might wonder whether the Americans' meanings were less retrievable there than in Puerto Rico; or whether the size of the archipelago might have in other ways restricted the dissemination of the Americans' political influence. Yet, the American officials themselves were aware of this issue and took steps to change. For example, as I will show in chapter 5, they assigned American agents to each province. If anything, then, American influence was probably more capable of dissemination in the Philippines than in Puerto Rico, where American agents were not assigned to local governments.

10. Burke 1997: 208.

11. The world can be thought of as a *referential field*: the dimensions of life that symbols reckon and render apprehensible, and to which they give meaningful form. Depending on the categories deployed, the world might then include other people and their relationships, ecological systems or electoral ballots, even concrete buildings and spatial arrangements. It might include anything cultural struc-

tures conjure as nouns: objects, events and happenings, people, their activities or products, and ideas.

12. Johnson 1997: 8.

13. Ricoeur 1984; Somers and Gibson 1994.

14. See also Roland Barthes (1977: 86–87) who suggests that codes and narratives are always "bundled" together. Classification therefore entails narrative and vice versa.

15. Keesing 1974: 89.

16. Sahlins alludes to disjunction when he speaks of the "recalcitrance" of the world, but the kind of recalcitrance I posit is different: it involves devaluation of a schema, not a revaluation.

17. DiMaggio 1997.

18. L. Amadeo in U.S. Congress 1904: 382.

19. *Boletín Mercantil de Puerto Rico*, Sept. 1899, 1, quoted in Schwartz 1992:304.

20. Carroll 1899: 68, see also 507–8.

21. Quoted in Negrón Portillo 1991: 36.

22. SJN Dec. 17, 1899, 1.

23. Commissioner of the Interior for Puerto Rico 1900: 32; 1901: 39; Carroll 1899: 763.

24. Carroll 1899: 106.

25. Ibid.: 507. See also LCPR, May 30, 1898, 1.

26. LCPR, Aug. 8, 1898, 2; AGPR, FF, Munic., San Juan, box 34, files 27–30.

27. Coll y Toste to Gen. Geo. Davis, Sept. 27, 1899 (AGPR, FF, Munic., Arecibo, box 75, file 6013); LD, Jan. 17, 1898, 2.

28. Carroll 1899: 738; USWD 1902: 182, 371–72, 376–77, 455–64, 657–65; USWD 1899: 45.

29. USWD 1902: 730, 739; SJN, March 20, 1900, 1; "Residents of Quebradillas to Secretary of Interior," May 13, 1899 (USNA, RG 350, entry 101-719, item 2); Circular of Director of Public Works, June 2, 1899, in ibid., item 1.

30. Guy Henry to Gen. Gilmore, Aug. 10, 1898 USNA, RG 108, vol. 190.

31. USWD 1900: 5; USWD 1902: 741, n. 4088; GPR 1901: 161.

32. SJN, Sept. 4, 1900, 2; for municipal finances, see USWD 1900: 73–74.

33. Alcalde of Utuado to Governor General, March 13, 1900 (AGPR, FF/GC/Gob-Munic., box 107, file 7591).

34. Gen. Geo. Davis to Secretary of State, July 10, 1899 (AGPR, FF, GC, Gob-Munic., Aguadilla, box 72, file 4275); E. Pujal to Governor, Dec. 10, 1899 (AGPR, FF, GC, Gob-Munic., Mayaguez, box 95, file 1032); Rafael Cordova y Ramirez to Secretary of PR, Feb 28, 1901 (AGPR, FF, GC, Gob-Munic., Arecibo, box 75, file 1527).

35. Picó 1998:47; LD, March 13, 1900, 2.

36. Gen. George Davis to Asst. Secretary of War, March 23, 1900 (USNA, BIA, RG 350, 975-5).

37. LD March 13, 1900, 2.

38. USWD 1900: 45, Pablo Villela Pol quoted in Bergad 1983.

39. Picó 1997: 341; Pubill 1990: 103–4.

40. Pubill 1990: 103–4.

41. Quoted in Carroll 1899: 507.

42. Carroll 1899: 601–2, 604. Federico E. Virella to Commanding U.S. General, Nov. 17, 1898 (AGPR, FF, box 16, unnumbered file; also box 58, file titled "Attorney General," May 1, 1902). Also see Picó 1987: 129–30 and Santiago-Valles 1994.

43. LCPR, Aug. 30, 1898: 1; SJN, Dec. 31, 1899, 1, April 29, 1900, 1.

44. Carroll 1899: 602.

45. Ibid.: 795; see also Picó 1997: 47.

46. On the town plaza as the site for the traditional elite, see Picó 1997; Quintero-Rivera 1988: chap. 1. For these incidents, see SJN, Dec. 27, 1900, 1; Ramon Yrizarri to Secretary of PR, Oct. 1, 1903 (AGPR, FF, GC, Gob-Munic., Mayaguez, box 96, file 97); Mayor of Mayaguez to Governor, Oct. 8, 1903 (AGPR, FF, GC, Gob-Munic., Mayaguez, box 96, file 97).

47. LD, Feb. 28, 1901; Negrón Portillo 1997; Santiago-Valles 1994: 103.

48. Bernardino Diaz to Secretary of PR (AGPR, FF, box 110); Rowe 1904: 147–48.

49. USWD 1902: 105. Local newspapers seemed to cover only some of these incidents in 1899. They initially censured reports about violence out of fear that Puerto Rican's image would be tainted (Carroll 1899: 603).

50. Matias 1903.

51. Fuster Morales 1903.

52. LD, Nov. 1, 1901, 1; see also LD Nov. 27, 1902, 2; PRH, July 26, 1902, 24.

53. Felipe Cuebas in Carroll 1899: 604.

54. LD, Feb 6, 1900, 2; Diego 1901: 33; also Santiago-Valles 1994: 96.

55. SJN, Sept. 18, 1900, 4.

56. Alcalde of Fajardo (José M. Rivera) to Gov. Allen, Sept 27, 1900 (AGPR, FF/GC/Gob., Munic., caja 11).

57. Principe Juan to Governor, n.d. (AGPR, FF, GC, Legislation, box 167, file 1044).

58. OGPR, Dec. 14, 1898, 1; GPR 1905: 40–41.

59. GPR 1902: 76.

60. GPR 1902: 57–58; 76. Also Willoughby 1905: 133 and Wilson 1905: 113. In 1901, the Americans ended up appointing 49 officials due to vacancies the total number of municipal seats across the island was around 846. In 1902, the number of appointments increased to 186. It is unclear from the data how many of these were actually Republicans, but a cursory look at the names suggests that the appointment of Republicans was indeed the practice (GPR 1901: 116–17; 1902: 85–89).

61. GPR 1902: 78. The Americans had complained early on that the municipal offices were excessive; see, e.g., A. C. Sharpe to General Davis, May 24, 1899 (AGPR, FF, Gob., GC, box 110, file 3142).

62. Willoughby to Bessie Talbot Willoughby, Sept. 2, 1902 (WP, folder 25).

63. Guy Henry to Adjutant General, Feb. 15, 1899 (USNA, RG 350, Gen. Classified Files, entry 168-3); Wilson 1905: 66; copy of the order in BHPR 4, no. 2: 106–7.

64. Guy Henry to Adjutant General, Feb. 15, 1899 (USNA, RG 350, Gen. Classified Files, entry 168-3).

65. Gen. George Davis to Elihu Root, April 19, 1900 (USNA, RG 350, entry 719-29).

66. Henry Allen to Elihu Root, Sept. 7, 1900 (ERP, box 7, folder A2). Also see Berbusse 1966: 175–76; SJN Sept. 4, 1900, 1.

67. Quoted in Picó 1998: 40.

68. "Resolution of the municipal council of Vieques," 1 (AGPR, FF, Gob., GC, box 110, file 7515); Alcalde of Maunabo (Rafael Ortiz) to President of Executive Council, March 14, 1902 (AGPR, FF, GC, Gob., box 112, file 821).

69. "Hon. William McKinley" (PRH, July 1901, 13, 1).

70. BHPR 4, no. 2: 107.

71. SJN Feb. 14, 1899, 1.

72. SJN Sep. 8, 1900, 1.

73. "Declaraciones Graves. Mr Allen y Puerto Rico," LD June 3, 1901, 3.

74. "The Discrediting of a Country," PRH Dec. 28, 1901, 1.

75. Manuel Rossy to Federico Degetau, May 7, 1901 (FDG 3, 1, 7).

76. Carrión 1983: 160; see also Berbusse 1966: 177–80.

77. "El Retraimiento," LD, Oct. 26, 1900, 1; see also "Se Consumó la injusticia" in BG 1979: 2:160–61.

78. Allen to Root, Sept. 7, 1900 (ERP, box 7, folder A2).

79. Ibid.

80. E. Wilson 1905: 92; GPR 1901: 42.

81. Sweet 1906: 53.

82. PRR, Feb. 10, 1906, 10–11.

83. Out of all eligible electors, only one-fifth voted. The voters were all avowed Republicans.

84. Rowe 1904b: 253.

85. Quote from GPR 1901: 402; see also 167, 177–80. See J. H. Hollander to Secretary, June 20, 1900 (AGPR, FF, Gob., GC, box 110, file 10733); Hollander 1901: 571–72; Rowe 1904b: 191–95; Willoughby 1909: 431–42; 1910: 90. The Republicans in the House of Delegates and the Americans found a happy marriage. The Americans wanted to intensify political education and uproot corruption, which meant undermining municipal powers long dominated by the Federals and enacting policies that would further undo the Federals' control. The Republicans likely saw themselves as the new favored party, enjoying the benefits of patronage from the metropole.

86. Moses, diary, entry for Aug. 27, 1901 (BM).

87. USWD 1901: 1:21.

88. USWD 1901: 1:40. Cullinane 1971 provides an excellent discussion of these developments in local government.

89. Forbes 1928: 1:156.

90. Taft to Root, Nov. 11, 1902 (ERP, container no. 164); see also Paredes 1990: 309, 312.

91. Dean Worcester quoted in Paredes 1990: 31.

92. MT March 1, 1901, 1, emphasis added.

93. Taft to Jose de la Vina, Don Justo Lukban, Leon M. Guerrero, and Alberto Barretto, Nov. 7, 1902 (ERP, container no. 164).

94. Moses, diary, part 5, entry for Aug. 28, 1901 (BM).

95. Ibid., entry for Aug. 27, 1901 (BM).

96. Taft to Paterno, July 28, 1900, quoted from Kalaw 1927: 267. See also Williams 1913: 68–69.

97. REN, Aug. 28, 1904, 1.

98. "Are Not of the People," orig. *El Renacimiento*, reprinted in MT, Nov. 14, 1905 2.

99. Ibid. See also "El Problema del Bandolerismo," *El Renacimiento*, April 6, 1905; "La cuestion de la constabularia" *El Renacimiento*, July 27, 1905.

100. Forbes, journal, 1:89, WCF.

101. Kaut 1961: 260.

102. Forbes, journal, 2:312, WCF.

103. Ibid., 1:116, WCF.

104. In 1902, for instance, after the economic crisis had abated, the insular government lent about $1.1 million in loans for infrastructural development to the major municipalities, which amounted to close to 40 percent of the insular government's budget (Willoughby 1910, 81; GPR 1903: 101).

105. In the Philippines, percentage calculated for 1904–5 from RPC 1903: part 3, 294 and 1904: part 3, 402.

106. Lesada to Taft, Aug. 15, 1906 (USNA, BIA, RG 350, entry 3047-37).

107. Larkin 1993: 56, 249. The decline in sugar production was in large part due to increased competition from beet-sugar producers in Europe and the United States.

108. USNA, BIA, RG 350, files 2058, 3597, 3018, 3019; USPC 1903; USPC 1904; USPC 1905; U.S. Senate 1902.

109. Valdepeñas and Bautista 1977: 49; Lewis 1970: 294.

110. Valdepeñas and Bautista 1977: 114.

111. Exec. Sec. Fergusson to Gov. Wright, May 12, 1902, 2 (USNA, BIA, RG 350, entry 3022-7).

112. Luke Wright to Secretary of War, June 15, 1904 (CE, I, 3.20 "1904, June 15").

113. To determine this, I examined the provincial governors' reports to the American authorities for this five-year period (USNA, BIA, RG 350, entries 2058, 3597, 3018,

3019; USPC 1903; USPC 1904; USPC 1905; and U.S. Senate Committee on the Philippines 1902).

114. Valdepeñas and Bautista 1977: 93; U.S. Bureau of the Census 1905: 4:12–14.

115. Economic data from U.S. Bureau of Insular Affairs 1902: 118–26; Foreman 1906: 648–50.

116. U.S. Bureau of the Census 1899: 149; 1905: 4:325–28.

117. Larkin 1993: 81, 89–97; Lewis 1970: 290; USPC 1907: 2:800–12; USPC 1904: 1:891.

118. Governors' report, USNA, RG 350, entry 3018-3. The relatively well-off economy of Capiz Province is seen in USPC 1905: 1:198–207; similar responses are seen in Governors' report, Jan. 10, 1903, USNA, BIA, RG 350, entry 3597-6.

119. USPC 1906: 1:191. These reports were consistent across the provinces and throughout the period from 1902 to 1910.

120. For example, see REN April 6, 1905, 1. There was indeed sporadic resistance to the elite, particularly from peasant movements for independence that accused the elite of betraying national ideals (Ileto 1979). But this resistance was not sustained in the way it was in Puerto Rico. The point is not whether or not there actually was resistance, but how any resistance related to the elites' cultural structures and therefore their expectations. In Puerto Rico, the resistance was entirely new. There had not been such resistance before American arrival. In the Philippines, however, sporadic resistance had existed even during Spanish rule. Thus the Filipino elite were not strangers to anti-elite peasant movements; and indeed had a conceptual vocabulary for making sense of, and thereby taming them: they called them, for example, *ladrones* (Ileto 1979).

121. Governors' report, Jan. 1903, USNA, BIA, RG 350, entry 2058.

122. USPC 1905: vol. 1.

123. USPC 1906: 1:361.

124. Ibid.: 1:418; USPC 1905: 1:124.

125. USPC 1904: 1:364–65; USPC 1906: 1:461. Admittedly, such discourse is suspect. It could have been the case that the Filipino elite were painting rosy pictures to American authorities in order to demonstrate their capacities of governing and thereby receive more "self-government." But again the comparison with Puerto Rico helps us see that the discourse is not as suspect as we might assume. If it was the case that the Filipino elite were performing their capacities, then we would have expected the Puerto Rican elite to also paint rosy pictures, for they too had an interest in demonstrating their governing capacities. Yet the Puerto Rican elite did not do this. As seen, they incessantly complained and expressed fear of their loss of local power.

126. Forbes, journal, vol. 1, April 14, 1906 (WCF).

127. We will see in later chapters that the Puerto Rican Federals also later took up seats in the House of Delegates, even as they had initially been locked out of the state

center due to retraimiento. The difference is that by the time they had occupied seats, they had already experienced convergent and recurrent recalcitrance.

128. Alfonso Doneza to Taft, Oct. 13, 1907 (TP, 70-3); Muni, Gov. of Batangas, to Taft, Oct. 15, 1907 (TP, 70-3); Felix Unson to Taft, Oct. 15, 190 (TP, 70-3).

129. Forbes 1928: 2:135–37, emphasis added.

5. DIVERGENT PATHS

1. Emirbayer and Mische 1998: 994.

2. SJN, June 19, 1901, 1.

3. LD, June 29, 1901, 3; LD, July 2, 1901, 3.

4. SJN, June 19, 1901, 1, 2.

5. LD, June 26, 1901, 2.

6. PRH, July 27, 1901, 1.

7. LD, June 26, 1901, 2; emphasis added; see also PRH, July 20, 1901, 2.

8. Rowe 1904b: 255.

9. Van Buren 1905: 127.

10. LD, March 21, 1904.

11. LD, May 19, 1903, 1.

12. Palmer to Theodore Roosevelt, Nov. 5, 1902 (USNA, RG 48, MF #824, roll 2), emphasis added.

13. Hunt to Theodore Roosevelt, Dec. 2, 1902 (USNA, DI, RG 48, MF #824, roll 2).

14. LD, Oct. 6, 1902, 4.

15. LD, Oct. 21, 1902. In 1909, the Federals adopted a different kind of retraimiento when, in the House of Delegates, they failed to pass an appropriation law. But this was an American tactic, used also by the U.S. Congress. The Federals thus learned how to manipulate power, but on the Americans' own terms.

16. LD, July 2, 1901, 3; orig. emphasis.

17. Muñoz Rivera started the *Puerto Rican Herald*, a bilingual newspaper distributed in New York and Washington, D.C., which reproduced local editorials and reports from the island's periodicals.

18. Sweet 1906: 17, and GPR 1907: 66, USNA, RG 126, file 9-8-22.

19. LD, Oct. 15, 1901, 3.

20. The Americans did not dismantle the police forces in the larger cities like San Juan, instead leaving them in the hands of local officials (Willoughby 1909b: 431–32).

21. GPR 1902: 336–37.

22. Ibid.: 339–40.

23. The address was published in local newspapers and as a pamphlet ("Inaugural Address of Hon. Wm. H. Hunt," San Juan, Tip. El Pais, 1901).

24. LD, Oct. 15, 1901, 3.

25. S. Palmer to Governor of Puerto Rico, May 15, 1902 (AGPR, FF, GC, box 167-

433-69). The Federals' newspaper had previously quoted Hunt's utterance about political differences in opinion verbatim and then stated: "Mr. Hunt makes an appeal to the political parties which seems to us very fitting . . . it is the duty of every citizen to respect the opinions of every other, *no matter how far they may differ from his own*" (LD, Oct. 12, 1901, 3).

26. Palmer to Hunt, Aug. 4, 1902 (AGPR, FF, GC, Tribunales, box 163-1203); GPR 1901: 103; 1902: 76, 336–39, emphasis added.

27. LD, May 18, 1903, 3.

28. LD, Sept. 5, 1901, 3.

29. LD, June 25, 1901, 3.

30. PRH, Aug. 31, 1901, 1–2; capitalization original.

31. GPR 1901: 418.

32. PRH, Nov. 2, 1901, 2.

33. After Governor Allen had been inaugurated, for example, *La Democracia* reproduced the text of his speech, but its only discussion of it expressed fear that Allen's new regime might continue to undermine autonomía (LD, May 2, 1900, 2). Yet Allen's speech had uttered the exact same themes that Hunt's speech later did (for Allen's speech, see GPR 1901).

34. LD, Oct. 12, 1901, 3; PRH, Jan. 18, 1902, 2; ibid; PRH, Aug. 31, 1901, 1–2; LD, Dec. 23, 1901, 3; LD, Jan. 2, 1902, 3; LD, Jan. 29, 1903, 3.

35. These letters are found in the Archivo General de Puerto Rico: J. L. Sobá, Councilman of Adjuntas, to Secretary of PR, July 6, 1902 (AGPR, FF, GC, Gob., Munic., box 114, file 1084A). Alcalde of Aguada to Secretary, April 1, 1902 (AGPR, FF, GC, Gob., Justicia, Procurador General, box 145-2799); Secretary of PR to Attorney General, July 7, 1902 (AGPR, FF, GC, Legislación, box 168-2084); Santiago Palmer to Secretary of PR, May 5, 1903 (AGPR, FF, GC, Legislación, box 168-708); J. R. Colon to Atty. Gen, Jan. 25, 1905 (AGPR, FF, GC, Gob. Munic., box 107-1143); Alcalde of Ponce to Secretary of PR, June 6, 1905 (AGPR, FF, GC, Gob., Justicia, Procurador General, box 146-1176).

36. Coll Cuchí 1904: 132.

37. Ibid.: 71, 106, 108, 151–52; Coll Cuchí 1972: 74.

38. LD, Jan 11, 1905, 1, emphasis added.

39. PRR, Feb. 3, 1906, 1.

40. Guha 1997.

41. Cullinane's excellent study (1989) has detected this new campaign. As he notes, after nationalists failed to receive favor from the state center, they "were forced to engage in politics by other means," turning to a "wide range of political propaganda in the more liberal atmosphere of post-war Manila and its environs" (Cullinane 1989: 169). The result was that the influence of *El Renacimiento* "increased by leaps and bounds" in this period (188).

42. James LeRoy, "Memorandum of what occurred at the dinner of the governors of provinces in the Hotel Metropole on Monday, noon, Aug. 7, 1905" (Travelogue of 1905 trip, LeRoy Papers, Bentley); Morgan Shuster to Henry Ide, Aug. 30, 1905 (WHT, series 3, r. 52).

43. REN, Aug. 4, 1905, 2; also REN, Oct. 18, 1905, 1.

44. REN, March 16, 1905, 1.

45. Reproduced in Cristobal 1918: 7; Rizal 1928: 162.

46. Jose de Vera, speech at Sorsogon province, Aug. 26, 1905 (WHT, ser. 3, r. 52).

47. *El Grito del Pueblo*, Aug. 1, 1905, 2.

48. LeRoy, "Memorandum . . . 1905" (LeRoy Papers, Bentley). See also Morgan Shuster to Henry Ide, Aug. 30, 1905 (WHT, ser. 3, r. 52); and *El Grito del Pueblo*, Dec. 15, 1906, 1.

49. REN, Aug. 4, 1905, 2.

50. *El Grito del Pueblo*, Sept. 16, 1903, 2, also Aug. 30, 1903, 2; Dec. 24, 1903, 2.

51. *El Grito del Pueblo*, Dec. 24, 1903, 2.

52. *La Patria*, Aug. 13, 1904 (WHT, ser. 3, r. 45). Before U.S. rule, Paterno had authored historical tracts that recast ancient Tagalog society as a flourishing "civilization," portraying chiefs like Lapu as protonationalist nobles and aristocrats (Paterno 1892).

53. Felipe Meniamis to Col. Edwards and Judge Magoon, Sept. 20, 1902 (CE, I, 2.12).

54. Dauncey 1906: 142, 308.

55. Moses, diary, part 7, entry for Dec. 24, 1901 (BM).

56. "Speech Delivered by Governor Taft at Iloilo, February 18, 1903" (WHT, ser. 9A, r. 563); "Address Delivered before the Union Reading College, December 17, 1903" (WHT, ser. 9A, r. 563).

57. "Speech . . . at Iloilo" (WHT, ser. 9A, r. 563).

58. W. Taft to Charley Taft, Sept. 24, 1903, as quoted in Alfonso 1969: 239.

59. REN, Dec. 14, 1903, 1.

60. REN, Dec. 12, 1903, 1. See also *El Grito del Pueblo*, Dec. 20, 1903, 2.

61. MT March 18, 1904, quoted in Paredes 1990: 347; *Manila American* quoted in Blount 1913: 437.

62. Alfonso 1969: 241.

63. Dauncey 1906: 313.

64. RPC 1901: 2:283–84. The elites' own newspapers had reprinted this particular speech, but they had not commented on these utterances.

65. "Speech . . . at Iloilo" (WHT, ser. 9A, r. 563).

66. LeRoy, travelogue, Aug. 15, 1905 (LeRoy Papers, Bentley).

67. Whenever the elite in this period referred to the Americans' discourse, including the discourse of President Roosevelt, they appropriated only those elements that supported their claim that the Americans were not fulfilling their initial "obligations" and meeting their "debts" (e.g., REN, Aug. 28, 1904, 1; Aug. 28, 1904, 1).

68. On hidden transcripts of resistance, see Scott 1985.

69. Francisco Morales to Taft, Aug. 22, 1902 (WHT, ser. 3, r. 40).

70. Macario Favila to Executive Secretary, Aug. 22, 1902 (WHT, ser. 3, r. 36).

71. Poblete et al. to Taft, Aug. 22, 1902 (WHT, ser. 3, r. 40).

72. Moses, diary, part 7, Dec. 24, 1901 (BM); see also Dauncey 1906: 142.

73. Aniceto Clarin to Taft, Nov. 30, 1903 (WHT, ser. 3, r. 41).

74. See also J. Clímaco to Taft, Oct. 16, 1903 (WHT, ser. 3, r. 40); Juan Cailles to Taft, Aug. 4, 1904, WHT, ser. 3, r. 45.

75. REN, Aug. 3, 1905, 1.

76. Ibid.

77. REN, Aug. 6, 1905, 1.

78. Delegation from Cagayan to Taft and Visiting Party, Aug. (n.d.), 1905 (USNA, BIA, RG 350 entry 3602-11).

79. Munic. of Balayan to Alice Roosevelt, Aug. 26, 1905 (USNA, RG 350, entry 3047-35), emphasis added.

80. USPC 1905: 38–39, 42; see also 78–80 for the petition from the *Comité de Intereses Filipinos*.

81. USPC 1905: 13; see also USPC 1906: 1:254–55 for more.

82. REN, Aug. 12, 1905, 2.

83. USPC 1905: 11–12; Spanish version in REN, Aug. 29, 1905, 3. The petitioners were prominent Manila ilustrados who headed major political factions of the elite. They likewise held official positions, and some were writers for the newspaper *El Renacimiento*. They were the core of the Filipinos who were leading the charge against American centralization, and many would remain prominent politicians for years to come.

84. Ibid.: 12. The equation between the "intelligent Filipinos" and the directing class is made by Vicente Ilustre during his preface to the submission of the petition (8).

85. Talk of "candor" from Taft 1908: 8, 25; second quote from Taft in Forbes 1928: 2:497.

86. USPC 1905: 45–46.

87. Forbes, journal, Aug. 11, 1905, 1:284–85 (WCF). In 1910, Filipino newspapers reflected upon the 1905 hearings at which they had so offended American administrators with their talk of "directing classes," but while they recognized that something had been amiss at those hearings, that there had been a "capital defect," they did not say that the defect was their own discourse. Rather, the problem had been that they let themselves be subject to "an unmerciful questioning [by the Americans] before a numerous public" (La Vanguardia, June 17, 1910, 2, clipping in USNA, BIA, RG 350, entry 2143-71).

88. Fox 1985; Obeyeskere 1992; cf. Sahlins 1995.

89. Chong 2003.

90. In addition, the violence and protests did not persist. They subsided as the Ameri-

can authorities repressed it, yet the elite continued to disavow their prior meanings nonetheless. The damage had already been done.

6. STRUCTURAL TRANSFORMATION IN PUERTO RICO

1. The Federal party changed its name in 1904 to the Union Party, and membership remained the same. The only difference was that some Republican Party members joined them.

2. GPR 1907: 39.

3. Existing scholarship has instead examined class formation, the elites' economic fortunes, their attitudes toward statehood, or attempts to restore lost economic privileges (Bernabe 1996; Caban 1999; Quintero Rivera 1981: 60–61).

4. Outbreaks of disorder and violence began to subside due to the Americans' use of police power (see reports of the insular police, e.g., GPR 1901: 404; GPR 1902).

5. Sweet 1906: 53.

6. Pagan 1959: 85.

7. PRH, Jan. 4, 1902 3; LD, Jan. 4, 1902.

8. *Porto Rico Eagle*, April 22, 1903); Rivas 1903: 10.

9. Manuel Rossy to F. Degetau, May 12, 1903 (FDG, Caja 4, II, 176).

10. LD, Nov. 24, 1902, 2; also LD, Jan. 24, 1902, 3.

11. LD, March 12, 1903, 4.

12. LD, Oct. 7, 1901, 3.

13. LD, Nov. 2, 1901, 2.

14. LD, Aug. 20, 1903, 3.

15. LD, July 7, 1904, 2.

16. LD, July 9, 1901, 3, emphasis added; see also SJN, July 27, 1901, 3.

17. LD, Jan. 5, 1903, 3; PRH, Nov. 2, 1901, 2–3; also LD, April 28, 1903, April 13, 1903, 3.

18. PRH, Oct. 12, 1901, 2, also PRH, Feb. 15, 1902, 1.

19. LD, Dec. 2, 1902, 4; also LD, Jan. 30, 1905, 5.

20. SJN, April 19, 1903, 2.

21. LD, April 20, 1903, 3.

22. LD, April 27, 1903, 2.

23. LD, Oct. 12, 1901, 3.

24. PRH, Sept. 14, 1901, 2.

25. PRH, Oct. 12, 1901, 2.

26. LD, Sept. 17, 1901, 3.

27. LD, Nov. 1, 1901, 2.

28. Circular of the Subcomité Obrero Federal of Arecibo (AGPR, FF, PP, Caja 181).

29. E.g., PRH, Jan. 18, 1902, 2.

30. LCPR, Nov. 7, 1904. See also "El deber de los patriotas" (LD, Nov. 7, 1910, 1), which

warned against selling the vote (the "most sacred rights of citizenship"): "Jibaros [Peasant] of Puerto Rico! Jibaros of Caguas and Gurabo! . . . If you are approached by a Republican or Izquerdista to offer you money in exchange for your vote, reject it indignantly and tell them that the Puerto Rican jibaro is a man of honor and as such is not sold to anyone for anything."

31. LD, Nov. 5, 1910, 2.

32. LD, Jan. 20, 1904, 3.

33. "Ante las elecciones" (BG 1979: vol. 2, doc. no. 60).

34. Coll Cuchí (1904: 151–52).

35. Coll Cuchí (1904: 195, 206).

36. Matienzo Cintron to W. Sweet, Sept. 18, 1906 (PRR, Sept. 29, 1906, 13–15).

37. LD, July 25, 1905, 1. These demands and signifying equations proceeded unabated in countless platforms, manifestos, and petitions (LD, July 12, 1905, 2; House of Delegates to Theodore Roosevelt, Aug. 13, 1907, USNA, RG 126, entry 9-8-18; House of Delegates to Elihu Root, July 8, 1906, BG 1979: 2:219–20; "Report and Tally on Interrogatories Sent Out by Governor Post to Various Citizens of Porto Rico in September, 1909," USNA, BIA, RG 350, NARA, entry 168-58, 3).

38. Bayron Toro 1977: 125–26; "Results of Elections, Nov. 6, 1906" (unpublished ms., Biblioteca y Hemeroteca Puertorriqueña, UPRL); GPR 1909: 42–43.

39. Miguel Rodriguez Sierra to Guerra Mondragon, Dec. 6, 1906 (MGM Doc. 604).

40. Republican Party leaders saw things this way, as did some others. See Todd 1943: 29; Beekman Winthrop to Taft, Oct. 10, 1904 (TP, ser. 1, r. 48); Pagan 1959: 1:118.

41. GPR 1901: 106–7; Willougby 1910: 86.

42. Willougby 1910: 78–79.

43. GPR 1902: 58. Also affirmed by Marvin 1903: 650.

44. GPR 1905: 38–39.

45. Willoughby 1910: 99.

46. GPR 1906: 43.

47. GPR 1907: 60–61.

48. GPR 1909: 422; also Willoughby 1910: 104.

49. GPR 1905: 38–39.

50. GPR 1906: 49.

51. GPR 1902: 76.

52. GPR 1912: 105. There is no systematic data on corruption in Puerto Rico. The Americans did not keep track in their published reports or private records. But this absence is telling in itself. It was in the Philippines where the administrators bothered to count and compile the Filipinos' corrupt activities, because only in the Philippines (as I will show in chapter 7) and not in Puerto Rico was corruption such a pressing problem. Dickinson's report in 1910 is assuring. Dickinson was sent to both Puerto Rico and the Philippines to investigate political conditions in the

colonies, and made no mention of corruption in the former, but found much corruption in the latter (U.S. Congress, House of Representatives 1910). A Brookings Institution investigation into Puerto Rico in the 1920s led one writer to conclude that "Puerto Rico's political leaders and politicians have on the whole almost always been the most honest to be found anywhere" (Hanson 1955: 46; see Clark and Brookings Institution 1930).

53. The numbers of protested and void ballots are given only for the elections of 1899, 1906, and 1908. The 1899 and 1906 numbers are for local elections only, while the 1908 numbers are only for the elections for commissioner to the United States. These are found in Report of the Military Governor of Puerto Rico (USWD 1902: 275–76), GPR, Annual Report (1909: 42–45) and "Results of Elections" (pamphlet in Biblioteca y Hermereoteca Puertorriqueña, UPRL).

54. The data does not cover all forms of corruption. Since it deals only with the number of voided ballots, it does not include activities like voter intimidation. Furthermore, the data encompasses only the corruption discovered by American agents. There were probably many other instances of corruption. This is perhaps why the actual percentage of voided ballots is relatively low. On the other hand, of interest here is the percentage of voided ballots over time, not their actual numbers.

55. Boyce 1914: 92.

56. R. H. Delgado, L. M. Rivera, and Carlos M. Soler to Don Miguel Guerra, Sept. 28, 1906 (MGM, G-6, 804-a)

57. The very fact that the Union leadership sent letters asking for contributions is suggestive of a change in the elites' conduct. Even if the money collected had then been used for bribery (and the letter does not suggest this), the lines of circulation were significantly different. No longer moving along the socioeconomic lines of merchant-landowner-tenant, as had been the case during late Spanish rule, the money circulated through the party leaders.

58. PRR, Nov. 2, 1910, 5.

59. Ibid.: 15.

60. GPR 1905: 1–2.

61. Ibid.: 46.

62. GPR 1907: 36; see also 1906: 11, 56.

63. GPR 1909: 34.

64. GPR 1915: 132–33.

65. The reports came from administrators, residents, and police officers. For 1899 to 1904, these files are found in various boxes of the General Archive of Puerto Rico. After 1904, they are found in the boxes of the Bureau of Insular Affairs at the United States National Archives.

66. Hollander 1901: 571–72. The system clearly resembled Foucault's panopticon. See Willoughby 1910: 90.

67. "People change both their attitudes and their behaviour when changes in social and legal institutions make it detrimental for them to continue to conform to old norms" Chong 2003: 10.

68. GPR 1912: 104.

69. Riera Palmer 1907: 1–2.

70. Ibid.: 77.

71. Augustin Aponte 1908: 11–12.

72. LD, July 19, 1904, 2.

73. Wilson 1905: 100–101.

74. LD, Jan. 9, 1906, 2.

75. LD, Aug. 7, 1901, 3.

76. LD, April 18, 1904, 3.

77. LD, Oct. 6, 1902, 4.

78. "Ante las elecciones" (BG 1979: vol. 2, doc. no. 60).

79. "Circular of Oct. 8, 1910, by the Hon. Carlos M. Soler, Acting President of the Union of Porto Rico, to the Unionist Alcaldes of the island" (USNA, BIA, RG 350, entry 719-11).

80. LD, Nov. 14, 1910, 1.

81. LD, Nov. 12, 1910, 3.

82. Augustin Aponte 1908: 77.

83. LD, March 14, 1905, 1.

84. LD, Jan. 9, 1906, 2.

85. LD, Jan. 18, 1906.

86. Bayron Toro 1977: 262.

87. GPR 1905: 46. It should be clear that the new law was not an attempt to secure the Unionists' own victory, for the Unionists had already won.

88. GPR 1906: 41–42.

89. GPR 1908: 30.

90. LD, Feb. 2, 1906, 6.

91. LD, Jan. 17, 1906, 5.

92. "Carta del Sr. Matienzo" (LCPR, Oct. 13, 1906, 1).

93. Sweet's stance on the county bill is seen in Sweet 1906. See also "Letter of Matienzo" (PRR, Sept. 29, 1906, 13–15). Governor Allen in 1900 had proposed the idea of the county system in his address to the first legislative assembly, but it was not taken further (GPR 1901: 425).

94. LD, Feb. 14, 1905, 1.

95. GPR 1906: 39, 43–44; Executive Council, *Journal*, Sixth Regular Session (1906: 13).

96. Report of the Governor, fiscal year 1906–7, manuscript copy in USNA, RG 126, entry 9-8-22, 66.

97. LD, Feb. 28, 1905, 1.

98. GPR 1906: 11. It was around this time that some American officials changed their

initial views. Noting the elites' changed conduct, they began requesting that Congress pass a bill granting U.S. citizenship to Puerto Ricans. Roosevelt himself supported the plan (GPR 1904: 15; GPR 1907: 39, appendix; Sweet 1906; also see House of Delegates to President T. Roosevelt, March 14, 1907, USNA, RG 126, entry 9-8-18). The tragedy is that Congress, still working from their prior racial assumptions, resisted the calls. It was not until 1917 that citizenship was granted. This is an entirely different story, and I do not have the space to cover it here.

99. LD, Jan. 9, 1906, 1.

100. PRH, April 19, 1902, 3.

101. Augustin Aponte 1908: 84.

7. CULTURAL REVALUATION IN THE PHILIPPINES

1. A parallel to revaluation can be found in studies that show subtle shifts in word meaning. In this literature, then, tracking change involves a lexical semantics (Richter 1995). My analysis, however, is concerned not with lexical semantics but with elaborations of schemas in conduct as well as discourse.

2. Worcester quoted in Cullinane 1971: 27.

3. Forbes, journal, July 31, 1909, 3:240 (WCF).

4. The data fit our needs. Our interest lies primarily in the time period between 1903, when the data begin, and 1912, when the present study ends its main focus. This was also the period in Puerto Rico when corruption declined as the elite reorganized their line of conduct to fit American methods.

5. USWD 1910: 7.

6. U.S. Congress, House of Representatives 1921: 43; Hoyt 1963: 116, 121, 125–26, 173–74, 183.

7. "Memo of Chief of Law Division regarding voluntary contributions, March 6, 1907 by Mr. Putnam" (WPC, Documents and Papers, vol. 1, item 26).

8. "Report of the Chief of the Law Division in the matter of the charges against the Vice-President and Councilors of the municipality of Cebu" (WPC, Documents and Papers, vol. 1, item 31); also Cullinane 1971: 32.

9. Taft 1908: 23; also Forbes, misc. clippings, 1904 (WCF, "Philippine data: political," 1:5–7, 13–16); Forbes, journal, Dec. 5, 1904, 1:132 (WCF); Hart 1928: 156–57; "Record in the matter of the charges against Nicolas de las Reyes," 1908 (WPC, Documents and Papers, vol. 1, item 38). For secondary sources, see Cullinane 1971; McCoy 1993; and Sidel 1999; cf. Ileto 1999.

10. Forbes, journal, May 31, 1905, 1:219 (WCF).

11. Forbes 1928: 1:154–55; also Cullinane 1971: 41.

12. Hayden 1942: 285.

13. Forbes, journal, Dec. 5, 1904, 1:117 (WCF).

14. USPC 1905: 1:33. See also USPC 1904: 1:315.

15. I read all the articles that mentioned elections in 1902, 1906, 1912, and 1916, which gives a broad longitudinal view. I limited the newspaper analysis to the electoral period: two months before the date of each election (when election campaigns and registration began) and one month afterward. Counts for corruption include references to "bribery," "vote-buying," "intimidation," "electoral violence," "irregularities," and "fraud."

16. Forbes 1928: 1:166–67.

17. Quoted in Cullinane 1971: 30.

18. Forbes, journal, July 26, 1909, 3:236 (WCF); USPC 1904: 1:694.

19. Forbes, journal, Aug. 1, 1909, 3:241; Aug. 25, 1904, 1:52.

20. Romualdez 1925: 30.

21. Taft 1908: 34.

22. USPC 1904: 1:694.

23. Worcester 1914: 2:954.

24. Ibid.

25. The documents related to this are in WPC, Documents and Papers, vol. 1, items 27 ("Results of the Investigation of Joaquin Gil") and 40 ("Report of the Chief, Law Division, in the matter of charges against Quintin Salas"). See also Cullinane 1971.

26. Mabini reproduced in LeRoy 1906: 858.

27. Lopez had been aid to General Artemio Ricarte during the revolution. He also had served under General Mariano Trias. Under U.S. rule he was a prolific writer, dramatist, essayist, and journalist. He was editor of the Tagalog sections of various nationalist papers (National Historical Institute 1992: 3:154).

28. Lopez 1905: 21.

29. Ileto 1979: 106–7.

30. I have discussed the connections between razón and katwiran in chapter 3, but for the equations in the American period, see the word entries in Calderon 1915 and Nigg 1904 and the illuminating discussion in Diokono 1983: 6.

31. But what about the Americans' findings that some of the elite suspended their corruption in the presence of Americans? Suspension of a practice in the presence of authority is not the same as structural transformation, such as the kind seen in Puerto Rico. In Puerto Rico, the elite did not only suspend their prior corruption, they actively changed their ways, adopted new categories for making sense of it, and publicly articulated those categories in their discourse. Further, even if a handful of elites in the Philippines obtained a new consciousness, a new consciousness is not the same thing as transformation in prior cultural categories and conduct; nor does it mean that everyone else will adopt a new consciousness and change culture.

32. USPC 1904: 1:37. See also MT, Dec. 7, 1905, 5, and USPC 1908: 1:164.

33. USPC 1907: 1:165–66; MT, Jan. 9, 1907, 1.

34. See chapter 3.

35. USPC 1904: 1:436. Recall that during the first years of U.S. rule the electorate was restricted.

36. "Report of the Governor of Albay," USPC 1904: 1:368.

37. The impersonalism of the provincial elections is seen in the electoral procedures. See "Report of Frederick S. Young, Treasurer of Cebu" (USNA, BIA, RG 350, entry 3019-15). For size of electorate, see "Result of Elections of February 3, 1902" (USNA, BIA RG 350, entry 2710-26).

38. Philippine Constabulary, "Confidential Report," June 7, 1912 (USNA, BIA, RG 350, entry 10265-51).

39. Director of Constabulary, Circular, Feb. 11, 1913 (USNA, BIA, RG 350, entry 10265-60); MT Feb. 13, 1902, 5; Feb. 12, 1902, 1; Jan. 22, 1904, 4; Feb. 21, 1906, 5; June 15, 1912, 1; USPC 1907: 1:168; 1906: 1:39–40; 1912: 46.

40. Forbes 1928: 1:166 and journal, July 9, 1910, 4:135 (WCF).

41. Quoted in the *Official Gazette of the Philippines*, April 24, 1912, 900 (clipping in USNA, BIA, RG 350, entry 10265-46).

42. MT, Feb. 12, 1906, 4.

43. For an analysis of how the use of cultural schemas in practice, rather than discourse, also entails certain implicit classifications, see Biernacki 1999. My point here is to show how the use of preexisting cultural schemas in new referential contexts carries new implicit meanings, however still delimited by old meanings (e.g., in practice, patrons are still patrons, and clients are still clients, but the people encompassed by the category are different than before).

44. Chief, Law Division, "Result of investigation of Joaquin Gil, Benito Lopez, Governor of Iloilo" (WPC, Documents and Papers, vol. 1, file 108447-a8.)

45. Reyes 1930: 191–92; also see Larkin 1972: 185; REN, Nov. 5, 1903, 1.

46. MT, Feb. 28, 1902, 1; Feb. 14, 1906, 4; USPC 1906: 39.

47. MT, March 4, 1902, 4. The first record of illiterate voters was for the election of 1912, when they made up 15 percent of the total voters (Forbes 1928: 2:125).

48. MT, June 6, 1912, 4. See also MT, June 17, 1912, 1, and June 21, 1912, 1. On paying tax money for voters, see MT, Nov. 30, 1903, 1.

49. Larkin 1972: 197.

50. MT, Jan. 29, 1906, 2.

51. WPC, Documents and Papers, vol. 1, file 108447-a8, 13.

52. Fee 1910: 139.

53. Forbes, journal, Aug. 26, 1909, vol. 3 (WCF).

54. MT, Dec. 3, 1903, 4.

55. MT, Dec. 2, 1903, 2.

56. MT, June 6, 1912, 4; see also MT, June 4, 1912, 1, and Fee 1910: 140.

57. MT, June 2, 1916, 1.

58. Hollsteiner 1969: 164. See also Fegan 1993.

59. Machado 1974: 532–33.

60. Larkin 1972: 192–93; see also Lande 1965 and Meimban 1997: 214–16.

61. Sidel 1993: 119.

62. Hollsteiner 1969: 163.

63. The political parties discussed in chapter 5 quickly dismantled after they did not receive recognition. It was only later that parties besides the Federal Party emerged and remained.

64. USPC 1907: 1:166. See also Report of James F. Smith to William Taft, Sept. 24, 1906 in BIA, RG 350, box 344, file 3427, "Political Parties."

65. Mabini 1931: 2:23.

66. Taft 1908: 42.

67. USPC 1907: 224, 240.

68. Census Office of the Philippine Islands 1920: 1:3.

69. USPC 1907: 236.

70. USPC 1908: 240–41.

71. Ibid.: 38–39, emphasis added.

72. May 1980: 187–88.

73. Forbes, journal, Oct. 16, 1907, 2:319 (WCF).

74. Adriatico 1917: 42–43. Adriatico had signed the petition of 1905 that tried to convince the American visiting party that the Filipinos were capable of self-government because the Philippines had a directing class.

75. Lopez 1915: 26–27.

76. Jenista 1971: 85–89, 92–97.

77. "A List of Assembly bills" and "Notes on certain Assembly bills . . . ," items 12 and 13 in WPC, Documents and Papers, vol. 11; Forbes, journal, May 14, 1908, 3:20 (WCF); Forbes 1928: 2:160; Worcester 1921: 2:774.

78. See also Cullinane 1989: 471 and Sidel 1993: 119.

79. If we return to Honorio Lopez's description of what the duties of the legislature are, we can glimpse this sense of indebtedness. To wit, Lopez says that "Honor is necessary for the deputy [assemblyman]," and he uses the word *karangalan* for honor. *Karangalan* derives from combining *dangal* and *puri*, meaning, respectively, "self-dignity" and "praise" or "accolade." Karangalan is thus the effect of joining one's self-ascribed sense of dignity, on the one hand, and social approval/praise, on the other, which happens only through reciprocal exchange between oneself and others. For this meaning, see Enriquez 1994: 48.

80. Forbes 1928: 1:375.

81. Jenista 1971: 93, 95–97.

82. USPC 1908: 432. Quezon added that their legislation sought to "grant the provinces autonomy in the expenditure of their funds . . . because it is supposed that the provinces know their own needs best and will spend the money in accordance with such needs" (ibid.).

83. Forbes 1928: 2:153.

84. "A List of Assembly bills" (WPC, Documents and Papers, vol. 11, item 12).

85. Adriatico 1917: 43.

86. M. Quezon quoted in Worcester 1913: 39; see also Osmeña 1911.

87. Ibid.: 44.

88. Paterno 1910: 44–45.

89. I consulted both Nigg's English-Tagalog dictionary of 1904 and Nocea's comprehensive Spanish-Tagalog dictionary (1860).

90. Sidel 1995: 150. Benedict Anderson (1990: 17–77) finds a similar notion of Indonesian political cosmologies.

91. See Rafael 1993b: 14, 139–40; Sidel 1995: 150.

92. See especially Ileto 1979: 115 and Osias 1971: 49.

93. Schumacher 1991: 102–17.

94. Adriatico 1917: 44.

95. Alejo, Rivera, and Valencia 1996: 88.

96. Sidel 1995: 152.

CONCLUSION: RETURNING TO CULTURE

1. May 1980: 17; Karnow 1989. For more on exceptionalism, see Go 2003 and Kaplan 1993.

2. See, most recently, the excellent studies by Kaplan 2005 and Kramer 2006.

3. Studies that reduce culture to subjective values overlook these complexities and therefore fail to address a critical question raised by their own analyses: If tutelage reflected America's deep democratic values and anticolonial beliefs, why did the American officials try to impose democracy through colonial rule, an exercise that belied those very values and beliefs?

4. For a deeper discussion of this point and the formation of the tutelage project in comparison with U.S. policies in Guam and Samoa, see Go 2007.

5. Berbusse 1966: 25.

6. Rosenberg 1998: 510.

7. Some studies provide rich descriptions of processes akin to domestication while alluding to processes of change (Rafael 1993b). But because they do not put their analyses to the comparative test, the causal mechanisms they intimate are worth reconsidering. Some suggest, for example, that indigenization or "localization" follows from linguistic translation (Rafael 1993b), but is this to say that localization would not have occurred if the actors involved spoke the same language? Without a sustained comparative perspective, it is difficult to address this question.

8. Sahlins 1985: ix.

9. Sahlins 1981: 31, 52; 1985: 140.

10. Friedman 1997; Fox 1985; Obeyeskere 1992; cf. Merry 2000: 333. Later Sahlins does discuss the marginalization of prior schemas, such as when he shows that

chiefs eventually disavowed the taboo system. The problem is this part of the story is undertheorized: it happens only after the initial change of functional revaluation. Furthermore, the actors effecting the change were not the ones who initially effected reproduction (1981; cf. 1985, chap. 4).

11. See also Emirbayer and Mische 1998 on different types of agency.

12. Sahlins 1995.

13. Swidler 1986.

14. Tsebelis 1997.

15. Laitin 1986: 108.

16. Proponents of the strategic uses approach admit that one of the ways in which their theory could be falsified is if we find a case wherein people have "inaccurate beliefs about the situations they face" — that is, when people have incomplete information or if "information that would lead to a better decision is not processed" (Chong 2000: 222. See also Adams 1999).

17. Geddes 1995: 87; Chwe 2001. As Wedeen 2002: 719 notes, therefore, rational choice models are similar to structural-functionalist theories of culture in that they both treat "culture" (i.e., "information") as a "fixed, frozen, — always already there — category." An explanation rooted in changing incentive structures (Chong 2000) cannot resuscitate the theory either. Even if incentives had changed in Puerto Rico, a change in incentives does not mean that information or common knowledge changes, it simply means that the costs of using one bit from the repertoire of knowledge are raised or lowered. Incentive changes, according to the theory, does not mean repertoire *expansion*.

18. Paredes 1988: 65–66. On Puerto Rico, see Clark 1973: 224.

19. True, a look at culture from the top down helps us better understand the formation of the elites' political culture during *Spanish* rule. The particular policies and practices of the Spanish colonial state helped shape the contours, content, and institutionalization of the elites' political culture before American arrival. But the problem arises when we try to explain why the elites' initially similar cultural paths during American occupation later diverged.

20. Skocpol 1984.

21. On historical sociology that has theorized turning points, events, sequence, and process in time, see Abbott 2001 and Sewell 1996a.

22. Thus, as we have seen, the elite did not engage in "corruption" because their putatively essential "culture" told them to, but because they had a distinct meaning of democracy that they then tried to realize amid tutelage. It follows that if the meanings the elite made had been different, so too would the conduct. This happened exactly in Puerto Rico: once the elite reclassified their original meaning of self-government, their so-called corruption subsided.

23. Sahlins 1981 offers inspiration for this point about conjuncture. It is not, to be

clear, a "correspondence" model in structural-functionalist theories, where "correspondence" implies a logically necessary connection between the cultural system and other systems (Geertz 1973: 144). Even Geertz admitted "correspondence" and "noncorrespondence" were problematic terms needing refinement and thus abandoned them (reported in Aronoff 1983: 5).

24. The theory is not obliged to deductively explain when or why recalcitrance occurs, it only predicts that: (a) if there is convergent and recurrent recalcitrance, social actors will question their assumptions and seek out new schemas and (b) if schemas are validated, social actors will continue to employ their preexisting schemas while elaborating upon them. Furthermore, whether or not recalcitrance occurs depends partially upon the particular schemas at stake. Thus we cannot deduce when recalcitrance will occur in the absence of examinations of particular cases.

25. In political science, discussions by Laitin 1985 and Rogowski 1997 are informative here. See also Suny 2002 for a discussion of parallel movements in other fields. For studies of U.S. colonialism in the Philippines, one alternative is to focus upon "discourse" or language in the vein of the linguistic turn (e.g., Rafael 1993b; Salman 2001); while another proposal is to focus upon the more material processes of economic accumulation and political coercion (Sidel 1999).

26. For studies that have begun such examinations, see Briggs 2002, Findlay 1999, Kramer 2006, and Salman 2001.

27. Ileto 1979: 9. See also Rafael 1993b on utang na loób and Salman's 2001 study of Filipino elite and American authorities' discourses of slavery.

28. May 1988: 36.

29. For an incisive critique of this portrayal of U.S. rule in extant studies, see Ileto 1999.

30. This approach also offers an alternative to scholarship that has replaced *culture* with *discourse*. The turn to discourse often reinscribes some of the problems of the culture concept it seeks to transcend. If some studies of culture run into the problem of cultural determinism, studies of discourse — as critics note — simply replace it with a discursive determinism. Further, "discourse" is typically conjured to refer to linguistic phenomena of verbal or written speech; it thereby overlooks symbolic gestures or tacit actions that nonetheless communicate (Biernacki 1999). Finally, a focus on discourse cannot capture the sorts of changes we have captured. Studies of discourse root change in tensions or conflicts within discourses or between them — a conflict between different "language games" (e.g., K. Baker 1990: 16). But these studies have not specified when such discursive conflicts would lead to structural transformation in one case and revaluation in another.

31. This was likely true of Manuel Quezon. Yet my focus has been on group-level dynamics in comparison with group-level dynamics in Puerto Rico; in this sense, Quezon was the exception that proves the rule.

32. Countless works discuss nation building or "exporting democracy" (e.g., Smith 1994), but when they raise the problems of such a project, they discuss only armed resistance or institutional development. None of them raise the possibility of domestication.

33. Ferguson 2004; Ignatieff 2003.

34. Fernandez 1988.

REFERENCES

ABBREVIATIONS AND CITATION PROTOCOL

AGPR   Archivo General de Puerto Rico (General Archive of Puerto Rico), San Juan, Puerto Rico

      FF: Fondo Fortaleza

      GC: Correspondencia General

      Gob.: Gobierno

      Munic.: Municipalities

      PP: Partidos Politicos

BG   Bothwell-Gonzalez

BHPR   *Boletín Historico de Puerto Rico*

BM   Bernard Moses Papers, Bancroft Library, University of California at Berkeley

CE   Clarence R. Edwards Papers, Massachusetts Historical Society

DCIA   Division of Customs and Insular Affairs

EP   *El País*

ERP   Papers of Elihu Root. Library of Congress, Manuscript Division. Washington, D.C.

FDG   Papers of Federico Degetau y Gonzalez, Dr. Angel M. Mergal Collection, Centro de Investigaciones Historicas, University of Puerto Rico (box no., file no., document no.)

GPR   Governor of Puerto Rico, *Annual Report of the Governor of Puerto Rico* (listed year is year of publication)

HR   *El Heraldo de la Revolución*

LCPR   *La Correspondencia de Puerto Rico*

LD   *La Democracía*

MGM	Papers of Miguel Guerra Mondragon, University of Puerto Rico (box, folder no. or range in folder, document no.)
MP	Papers of William McKinley, Library of Congress
MT	*Manila Times*
OGPR	*Official Gazette of Puerto Rico*
PRH	*Puerto Rico Herald*
PRR	*Porto Rico Review/Revista de Puerto Rico*
REN	*El Renacimiento*
RG	Record Group, USNA
SJN	*San Juan News*
TP	Papers of Theodore Roosevelt, Library of Congress
UPRL	University of Puerto Rico at Río Piedras Library
USMG	U.S. Major-General Commanding the Army
USNA	U.S. National Archives, Washington, D.C.
USPC	U.S. Philippine Commission
USSC	U.S. Congress, Senate, Committee on the Philippines
USWD	U.S. War Department
WCF	William Cameron Forbes Papers, Houghton Library, Harvard University
WHT	William Howard Taft Papers, Library of Congress
WPC	Worcester Philippine Collection, Rare Books and Special Collections, Hatcher Library, University of Michigan, Ann Arbor

BIBLIOGRAPHY

Archives and Archival Collections

American Historical Collection, Ateneo de Manila University Library, Quezon City Philippines

Archivo General de Puerto Rico, San Juan, Puerto Rico

Ayer Philippine Collection, Newberry Library, Chicago

Bancroft Library, University of California, Berkeley

Harry J. Bandholtz Papers

David P. Barrows Papers

Bentley Historical Library, Michigan Historical Collections, Ann Arbor

La Biblioteca y Hemeroteca Puertorriqueña, University of Puerto Rico at Río Piedras

Papers of Federico Degetau y Gonzalez, Dr. Angel M. Mergal Collection, Centro de Investigaciones Históricas, University of Puerto Rico at Río Piedras

Clarence R. Edwards Papers, Massachusetts Historical Society, Boston

Executive Minutes of the United States Philippine Commission (bound ms.)

Filipinania Collection, University of the Philippines-Diliman

William Cameron Forbes Papers, Houghton Library, Harvard University

James A. LeRoy Papers

Colección Miguel Guerra Mondragon, Lazaro Collection, University of Puerto Rico at Río Piedras

Library of Congress, Manuscript Division, Washington, D.C.

William McKinley Papers

Bernard Moses Papers

Philippine National Archives, Manila

Philippine Revolutionary Papers

Theodore Roosevelt Papers

Elihu Root Papers

Manuel L. Quezon Papers

William Howard Taft Papers

United States National Archives, Washington, D.C., and College Park, MD

RG 48: Department of the Interior

RG 108: Records of the Headquarters of the Army

RG 126: Records of the Office of Territories

RG 350: Bureau of Insular Affairs

RG 395: Records of US Army Overseas Operations and Commands, 1898–1942

University of California Doe Library, Berkeley

William F. Willoughby Papers, William and Mary College, Virginia

Dean C. Worcester Papers

Worcester Philippine Collection, Rare Books and Special Collections, Hatcher Library, University of Michigan, Ann Arbor

Newspapers

Philippines

Cultura Filipina

El Eco de Panay (Iloilo)

El Grito del Pueblo

El Heraldo de la Revolución

La Independencia

La Justicia (Cebu)

The Manila Times

El Renacimiento

La Republica Filipina

La Solidaridad

Puerto Rico

La Correspondencia de Puerto Rico

La Democracia

El País

Puerto Rico Herald/El Heraldo de Puerto Rico

Puerto Rico Eagle/Aguila de Puerto Rico
Porto Rico Review/Revista de Puerto Rico
San Juan News

Books, Articles, and Other Materials

Abbott, Andrew. 2001. *Time Matters: On Theory and Method*. Chicago: University of Chicago Press.

Abinales, Patricio. 2003. "Progressive Machine Conflict in Early Twentieth-Century U.S. Politics and Colonial State Building in the Philippines." In *The American Colonial State in the Philippines: Global Perspectives*, ed. Julian Go and Anne Foster, 148–81. Durham, N.C.: Duke University Press.

Adams, Julia. 1999. "Culture in Rational-Choice Theories of State-Formation." In *State/Culture: State-Formation after the Cultural Turn*, ed. George Steinmetz. Ithaca, N.Y.: Cornell University Press.

Adas, Michael. 1998. "Improving on the Civilising Mission? Assumptions of United States Exceptionalism in the Colonisation of the Philippines." *Itinerario* 22:44–66.

Adriatico, Macario. 1917. "Our Directing Class, or The Aristocracy of the Intellect/ Nuestra Clase Directora o la Aristocracia Intelectual." *Philippine Review* 2:41–45.

Agoncillo, Teodoro A. 1960. *Malolos: The Crisis of the Republic*. Quezon City: University of the Philippines Press.

Aguilar, Filomeno. 1998. *Clash of Spirits*. Honolulu: University of Hawai'i Press.

Alegria, Ricardo. 1972. "Muñoz Rivera y de Diego ante la invasion norteamericana." *Revista del Instituto de Cultural Puertorriquena* 15.

Alejo, Myrna J., Maria Elena P. Rivera, and Noel Inocencio P. Valencia. 1996. *[De]Scribing Elections: A Study of Elections in the Lifeworld in San Isidro*. Quezon City: Institute for Popular Democracy.

Alexander, Jeffrey C., and Philip Smith. 1993. "The Discourse of American Civil Society: A New Proposal for Cultural Studies." *Theory and Society* 22:151–207.

Alfonso, Oscar. 1969. "Taft's Early Views on the Filipinos." *Solidarity* 4:52–58.

Almond, Gabriel A., and Sidney Verba. 1963. *The Civic Culture*. Princeton, N.J.: Princeton University Press.

Altamirano y Salcedo, Enrique. 1902. *Filipinas: Relato histórico de actos y hechos Realizados en los últimos días de nuetra dominación*. Madrid: Imprenta de Cárlos Perrín.

Alvarez Curbelo, Silvia. 1998. "Las fiestas públicas en Ponce: Políticas de la memoria y cultura cívica." In *Los Acros de la Memoria*, ed. Silvia Alvarez Curbelo, Mary Frances Gallart, and Carmen I. Raffucci, 208–31. San Juan: Oficina del Presidente de la Universidad de Puerto Rico.

Alvarez, Juan Guerra. 1887. *Viajes por Filipinas de Manila a Tayabas*. Madrid: Fortanet.

Alvarez, Santiago V. 1992. *The Katipunan and the Revolution: Memoirs of a General (With the Original Tagalog Text)*. Quezon City: Ateneo de Manila.

Amoroso, Donna. 2003. "Inheriting the 'Moro Problem': Muslim Authority and Colonial Rule in British Malaya and the Philippines." In *The American Colonial State in the Philippines: Global Perspectives*, ed. Julian Go and Anne Foster, 92–117. Durham, N.C.: Duke University Press.

Anderson, Benedict. 1990. *Language and Power: Exploring Political Cultures in Indonesia*. Ithaca, N.Y.: Cornell University Press.

———. 1995. "Cacique Democracy in the Philippines." In *Discrepant Histories: Translocal Essays on Filipino Cultures*, ed. Vicente L. Rafael, 3–47. Philadelphia: Temple University Press.

Anderson, Warwick. 1995. " 'Where Every Prospect Pleases and Only Man is Vile': Laboratory Medicine and Colonial Discourse." In *Discrepant Histories: Translocal Essays on Filipino Cultures*, ed. Vicente L. Rafael, 83–112. Philadelphia: Temple University Press.

Aronoff, Myron J. 1983. "Conceptualizing the Role of Culture in Political Change." In *Political Anthropology Yearbook*, ed. Myron J. Aronoff, 1–18. New Brunswick, N.J.: Transaction Books.

Asamblea Filipina. 1907. *Diario de Sesiones de la Primera Asamblea Filipina (Volume I, Number 1)*. Manila: Bureau of Printing.

Atkinson, F. 1904. "An Inside View of Philippine Life." *World's Work* 9, no. 2: 5571–5589.

Augustin Aponte, José. 1908. *Vida Politica y Literaria: Campaña Unionista de 1906*. Mayaguez, Puerto Rico: Imp. "Gloria."

Ayala, César J. 1999. *American Sugar Kingdom: The Plantation Economy of the Spanish Caribbean, 1898–1934*. Chapel Hill: University of North Carolina Press.

Baker, Jean H. 1998. *Affairs of Party: The Political Culture of Northern Democrats in the Mid-Nineteenth Century*. New York: Fordham University Press.

Baker, Keith. 1990. *Inventing the French Revolution: Essays on French Political Culture in the Eighteenth Century*. Cambridge: Cambridge University Press.

Bankoff, Greg. 1992. "Big Fish in Small Ponds: The Exercise of Power in a Nineteenth-Century Philippine Municipality." *Modern Asian Studies* 26:679–700.

Baralt, Guillermo A. 1999. *Buena Vista: Life and Work on a Puerto Rican Hacienda, 1833–1904*. Chapel Hill, NC: University of North Carolina Press.

Barceló Miller, María de Fátima. 1979. "Un Capitulo de Historia Municipal: Isabela (1873–1886)." PhD diss., Department of History, University of Puerto Rico at Río Piedras.

———. 1984. *Política Ultramarina y Gobierno Municipal: Isabela, 1873–1887*. Santurce, Puerto Rico: Ediciones Huracán.

Barthes, Roland. 1977. *Image, Music, Text*. London: Fontana.

Bayron Toro, Fernando. 1977. *Elecciones y Partidos Politicos de Puerto Rico (1809–1976)*. Mayagüez: Editorial Isla.

Bennagen, Ponciano L. 1985. "Social Development in the Philippines." In *Asian Perspectives in Social Science*, ed. W. R. Geddes, 91–98. Seoul: Seoul National University Press.

Berbusse, Edward. 1966. *The United States in Puerto Rico, 1898–1900*. Chapel Hill: University of North Carolina Press.

Bergad, Laird. 1978. "Agrarian History of Puerto Rico, 1870–1930." *Latin American Research Review* 8:63–94.

———. 1983. *Coffee and the Growth of Agrarian Capitalism in Nineteenth-Century Puerto Rico*. Princeton, N.J.: Princeton University Press.

Bernabe, Rafael. 1996. *Respuestas al Colonialismo en la Política Puertorriqueña 1899–1929*. Río Piedras, Puerto Rico: Ediciones Huracán.

Beveridge, Albert J. 1907. "The Development of a Colonial Policy for the United States." *Annals of the American Academy of Political and Social Science* 30:3–15.

Bhabha, Homi K. 1994. *The Location of Culture*. London: Routledge.

Biernacki, Richard. 1999. "Method and Metaphor after the New Cultural History." In *Beyond the Cultural Turn: New Directions in the Study of Society and Culture*, ed. Victoria E. Bonnell and Lynn Hunt, 62–92. Berkeley: University of California Press.

Blair, Emma H., and James A. Robertson 1903. *The Philippine Islands (1493–1898)*. Cleveland: The A. H. Clark Company.

Blanch, Jose. 1894. *Noticías Geográficas é Históricas de la Isla de Puerto Rico*. Mayaguez: Tip. al vap. de "La Correspondencia."

Blount, James H. 1913. *American Occupation of the Philippines, 1898–1912*. New York: G.P. Putnam's Sons.

Blumer, Herbert. 1969. *Symbolic Interactionism*. Englewood Cliffs, N.J.: Prentice-Hall.

Bonnell, Victoria E., and Lynn Hunt, eds. 1999. *Beyond the Cultural Turn*. Berkeley: University of California Press.

Borromeo, Soledad Masangkay. 1973. "El Cadiz Filipino: Colonial Cavite, 1571–1896." PhD diss., Department of History, University of California, Berkeley.

Bothwell-Gonzalez, Reece B. 1979. *Puerto Rico: Cien Años de Lucha Política*. Río Piedras: Editorial Universitaria.

Bourdieu, Pierre. 1977. *Outline of a Theory of Practice*. Cambridge: Cambridge University Press.

Boyce, William. 1914. *The Hawaiian Islands and Puerto Rico*. Chicago: Rand McNally.

Brands, H. W. 1992. *Bound to Empire: the United States and the Philippines*. Oxford: Oxford University Press.

Brau, Salvador. 1956. *Disquisiciones Sociológicas y Otros Ensayos*. San Juan: Universidad de Puerto Rico.

———. 1973. "En plena luz." In *Libertad y Crítica en el Ensayo Político Puertorriqueño*, ed. Iris M. Zavala and Rafael Rodríguez, 121–27. Río Piedras, Puerto Rico: Ediciones Puerto.

Brewer, Anthony. 1990. *Marxist Theories of Imperialism: A Critical Survey*. London: Routledge.

Briggs, Laura. 2002. *Reproducing Empire: Race, Sex, Science, and U.S. Imperialism in Puerto Rico*. Berkeley: University of California Press.

Brownell, Blaine, and Warren E. Stickle. 1973. *Bosses and Reformers*. Boston: Houghton Mifflin Company.

Buenker, John D. 1988. "Sovereign Individuals and Organic Networks: Political Culture in Conflict During the Progressive Era." *American Quarterly* 40:187–204.

Buitrago Ortiz, Carlos. 1976. *Los orígines históricos de la sociedad precapitalista en Puerto Rico*. Río Piedras, Puerto Rico: Ediciones Huracán.

———. 1982. *Haciendas Cafetaleras y Clases Terratenientes en el Puerto Rico Décimonónico*. Río Piedras, Puerto Rico: Editorial de la Universidad de Puerto Rico.

Bulatao, Jamie C. 1964. "Hiya." *Philippine Studies* 12:424–38.

Burch, Henry. 1902. "Suffrage in Colonies." *Annals of the American Academy of Political and Social Science* 19: 78–101.

Burgos Malave, Eda Milagros. 1997. *Genesis y Praxis de la Carta Autonomica de 1897 en Puerto Rico*. San Juan: Centro de Estudios Avanzados de Puerto Rico y El Caribe (in collaboration with Instituto de Cultura Puertorriqueña and the Luis Muñoz Foundation).

Burke, Peter. 1997. *Varieties of Cultural History*. Ithaca, NY: Cornell University Press.

Caban, Pedro A. 1999. *Constructing a Colonial People: Puerto Rico and the United States, 1898–1932*. Boulder, Colo.: Westview.

Calderon, Felipe. 1919. "The Memoirs of Felipe Calderon, part 1." *Philippine Review* 4:462–76.

Calderon, Sofronio G. 1915. *Diccionario Ingles-Español-Tagalog*. Manila: Libería y Papelería de J. Martinez.

Cancel, Mario. 1998. "Mayaguez 1898: La ciudad y los manejos de poder." In *Los Arcos de la Memoria*, ed. Silvia Alvarez Curbelo, Mary Frances Gallart, and Carmen I. Raffuci, 39–55. San Juan: Asociación Puertorriqueña de Historiadores.

Carr, Raymond. 1984. *Puerto Rico, a Colonial Experiment*. New York: Vintage Books.

Carrión, Arturo Morales. 1983. *Puerto Rico: A Political and Cultural History*. New York: W. W. Norton & Company.

Carroll, Henry K. 1899a. "How Shall Puerto Rico Be Governed." *Forum* 28:256–57.

———. 1899b. *Report on the Island of Porto Rico; its Population, Civil Government, Commerce, Industries, Productions, Roads, Tariff, and Currency, with recommendations by Henry K. Carroll*. Washington, D.C.: Government Printing Office.

Census Office of the Philippine Islands. 1920. *Census of the Philippine Islands*. Manila: Bureau of Printing.

Cepeda, Francisco. 1888. *Catecismo Autonomista ó La Autonomia Colonial*. Ponce: Tipografia de la Revista de Puerto Rico.

Chong, Dennis. 2000. *Rational Lives*. Chicago: University of Chicago Press.

Choudons, Juan de, Jr. 1911. *Guia Postal y Directorio General de Puerto Rico*. San Juan: Tip y Litografíca del Boletin Mercantil.

Chwe, Michael Suk-Young. 2001. *Rational Ritual: Culture, Coordination, and Common Knowledge*. Princeton, N.J.: Princeton University Press.

Clark, Victor S., and Brookings Institution. 1930. *Porto Rico and Its Problems*. Washington, D.C.: The Brookings Institution.

Clifford, James, and George Marcus, eds. 1986. *Writing Culture: The Poetics and Politics of Ethnography*. Berkeley: University of California Press.

Cohen, Abner. 1974. *Two-Dimensional Man: An Essay on the Anthropology of Power and Symbolism in Complex Society*. Berkeley: University of California Press.

Cohn, Bernard S. 1996. *Colonialism and Its Forms of Knowledge*. Princeton, N.J.: Princeton University Press.

Cole, Michael. 1996. *Cultural Psychology: A Once and Future Discipline*. Cambridge, Mass.: Belknap.

Coll Cuchí, Cayetano. 1904. *La Ley Foraker. Estudio Histórico-Político Comparado*. San Juan: Tipgrafia del Boletin Mercantil.

———. 1972. *Historias que parecen cuentos*. Río Piedras: Colección Uprex, Editorial Universitaria, Universidad de Puerto Rico.

Comaroff, Jean, and John Comaroff. 1991. *Of Revelation and Revolution: Christianity, Colonialism, and Consciousness in South Africa*. Vol. 1. Chicago: University of Chicago Press.

———. 1997. *Of Revelation and Revolution. The Dialectics of Modernity on a South African Frontier*. Vol. 2. Chicago: University of Chicago Press.

Commissioner of the Interior for Puerto Rico. 1900. *Report of the Commissioner of Interior for Porto Rico to the Secretary of the Interior, U.S.A.* Washington, D.C.: Government Printing Office.

———. 1901. *Report of the Commissioner of Interior for Porto Rico to the Secretary of the Interior, U.S.A.* Washington, D.C.: Government Printing Office.

Cooper, Frederick. 1992. "Colonizing Time: Work Rhythms and Labor Conflict in Colonial Mombasa." In *Colonialism and Culture*, ed. Nicholas B. Dirks, 209–45. Ann Arbor: University of Michigan Press.

Cora y Mora, Juan. 1897. *La Situación del Pais. Colección de articulos publicados por "La Española" acerca de la insurreción tagala, sus causas principales, cuestiones que afectan a Filipinas*. Manila: Imprenta de "Amigos del Pais."

Corpuz, Onofre D. 1957. *The Bureaucracy in the Philippines*. Diliman: Institution of Public Administration, University of the Philippines.

Cruz Monclova, Lidio. 1964. *Historia de Puerto Rico (Siglo XIX)*. Rio Piedras: Editorial Universitaria.

Cubano-Iguina, Astrid. 1988–89. "La Politica de la Elite Mercantil y el Establecimiento del Regimen Autonomico en Puerto Rico, 1890–1898." *Op. Cit. Boletin del Centro de Investigaciones Históricas* 3:153–73.

——. 1998. "Political Culture and Male Mass-Party Formation in Late Nineteenth-Century Puerto Rico." *Hispanic American Historical Review* 78:631–62.

Cullinane, Michael. 1971. "Implementing the "New Order": The Structure and Supervision of Local Government During the Taft Era." In *Compadre Colonialism: Studies on the Philippines Under American Rule*, ed. Norman Owen, 13–76. Ann Arbor: Michigan Papers on South and Southeast Asia, no. 3.

——. 1982. "The Changing Nature of the Cebu Urban Elite in the Nineteenth Century." In *Philippine Social History*, ed. Alfred W. McCoy and Ed. C. de Jesus, 251–96. Quezon City: Ateneo de Manila University Press.

——. 1989. "Ilustrado Politics: The Response of the Filipino Educated Elite to American Colonial Rule, 1898–1907." PhD diss., Department of History, University of Michigan.

Dauncey, Mrs. Campbell. 1906. *An Englishwoman in the Philippines*. London: John Murray.

Davis, General George W. 1900. *Report of General Davis: Civil Affairs in Puerto Rico, 1899*. Washington, D.C.: Government Printing Office.

Davis, Richard Harding. 1898. *The Cuban and Porto Rican Campaigns*. New York: Charles Scribner's Sons.

Díaz Hernández, Luis Edgardo. 1983. *Castañer. Una Hacienda Cafetalera en Puerto Rico (1868–1930)*. Río Piedras: Editorial Edil.

Díaz Soler, Luis M., and Rosendo Matienzo Cintrón. 1960. *Rosendo Matienzo Cintrón*. [Río Piedras]: Instituto de Literatura Puertorriqueña Universidad de Puerto Rico.

Díaz-Quiñones, Arcadio. 1999. "Salvador Brau: The Paradox of the *Autonomista* Tradition." In *The Places of History. Regionalism Revisited in Latin America*, ed. Doris Sommer, 104–18. Durham, N.C.: Duke University Press.

Diego, Jose de. 1890. *La Codificación Administrativa*. Mayaguez, Puerto Rico: Imp. de La Razon.

——. 1901. *Apuntes sobre la delincuencia y la penalidad*. San Juan: Tipografía La Correspondencia.

Dietz, James L. 1986. *Economic History of Puerto Rico: Institutional Change and Capitalist Development*. Princeton, N.J.: Princeton University Press.

DiMaggio, Paul. 1997. "Culture and Cognition." *Annual Review of Sociology* 23:263–87.

Diokono, Jose. 1983. "A Filipino Concept of Justice." *Solidarity* 3:5–12.

Director Census of Porto Rico, United States War Department. 1900. *Report on the Census of Porto Rico*. Washington, D.C.: Government Printing Office.

Dirks, Nicholas B. 1992. "Castes of Mind." *Representations* 37:56–78.

——. 2001. *Castes of Mind: Colonialism and the Making of Modern India*. Princeton, N.J.: Princeton University Press.

Domínguez, José de Jesús. 1887. *La Autonomía Administrativa en Puerto Rico*. Mayaguez: Tip. Comercial.

E.S.L. 1898. *Derechoes y Deberes del Ciudadano*. Aguadilla, Puerto Rico: Tip. de "La Voz del Pueblo."

Echauz, Robustiano. 1894. *Apuntes de la isla de Negros*. Manila: Tipo-Litografia de Chofre y Compaoia.

Elliot, Charles. 1917. *The Philippines to the End of the Commission Government*. Indianapolis: Bobbs-Merrill.

Elzaburu, D. Manuel. 1889. *El Sentimiento de Nacionalidad*. San Juan: Imprenta de Jose Gonzalez y Font.

Emirbayer, Mustafa, and Ann Mische. 1998. "What is Agency?" *American Journal of Sociology* 103:962–1023.

Engels, Dagmar, and Shula Marks. 1994. *Contesting Colonial Hegemony: State and Society in Africa and India*. London: British Academic Press/German Historical Institute, London.

Enriquez, Virgilio. 1994. *From Colonial to Liberation Psychology*. Manila: De La Salle University Press.

Executive Council of Porto Rico. 1901–7. *Journal of the Executive Council of Porto Rico*. San Juan: Press of Luis E. Tuzo and Company.

Fajardo, Reynaldo S. 1998. "Masonry and the Philippine Revolution." In *The Philippine Revolution and Beyond*, ed. Elmer A. Ordoñez, 1:337–52. Manila: Philippine Centennial Commission, National Commission for Culture and the Arts.

Fanon, Frantz. 1965. *A Dying Colonialism*. New York: Grove.

Fast, Jonathan, and Jim Richardson. 1979. *Roots of Dependency: Political and Economic Revolution in Nineteenth-Century Philippines*. Quezon City: Foundation for Nationalist Studies.

Feced y Temprado, Pablo. 1888. *Filipinas: Esbozos y pinceladas por Quioquiap*. Manila: Estab. Tipog de Ramirez y Companía.

Fee, Mary H. 1910. *A Woman's Impression of the Philippines*. Chicago: A.C. McClurg.

Fegan, Brian. 1982. "The Social History of a Central Luzon Barrio." In *Philippine Social History: Global Trade and Local Transformations*, ed. Alfred W. McCoy and Ed C. de Jesus, 91–130. Quezon City: Ateneo de Manila.

———. 1993. "Entrepeneurs in Votes and Violence: Three Generations of a Peasant Political Family." In *An Anarchy of Families: State and Family in the Philippines*, ed. Alfred W. McCoy, 33–107. Madison: University of Wisconsin Press.

Ferguson, Niall. 2004. *Colossus: The Price of America's Empire*. New York: Penguin Press.

Fernandez, Ronald. 1988. *Los Macheteros: The Violent Struggle for Puerto Rican Independence*. Westport, Conn.: Greenwood.

Fernández Méndez, Eugenio, ed. 1975. *Antología del Pensamiento Puertorriqueño (1900–1970)*. Río Piedras: Editorial Universitaria.

Findlay, Eileen J. 1998. "Love in the Tropics: Marriage, Divorce and the Construction of Benevolent Colonialism in Puerto Rico, 1898–1910." In *Close Encounters of Empire: Writing the Cultural History of U.S.-Latin American Relations*, ed. Gilbert M. Joseph, Catherin E. LeGrand, and Ricardo D. Salvatore, 139–72. Durham, N.C.: Duke University Press.

———. 1999. *Imposing Decency: The Politics of Sexuality and Race in Puerto Rico, 1870–1920*. Durham, N.C.: Duke University Press.

Fisher, Horace. 1899. *Principles of Colonial Government Adapted to the Present Needs of Cuba and Porto Rico, and of the Philippines*. Boston: L.C. Page.

Forbes, Cameron W. 1928. *The Philippine Islands*. 2 vols. Boston: Houghton Mifflin Company.

Foreman, John. 1906. *The Philippine Islands*. Shanghai: Kelly and Walsh.

Formisiano, Ronald. 2001. "The Concept of Political Culture." *Journal of Interdisciplinary History* 31:393–426.

Foucault, Michel. 1979.

———. 1990. *The History of Sexuality: An Introduction*. New York: Vintage Books.

Foucault, Michel, Graham Burchell, Colin Gordon, and Peter Miller. 1991. *The Foucault Effect: Studies in Governmentality (with Two Lectures by and an interview with Michel Foucault)*. Chicago: University of Chicago Press.

Fowles, George Milton. 1910. *Down in Porto Rico*. New York: Young People's Missionary Movement of the United States and Canada.

Fox, Richard G. 1985. *Lions of the Punjab: Culture in the Making*. Berkeley: University of California Press.

Frances Gallart, Mary. 1998. "Guayama: Resentimientos soterrados y ajustes de cuentas, 1898–1902." In *Los Arcos de la Memoria*, ed. Silvia Alvarez Curbelo, Mary Frances Gallart, and Carmen I. Raffuci, 128–40. San Juan: Asociación Puertorriqueña de Historiadores.

Friedman, Jonathan. 1988. "No History Is an Island." *Critique of Anthropology* 8:7–39.

Freer, William. 1906. *The Philippine Experiences of an American Teacher*. New York: Charles Scribner's Sons.

Frisch, Michael H. 1982. "Urban Theorists, Urban Reform, and American Political Culture in the Progressive Period." *Political Science Quarterly* 97:295–315.

Fuster Morales, C. 1903. *Miserias Políticas. Historia de un Alcalde y dos propagandistas*. Caguas, Puerto Rico: Tipografia "La Democracia."

Garcia, Gervasio L. 1989. *Historia crítica, historian sin coartadas*. Río Piedras: Ediciones Huracán.

Gates, John Morgan. 1973. *Schoolbooks and Krags: The United States Army in the Philippines*. Westport, Conn.: Greenwood.

Gaudier Texidor, Benito. 1957. *Nuetro Mayaguez de ayer y el verdadero origin de "La Borinqueña."* Río Piedras: Unpublished monograph, University of Puerto Rico, Jose M. Lazaro Library.

Geddes, Barbara. 1995. "Uses and Limitations of Rational Choice." In *Latin America in Comparative Perspective: New Approaches to Methods and Analysis*, ed. Peter H. Smith, 81–108. Boulder, Colo.: Westview.

Geertz, Clifford. 1973. *The Interpretation of Cultures: Selected Essays*. New York: Basic Books.

———. 1980. *Negara: The Theatre State in Nineteenth-Century Bali*. Princeton, N.J.: Princeton University Press.

———. 1990. "History and Anthropology." *New Literary History* 21:321–35.

Giddens, Anthony. 1986. *The Constitution of Society: Outline of the Theory of Structuration*. Berkeley: University of California Press.

Giddings, Franklin H. 1898. "Imperialism?" *Political Science Quarterly* 13:585–605.

Gillete, H. 1973. "The Military Occupation of Cuba, 1899–1902." *American Quarterly* 25(4):410–425.

Gleeck, Lewis E., Jr. 1976. *American Institutions in the Philippines (1898–1941)*. Manila: Historical Conservation Society.

———. 1981. *Laguna in American Times: Coconuts and Revolucionarios*. Manila: Historical Conservation Society.

Go, Julian. 2000. "Chains of Empire, Projects of State: Political Education and U.S. Colonial Rule in Puerto Rico and the Philippines." *Comparative Studies in Society and History* 42:333–62.

———. 2003. "Introduction: Global Perspectives on the U.S. Colonial State in the Philippines." In *The U.S. Colonial State in the Philippines in Comparative Perspective*, ed. Julian Go and Anne Foster. Durham, N.C.: Duke University Press.

———. 2004. " 'Racism' and Colonialism: Meanings of Difference and Ruling Practices in America's Pacific Empire." *Qualitative Sociology* 27:35–58.

———. 2007. "The Provinciality of American Empire." *Comparative Studies in Society and History* 49, no. 1: 74–108.

Goberino de Philippines. 1898. *Guia Oficial de Filipinas*. Manila: Chofré.

Gobierno de Puerto Rico. 1897. *Guía Oficial de Puerto Rico*. San Juan: Imprenta de La Gaceta.

Golay, Frank H. 1998. *Face of Empire: United States–Philippine Relations, 1898–1946*. Madison: University of Wisconsin, Madison, Center for Southeast Asian Studies, Monograph no. 14.

Gonzales, Andrew B. 1982. "Filipinization of the Social Sciences: A Red Herring?" *Social Sciences Information* 10:9–13.

Goodnow, Frank. 1906. "Colonial Administration: Territories and Dependencies of the United States, Their Government and Administration." *Political Science Quarterly* 21:135–38.

Gossett, Thomas F. 1997. *Race: The History of an Idea in America*. New York: Oxford University Press.

Governor of Porto Rico. 1900–1915. *Annual Reports*. Washington, D.C.: Government Printing Bureau.

Groff, George C. 1900. "A Successful Colonial Government." *Independent* 52:102–5.

✓ Guerra, Francois-Xavier. 1994. "The Spanish-American Tradition of Representation and its European Roots." *Journal of Latin American Studies* 26:1–35.

Guha, Ranajit. 1997. *Dominance without Hegemony: History and Power in Colonial India*. Cambridge, Mass.: Harvard University Press.

Guillermety, Carlos D'Alzina. 1995. *Evolucion y desarollo del autonomismo puertorriqueño*. San Juan: Carlos D'Alzina Guillermety.

Hannerz, Ulf. 1996. *Transnational Connections: Culture, People, Places*. London: Routledge.

Hanson, Earl. 1955. *Transformation: The Story of Modern Puerto Rico*. New York: Simon and Schuster.

Hart, Robert W. 1928. *The Philippines Today*. New York: Dodd, Mead, and Company.

Hartzell, Charles. 1909. "What is Just to Porto Rico." *Report of the Twenty–Seventh Annual Meeting of the Lake Mohonk Conference of Friends of the Indian and other Dependent Peoples, October 20th, 21st, and 22nd, 1909*, ed. Charles F. Meserve, 169–173. Lake Mohonk Conference of Friends of the Indian and other Dependent Peoples.

Hayden, Joseph R. 1942. *The Philippines: A Study in National Development*. New York: Macmillan and Company.

Herrmann, Karl. 1907. *A Recent Campaign in Puerto Rico*. Boston: E. H. Bacon.

Hofstadter, Richard. 1955. *The Age of Reform*. New York: Basic Books.

Hollander, J. H. 1901. "The Finances of Porto Rico." *Political Science Quarterly* 14:553–81.

Hollsteiner, Mary R. 1969. "The Development of Political Parties in a Town." In *The Foundations and Dynamics of Filipino Government and Politics*, ed. Jose Veloso Abueva and Raul P. de Guzman, 158–80. Manila: Bookmark.

———. 1973. "Reciprocity in the Lowland Philippines." In *Four Readings on Philippine Values*, ed. Frank Lynch and Alfonso de Guzman, 69–92. Quezon City: Ateneo de Manila University Press.

Hoyt, Frederick. 1963. "The Wood-Forbes Mission to the Philippines, 1921." PhD diss., Department of History, Claremont University.

Huntington, Samuel. 1997. *The Clash of Civilizations and the Remaking of World Order*. New York: Touchstone.

Hyslop, James H. 1899. "Responsibility in Municipal Government." *Forum* 28:409–81.

Ignatieff, Michael. 2003. "The American Empire: the Burden." *New York Times Sunday Magazine*, January 5. Pp. 22–31.

Ileto, Reynaldo C. 1979. *Payson and Revolution: Popular Movements in the Philippines*. Quezon City: Ateneo de Manila University Press.

——. 1995. "Cholera and the Origins of the American Sanitary Order in the Philippines." In *Discrepant Histories: Translocal Essays on Filipino Cultures*, ed. Vicente Rafael, 51–82. Philadelphia: Temple University Press.

——. 1999. *Knowing America's Colony: A Hundred Years from the Philippine War*. Manoa: Center for Philippine Studies.

Inglehart, Ronald. 1990. *Cultural Shift in Advanced Industrial Society*. Princeton: Princeton University Press.

Jackman, Robert W., and Ross A. Miller. 1996. "A Renaissance of Political Culture?" *American Journal of Political Science* 40:632–59.

Jackson, F. E. 1906. *The Representative Men of the Philippines*. Manila: E. C. McCullough & Co.

——. 1910. *The Representative Men of Porto Rico*: F. E. Jackson & Son.

Jacobson, Matthew Frye. 2000. *Barbarian Virtues: The United States Encounters Foreign Peoples at Home and Abroad*. New York: Hill and Wang.

Jenista, Frank. 1971. "Conflict in the Philippine Legislature: The Commission and Assembly from 1907 to 1913." In *Compadre Colonialism: Studies on the Philippines under American Rule*, ed. Norman Owen. Ann Arbor: University of Michigan, Papers on South and Southeast Asia, no. 3.

Jepperson, Ronald L., and Ann Swidler. 1994. "What Properties of Culture Should We Measure?" *Poetics* 22:359–71.

Jernegan, Prescott F. 1910. *The Philippine Citizen: A Text-Book of Civics, Describing the Nature of Government, the Philippine Government, and the Rights and Duties of Citizens of the Philippines*. Manila: Philippine Education Publishing Co.

Jessup, Philip. 1938. *Elihu Root*. New York: Dodd, Mead & Company.

Jesus, Edilberto C. de. 1978. "Gobernadorcillo Elections in Cagayan." *Philippine Studies* 26:142–56.

Johnson, James. 1997. "Symbol and Strategy in Comparative Political Analysis." *APSA–Comparative Politics Newsletter* 8:6–9.

Joseph, Gilbert M. 1998. "Close Encounters: Toward a New Cultural History of U.S.-Latin American Relations." In *Close Encounters of Empire: Writing the Cultural History of U.S.-Latin American Relations*, ed. Gilbert M. Joseph, Catherin E. LeGrand, and Ricardo D. Salvatore, 3–46. Durham, N.C.: Duke University Press.

Kalaw, Maximo M. 1927. *The Development of Philippine Politics (1872–1920)*. Manila: Oriental Commercial Co.

Kalaw, Teodoro M. 1956. *Philippine Masonry*. Manila: McCullough Printing Company.

——. 1913. *Directorio Oficial de la asamblea filipina: Tercera legislature Filipina*. Manila: Bureau of Printing.

Kaplan, Amy. 1993. "Left Alone in America." In *Cultures of United States Imperialism*, ed. Amy Kaplan and Donald E. Pease, 3–21. Durham, N.C.: Duke University Press.

———. 2003. *Anarchy of Empire in the Making of American Culture*. Cambridge, Mass.: Harvard University Press.

Kaplan, Amy, and Donald Pease, eds. 1993. *Cultures of United States Imperialism*. Durham, N.C.: Duke University Press.

Kane, Anne. 1991. "Cultural Analysis in Historical Sociology: The Analytic and Concrete Forms of the Autonomy of Culture." *Sociological Theory* 9:53–69.

———. 1997. "Theorizing Meaning Construction in Social Movements: Symbolic Structures and Interpretation during the Irish Land War, 1879–1882." *Sociological Theory* 15:249–76.

Karnow, Stanley. 1989. *In Our Image: America's Empire in the Philippines*. New York: Ballantine Books.

Kaut, Charles. 1961. "Utang na loób: A System of Contractual Obligation among Tagalogs." *Southwestern Journal of Anthropology* 17:256–72.

Kaye, Perey Lewis. 1903. "Suffrage and Self-Government in Porto Rico." *Yale Review* 12:169–190.

Keesing, Roger. 1974. "Theories of Culture." *Annual Review of Anthropology* 3:73–97.

Kerkvliet, Benedict. 1977. *The Huk Rebellion: A Study of Peasant Revolt in the Philippines*. Berkeley: University of California Press.

Kertzer, David. 1988. *Ritual, Politics, and Power*. New Haven, Conn.: Yale University Press.

Kidder, Frederick Elwyn. 1965. "The Political Concepts of Luix Munoz Rivera (1859–1916) of Puerto Rico." PhD diss., Department of Political Science, University of Florida, Gainesville.

Kramer, Paul. 2006. *The Blood of Government: Race, Empire, the United States, and the Philippines*. Chapel Hill: University of North Carolina Press.

LaFeber, Walter. 1963. *The New Empire: An Interpretation of American Expansionism, 1860–1898*. Ithaca: Cornell University Press.

Laitin, David D. 1986. *Hegemony and Culture: Politics and Religious Change among the Yoruba*. Chicago: University of Chicago Press.

———. 1988. "Political Culture and Political Preferences." *American Political Science Review* 82:589–93.

Laktaw, Pedro Serrano. 1965. *Diccionario Hispano-Tagalog*. Madrid: Ediciones Cultura Hispanica.

Lamont, Michèle, and Laurent Thévenot. 2000. "Introduction: Toward a Renewed Comparative Cultural Sociology." In *Rethinking Comparative Cultural Sociology. Repertoires of Evaluation in France and the United States*, ed. Michèle Lamont and Laurent Thévenot, 1–22. Cambridge: Cambridge University Press.

Lande, Carl H. 1965. *Leaders, Factions, and Parties: The Structure of Philippine Politics*. New Haven, Conn.: Yale University, Southeast Asia Studies Monograph Series, no. 32.

Larkin, John. 1972. *The Pampangans: Colonial Society in a Philippine Province*. Berkeley: University of California Press.

——. 1993. *Sugar and the Origins of Modern Philippine Society*. Berkeley: University of California Press.

LeRoy, James. 1902. "Race Prejudice in the Philippines." *Atlantic Monthly* 90:100–112.

——. 1906. "Mabini on the Failure of the Filipino Revolution (Document no. 2)." *American Historical Review* 11:843–61.

Lewis, W. Arthur. 1970. *Tropical Development 1880–1913*. Evanston, Ill.: Northwestern University Press.

Liang, Dapen. 1970. *Philippine Parties and Politics: A Historical Study of National Experience in Democracy*. San Francisco: The Gladstone Company.

Limon de Arce, Jose. 1938. *Arecibo Historico*. Arecibo: Jose Limon de Arce.

Lipset, Seymour M. 1960. *Political Man*. Garden City: Doubleday Anchor Books.

Liu, Lydia H. 1999. *Tokens of Exchange: The Problem of Translation in Global Circulations*. Durham, N.C.: Duke University Press.

López Giménez, Esteban. 1998. *Crónica del '98. El Testimonio de un médico puertorriqueño*. Madrid: Ediciones Libertarias Prodhufi.

Lopez, Honorio. 1905. *Mga Katuiran ng Filipino*. Manila: Limbagan ni Santos at Bernal.

——. 1915. *Marunong ng Pamahalá sa sariling Bayan*. Manila: Limbagang Magitang, Daang J. Luna.

Lowenthal, Abraham F. 1991. *Exporting Democracy: The United States and Latin America*. Baltimore: Johns Hopkins University Press.

Luis García, Gervasio. 2000. "I Am the Other: Puerto Rico in the Eyes of North Americans." *Journal of American History* 87: 39–64.

Luque de Sánchez, María Dolores. 1980. *La Ocupación Norteamericana y la Ley Foraker*. Río Piedras: University of Puerto Rico.

Lynch, Frank. 1973. "Social Acceptance Reconsidered." In *Four Readings on Philippine Values*, ed. Frank Lynch and Alfonso de Guzman, 1–68. Quezon City: Ateneo de Manila University Press.

Mabini, Apolinario. 1931. *La Revolución Filipina (Con Otras Documentos de la época). Complicados y publicados bajo la dirrección de Teodoro M. Kalaw*. 2 vols. Manila: Bureau of Printing.

Machado, K. G. 1974. "From Traditional Faction to Machine: Changing Patterns of Political Leadership and Organization in the Rural Philippines." *Journal of Asian Studies* 33:523–47.

Magalhaes, M. 1898. *Colonial Business Directory of the Island of Puerto Rico*. New York: M. De Magalhaes.

Majul, Cesar A. 1967. *The Political and Constitutional Ideals on the Philippine Revolution*. Quezon City: University of the Philippines Press.

———. 1996. *Mabini and the Philippine Revolution.* Quezon City: University of the Philippines Press.

Mamdani, Mahmood. 1996. *Citizen and Subject: Contemporary Africa and the Legacy of Late Colonialism.* Princeton, N.J.: Princeton University Press.

Marcus, George. 1997. "The Uses of Complicity in the Changing Mise-en-Scene of Anthropological Fieldword." *Representations* 59:85–108.

Martínez-Vergne, Teresita. 1999. *Shaping the Discourse on Space: Charity and Its Wards in Nineteenth-Century San Juan, Puerto Rico.* Austin: University of Texas Press.

Marvin, George. 1903. "Porto Rico, 1900–1903." *Outlook* 74:649–55.

Matias, Fernando J. 1903. *La Anarquia en Puerto Rico. Con motivo de los sucesos políticos más importantes ocurridos durante el año 1902.* Ponce, Puerto Rico: Tipografia de Manuel Lopez.

Matos Bernier, Félix. 1896. *Cromos Ponceños.* Ponce, Puerto Rico: Imp. La Libertad.

May, Glenn. 1979. "Filipino Resistance to American Occupation: Batangas, 1899–1902." *Pacific Historical Review* 48:531–56.

———. 1980. *Social Engineering in the Philippines: The Aims, Execution, and Impact of American Colonial Policy, 1900–1913.* Westport, Conn.: Greenwood.

———. 1988. "Civil Ritual and Political Reality: Municipal Elections in the Late Nineteenth Century." In *Philippine Colonial Democracy*, ed. Ruby R. Paredes, 13–40. New Haven, Conn.: Yale University, Southeast Asia Studies, Center for International and Area Studies.

Mayol Alcover, Esperanza. 1974. *Islas.* Río Piedras, Puerto Rico: Palma de Mallorca.

McCoy, Alfred W., ed. 1993. *An Anarchy of Families: State and Family in the Philippines.* Madison: University of Wisconsin Press.

———, and Ed. C. de Jesus, eds. 1982. *Philippine Social History: Global Trade and Local Transformations.* Quezon City: Ateneo de Manila University Press.

McKinley, William. 1900. *Speeches and Addresses of William McKinley, from March 1, 1897, to May 30, 1900.* New York: Doubleday & McClure Co.

Meimban, Adriel Obar. 1997. *La Union: The Making of a Province, 1850–1921.* Quezon City, Philippines: Adriel Obar Meimban.

Merry, Sally. 2000. *Colonizing Hawai'i: the Cultural Power of Law.* Princeton, N.J.: Princeton University Press.

Miles, Nelson A. 1911. *Serving the Republic: Memoirs of the Civil and Military Life of Nelson A. Miles.* New York: Harper & Brothers Publishers.

Miles, William F. S. 1994. *Hausaland Divided: Colonialism and Independence in Nigeria and Niger.* Ithaca, N.Y.: Cornell University Press.

Miller, Stuart Creighton. 1982. *"Benevolent Assimilation": The American Conquest of the Philippines, 1899–1903.* New Haven, Conn.: Yale University Press.

Mitchell, Timothy. 1991. *Colonizing Egypt.* Berkeley: University of California Press.

Mojares, Resil B. 1999. *The War against the Americans: Resistance and Collaboration in Cebu, 1899–1906.* Quezon City: Ateneo de Manila University Press.

Montero y Vidal, D. José. 1886. *El Archipiélago Filipino y las Islas Marianas, Carolinas y Palaos. Su Historia, Geografía y Estadística*. Madrid: Imprenta y Fundición de Manuel Tello.

Morales Carrión, Artuto. 1983. *Puerto Rico: A Political and Cultural History*. New York: W. W. Norton & Company, Inc.

Morse, Richard. 1989. *New World Soundings: Culture and Ideology in the Americas*. Baltimore: Johns Hopkins University Press.

Moses, Bernard. 1905. "Control of Dependencies Inhabited by the Less Developed Races." *University of California Chronicle* 7:3–18.

Moses, Edith. 1908. *Unofficial Letters of an Official's Wife*. New York: D. Appleton and Company.

Muñoz Rivera, Luis. 1899. *Petition to the President of the United States of the Agriculturalists of Puerto Rico*. Washington, D.C.: Gibson Bros.

———. 1960. *Obras Completas. Prosa (Febrero-Diciembre, 1893)*. San Juan: Instituto de Cultura Puertorriqueña.

National Historical Institute. 1992. *Filipinos in History*. Manila: National Historical Institute.

Nazaro Velasco, Ruben. 1996. "Negociacion en la tradicion legal: Los abogados y el Estado Colonial de Puerto Rico, 1898–1905." PhD diss., Department of History, University of Puerto Rico, Río Piedras.

Negrón Portillo, Mariano. 1990. *Las Turbas Republicanas, 1900–1904*. Río Piedras: Ediciones Huracán.

———. 1991. *Ruptura Social y Violencia Política: Antología de Documentos*. Rio Píedras: Centro de Investigaciones Sociales.

———. 1997. "Puerto Rico: Surviving Colonialism and Nationalism." Pp. 39–56 in *Puerto Rican Jam: Rethinking Colonialism and Nationalism*, ed. Frances Negrón-Muntaner and Ramón Grosfoguel. Minneapolis/London: University of Minnesota Press.

Neumann, Eduardo. 1896. *Verdadera . . . y Benefactores y hombres notables de Puerto Rico*. Ponce: Tip. La Libertad.

Nieves, Juan. 1898. *La Anexion de Puerto Rico*. Ponce, P.R.: Tipografia del "Listin Comercial."

Nigg, Charles. 1904. *A Tagalog English and English Tagalog Dictionary*. Manila: Imp. de Fajardo y Company.

Ninkovich, Frank A. 2001. *The United States and imperialism*. Malden, Mass.: Blackwell Publishers.

Noceda, P. Juan de, and P. Pedro Salucar. 1860. *Vocabulario de la lengua tagala*. Manila: Ramírez y Giraudier.

Normandía Ayala, Angel D. 1984. "Apuntes Sobre el Desarrollo Administrativo, Social, y Economico del Municipio de Toa Alta," in *Public Administration*. Río Piedras: University of Puerto Rico.

Obeyeskere, Gannath. 1992. *The Apotheosis of Captain Cook*. Princeton, N.J.: Princeton University Press.

O'Donnell, Guillermo. 1994. "Delegative Democracy." *Journal of Democracy* 5:55–69.

Ohnuki-Tierney, Emiko. 1991. "Introduction: The Historicization of Anthropology." Pp. 1–25 in *Culture Through Time*, ed. Emiko Ohnuki-Tierney. Stanford: Stanford University Press.

Olick, Jeffrey K., and Daniel Levy. 1997. "Collective Memory and Cultural Constraint: Holocaust Myth and Rationality in German Politics." *American Sociological Review* 62:921–936.

Oliver, Wm. H. 1901. *Roughing It with the Regulars*. New York: William F. Parr.

Ortiz, Fernando. 1995. *Cuban Counterpoint: Tobacco and Sugar*. Durham and London: Duke University Press.

Ortner, Sherry. 1991. "Patterns of History: Cultural Schemas in the Foundings of Sherpa Religious Institutions." Pp. 57–93 in *Culture Through Time: Anthropological Approaches*, ed. Emiko Ohnuki-Tierney. Stanford: Stanford University Press.

——. 1994. "Theory in Anthropology since the Sixties." Pp. 372–411 in *Culture/Power/History*, ed. Nicholas B. Dirks, Geoff Eley, and Sherry B. Ortner. Princeton, N.J.: Princteon University Press.

——. 1997. "Introduction." *Representations* 0:1–13.

Osborne, John. 1904. "The Americanization of Porto Rico." *The World's Work* 8:4759–4766.

Osias, Camilo. 1971. *The Story of a Long Career of Varied Tasks*. Quezon City: Manlapuz Publishing Co.

Osmeña, Sergo. 1911. *Speech of the Speaker of the Philippine Assembly at San Miguel de Mayumo, Bulacan, P. I., May 7, 1910*. Manilla: Bureau of Printing.

Otis, Major-General E.S. 1900. "The Next Steps in the Philippines." *The Independent* LII:2904–2909.

Owen, Norman. 1974. "The Principalia in Philippine History: Kabikolan, 1790–1898." *Philippine Studies* 22:297–324.

——. (Ed.). 1971. *Compadre Colonialism: Studies in the Philippines under American Rule*. Ann Arbor: Michigan Papers on South and Southeast Asia, no. 3.

——. 1979. "Winding Down the War in Albay, 1900–1903." *Pacific Historical Review* 48:557–89.

Pagan, Bolivar. 1959. *Historia de los Partidos Politicos Puertorriqueños, 1898–1956*. San Juan: Libreria Campos.

Pardo de Tavera, Dr. T.H. 1901. "A History of the Federal Party, by Dr. T.H. Pardo de Tavera." Pp. 161–169 in *Report of the U.S. Philippine Commission to the Secretary of War, Part I*. Washington, D.C.: Government Printing Office.

Paredes, Ruby R., ed. 1988. *Philippine Colonial Democracy*. New Haven, Conn.: Yale University, Southeast Asia Studies, Monograph Series no. 32.

———. 1990. "The Partido Federal, 1900–1907: Political Collaboration in colonial Manila." PhD diss., Department of History, University of Michigan.

Parekh, Bhikhu. 1993. "The Cultural Particularity of Liberal Democracy." In *Prospects for Democracy: North, South, East, West*, ed. David Held, 156–75. Stanford, Calif.: Stanford University Press.

Partido Liberal Comité Provincial. 1897. *Instrucciones electorales*. Ponce: Imp. al vapor de "La Correspondencia."

Paterno, Pedro. 1892. *El Barangay*. Madrid: Cuesta.

———. 1900. *El Problema Politico de Filipinas. Solucion Dada por Pedro A. Paterno* (pamphlet). Rare Books and Manuscripts Division, Harlan Hatcher Library, University of Michigan, Ann Arbor.

———. 1910. *Gobierno Civil de las Islas Filipinas*. Manila: University of Philippines, Filipinia Collection.

Phelan, John Leddy. 1960. "Authority and Flexibility in the Spanish Imperial Bureaucracy." *Administrative Science Quarterly* 5:47–65.

Picó, Fernando. 1981. "Deshumanización del trabajo, cosificación de la naturaleza: los comienzos del café en el Utuado del siglo XIX." In *Inmigración y Clases Sociales en el Puerto Rico del Siglo XIX*, ed. Francisco A. Scarano, 187–206. Río Piedras: Ediciones Huracán.

———. 1985. *Amargo Café*. Río Piedras: Ediciones Huracán.

✓ ———. 1987. *La Guerra Despues de La Guerra*. Río Piedras: Ediciones Huracán.

———. 1993. *Al Filo del Poder*. Río Piedras: Editorial de la Universidad de Puerto Rico.

———. 1995. "Coffee and the Rise of Commercial Agriculture in Puerto Rico's Highlands: The Occupation and Loss of Land in Guaonico and Roncador (Utuado), 1833–1900." In *Coffee, Society, and Power in Latin America*, ed. William Roseberry, Lowell Gudmundson, and Mario Samper Kutschbach, 94–111. Baltimore: Johns Hopkins University Press.

———. 1997. "Transgresiones Populares de los Espacios Públicos Urbanos en el 1898 Puertorriqueño." In *1898: Enfoques y Perspectivas*, ed. Luis E. González Vales, 337–49. San Juan: First Book Publishing.

———. 1998. *Cada Guaraguao . . . Galería de oficiales norteamericanos en Puerto Rico (1898–1899)*. Río Piedras: Ediciones Huracán.

Pierce, Charles. 1901. "The Races of the Philippines—The Tagals." *Annals of the American Academy of Political and Social Science* 18:21–39.

Platt, Orville H. 1901. "Our Relation to the People of Cuba and Porto Rico." *Annals of the American Academy of Political and Social Science* 18:145–59.

Pomeroy, Earl S. 1944. "The American Colonial Office." *Mississippi Valley Historical Review* 30:521–32.

Post, Regis. 1909. "Some Facts of Interest Concerning Porto Rico." In *Report of the Twenty-Seventh Annual Meeting of the Lake Mohonk Conference*, ed. secretary of the

Lake Mohonk Conference, 181–88. Lake Mohonk, N.Y.: Lake Mohonk Conference of Friends of the Indian and Other Dependent Peoples.

Prakash, Gyan. 1999. *Another Reason: Science and the Imagination of Modern India*. Princeton, N.J.: Princeton University Press.

Pratt, Julius. 1936. *Expansionists of 1898*. Baltimore: Johns Hopkins University Press.

Pratt, Mary Louise. 1992. *Imperial Eyes: Travel Writing and Transculturation*. London: Routledge.

Pubill, Felix. 1900. *La Administracion Municipal de Ponce*. Ponce, Puerto Rico: Tip. José Picó Matos.

Puerto Rico Board of Elections. 1908. "Results of Elections." Unpublished manuscript. UPRL.

Pumarada O'Neill, Luis. 1990. *La industria cafetalera de Puerto Rico, 1736–1969*. San Juan: Oficina Estatal de Preservación Histórica.

Pye, Lucien, and Sidney Verba, eds. 1965. *Political Culture and the Politics of Development*. Princeton, N.J.: Princeton University Press.

Quezon, Manuel Luis. 1946. *The Good Fight*. New York: D. Appleton-Century Company.

Quintero Rivera, Angel. 1980. "Background to the Emergence of Imperialist Capitalism in Puerto Rico." In *The Puerto Ricans: their History, Culture, and Society*, ed. Adalberto López, 87–117. Cambridge, Mass.: Schenkman Publishing Company.

———. 1981. *Conflictos de Clase y Política en Puerto Rico*. Río Piedras: Ediciones Huracán.

———. 1988. *Patricios y plebeyos: Burgueses, hacendados, artesanos y obreros*. Río Piedras: Ediciones Huracán.

Rafael, Vicente. 1993a. "White Love: Surveillance and Nationalist Resistance in the U.S. Colonization of the Philippines." In *Cultures of United States Imperialism*, ed. Amy Kaplan and Donald Pease, 185–218. Durham, N.C.: Duke University Press.

———. 1993b. *Contracting Colonialism: Translation and Christian Conversion in Tagalog Society under Early Spanish Rule*. Durham, N.C.: Duke University Press.

———. 1995. "Nationalism, Imagery, and the Filipino Intelligensia of the Nineteenth Century." In *Discrepant Histories: Translocal Essays on Filipino Cultures*, ed. Vicente Rafael, 133–158. Philadelphia: Temple University Press.

Rambo, Eric, and Elaine Chan. 1990. "Text, Structure, and Action in Cultural Sociology." *Theory and Society* 19:635–48.

Ramos, Francisco. 1946. *Viejo Rincón Utuadeño*. Utuado, Puerto Rico: Farmacia Central Utuado.

Ranger, Terence. 1983. "The Invention of Tradition in Colonial Africa." In *The Invention of Tradition*, ed. Eric Hobsbawm and Terence Ranger, 211–62. Cambridge: Cambridge University Press.

Retana, W. E. 1892. *Avisos y Profecias*. Madrid: Imprenta de la Viuda de M. Minuesa de los Rios.

————. 1888. *Indio Batangueño*. Manila.

Reyes, Baldomero B. 1930. *Philippine Elections from Pre-Spanish to the Present Time*. Diliman: University of the Philippines Library, Filipiniana Collection.

Richter, Melvin. 1995. *The History of Political and Social Concepts: A Critical Introduction*. New York: Oxford University Press.

Ricoeur, Paul. 1974. *The Conflict of Interpretations: Essays in Hermeneutics*. Evanston, Ill.: Northwestern University Press.

Riera Palmer, Mariano. 1907. *Memorandum presentado al Honorable Ayuntamiento de Mayaguez*. Mayaguez, Puerto Rico: Tip. "La Voz de la Patria."

Rivas, Nicolas F. 1903. *Política del Partido Republicano Puertorriqueño y Perfiles de Jovenes Obreros Republicanos*. San Juan: Tip. de L. Ferreras.

Rivero Méndez, Angel. 1922. *Crónica de la Guerra Hispano Americana en Puerto Rico*. Madrid: Sucesores de Rivadenyera (S.A.) Artes Gráficas.

Rizal, Jose. 1922. *Filipinas dentro de cien años*. Manila: Libereria Manila Filatelica.

————. 1928. "The Indolence of the Filipino." In *Thinking for Ourselves: A Collection of Representative Filipino Essays*, ed. Vicente M. Hilario and Eliseo Quirino, 146–66. Manila: Oriental Commercial Company.

Robinson, Ronald. 1972. "Non-European Foundations of European Imperialism: Sketch for a Theory of Collaboration." In *Studies in the Theory of Imperialism*, ed. Roger Owen and Bob Sutcliffe, 117–40. London: Longman.

Robles, Elidoro G. 1969. *The Philippines in the Nineteenth Century*. Quezon City: Malaya Books.

Rodgers, Daniel T. 1982. "In Search of Progressivism." *Reviews in American History* 10:113–32.

Rogowski, Ron. 1997. "Rational Choice as a Weberian View of Culture." *APSA–Comparative Politics Newsletter* 8:14–15.

Romualdez, Norberto. 1925. *The Psychology of the Filipino*. Unpublished typescript: Filipiniana Collection, University of Philippines.

Roosevelt, Archibald, ed. 1968. *Theodore Roosevelt on Race, Riots, Reds, and Crime*. West Sayville, N.Y.: Probe.

Roosevelt, Theodore, and Elting Elmore Morison. 1951. *The Letters of Theodore Roosevelt*. Cambridge, Mass.: Harvard University Press.

Root, Elihu. 1907. *The Citizen's Part in Government*. New York: Charles Scribner's Sons.

————. 1917a. "The Effect of Democracy on International Law." In *Miscellaneous Addresses by Elihu Root*, ed. Robert Bacon and James Brown Scott, 281–94. Cambridge, Mass.: Harvard University Press.

————. 1917b. "The Preservation of American Ideals. Address at a dinner of the Union League Club, Chicago Illinois, in commemoration of the birth of Washington, February 22, 1904." In *Miscellaneous Addresses by Elihu Root*, ed. Robert Bacon and James Brown Scott, 259–66. Cambridge, Mass.: Harvard University Press.

———, Robert Bacon, and James Brown Scott. 1916. *Addresses on Government and Citizenship*. Cambridge, Mass.: Harvard University Press.

Rosaldo, Renato. 1989. *Culture and Truth: The Remaking of Social Analysis*. Boston: Beacon.

Rosario Natal, Carmelo. 1975. *Puerto Rico y la Crisis de La Guerra Hispanoamericana (1895–1898)*. Hato Rey, Puerto Rico: Ramallo Brothers Printing Co.

Rosenberg, Emily. 1998. "Turning to Culture." In *Close Encounters of Empire*, ed. Gilbert M. Joseph, Catherine C. LeGrand, and Ricardo A. Salvatore, 497–514. Durham, N.C.: Duke University Press.

Ross, Dorothy. 1984. "Liberalism." In *Encyclopedia of American Political History: Studies of the Principal Movements and Ideas*, ed. Jack P. Greene. New York: Charles Scribner's Sons.

Ross, Edward A. 1901. "The Causes of Race Superiority." *Annals of the American Academy of Political and Social Science* 18:67–89.

Rothbard, Murray N. 1958. "A Note on Burke's Vindication of the Natural Society." *Journal of the History of Ideas* 19:114–18.

Rowe, L. S. 1904a. "The Legal and Domestic Institutions of Our New Possessions." In *Proceedings of the Twenty-Second Annual Meeting of the Lake Mohonk Conference of Friends of the Indian and Other Dependent Peoples*, ed. Wm. J. Rose, 38–43. Lake Mohonk, N.Y.: Lake Mohonk Conference.

———. 1904b. *The United States and Puerto Rico*. New York: Longsman, Green.

Rydell, Robert W. 1984. *All the World's a Fair: Visions of Empire at American International Expositions, 1876–1916*. Chicago: University of Chicago Press.

Sahlins, Marshall. 1981. *Historical Metaphors and Mythical Realities*. Ann Arbor: University of Michigan Press.

———. 1985. *Islands of History*. Chicago: University of Chicago Press.

———. 1995. *How "Natives" Think: About Captain Cook, for Example*. Chicago: University of Chicago Press.

Said, Edward. 1979. *Orientalism*. New York: Vintage Books.

Salman, Michael. 1991. "In Our Orientalist Imagination: Historiography and the Culture of Colonialism in the United States." *Radical History Review* 50:221–32.

———. 1995. "'Nothing without Labor': Penology, Discipline and Independence in the Philippines under United States Rule." In *Discrepant Histories: Translocal Essays on Filipino Cultures*, ed. Vicente Rafael, 113–29. Philadelphia: Temple University Press.

———. 2001. *The Embarrassment of Slavery*. Berkeley: University of California Press.

Santiago-Valles, Kelvin. 1994. *"Subject People" and Colonial Discourses: Economic Transformation and Disorder in Puerto Rico, 1898–1947*. Albany: State University of New York Press.

Santos Cristóbal, Epifanio de los. 1918. "Emilio Jacinto." *Philippine Review/Revista Filipina* 3:412–30.

Santos, Epifanio de los. 1918. "Marcelo H. del Pilar (Plaridel)." *Philippine Review/Revista Filipina* 3:10–12.

Saussure, Ferdinand de. 1966. *Course in General Linguistics*. New York: McGraw-Hill Book Company.

Schumacher, John N. 1973. *The Propoganda Movement, 1880–1895*. Manila: Solidaridad Publishing House.

———. 1991. *The Making of a Nation: Essays on Nineteenth-Century Filipino Nationalism*. Quezon City: Ateneo de Manila University Press.

Schwartz, Stuart. 1992. "The Hurricane of San Ciriaco: Disaster, Politics, and Society in Puerto Rico, 1899–1901." *Hispanic American Historical Review* 72:303–34.

———. 1994. *Implicit Understandings: Observing, Reporting, and Reflecting on the Encounters between Europeans and Other Peoples in the Early Modern Era*. Cambridge: Cambridge University Press.

Scott, David. 1995. "Colonial Governmentality." *Social Text* 43:191–220.

Scott, James C. 1972. "The Erosion of Patron-Client Bonds and Social Change in Rural Southeast Asia." *Journal of Asian Studies* 32:5–37.

———. 1985. *Weapons of the Weak: Everyday Forms of Peasant Resistance*. New Haven, Conn.: Yale University Press.

Scott, William Henry. 1986. *Ilocano Responses to American Aggression, 1900–1901*. Quezon City: New Day Publishers.

Sewell, William H., Jr. 1992. "A Theory of Structure: Duality, Agency, and Transformation." *American Journal of Sociology* 98:1–29.

———. 1996a. "Three Temporalities: Toward an Eventful Sociology." In *The Historic Turn in the Human Sciences*, ed. Terrence J. McDonald, 245–80. Ann Arbor: University of Michigan Press.

———. 1996b. "Historical Events as Transformations of Structures: Inventing Revolution at the Bastille." *Theory and Society* 25:841–81.

———. 1999. "The Concept(s) of Culture." In *Beyond the Cultural Turn*, ed. Victoria E. Bonnell and Lynn Hunt, 35–61. Berkeley: University of California Press.

Sidel, John. 1993. "Walking in the Shadow of the Big Man: Justiniano Montano and Failed Dynasty Building in Cavite, 1935–1972." In *An Anarchy of Families: State and Family in the Philippines*, ed. Alfred W. McCoy, 109–61. Madison: University of Wisconsin Press.

———. 1995. "The Philippines: The Languages of Legitimation." In *Political Legitimacy in Southeast Asia*, ed. Muthiah Alagappa, 136–169. Stanford, Calif.: Stanford University Press.

Silverstrini de Pacheo, Blanca. 1980. *Violencia y Criminalidad en Puerto Rico (1898–1973)*. Río Piedras: Editorial Universitaria, Universidad de Puerto Rico.

Skocpol, Theda. 1984. "Emerging Agendas and Recurrent Strategies in Historical Sociology." In *Visions and Method in Historical Sociology*, ed. Theda Skocpol, 356–391. Cambridge: Cambridge University Press.

Skowronek, Stephen. 1982. *Building a New American State: the Expansion of Administrative Capacities, 1877–1920*. New York: Cambridge University Press.

Smith, Philip, ed. 1998. *The New American Cultural Sociology*. Cambridge: Cambridge University Press.

Smith, Tony. 1994. *America's Mission: The United States and the Worldwide Struggle for Democracy in the Twentieth Century*. Princeton, N.J.: Princeton University Press.

Somers, Margaret R. 1995. "What's Political or Cultural about Political Culture and the Public Sphere? Toward an Historical Sociology of Concept Formation." *Sociological Theory* 13:113–14.

——, and Gloria D. Gibson. 1994. "Reclaiming the Epistemological 'Other': Narrative and the Social Constitution of Identity." In *Social Theory and the Politics of Identity*, ed. Craig Calhoun, 37–99. Cambridge, Mass: Blackwell Publishers.

Stanley, Peter. 1974. *A Nation in the Making: The Philippines and the United States, 1899–1921*. Cambridge, Mass.: Harvard University Press.

Steinmetz, George. 1992. "Reflections on the Role of Social Narratives in Working-Class Formation." *Social Science History* 16:489–516.

——. 1998. "Critical Realism and Historical Sociology: A Review Article." *Comparative Studies in Society and History* 39:170–86.

Stern, Steve J. 1998. "The Decentered Center and the Expansionist Periphery: The Paradoxes of the Foreign-Local Encounter." In *Close Encounters of Empire*, ed. Gilbert M. Joseph, Catherine C. LeGrand, and Ricardo D. Salvatore, 47–68. Durham, N.C.: Duke University Press.

Stocking, George W., Jr. 1968. *Race, Culture, and Evolution*. Chicago: University of Chicago Press.

Stoler, Ann Laura. 1995. *Race and the Education of Desire*. Durham, N.C.: Duke University Press.

Suny, Ronald Grigor. 2002. "Back and Beyond: Reversing the Cultural Turn?" *American Historical Review* 107:1476–99.

Sweet, Willis. 1906. *Self-Government for Porto Rico. A Proposed County Bill*. San Juan: Tip. la Republica Española.

Swidler, Ann. 1986. "Culture in Action: Symbols and Strategies." *American Sociological Review* 51:273–86.

——. 2001. *Talk of Love: How Culture Matters*. Chicago: University of Chicago Press.

Taft, William H. 1906. *Four Aspects of Civic Duty*. New York: Charles Scribner's Sons.

——. 1908. *Special Report of Wm. H. Taft Secretary of War to the President on the Philippines*. Washington, D.C.: Government Printing Office.

Taylor, Charles. 1985. *Philosophy and the Human Sciences*. Cambridge: Cambridge University Press.

Taylor, R. M. 1971. *The Philippine Insurrection against the United States*. 4 vols. Pasay City, Philippines: Eugenio Lopez Foundation.

Thomas, Nicholas. 1994. *Colonialism's Culture: Anthropology, Travel, Government.* Princeton, N.J.: Princeton University Press.

Thompson, Lanny. 2002. "Representation and Rule in the Imperial Archipelago." *American Studies Asia* 1:3–39.

Todd, Roberto H. 1943. *Desfile de Gobernadores de Puerto Rico.* San Juan: Impreso en Casa Baldrich.

Todorov, Tzvetan. 1984. *The Conquest of America.* New York: Harper & Row.

Totanes, Stephen Henry. 1990. "Sorsogon's Principalia and the Policy of Pacification, 1900–1903." *Philippine Studies* 38:477–99.

Tsebelis, George. 1997. "Rational Choice and Culture." *APSA–Comparative Politics Newsletter* 8:15–18.

Tuohy, Anthony R. 1908. *Album histórico de la primera asamblea filipina.* Manila: I. F.

Turner, Frederick C. 1995. "Reassessing Political Culture." In *Latin America in Comparative Perspective*, ed. Peter H. Smith, 195–224. Boulder, Colo.: Westview.

U.S. Adjutant-General's Office, Military Information Division. 1900. *Report on the Island of Guam by Brig. General Joseph Wheeler, U.S. Army. June, 1900.* Washington, D.C.: Government Printing Office.

U.S. Bureau of Insular Affairs. 1902. *A Pronouncing Gazetter and Geographical Dictionary of the Philippine Islands.* Washington, D.C.: Government Printing Office.

U.S. Bureau of the Census. 1905. *Census of the Philippine Islands Taken under the Direction of the Philippine Commission.* Washington, D.C.: Government Printing Office.

U.S. Commission to Review and Compile the Laws of Porto Rico. 1901. *Report of the U.S. Commission to Review and Compile the Laws of Porto Rico.* Washington, D.C.: Government Printing Office.

U.S. Congress, House Committee on Insular Affairs. 1903. *Committee Reports, Hearings, and Acts of Congress Corresponding Thereto, Fifty-Seventh Congress, First and Second Sessions, 1901–1903.* Washington, D.C.: Government Printing Office.

———. 1904. *Committee Reports, Hearings, and Acts of Congress Thereto. U.S. Congress. House. Committee on Insular Affairs. Fifty-Sixth Congress, First and Second Session, 1900–1901.* Washington, D.C.: Government Printing Office.

———. 1906. *Hearing Before the Committee on Insular Affairs, House of Representatives.* Washington, D.C.: Government Printing Office.

U.S. Congress, House of Representatives. 1910. *Conditions in Porto Rico. Message from the President of the United States. A report made by the Secretary of War upon conditions existing in Porto Rico.* Washington, D.C.: House Document no. 615, 61st Congress, 2nd Session.

———. 1921. *Report of the Wood-Forbes Commission. House Document 325. 67th Congress, 2nd Session.* Washington, D.C.: Bureau of Printing.

U.S. Congress, Senate, Committee on Pacific Islands and Puerto Rico. 1900. *Hearings before the Committee on Pacific Islands and Puerto Rico of the United States Senate on senate Bill 2264, to Provide A Government for the Island of Puerto Rico (Industrial and Other Conditions of the Island of Puerto Rico and the Form of Government Which Should be Adopted for it). 56th Congress, Senate, 1st session. Document no. 147*. Washington, D.C.: Government Printing Office.

———. 1906. *Hearings before the Committee on Pacific Islands and Puerto Rico, United States Senate*. Washington, D.C.: Government Printing Office.

U.S. Congress, Senate, Committee on the Philippines. 1902. *Affairs in the Philippines. Hearings before the Committee on the Philippines of the United States Senate*. Senate Document no. 331, 57th Congress, 1st Session. Washington, D.C.: Government Printing Office.

U.S. Insular Commission. 1899. *Report to the Secretary of War Upon Investigations into the Civil Affairs of Puerto Rico*. Washington, D.C.: Government Printing Office.

U.S. Major-General Commanding the Army. 1899. *Annual Report of the U.S. Major-General Commanding the Army. 1899. In Three Parts*. Washington, D.C.: Government Printing Office.

U.S. Navy Department. 1900. *Annual Reports of the Navy Department for the Year 1900. Report of the Secretary of the Navy. Miscellaneous Reports*. Washington, D.C.: Government Printing Office.

———. 1901. *Annual Reports of the Navy Department for the Year 1901. Report of the Secretary of the Navy. Miscellaneous Reports. In Two Parts. Part 1*. Washington, D.C.: Government Printing Office.

———. 1904a. *Annual Reports of the Navy Department for the Year 1904. Report of the Secretary of the Navy. Miscellaneous Reports*. Washington, D.C.: Government Printing Office.

———. 1904b. *Data Relating to the Island of Guam*. Washington, D.C.: Government Printing Office.

———. 1905. *Brief extracts from publications, Memoranda furnished, Congress, General Orders and Annual Reports from 1901–1904, relative to the Island of Guam*. Washington, D.C.: Government Printing Office.

U.S. Philippine Commission. 1900. *Report of the Philippine Commission to the President (January 31, 1900)*. Washington, D.C.: Government Printing Office.

———. 1901. *Report of the United States Philippine Commission to the Secretary of War for the period from December 1, 1900 to October 15, 1901*. Washington, D.C.: Government Printing Office.

———. 1902–14. *Annual Reports*. Washington, D.C.: Government Printing Office.

———. 1905. *Hearings Before the Secretary of War and the Congressional Party Accompanying Him to the Philippine Islands, Held at Manila August 29–30, 1905*. Manila: Bureau of Public Printing.

U.S. War Department. 1899a. *Annual Reports of the War Department for the Fiscal year*

Ended June 30, 1899. Report of the Secretary of War. Miscellaneous Reports. Washington, D.C.: Government Printing Office.

——. 1899b. *Puerto Rico, embracing the Reports of Brig. Gen. Geo. W. Davis, Military Governor, 1899.* Washington, D.C.: Government Printing Office.

——. 1899c. *Report of the US Insular Commission to the Secretary of War upon Investigations Made into the Civil Affairs of Porto Rico.* Washington, D.C.: Government Printing Office.

——. 1899d. *Translation of Constitution Establishing Self-Government in the Islands of Cuba and Porto Rico, Promulgated by Royal Decree of November 25, 1897.* Washington, D.C.: Government Printing Office.

——. 1899e. *Translation of the Provincial and Municipal Laws of Porto Rico.* Washington, D.C.: Government Printing Office.

——. 1900a. *Annual Reports of the War Department for the Fiscal Year Ended June 30, 1900. Report of the Lieutenant-General Commanding the Army. In Seven Parts. Part 2.* Washington, D.C.: Government Printing Office.

——. 1900b. *Puerto Rico, embracing the reports of Brig. Gen. Geo. W. Davis, Military Governor, and Reports on the Districts of Arecibo, Aguadilla, Cayey, Humacao, Mayaguez, Ponce, San Juan, Vieques, and the Subdistrict of San German.* Washington, D.C.: Government Printing Office.

——. 1901. *Annual Reports of the War Department for the Fiscal Year Ended June 30, 1901. Report of the Philippine Commission. In Two Parts.* Washington, D.C.: Government Printing Office.

——. 1902. *Annual Reports of the War Department for the Fiscal Year Ended June 30, 1900. Part 13. Report of the Military Governor of Porto Rico on Civil Affairs.* Washington, D.C.: Government Printing Office.

——. 1910. *Special Report of J. M. Dickinson, Secretary of War, to the President on the Philippines.* Washington, D.C.: Government Printing Office.

Valdepeñas, Vicente B., and Gemelino M. Bautista. 1977. *The Emergence of the Philippine Economy.* Manila: Papyrus.

Valle, Jose G. del. 1907. *A Través de Diez Años (1897–1907).* Barcelona: Establecimieno Tipográfico de Feliu y Susanna.

Van Buren, James Heartt. 1905. "Present-Day Porto Rico." *Outlook* 79:127–31.

Velasco Shaw, Angel, and Luis H. Francia, eds. 2002. *Vestiges of War.* New York: New York University Press.

Vergara, Benito M. 1995. *Displaying Filipinos.* Quezon City, Philippines: University of the Philippines Press.

Vincent, Joan. 1988. "Sovereignty, Legitimacy, and Power: Prologomena to the Study of the Colonial State." In *State Formation and Political Legitimacy*, ed. Ronald Cohen and Judith D. Toland, 137–54. New Brunswick, N.J.: Transaction Books.

Wedeen, Lisa. 2002. "Conceptualizing Culture: Possibilities for Political Science." *American Political Science Review* 96:713–28.

Weinberg, Albert K. 1935. *Manifest Destiny: A Study of National Expansionism in American History*. Chicago: Quadrangle Books.

Wells, Henry. 1969. *The Modernization of Puerto Rico*. Cambridge, Mass.: Harvard University Press.

Wiebe, Robert H. 1995. *Self-Rule: A Cultural History of American Democracy*. Chicago: University of Chicago Press.

Williams, Daniel R. 1913. *The Odyssey of the Philippine Commission*. Chicago: A. C. McClurg & Co.

Williams, Walter. 1980. "United States Indian Policy and the Debate over Philippine Annexation: Implications for the Origins of American Imperialism." *Journal of American History* 66:810–31.

Williams, William Appleman 1969. *The Roots of the Modern American Empire*. New York: Random House.

Willoughby, William F. 1905. *Territories and Dependencies of the United States*. New York: Century.

——. 1909a. "The Problem of Political Education in Porto Rico." In *Report of the Twenty-Seventh Annual Meeting of the Lake Mohonk Conference of Friends of the Indian and Other Dependent Peoples, October 20th, 21st and 22nd, 1909*, ed. Charles F. Meserve, 160–68. Lake Mohonk, N.Y.: Lake Mohonk Conference of Friends of the Indian and Other Dependent Peoples.

——. 1909b. "The Reorganization of Municipal Government in Porto Rico: Political." *Political Science Quarterly* 24:409–43.

——. 1910. "The Reorganization of Municipal Government: Financial." *Political Science Quarterly* 25:69–104.

Wilson, Edward S. 1905. *Political Development of Porto Rico*. Columbus, Ohio: Fred J. Heer.

Wilson, James Harrison. 1912. *Under the Old Flag: Recollections of Military Operations in the War for the Union, the Spanish War, the Boxer Rebellion, Etc.* New York: D. Appleton and Company.

Wilson, Woodrow. 1887. "The Study of Administration." *Political Science Quarterly* 2:197–222.

——. 1901. "Democracy and Efficiency." *Atlantic Monthly* 87: 289–99.

Wolf, Eric. 1956. "San Jose: 'Traditional' Coffee Municipality." In *The People of Puerto Rico*, ed. Julian et al. Steward, 171–264. Urbana: University of Illinois Press.

Wolfe, Patrick. 1997. "History and Imperialism: A Century of Theory, from Marx to Postcolonialism." *American Historical Review* 102(2):388–420.

Wolff, Leon. 1991. *Little Brown Brother: How the United States Purchased and Pacified the Philippines*. Oxford: Oxford University Press.

Worcester, Dean C. 1913. *Slavery and Peonage in the Philippine Islands*. Manila: Bureau of Printing.

———. 1914. *The Philippines Past and Present*. New York: Macmillan.

Young, James T. 1902. "Colonial Autonomy." *Annals of the American Academy of Political and Social Science* 19:62–77.

INDEX

Colonialism and culture, 4–10, 25–53, 131–132, 188–189, 205–206, 274–278, 287–289, 290–294

Colton, George, 90–91

Corruption, political: in United States, 33, 41–42, 308 nn.24, 25, 320 n.137

Culture: and change, 7–10, 12–18, 131–140, 205–209, 213–214, 238–239, 269–271, 277–289, 320 n.6, 339 n.23, 340 n. 30; and power, 4–7, 14, 18, 45–53, 91, 276, 290; as repertoire, 16–18, 184–189, 205–209, 224–225, 301 n.56; as semiotic system in practice, 16–18, 62, 273, 275, 283, 287–289; theories of, 4, 12–18, 131–140, 205–209, 269–271, 273, 275–283, 288–294, 340 n. 30. *See also* Colonialism and culture; Rational choice theory; Structural-functionalism; Values

Davis, George, 61, 145

Democracia, La, 184–185, 218–219

Democracy: American conceptions of, 39–44, 249, 305 nn.64, 67, 306 n.69, 308 n.24; Puerto Rican ideologies of, 57–58, 62–74, 79–84, 140, 221–222; Philippine ideologies of, 105–109, 118–122, 125, 140, 203–204. *See also* Self-government

Democratic Party: in the United States, 153, 302 n.62

Dewey, John, 34

Diaz, Herminio, 176–177

Diego, Jose de, 56, 70–71, 236, 238

Discipline: colonialism and, 8–9; democracy and, 39–44, 48, 83, 223–224, 230–235, 242–251. *See also* Foucault, Michel

Domestication, 11, 57, 276–277, 285–288, 293, 339 n.22; explanation of, 129–130, 131, 278–285; in the Philippines, 94, 129–130, 131, 173, 191–205, 242–251, 278–285; in Puerto Rico, 77–92, 129–130, 131, 278–285. *See also* Localization

Education: of American colonial officials, 19; in colonies, 22–23, 29–30, 36, 94, 297; during U.S. occupation, 49. *See also* Political education

Elections: and corruption, 51, 72–75, 88–89, 126–129, 222–223, 245–248, 252–259; electorates in colonies, 20, 253, 307 n.104, 323 n.83; in the Philippines during Spanish rule, 97–98; in the Philippines during U.S. rule, 126–129, 245–248, 252–259; in Puerto Rico during Spanish rule, 65, 71–76, 310 n.72; in Puerto Rico during U.S. rule, 88–89, 153–154, 177, 222–223, 227–230, 232–235, 236, 330 n.30; and tutelage, 51

Elite: political, 3, 15, 18–23, 163, 279; definition and characteristics of, 3, 295–297; socioeconomic, 22–23, 65, 163, 297, 309 n.45

Empire, 2–4, 8, 31, 293–294

Ethnicity, 21, 23, 134, 278, 280, 302 n.62. *See also* Race

Exceptionalism. *See* American exceptionalism

Executive Council of Puerto Rico, 52, 150, 187

Federal Party: in the Philippines, 21, 109, 111–112, 115, 128, 134–135, 157, 158, 168, 258–259; in Puerto Rico, 20, 79–82, 143, 148–155, 166–168, 174–188, 212–224, 323 n.85, 330 n.1

Foraker Act, 150, 186–188, 224

Forbes, W. Cameron, 27, 40, 53, 123, 125, 159–160, 168, 243, 245, 247–248, 257, 260, 262, 303 n.21

Foucault, Michel, 8, 43, 251, 306 n.86, 332 n.66

Geertz, Clifford, 14–15, 300 nn.38, 39, 339 n.23

Governance: compared with discipline, 48, 306 n.86. See also Colonial government; Foucault, Michel

Great Puerto Rican Family (gran familia puertorriquena), 66–68, 71–73, 75, 76, 142

Henry, Guy, 47, 55, 56, 87, 149–150

House of Delegates: in Puerto Rico, 150, 153–154, 168–169, 175, 213, 235–237, 326 n.15

Hunt, William, 42, 50, 179–183, 184–186, 215, 219, 220, 304 n.36

Ileto, Reynaldo, 6, 9, 105, 268

Ilustrado, 98, 107, 157–158, 189, 315 n.30

Imperialism. See Empire

Incondicional Party: in Puerto Rico, 65, 71–74, 152–153, 219

Independence: Philippine demands for, during U.S. occupation, 23, 112–113, 203–204, 281, 317 n.80

Indigenization. See Localization

Kalayaan, 104–105, 113

Kapangyarihan, 268–269

Katwiran, 107, 250–251, 263–264. See also Razón

Kinship: American views of, 42; in Puerto Rico, 63–64

Laitin, David, 15, 281–282

Language, 21, 23, 50–51, 133–134, 338 n.7

Legislature. See House of Delegates; Philippine Assembly

Localization, 8–9, 11, 131, 276–277, 338 n.7. See also Domestication

Lopez de Legaspi, Miguel, 101, 102

Lopez, Benito, 255–257

Lopez, Enrique, 117–121

Lopez, Honorio, 250–251, 263–264, 265, 267–268

Lukban, Vicente, 204–205

Mabini, Apolinario, 99–100, 104, 105–108, 250, 260, 266, 315 nn.25, 27

Makapangyarihan, 268–269, 270

Malolos: American views of, 40, 44, Constitution and Government, 107–108, 120–121, 125, 242, 249, 259–260

Manila Times, 245–246

McKinley, William, 19, 33, 46, 47, 55, 87, 109, 110, 111, 112, 128, 150–151, 193

Meaning. See Culture

Method: comparative, 18–23, 138–140, 283–287

Miles, Nelson, 45–46, 55, 77, 90

Moses, Bernard, 31, 47, 123, 124, 195, 199, 304 n.33

Muñoz Rivera, Luis, 67, 68–72, 74, 78, 83–84, 86, 143, 146–147, 148, 150–152, 179, 221, 224, 312 n.119

Nationalist Party: in the Philippines, 21, 133–134, 157, 194, 258–259

Organic Act, 156, 158

Orthodox-Reformist Party: in Puerto Rico, 75–76, 85, 87

Paredes, Ruby, 157, 317 n.80

Paterno, Pedro, 112, 125, 158, 169, 194, 262, 267, 328 n.52

Patron-clientelism: in the Philippines, 22, 95–101, 128, 159–161, 164–168, 190, 199–202, 245, 254–256, 258, 309 n.31, 316 n.40; in Puerto Rico, 22, 63–65, 70, 86, 141–148, 164–168, 309 n.31

Peasantry: in the Philippines, 22, 95, 96, 97, 164–165; revolt in the Philippines, 164, 325 n.120; in Puerto Rico, 22, 63–64, 66, 142–143, 145–148, 325 n.120

Philippine Assembly, 135, 169–170, 189, 201, 242, 259–269

Philippine Commission, 52, 109–110, 112–117, 125, 156, 157

Philippine Revolution against Spain, 37–38, 98–99, 102–105, 317 n.70; ideology of, 106–109

Philippine-American War, 6, 34–35, 46, 93, 109–111, 162, 279–280, 282

Pilar, Marcelo del, 101, 102–103, 104, 116

Poblete, Pascual, 194, 199

Political education, 3, 7, 20, 29, 48, 49–53, 122–123, 156, 260–261

Political parties, 20–21. *See also individual parties*

Progressivism/Progressive movement, 19, 32–34, 41–42, 51, 88, 122, 275, 304 n.26, 308 n.24

Quezon, Manuel, 111, 265, 267, 340 n.31

Race, 28–32, 274, 278, 280, 303 n.20, 307 n.110

Rafael, Vicente, 6, 9, 48, 268

Rational choice theory, 15, 59–61, 92, 94, 129–130, 135–136, 214, 231, 238,

281–282, 300 n.40, 301 nn.40, 53, 333 n.67, 339 nn.16, 17, 340 n.25

Razón, 98–104, 105–108, 113–114, 118–119, 120–121, 126, 165–166, 193–194, 202, 249–251, 260, 262–264, 266–267

Renacimiento, El, 114, 126, 164, 190, 191, 327 n.41, 329 n.83

Republican Party: in Puerto Rico, 87, 144–143, 149, 152–153, 167, 174, 175, 178–184, 186, 213–224, 322 n.60, 323 n.85, 330 n.1; in the United States, 19, 153

Retraimiento, 74, 152–155, 168, 174, 175–178, 183–184

Riera Palmer, Santiago, 177

Rights. *See* Razón

Rizal, Jose, 115, 195

Roosevelt, Theodore, 44, 47, 48, 177, 179, 304 n.30

Root, Elihu, 2, 19, 29, 37, 43, 51, 53, 82, 150, 158, 304 n.34

Rowe, Leo, 36, 89, 176, 304 n.33

Sagasta, Mateo, 74–75, 79, 85, 140–141, 151, 174

Sahlins, Marshall, 277, 321 n.16, 333 n.10, 339 n.23

Said, Edward, 5, 6

Salman, Michael, 48

Schurman, Jacob, 34, 109. *See also* Philippine Commission

Self-government: American views on capacity for, 1, 25, 27–31, 40–44, 60–61, 76, 95, 132, 153, 196, 275–276, 333 n.98; Filipino ideologies of, 105–109, 117–122, 125, 140, 158–159, 203–204; Puerto Rican ideologies of, 62–74, 79–84, 224, 235–237. *See also* Autonomy

Sidel, John, 268, 269

Social Class: of Political elite, 22–23, 163. *See also* Elite

Spanish colonialism: American views of, 29–30, 36, 38, 45; in the Philippines, 96–102; in Puerto Rico, 64–65, 71–76, 77, 80–82, 150–155, 311 n.98; similarities between Puerto Rico and the Philippines, 21–22

Spanish-American War, 1, 45, 58–59, 76, 93, 146

Statehood: for the Philippines, 307 n.110; for Puerto Rico, 23, 36–37, 56, 58–61, 79–84, 90, 133, 178, 233–234, 238, 305 n.51, 311 n.100, 333 n.98

Structural-functionalism, 13–14, 57, 135–136, 274–275, 280–281, 288–289, 291–292, 300 n.32, 320 n.6, 339 n.23

Sweet, Willis, 179, 213, 228–229

Taft, William Howard, 1, 30, 33–34, 40, 42, 47, 49–50, 53, 109, 112, 119, 122, 123, 158, 191, 260, 304 n.36; as patron in the Philippines, 114–116, 140, 161, 170, 193–200

Taxation: in Philippines during Spanish rule, 95, 97. See also *Buwis*

Tutelage, 1–2, 7, 20, 37–39, 260–261, 274–276, 279–280, 282–283, 307 n.111. *See also* Political education

Union Party: in Puerto Rico, 20, 225–237, 330 n.1

Utang na loób, 96, 104, 116, 140, 170, 249, 291, 314 n.11, 340 n.27

Values, 13–14, 17, 26, 39, 57–59, 92, 94, 129–130, 135, 274–275, 280–281, 288–289, 291–292, 300 n.31, 314 n.11, 315 n.24, 338 n.3. *See also* Structural-functionalism

Williams, Daniel, 113, 125

Willoughby, William, 41, 43, 44, 149, 304 n.36

Wilson, Woodrow, 31–32, 33, 44, 304 nn.30, 33, 306 n.69

Worcester, Dean, 110, 304 n.33

Wright, Luke, 26, 162, 191–193, 196

Julian Go is an assistant professor of sociology at Boston University. He is the coeditor, with Anne L. Foster, of *The American Colonial State in the Philippines: Global Perspectives* (also published by Duke University Press).

Library of Congress Cataloging-in-Publication Data
Go, Julian, 1970–
American empire and the politics of meaning : elite political cultures in the Philippines and Puerto Rico during U.S. colonialism / Julian Go.
p. cm. — (Politics, history, and culture)
Includes bibliographical references and index.
ISBN 978-0-8223-4211-3 (cloth : alk. paper)
ISBN 978-0-8223-4229-8 (pbk. : alk. paper)
1. United States — Insular possessions — History. 2. Elite (Social sciences) — Philippines — History. 3. Elite (Social sciences) — Puerto Rico — History. 4. Political culture — Philippines — History. 5. Political culture — Puerto Rico — History. 6. Philippines — Colonial influence. 7. Puerto Rico — Colonial influence. I. Title.
F970.G6 2008
306.209599'09041 — dc22   2007042559

21/5/